ProgressionSeries

Economics, Finance and Accountancy

For entry to university and college in 2011

Published by: UCAS Rosehill New Barn Lane Cheltenham GL52 3LZ

Produced in conjunction with GTI Media Ltd

UCAS, a company limited by guarantee, is registered in England and Wales number: 2839815
Registered charity number: 1024741 (England and Wales) and SC038598 (Scotland)

UCAS reference number: PU032011
Publication reference: 10_059
ISBN: 978-1-84361-127-1
Price £15.99

Further copies available from UCAS (p&p charges apply):

Contact Publication Services PO Box 130 Cheltenham GL52 3ZF

email: publicationservices@ucas.ac.uk or fax: 01242 544806

For further information about the UCAS application process go to www.ucas.com.

If you need to contact us, details can be found at www.ucas.com/about_us/contact_us

MIX
Paper from responsible sources
FSC® C015900
www.fsc.org

Foreword

THINKING ABOUT ECONOMICS, FINANCE OR ACCOUNTANCY?

Finding the course that's right for you at the right university or college can take time and it's important that you use all the resources available to you in making this important decision. We at UCAS have teamed up with GTI Media Ltd to provide you with Progression to Economics, Finance and Accountancy to show you how you can progress from being a student to careers in economics, finance and accountancy. You will find information on what the subject includes, entry routes and real-life case studies on how it worked out for others.

Once you know which subject area you might be interested in, you can use the listings of all the full-time higher education courses in economics, finance and accounting to see where you can study your subject.

The course entry requirements are listed so you can check if getting in would be achievable for you. There's also advice on applying through UCAS, telling you what you need to know at each stage of the application process in just six easy steps to starting university or college.

We hope you find this publication helps you to choose a course and university or college that is right for you.

On behalf of UCAS and GTI Media Ltd, I wish you every success in your research.

Mary Curnock Cook, Chief Executive, UCAS

Introducing economics

ProgressionSeries

It could be you...

Economics: "A study of mankind in the ordinary business of life" (Alfred Marshall)

WHY ECONOMICS?

We all make economic decisions every day in our lives, from whether we have enough money to buy the latest CD to how much we need to save for a summer holiday with friends. In this way, economics shows us how to live our lives and, hopefully, how to make better economic decisions.

On a bigger scale, economics is all about the production, distribution and consumption of wealth, both on a small scale (ie individuals) and on a large scale (ie countries). Economics is also about comparing ways to use the limited resources that countries and individuals have, and how fair these are. Basically, economics gives us ways to think about the world so that we can make the best of what we already have. And it's not just about money (although of course finance plays a huge role in this area): it's also about how the choices we make impact on society. Who could ask for a more responsible and challenging potential career?

YOUR SKILLS

Not only will you have an interesting degree course if you study economics but you will also improve your future career prospects. Economics graduates are highly sought after in the world of work because of the variety of skills they can bring to a job. Equally, economists are needed in so many different fields that you are bound to find something that will satisfy both your interests and skills set.

It's all very well talking about skills but what exactly will you learn? The following are just examples:

SKILL	THE ABILITY TO...
Analysis and problem-solving	... develop strategic ways of thinking and devise effective frameworks to solve economic problems or issues
Communication	... explain complex information in a user-friendly way (often to clients in different work areas) and be able to summarise and apply difficult concepts
Self-management	... work efficiently on your own, managing often quite hectic work schedules and tight deadlines
Political and commercial awareness	... understand government policy, while shrewdly assessing economic performance
Teamworking	... work well within a team to achieve shared goals
Numeracy	... understand and confidently interpret numerical information, often by using various mathematical and statistical techniques

YOUR CAREER

Economics graduates are spoilt for choice when it comes to careers. The skills they learn as part of their undergraduate degree stand them in good stead for a wide range of high-level jobs, including:

- actuary
- market researcher
- insurance underwriter
- statistician
- management consultant
- economist
- retail banker
- investment banker
- chartered accountant
- political party research officer
- investment analyst
- trader (equities, bonds, shares).

WHAT WILL YOU EARN?

The average starting salary for graduates paid by The Association of Graduate Recruiters member organisations in 2009 was £25,000 (source: *The Association of Graduate Recruiters (AGR) Graduate Recruitment Survey 2009)*. Due to their specific skills and knowledge, many economics graduates go into professions such as banking and investment, accountancy and taxation, and management consulting, which can offer substantially higher starting salaries as well as excellent long-term prospects. See page 22 for further information on graduate starting salaries.

WORKING AS AN ECONOMIST

Economists look at how society manages resources such as money, labour, businesses, services and raw materials. They study economic trends, produce economic forecasts and research issues such as interest rates, inflation, exchange rates, taxes, business cycles and employment levels. One of the key skills for an economist is the ability to present statistics and economic theories with clarity.

Economists can work for a range of organisations including government bodies, the media, charities and businesses.

OTHER CAREERS

For information on some of the financial jobs listed here, take a look at **Which area?** (starting on page 26) in the main finance and accountancy section, as well as the various **case studies** (starting on page 45).

Introducing finance and accountancy

ProgressionSeries

It could be you...

... calculating losses arising from a flood or earthquake – forensic accounting

... advising companies on mergers and acquisitions – corporate finance

... rescuing troubled businesses – corporate recovery

... making massive profits for clients – markets

... helping clients make multibillion-euro acquisitions – investment banking

... and lots more besides. Could a career in finance and accountancy be for you? The aim of this guide is to help you decide.

A CAREER IN FINANCE AND ACCOUNTANCY?

- Choose from a wide range of exciting career options. See **Which area?** starting on page 26.
- Learn about all the appropriate financial and technical language. See **Jargon buster** on page 23.
- Finance and accountancy professionals have good earnings potential. See how much in **A career in economics, finance and accountancy** on page 20.
- Make your UCAS application stand out from the crowd. Read **How will they choose you?** starting on page 76.

FINANCE AND ACCOUNTANCY IN CONTEXT

Mention a career in finance and accountancy to people outside the sector and, chances are, they will think you want to be an accountant. Worse still, thanks to unkind media portrayals, they may even stereotype accountants as grey-suit-wearing individuals with no sense of humour.

But who has the last laugh? **Accountancy** is far from dull. Nearly every business, whether an international conglomerate or a local handyman's company, needs an accountant to help with their business's planning and financial health. Someone, somewhere, will always need your expertise, with trainee accountants earning up to £28,000 per year and some senior accountants raking in over £100,000.

But let's not forget the other business areas in this sector. The **banking and investment** business is all about making money work as hard as possible. It's borrowed and invested in a number of different ways but it's never allowed to sit still. The financial markets are open 24/7 and cross various time zones, from Hong Kong and Tokyo in the Far East, to Frankfurt and London in Europe and New York in the US – there is always something going on somewhere with money. London is a key player in the financial world because it straddles the working days of both the Far East and America. Key employers include investment banks, specialist finance houses and universal banks. And in spite of the recent financial crisis, the median starting salary for graduates in investment banking in 2009 was a healthy 37,000 (the AGR Graduate Recruitment Survey 2009).

Finally, you could opt for a career in **insurance and financial services**, a very fast-moving sector, driven by the very capable 'brains' that are behind it. Most jobs contain aspects of project and people management so you'll need to have a great combination of both analytical and people skills, plus, obviously, an ability to number-crunch. This sector particularly appeals to people who love reading the deals pages of the *FT* or who like to manage money. If you find yourself giving your parents advice on the best mortgage offers, this could be your dream area!

If you're interested in a possible career in finance and accountancy, then this guide can help point you further in the right direction. Read on to discover:

- the main roles on offer
- the skills and educational grades that employers in finance and accounting look for
- how to get into university and what you could do after graduating
- advice and personal experience stories from recent graduates working in finance and accountancy.

ARE YOU INTERESTED IN STUDYING ECONOMICS?

The careers outlined in the sections on finance and accountancy are open to students of economics who can, of course, also aim to work as economists. For more details please see the **Which economics degree?** section, starting on page 18.

Why finance and accountancy?

Choose a career that is...

VARIED

The people who work in finance and accountancy come from all walks of life and have studied all sorts of things. You needn't study a numerate subject as long as you have a strong interest in all things financial. Just think: you will be paid for helping to manage, invest, advise on or use other people's or companies' money, from a sole trader to a multinational organisation. Read *What do recent graduates say?* opposite.

HIGHLY SKILLED

The chances of becoming professionally qualified in the accounting and financial management and the insurance and financial services sectors are excellent – and often essential to get ahead in your career. You can also study for a professional qualification linked to the banking and investment sector to add weight to your expertise. Such training not only helps you do your job more effectively but also makes you a very attractive potential employee, either in similar firms or in different career areas, where the transferable skills you gain can be used to great effect. Read **Routes to qualification** starting on page 58.

LUCRATIVE

Since your career is all about making money for other people, it's only fair that you should reap similar financial rewards. Finance and accountancy professionals can earn good salaries plus perks such as pension schemes, private healthcare and season ticket loans. It can be a work hard, play hard way of life. Check it out in **A career in economics, finance and accountancy** on page 20.

STIMULATING

Watching stock market changes in Tokyo and New York, managing cash flows, monitoring profits... all of these require a keen eye for detail and an interest in the financial status and health of both companies and individuals. Professionals in accounting and financial services work across a wide range of sectors, with a huge variety of companies, which means each day could bring a new challenge. Read **case studies** of people in the sector, starting on page 45.

INFLUENTIAL

It's true what they say: money does make the world go round. The fate of our economy, and of the industries within it, rests on the state of the country's (and the world's) financial status. Professionals in the finance and accounting arenas play a major role in determining a company's, or an individual's, financial future, ranging from advising on suitable investment opportunities to rescuing businesses in distress. Without this advice, companies couldn't function effectively and profitably, individuals might flounder with their tax returns and payments, and the country's economy would be in dire straits. Read **Which area?** on page 26 to see how you might be influencing future clients.

WHAT DO RECENT GRADUATES SAY?

'I am now in the final year of my degree and when I finish I will be starting a graduate job with in the restructuring division of Deloitte's corporate finance function.'
Arthur Callaghan, economics student

'I am working to improve planning and budgeting within the Ministry of Health, and to increase their capacity by training colleagues.'
Karishmah Bhuwanee, economist

'Recently I have taken on more managerial responsibilities, checking how all the staff are doing and helping them to achieve their targets.'
Rebecca Safurridin, retail management trainee

'There are always new projects going on and we constantly seek to improve our processes and practices, so there is never a dull moment.'
James Wadley, structured credit trading risk officer

Sign up for graduate jobs with real bite
targetjobs.co.uk has tastier graduate jobs than any other UK site. Over 65,000 of them, in fact. And if you register with us now, we'll e-mail you the ones that are the most relevant to your interests.
To register, visit targetjobs.co.uk/registration
Essential nutrition for your career
TARGETjobs.co.uk
more graduate jobs and careers intelligence

A career in economics, finance and accountancy

ProgressionSeries

Which economics degree?

In 2010, there were almost 1,500 economics-related courses on the UCAS website. How can you narrow those down to five?

SINGLE HONOURS

The first choice you will have to make is whether you would like to study economics on its own or as part of a combined degree. Since economics is a social science it links in well with other academic areas. Therefore, even if you opt for a straight single honours degree, you will almost certainly look at other related disciplines such as sociology, politics and international relations.

However, the mere fact that you have chosen to specialise in economics will mean that you will cover the subject and its related areas in far greater detail than students on a joint honours degree. This is great if you are fascinated by economics and want to focus solely on it but if you want to keep your options open, you may be better off combining it with another subject.

JOINT HONOURS

Economics combines well with many other subjects, including history, business studies, human geography, maths, management, politics, psychology and languages. All of these share some common components with economics, while languages can add an international flavour to your studies.

HOW LONG DO COURSES LAST?

Economics courses typically last for three years, unless you combine them with a language, when you will normally be expected to spend either your second or third year abroad to develop your linguistic ability. In this case, courses will stretch to four years. Equally, some universities offer a joint degree of economics and engineering, which would typically mean a four-year course.

ECONOMICS YEAR BY YEAR

As with all higher education courses, your economics degree will differ in focus throughout each of the three years. This enables the university to teach you common principles that are key to all economics degrees, while allowing you to choose options at a later date that are more suited to your areas of interest. Broadly speaking, however, all undergraduate economics courses will be structured like this:

Year 1

In this year, tutors will give a general introduction to the subject: what it's all about, why it is relevant and how it applies to different aspects of our everyday life. This introduction not only gives students an idea of the different areas in which they can specialise, but also teaches them useful studying skills that they can use throughout the rest of their degree.

Year 2

The theme of year two is 'application': you will, in effect, be applying the skills you learnt in year one to different fields of economics. You may cover such areas as industrial economics, international economics and political economy.

Year 3

The third year is all about specialising. After two years of intense study, you should be able to identify particular areas of economics that interest you, often culminating in a dissertation, which provides you with an opportunity to develop economic ideas and theories.

A career in economics, finance and accountancy

Finance and accounting degrees are hot topics at university. In the 2009 academic year around 6,400 students started accounting degree courses and around 1,350 started degree courses in finance. Careers in banking, accountancy and financial services offer graduates very attractive starting salaries, as you can see from the table on page 22. Equally encouraging for graduates in economics, accounting and finance is that these business sectors have a significant demand for graduates. In 2009, accounting firms and investment banks together offered 32.5% of the total of all graduate vacancies reported by 226 members of the Association of Graduate Recruiters.

WHERE THEY WORK

Where you work will depend on which business sector you choose. There are, broadly speaking, three main areas, which then break down into smaller sub-areas.

Banking and investment

Investment banks are global firms that carry out a full range of banking and investment services.

Specialist finance houses are smaller organisations that specialise in a particular area of work such as corporate finance.

Universal banks are financial services organisations that offer both corporate and investment banking.

Accounting and financial management

Professionals in these areas often work within general companies, or for specialist firms, providing a full range of advice and services in the following areas:

Assurance – the traditional side of financial work, involving auditing: independently reviewing a client's accounts and reassuring shareholders that a company's financial statements are accurate.

Corporate finance – advising companies on mergers and acquisitions, as well as financing for larger projects through loans or sales of assets.

Corporate recovery – saving ailing businesses, where possible, or putting them into liquidation if necessary.

Corporate treasury – managing a (normally large) company's cash flows, investing surpluses and controlling financial risk.

Forensic accounting – calculating losses arising from such natural disasters as floods and earthquakes, as well as thefts and accidents, helping with fraud allegations and assessing the financial impact of a disaster.

Tax – either advising companies on their liability and ways of minimising it, or working for Revenue & Customs in policy or as an inspector.

Insurance and financial services

Financial services providers – large employers (international companies with branches throughout the UK) offering a range of financial services (eg retail banking and savings accounts).

Large international corporates – businesses that have built their name in a different area but have diversified into financial services (such as food retailers).

Specialist firms – offer specialist services such as actuarial consulting, risk management, underwriting and reinsurance.

Regulation – the Financial Services Authority (FSA) regulates the industry and takes on graduates.

TRENDS

The 'credit crunch' and global recession were the most significant trends during 2008 and 2009. Banks were certainly hard hit, with mergers and job losses frequently in the news headlines. However, this doesn't mean you should give up an idea of a career in finance! Banks, accounting and financial services firms are taking a strategic approach to the future and continuing to recruit top graduates who can prove their commitment to the industry. This means it's a good idea to keep up with current affairs and accrue as much relevant work experience before you apply for a permanent job.

FINANCE AND ACCOUNTANCY STATISTICS

Average graduate starting salaries (2009)

Investment banks or fund managers	£36,000
Banking or financial services	£29,000
Consulting or business services firm	£31,000
Accountancy or professional services firm	£23,000
Average graduate starting salary (paid by The Association of Graduate Recruiters member organisations)	£25,000

Largest share of graduate vacancies by type of occupation

Accountancy	24.4%
Banking or financial services	13.6%
Law	9.4%

(Source: The Association of Graduate Recruiters (AGR) Graduate Recruitment Survey 2009)

Jargon buster

There is a lot of specialist vocabulary in finance and accounting. We define some of the more common words you'll come across both here and elsewhere.

ANALYST

A person who studies a number of different companies and makes buy-and-sell recommendations OR the entry position of someone starting their career in some investment banks.

BONDS

In simplest terms, an IOU! It is an agreement whereby a sum of money is repaid to an investor after a certain period of time, usually with interest.

BROKER

Either an intermediary between a buyer and a seller, receiving a commission typically based on the value of the transaction OR an insurance intermediary who advises clients and arranges their insurance or investments.

CAPITAL MARKET

The financial market in which investment products, such as stocks and bonds, are bought and sold.

CLAIM

A demand made by the insured, or the insured's beneficiary, for payment from a policy (eg insurance).

COMMODITIES
Commodities are goods such as oil, petrol, metal or grain traded on the commodity markets such as the London Metal Exchange.

DERIVATIVES
The group term for financial contracts between buyers and sellers of goods (commodities) or money (capital).

DUE DILIGENCE
An investigation into the true financial and commercial position of a company.

EQUITY
The risk-sharing part of a company's capital, usually referred to as ordinary shares.

FINANCIAL SERVICES AUTHORITY (FSA)
An independent, non-government body, which regulates the financial services industry in the UK.

FTSE 100/250 INDEX
The Financial Times Stock Exchange Index of the 100/250 companies with the largest market capitalisation on the UK stock market.

INDEMNITY
The legal principle that ensures that a policyholder is restored to the same financial position after a loss as he/she was in beforehand.

INDEPENDENT FINANCIAL ADVISER
A broker or other intermediary authorised to sell or advise on the policies of any life insurance company, as well as other financial products.

INSURANCE
A service that offers financial compensation for something that may or may not happen. Assurance is often used interchangeably for the same service.

INTEREST RATES
This is the 'rental' price for borrowing money and is charged to compensate for potential risk.

LIABILITY
Legal responsibility for injuring or damaging a person or their property.

LIQUIDATION
Selling a company's assets to pay off debts.

LIQUIDITY
The ease with which an asset or investment can be turned into money.

LLOYD'S OF LONDON
An insurance market, organised into syndicates, which underwrites most types of policy.

LONDON MARKET
A distinct, separate part of the UK insurance and reinsurance industry centred on the City of London, comprising insurance and reinsurance companies.

PERSONAL ACCIDENT INSURANCE
A policy that pays specified amounts of money if the policyholder is injured in an accident.

POLICY
A legal document confirming a contract between an insurer and a policyholder.

POLICYHOLDER
A person or organisation who takes out an insurance policy in cover of a particular risk.

PORTFOLIO
A collection of securities held by an investor.

PRIVATE EQUITY
High risk and high return investment in shares, which cannot easily be turned into cash, in new companies.

REINSURANCE
The cover insurance companies can purchase to protect themselves against large losses.

RISK MANAGEMENT
Evaluating and selecting alternative regulatory and non-regulatory responses to risk, normally through legal and economic considerations.

SECURITIES
This is a general term describing all types of bonds and shares.

SETTLEMENT
Once a deal has been made stock is transferred from seller to buyer to settle the deal.

STOCKS
A certificate of ownership in a company, rather like shares.

UNDERWRITER
A person who evaluates risks and decides whether or not to accept a risk. The underwriter also determines the rates and coverage that are associated with accepting a risk.

Which area?

Such is the range of career paths to choose from in this sector that finance and accounting students are spoilt for choice.

Those unfamiliar with the range of sectors within the finance and accounting worlds may think that the main work areas revolve around services offered by high street banks or accountancy firms. However, the situation is far more diverse and complex than that. There are many different disciplines to choose from, varying in location from a small town in the regions, to the City of London and beyond. We have summarised the main areas into which people are recruited to give you a flavour of what you might end up doing as a recent graduate.

ACTUARIAL WORK

Advice, assessment and calculations

The work

Three main business areas employ actuaries: pensions, insurance and investment. Actuaries advise clients on their schemes in each or any of these areas: this can be challenging as they have to explain quite technical information in layman's terms. Some of the typical tasks they undertake include working on risk-assessment models to set insurance premiums and monitoring the running and financial health of pension schemes. Not everyone working in an actuarial department is a qualified actuary: there are also IT, human resources and marketing experts.

Graduates will start off as trainee actuaries and will study, while working, for three to six years before taking their professional exams. Typical daily tasks include working on calculations and preparing papers for client meetings. Long hours should be expected when meeting client deadlines.

ASSURANCE

Reviewing financial data and procedures

The work

Assurance professionals review companies' financial data and procedures to ensure that the management is taking care of shareholders' money. It is impossible to check every single transaction, so it's important to assess areas that are considered higher risk. Clients vary from listed companies to small family businesses.

Everyone tends to work as part of a team in this area and a few weeks after joining, you would be heavily involved in all aspects of each process.

BUSINESS ADVISORY

Offering clients a wide range of services

The work

The main responsibility of people working in business advisory is to provide a high standard of service to clients based on the development of strong client relationships. The services provided range from audit, corporate and personal tax to corporate finance and business recovery.

Graduates in this area will normally work on projects as part of a small team. Opportunities for travel are huge, as are secondments to worldwide destinations on qualification.

COMMERCIAL FINANCE

Analysing and improving performance

The work

Commercial finance managers work in a variety of sectors including leisure, retail and fast-moving consumer goods to analyse the performances of their services or goods and recommend steps to maximise profits. The focus of analysis could be on one product or on broader strategic advice to drive a business forward. Pricing goods or services can fall within the remit of the commercial finance manager, who needs to find a balance between making a sufficient profit and being appealing to consumers.

Graduates can join a training programme in industry and commerce and gain a professional accountancy qualification. Commercial finance managers can move into a career in management, once they have acquired in-depth sector knowledge and an understanding of how businesses work.

CORPORATE BANKING

Managing financial flows for corporate customers

The work

Corporate bankers help corporate customers, financial institutions and public-sector organisations to manage their daily financial flows. They are the 'bread and butter' winners of any corporate bank. They will provide advice on such aspects as a potential merger or acquisition, investments or fund management, and making payments to suppliers on time. The services corporate banks provide to customers are similar, but more complex, to those offered by high street banks to their retail customers.

Employees can expect early, and high, levels of responsibility and autonomy, with their own portfolio of junior products and client contact, and with opportunities for travel.

CORPORATE FINANCE

Add value to businesses in the process of change

The work

Corporate finance involves adding value to businesses that are in the process of change, for example selling off a part of their business or acquiring a new one. There are three main areas of work: lead advisory (project management of a transaction), transaction support (including due diligence, valuations and business planning) and compliance work (regulatory work).

Graduates can gain professional qualifications in audit and accountancy or corporate finance. Excellent social skills are needed, as the role often involves communicating with senior business managers, as well as adaptability and the confidence to take on responsibility.

CORPORATE RECOVERY

Assisting companies in financial distress

The work

Professionals in this area provide services and advice to underperforming companies (mainly banks and private equity houses) and their stakeholders. Financial and restructuring solutions are normally offered, including restoring debt to reduce finance costs, improving cash management, and increasing operational performance. If it is too late in the day for the company to recover, insolvency is sometimes the only option.

Employees normally spend six months of a three-year training contract undertaking chartered accountancy exams. They will work mainly on insolvency assignments, helping an insolvent business continue to trade. Tasks include preparing financial projections and bank reports, dealing with a company's suppliers or debtors, or helping to sell the business.

CORPORATE TREASURY

Managing risks and looking forward

The work

This involves, broadly speaking, managing financial risks, such as bank facilities and capital markets, cash investments, foreign exchange dealing, mergers and acquisitions, insurance and pensions.

The starting point is normally as a treasury dealer, which involves reviewing bank balances, proposing, executing and recording transactions, and ensuring compliance with internal controls. Hours tend to be long, especially when projects near completion.

FINANCIAL ACCOUNTING

Communicating financial information with the outside world

The work

Financial accountants record and report a company's results to the outside world, according to strict accounting rules. The work involves: analysing and reviewing business financial results; providing advice and support on accounting issues, deals and projects; consolidating and analysing financial results and reporting on them; external reporting and planning; and interpreting and communicating accounting developments to ensure open and accurate disclosure of financial information.

FORENSIC ACCOUNTING

Putting together the accounting pieces

The work

Forensic accountants provide expert reports on, or attend court to give oral evidence in, cases involving accountancy matters. They may also assess the effect of applying legal issues to a case, and assist with dispute resolution (trying to solve matters through arbitration or mediation instead of going to court). Specialists in this field also help clients to investigate accounting irregularities and fraud by looking at any evidence such as witness interviews and paper and electronic sources.

Graduates are often offered a wealth of opportunities, including the chance to spend six months on secondment during training. A business understanding of corporate controls is normally gained by training in audit and then transferring to forensic accounting, enabling you to see a wider spectrum of businesses, not just the ones that are in conflict. Professionals normally work as part of a team, varying in size from two to 20 people, and new starters will normally be involved in research, analysis, evidence gathering and computer modelling.

INTER-DEALER BROKING

Buy and sell financial instruments for clients

The work

Inter-dealer brokers act as intermediaries to help clients – normally corporations rather than individuals – buy and sell financial instruments, such as bonds and equities. Sometimes clients use inter-dealer brokers for the purpose of trading anonymously, in order to get the best price.

To succeed in the field you need good people skills and an outgoing personality, as well as a passion for financial markets.

INSURANCE

Helping customers manage unforeseen risks

The work

Insurance companies help individuals and organisations protect themselves against unforeseen circumstances in exchange for an annual premium. If anything unexpected happens, the insurance claim should help get them back on their feet again as quickly as possible.

You could be employed within the engineering or surveyors' departments, which assess damage to cars and property, or work as a team leader in a contact centre. Some specific areas include **strategy:** business planning and support; **underwriting:** setting policy terms and evaluating the risk an individual or company presents; and **relationship management:** managing relationships with client companies for whom insurance schemes are provided and helping to develop new products for them.

INTERNAL AUDIT

Providing independent and objective financial opinions

The work

Internal audit is all about providing an independent and objective appraisal of an organisation's operations, in order to assess the effectiveness of their internal administrative and accounting controls and to ensure that they conform to relevant policies. Internal auditors will normally do this by testing the internal controls that are already in place and drafting a subsequent report on their findings.

Those employed in this area may find themselves working for clients throughout the UK and possibly overseas. Team sizes vary from one individual working on their own to four or five auditors. The sheer variety of the clients served keeps the job stimulating and interesting.

INVESTMENT BANKING

Offering advice on finance and risk management to clients

The work

Investment bankers provide advice on finance and risk management to a wide range of clients from corporates and financial institutions to government-related organisations. They analyse their financial needs and offer appropriate solutions. However, they do not force products onto their clients.

Long hours can be common. Investment bankers normally start their careers by helping senior bankers with their work. The job can sometimes be routine, eg when collating and repackaging data, but you will soon move on to enjoying more direct contact with clients.

INVESTMENT MANAGEMENT

Making and managing profits for clients

The work

Investment managers try to select stock for a client's portfolio that will outperform both the wider market and their competitors, with the result that they will hopefully make their clients a tidy sum of money. They meet with senior managers from a wide range of companies to research both the businesses themselves and the markets in which they operate before investing money entrusted to them from pension funds or private investors.

Employees normally work towards the Chartered Financial Analyst qualification, while still undertaking their professional duties. Normally you will be given one or two sectors to research and it's your job to then pass on any buy-and-sell ideas to your investment manager, who will ultimately decide where the money is invested. Travel opportunities are good, both nationally and internationally, but expect long hours and an intense working environment.

LIFE ASSURANCE

Providing financial security for life

The work

Companies in this area provide their customers with financial protection and money-management ideas. The main difference between general and life insurance is that this area is long term, providing three major product lines: **pensions:** financial protection at the end of your working life; **life assurance:** financial protection for your family if something unfortunate happens to you; and **investment:** life assurance companies invest their customers' premiums in the stock market, bonds and property.

Work in this area could be in one of many roles, including customer services, sales, marketing, risk management, finance, HR and IT.

MANAGEMENT ACCOUNTING

Enabling effective decision-making

The work

Management accountants work with company managers to help them make effective decisions about their business and how it is run. They provide financial interpretation and advice, report on financial performance within the company and give early warnings if underperformance is likely or suspected (and suitable plans of action if this is the case). They also help managers understand what drives the business and explain the financial consequences of their decisions.

Beginners normally support a management accountant team, often by covering a management accountant position. This carries with it a great deal of responsibility, as you get to influence business decisions. The area is constantly changing and consequently is never dull: but you must be happy to accept frequent challenges.

MARKETS

Providing investment solutions for clients and profits for the firm

The work

This sector provides both investment solutions for customers and profits for the firm, and covers three main areas: **sales:** providing a link between the firm and the financial institutions that want to invest money; **trading:** investing the firm's capital, or making markets or providing liquidity on financial products for clients; and **structuring:** developing large financial products for clients.

Starters normally work in small teams of up to ten, designing presentations, working on spreadsheets and modelling: basically helping out wherever possible. Expect long working hours: 7am to 6pm is normal, as are 12 hour days during big deals.

OPERATIONS

Ensuring banks comply with financial and legal regulations

The work

The main job of the operations department is to ensure that business activities within a bank are conducted in a controlled manner and comply with both banking and legal regulations. Roles in this area can have an accounting, settlement or risk-management bias.

Most people will be able to rotate around different operations groups for a couple of years to get an overview of the various jobs available. Not only does this give you excellent experience but it should also help you decide on where you would like to base your career. Early responsibility and accountability is likely, and typical jobs include initiating the introduction of a new product on behalf of your team. Working hours depend on the markets you support and the activity within them, so can fluctuate from one day to the next.

PRIVATE BANKING

Also known as private wealth management

The work

Private wealth management is about providing professional services to high net-worth clients to help them manage their finances to the best possible effect. Services offered include advisory, where the private banker advises the client about investment opportunities and the client makes the final decision, and discretionary, where, after an in-depth discussion, the bank manages the client's portfolio on their behalf.

Private banking tends to be an international business, so good language skills are invaluable. You also need to have excellent communication skills and a strong customer focus.

REGULATION

Setting regulations to protect consumers

The work

Employers in this area fall into two main categories:
Regulatory bodies: such as the Financial Services Authority (FSA), which oversees the UK financial

services industry, and the Office of Fair Trading (OFT), which ensures that markets work well for consumers.
Financial services providers: which employ compliance or risk officers to ensure their business and products meet with FSA regulations.

Professionals in this area are responsible for:

- making sure that each company's rules and regulations are financially trustworthy
- alerting consumers to the benefits and risks associated with different financial products
- looking into the type and level of risk associated with different investment products and transactions and taking action to lower that risk
- ensuring that regulated businesses cannot easily be used to commit financial crime.

Those working for a regulatory body will have a broad introduction to regulation before specialising in a specific sector, eg insurance. Financial services providers normally recruit graduates into a more general finance scheme before offering the chance to specialise later.

RETAIL BANKING

Supplying financial products to a wide range of clients

The work

This work not only involves front line sales staff and branch management but also covers jobs in human resources, marketing and finance, as is the case with any other retail business. Retail banks deal with a huge variety of clients, from individuals with personal accounts to multinational companies needing a range of financial services. This area is fast moving and exciting, requiring new initiatives to keep up-to-date with clients' needs.

There are opportunities for graduates in branch management, network support and project management. Many retail banks have an international element, so travel might be possible. Available training includes studying for relevant banking qualifications or a diploma in financial services.

RISK ASSESSMENT

Protecting business from potential risks

The work

Risk assessors help businesses to understand, prioritise and manage potential risks, thus avoiding future problems while making the most of opportunities. The role of the risk assessor is to identify and evaluate risks and then recommend appropriate strategies. It is an intellectually satisfying job but primarily advisory, which requires the ability to step back and let others make final decisions.

Graduates usually train in a broader area such as assurance, going on to specialise in risk assessment at a later stage, although some accountancy firms do employ graduates directly into risk assessment roles. Numerical and analytical skills are key, as are an ability to think logically and good interpersonal skills.

RISK MANAGEMENT

Understanding and controlling trading risks

The work

Risk management, or risk control, is the business function that ensures trading risks are understood by an organisation, which can then build a suitable strategy. Daily activities include running reports, analysing risks and communicating risk exposures to traders.

Graduates tend to join graduate training programmes. Numeracy and strong analytical skills are essential, and many graduates have a science or mathematics background.

SPECIALIST MARKETS

Advising and structuring deals for specific sectors

The work

Specialist market teams provide advice on mergers and acquisitions to clients from particular industry sectors, such as healthcare, the media and financial institutions. It's 'specialist' because you need an in-depth knowledge of your client's sector in order to effectively carry out transactions on your client's behalf, after you have made them aware of the different options available. You will also need to watch what is happening in their sector to both predict future transactions and approach clients with ideas.

You normally work in small teams of around four or five people and early responsibility is guaranteed. You will normally produce the financial analysis reports, prepare press materials, research the sector and oversee some aspects of a deal. Travel is common, depending on your clients' locations. Working hours tend to be long because of the project nature of the work.

STRUCTURED FINANCE

Providing tailor-made financing solutions to clients

The work

Specialists in this area use their in-depth knowledge of different industry sectors, such as telecommunications, gas and oil, and natural resources, to offer clients a variety of structured debt and equity products, while designing complex financing to meet their clients' requirements.

You will be involved with transactions from day one, as part of a small team. You will normally be responsible for such tasks as preparing pitch material, undertaking analysis and research, carrying out due diligence and helping to close a deal successfully. Since deals are becoming more complex, long days can be expected, often from 8.30am-8pm.

TAX

Giving clients the lowdown on taxation

The work

In most corporate tax departments, each member has their own portfolio of clients to deal with, from virtually every type of business and industry. Typical work includes preparing company tax returns, handling relationships with the tax inspector, and offering tax advice on any ongoing or potential business transactions. Basically, it's about making sure companies comply with current tax legislation, submit their tax return on time and pay the right amount of tax.

In larger firms, several graduates are taken on each year to train as chartered tax advisers and accountants. They often play a key role early on in their careers as tax assistants by preparing tax calculations for clients, helping to improve the client/company relationship and giving good tax advice.

Register
Sign up for the FREE UCAS Card if you're in Year 12, S5 or equivalent and thinking about higher education to receive all these benefits...
cdWOW!
Domino's Pizza
TOPSHOP
TOPMAN
BELLA ITALIA
Caffe • Bar • Ristorante
BSM
SAVE a packet on the high street with your card.*
ucascard
EXPERT help from Giles, the UCAS adviser with all the reminders, hints and tips.
INFO about the courses and universities you're interested in.
UNLIMITED use of yougofurther.co.uk, the UCAS student network website
FREE copies of The Independent's 'You Can' magazine delivered to your door.
YOU CAN
ucascard
* correct at time of printing.
UCAS

Is economics, finance or accountancy for you?

Building a successful career in finance and accountancy requires more than a head for numbers.

A career in these sectors requires certain skills and personal qualities and, to help you decide if this is the right working area for you, we suggest you think about the following three areas:

- what you want from your future work
- what a finance or accounting course typically involves
- which skills and qualities admissions tutors in this field typically seek in new recruits.

WHAT DO YOU WANT FROM YOUR CAREER?

You may not have an instant answer for this now but your current studies, work experience and even your hobbies can help give you clues about the kind of work you enjoy and the skills you have already started to develop. Start with a blank sheet of paper and note down the answers to the following questions to help get you thinking. Be as honest with yourself as you can: don't write what you think will impress your teachers or parents. Write what really matters to you, and you'll start to see a pattern emerging.

WHAT REALLY MATTERS TO YOU

- When you think of your future, what kind of environment do you see yourself working in, eg in an office, outdoors, nine-to-five, relaxed or high-pressured?
- What are your favourite hobbies outside of school?
- What is it about them that you enjoy, eg the numerical challenges of a Sudoku puzzle or the strategies of a chess game?
- What are your favourite subjects in school and what is it about them that you enjoy most, eg being able to solve mathematical problems or working with people to arrive at solutions?
- What do you dislike about the other subjects you're studying?
- If you've had any work experience, which aspects have you most enjoyed?

WHAT DO FINANCE AND ACCOUNTING COURSES INVOLVE?

Unsurprisingly, the skills you'll require as a successful accountant or financial services professional will also be required at various stages of your studies. Therefore, it is important to know what typical finance and accounting courses entail before you apply, to be sure it's the kind of work you will enjoy. For example, most university courses will involve a mixture of practical knowledge, which can be applied and used in the modern workplace, and more theoretical study, often concentrating on both essential and advanced concepts of such areas as business, finance economics, accounting and management. Are you happy to undertake such in-depth analysis of your subject?

WHAT SKILLS WILL YOU NEED?

Despite the many different career options within the finance and accountancy sectors, the skills set they all require is broadly the same. Number one is **numerical ability**, which employers will mostly discern from your GCSEs, A levels and degree subject. Beyond this, other key skills required of any potential finance and accountancy professional are:

- **analytical ability** - to assess a situation or issue and identify key elements that need to be addressed in order to move on
- **commercial awareness** - a knowledge and understanding of the business issues that affect the sector you are interested in, as well as their external factors and internal structures
- **problem-solving** - finding an appropriate solution to a problem using the information and resources to hand
- **decision-making** - confidently choosing the best way forward for you and your client by assessing the various available options and the pros and cons of each

- **negotiation** - discussing an issue or problem either face-to-face or by telephone or, more rarely, by email. The aim is for both parties to come to a mutually satisfactory conclusion and this may involve compromise on one or both sides
- **self-confidence** - when dealing with often contentious and sensitive issues, you need to feel confident in yourself and your abilities to help instil that belief in others to follow your recommendations
- **teamworking** - working with others to reach a desired goal: a key skill in virtually every working environment, finance-related or not
- **written communication** - an ability to make yourself clearly understood in text, whether in emails, letters or more formal documentation. With such large amounts of cash often at risk, it's vital people know where you're coming from
- **interpersonal skills** - since most, if not all, roles in these sectors involve working in teams and dealing with clients, you need to be comfortable working with, and relating to, other people.

Alternative economics, finance and accountancy careers

If a career in finance and accountancy isn't for you, there are plenty of other interesting possibilities...

There are many career paths that can be linked directly, or tenuously, to a degree in finance or accounting: the difficulty is choosing the right one. In broad terms, suitable career sectors can include the law (particularly commercial law), management consulting, property and quantity surveying.

COMMERCIAL LAWYERS

Commercial solicitors work with investment bankers to get the best possible deal for their clients and to ensure that their contracts comply with the appropriate investment-related regulations. Typical employers range from large London-based firms that specialise in handling high-value and often international commercial transactions, to sole practitioners based in high street firms, undertaking work for local companies.

If working as a barrister appeals more to you, you will normally work on a self-employed basis, from a set of chambers, again probably situated in London. Typical tasks include defending or prosecuting cases, of a commercial nature, on behalf of a client in the commercial court.

If the legal route wins your vote, you will need to complete a one-year postgraduate law conversion course, if your first degree subject is not law. After that, you will also need to study for either the Legal Practice Course (LPC) if you want to become a solicitor, followed by a two-year training contract with a firm; or the one-year Bar Vocational Course (BVC), followed by pupillage in a set or sets of chambers, if you want to be a barrister.

Further information

The Law Society of England & Wales, **www.lawsociety.org.uk**, for information on becoming a solicitor, or The Bar Council, **www.barcouncil.org.uk** for information on becoming a barrister.
Progression Series – Law
www.ucasbooks.com

MANAGEMENT CONSULTANTS

Management consultants provide organisations with strategies to improve their business. They identify potential problem areas and suggest, then implement, solutions. Employers range from the consultancy divisions of the four main accountancy firms (The Big Four: Deloitte Touche Tohmatsu, Ernst & Young, KPMG and PricewaterhouseCoopers) to specialist organisations that provide more specific advice on certain areas such as IT, healthcare, strategy, etc.

Further information

The Institute of Business Consulting
www.ibconsulting.org.uk

CHARTERED SURVEYORS

Chartered surveyors advise clients on how to maximise the value of their property while **quantity surveyors** manage the cost of construction projects. In order to gain professional status, you will need to take a one-year full-time (or two-year part-time) conversion course, if your first degree is not in quantity surveying, as well as completing the assessment of professional competence (APC), which is a two-year training scheme that all quantity surveyors undertake.

Property and quantity surveying are dominated by a few small international firms based both in London and regional centres and a larger number of smaller firms based throughout the UK.

Further information

The Royal Institution of Chartered Surveyors,
www.rics.org

There are various industry associations and institutes that provide information for aspiring graduates. To check them out, visit **www.targetjobs.co.uk**, select 'Career Sectors' and select 'Construction' or 'Property' from the list of options.

USING YOUR TRANSFERABLE SKILLS

While these three areas are great career matches for finance and accounting graduates, you don't have to limit yourself to these. The skills you will develop and hone as part of your degree are transferable to many other areas that require an ability with numbers, an analytical approach, an interest in financial processes and organisations, and an understanding of how companies work. Any business area would potentially benefit from the skills you'll develop through a finance or accounting related degree, as would any roles that require financial research and advice, including those in politics and government and even in specialist publishing and media (eg financial broadcasting and journalism).

Professional bodies

Professional bodies are responsible for overseeing a particular profession or career area, ensuring that people who work in the area are fully trained and meet ethical guidelines. Professional bodies may be known as institutions, societies and associations. They generally have regulatory roles: they make sure that members of the profession are able to work successfully in their jobs without endangering lives or abusing their position.

Professional bodies are often involved in training and career development, so courses and workplace training may have to follow the body's guidelines. In order to be fully qualified and licensed to work in your profession of choice, you will have to follow the professional training route. In many areas of work, completion of the professional training results in gaining chartered status – and the addition of some extra letters after your name. Other institutions may award other types of certification once certain criteria have been met. Chartered or certified members will usually need to take further courses and training to ensure their skills are kept up to date.

What professional bodies are there?

Not all career areas have professional bodies. Those jobs that require extensive learning and training are likely to have bodies with a regulatory focus. This includes careers such as engineering, law, construction, health and finance. If you want to work in one of these areas, it's important to make sure your degree course is accredited by the professional body – otherwise you may have to undertake further study or training later on.

Other bodies may play more of a supportive role, looking after the interests of people who work in the sector. This includes journalism, management and arts-based careers. Professional bodies may also be learned bodies, providing opportunities for further learning and promoting the development of knowledge in the field.

Can I join as a student?

Many professional bodies offer student membership – sometimes free or for reduced fees. Membership can be extremely valuable as a source of advice, information and resources. You'll have the opportunity to meet other students in the field, as well as experienced professionals. It will also look good on your CV, when you come to apply for jobs.

See below for a list of professional bodies in the fields of economics, finance and accountancy.

ECONOMICS

The Royal Economic Society
www.res.org.uk

Society of Business Economists
www.sbe.co.uk

FINANCE AND ACCOUNTANCY

The Actuarial Profession
www.actuaries.org.uk

The Association of Chartered Certified Accountants
www.acca.org.uk

Chartered Institute of Bankers in Scotland
www.ciobs.org.uk

Chartered Institute of Management Accountants
www.cimaglobal.com

The Chartered Institute of Public Finance and Accountancy
www.cipfa.org.uk

Chartered Institute for Securities and Investment
www.cisi.org

Institute of Bankers in Ireland
www.bankers.ie

Institute of Chartered Accountants in England & Wales
www.icaew.co.uk

The Chartered Insurance Institute (CII)
www.cii.co.uk

Insurance Institute of London
www.iilondon.co.uk

Graduate destinations

Economics and Accountancy
HESA Destination of Leavers of Higher Education Survey

Each year, comprehensive statistics are collected on what graduates are doing six months after they complete their course. The survey is co-ordinated by the Higher Education Statistics Agency (HESA) and provides information about how many graduates move into employment (and what type of career) or further study and how many are believed to be unemployed.

The full results across all subject areas are published by the Higher Education Careers Service Unit (HECSU) and the Association of Graduate Careers Advisory Services (AGCAS) in *What Do Graduates Do?*, which is available from **www.ucasbooks.com**.

	Economics	Accountancy
In UK employment	49.3%	47.6%
In overseas employment	2.0%	1.0%
Working and studying	18.5%	24.4%
Studying in the UK for a higher degree	6.6%	3.0%
Studying in the UK for a teaching qualification	0.6%	0.6%
Undertaking other further study or training in the UK	3.7%	4.1%
Studying overseas	0.2%	0.1%
Not available for employment, study or training	5.2%	3.4%
Assumed to be unemployed	9.7%	10.9%
Other	4.1%	4.8%

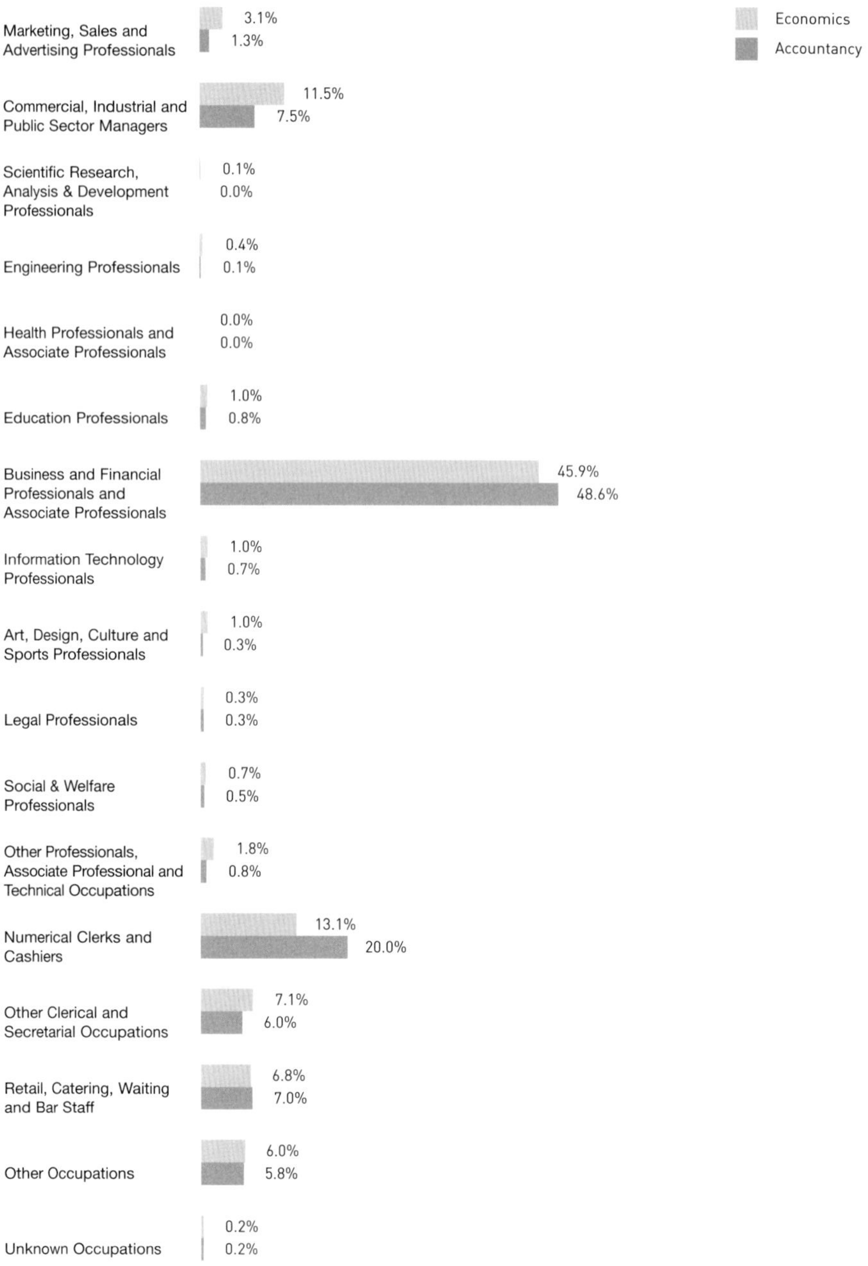

Reproduced with the kind permission of HECSU/AGCAS, *What Do Graduates Do? 2010.*
Data from the HESA Destinations of Leavers from Higher Education Survey 07/08

Case studies

ProgressionSeries

HEAR IT FROM THE EXPERTS

Still not sure whether you want to work in finance or accountancy? Read the following profiles to see where the world of work has taken recent graduates in the financial professions and beyond!

Tax and consulting work placements

Deloitte

ARTHUR CALLAGHAN

Route into accountancy:
A levels – economics, physics, maths, further maths, geography (AS) (2006); in third year of BSc economics degree, University College London

WHY ECONOMICS AND ACCOUNTANCY?

I enjoyed economics A level so decided to study it in greater depth but applied for deferred university entry because I wanted to do a work placement with a business services firm during my gap year. I hoped that this experience would help me choose the right career direction after my degree. I also knew that I would be able to do further placements during my degree and earn some money!

My degree has had a broad outlook but I've been most interested in the area of financial markets, which is a very practical application of economics.

HOW DID YOU GET TO WHERE YOU ARE TODAY?

I am now in the final year of my degree and when I finish I will be starting a graduate job within the restructuring division of Deloitte's corporate finance function. During my first three years I will also be studying for the ACA professional accounting qualification. I applied for the job once I had finished all my placements at the firm and was sure that I wanted to work there.

WHAT HAVE YOUR PLACEMENTS INVOLVED?

While on the Deloitte scholar scheme, I had a gap-year placement that lasted for seven months. I was based in the tax division of my employer's Cambridge office. I started out with and was given the same training and treatment as university graduates. The work involved calculating tax bills for such businesses as local pharmaceutical and science companies and trying to make them as tax efficient as possible. As well as attending compulsory training on tax issues including tax law, I was able to take voluntary training courses, for example in IT.

In my first university summer vacation, I did a four-week placement in the tax division of my employer's London office. I was placed in a specialist division working on the tax affairs of international companies. As well as tax calculations, I was sometimes asked to carry out market research into a particular industry before looking at a company from a tax perspective.

I did a third placement in my second summer vacation. This time I asked to work in my employer's consulting service line and was put onto a project dealing with the merger of two large banks from a human resources perspective. I was working in a small team, the hours were longer than I'd previously worked and there were tight deadlines, but I discovered that I enjoyed the pressure.

WHAT WAS YOUR BIGGEST CHALLENGE?

The placement in consulting was my biggest challenge. There were lots of meetings with the client where we had to get the information we needed, which wasn't always what they wanted to tell us. Diplomacy and communication skills were really important.

WHAT DO YOU MOST ENJOY ABOUT YOUR PLACEMENTS?

I was continually surprised by how friendly and open my colleagues were! I am still in contact with friends I made during my gap-year placement. I really enjoyed the chance to work on and learn about industries I was interested in but previously knew little about. Although I found it daunting at first to be treated the same as full-time graduate employees, I found that I loved being given so much responsibility during all my placements.

ARTHUR'S TOP TIPS

Choose a degree subject you are genuinely interested in – you'll be studying it for three years! If you take a gap year, make sure you spend some of it gaining valuable work experience.

Economist

Ministry of Health, Burundi
(Overseas Development Institute fellowship)

KARISHMAH BHUWANEE

Route into economics:
A levels – maths, economics, chemistry, German (2000); BA economics and management, University of Oxford (2003); MSc development management, London School of Economics (2006)

WHY ECONOMICS?

I enjoyed studying economics A level. It's a very logical subject and overlaps with many other areas, and I knew it would open up many career paths. I chose to work in development economics because I wanted a career where I could feel that I was genuinely contributing to something and having a positive impact. I also knew I would have the chance to visit different countries, meet many different types of people and experience different cultures.

HOW DID YOU GET WHERE YOU ARE TODAY?

My path into international development was somewhat unconventional. After my undergraduate degree, I spent two years in an investment bank, advising companies on mergers and acquisitions. At this point I had not yet decided on the best route into development work but knew that a job as a financial adviser would give me transferable skills and valuable private-sector experience. I then took a master's in international development at the London School of Economics (LSE), spending the summer before the course doing an internship with the Overseas Development Institute researching pro-poor policy.

While I was at LSE, a careers adviser mentioned Crown Agents, a development consultancy that provided graduate training programmes. I applied for the graduate scheme and worked there for three years, working on a variety of projects and getting a very useful insight into how the field of development operates. I also had the opportunity to travel to visit projects and clients.

Added to this I wanted to get some long-term experience in a developing country. I successfully applied for the Overseas Development Institute Fellowship, a scheme that sends economists to work in ministries in developing countries across the world. My posting was the Ministry of Health in Burundi. I will be spending two years here as an economic adviser in the planning and budgeting department.

WHAT DOES YOUR JOB INVOLVE?

I am working to improve planning and budgeting within the Ministry of Health, and to increase its capacity by training colleagues. On a day-to-day basis this involves analysing the ministry budget, collecting and analysing donor data, organising meetings between the ministry and the donors to improve cooperation and assisting with ministry reforms.

I am normally based at the central ministry office but often we have meetings with the donors as well as other Ministry of Health departments and other ministries. Sometimes there are field visits up-country which, work permitting, I can join.

WHAT HAS BEEN YOUR BIGGEST CHALLENGE?

My biggest challenge has been adjusting to working conditions in Burundi, where capacity and motivation can be very low. I have to be very self-motivated to get things done, and I cannot always get colleagues to assist. I've had to get used to a slower pace of working – it takes much longer to get things done here!

WHAT DO YOU LIKE MOST ABOUT YOUR JOB?

The best part is travelling to different countries and working with different governments to try to help them improve their efficiency and effectiveness. It's also rewarding being in an environment where you feel that your help is really needed. The variety of the projects makes the job fascinating.

KARISHMAH'S TOP TIPS

Get as much work experience as possible, as early as you can. It is a very competitive field, so be very flexible at the start – any foot in the door is useful.

Retail management trainee

HSBC

REBECCA SAFURRIDIN

Route into retail banking:
A levels – economics, politics, ITC (2004); BSc business management, University of Birmingham (2008)

WHY RETAIL BANKING?

I knew that I wanted to go into business, although I wasn't sure what kind. I chose a business management degree because I knew it would give me a range of career options. In my first year I studied accounting, finance, economics, marketing and customer relationships management.

HOW DID YOU GET WHERE YOU ARE TODAY?

Initially, I was attracted to investment banking, but the recession made me rethink my plans and I decided to apply for a retail banking graduate scheme. I had built up a lot of work experience during my summer vacations, although none of it specifically related to finance, I knew that I enjoyed working with people and that customer relationship management was an important part of retail banking. I applied for HSBC's graduate scheme in the summer after my final exams.

WHAT DOES YOUR JOB INVOLVE?

I have recently completed the first six months of a two-year graduate training programme. This involves starting 'at the bottom' so you can learn everything about how the business works. It also gains you more respect when you come to manage others.

I have spent the first few months learning all about basic banking, meeting and greeting customers and taking on a 'counsellor' role, which involves dealing with more complex issues such as opening accounts or transferring money abroad.

On a typical day I get into the branch at 8.30am. At 8.45am we have a branch meeting, which I sometimes lead, to talk through how things went the day before and how we can improve on our service. From then on my day is varied. I may start on reception, meeting and greeting our customers and allocating them to a member of staff who will be able to deal with their needs, before doing this myself. Recently I have taken on more managerial responsibilities, checking how all the staff are doing and helping them to achieve their targets.

My next six-month placement will be as a senior counsellor, where my managerial duties will be extended. I will then be placed in a business specialist role, which will involve getting new business clients, and in my final six months I will take on a leadership role, for example as a branch or a sales and service manager.

As a graduate trainee I also attend regular external meetings and conferences, and am required to work towards a professional qualification in corporate finance management.

WHAT HAS BEEN YOUR BIGGEST CHALLENGE?

Getting up at 6am! I've had to learn to be extremely organised to make sure I get everything done, for example, I use my commuting time to revise for exams and I keep a diary so that I manage my time properly and get to all my meetings. I often look back to my university days and wonder what I did with all that spare time...

WHAT DO YOU LIKE MOST ABOUT YOUR JOB?

On a day-to-day level, the people I work with are lovely. I really enjoy solving customers' problems and see them leaving the branch satisfied: it's a great opportunity to build on my customer management skills. I regularly meet senior personnel at conferences, which is exciting.

REBECCA'S TOP TIPS

I wasn't hindered by not doing an internship, but I know lots of people who were offered jobs after completing one. If you decide to apply for internships or graduate schemes while studying, check you know important dates in the application process so you can plan ahead for essays and exams.

Market risk management – Structured Credit Trading Risk Officer

Bank of America Merrill Lynch

JAMES WADLEY

Route into investment banking:
A levels – mathematics, physics, economics (2004); master of mathematics, operational research, statistics and economics, University of Warwick (M. Morse) (2008)

WHY BANKING / FINANCE?

I chose my degree because I was keen to further my numeracy skills and proficiency and to understand how the economy functioned in greater depth.

I wasn't sure what career path I wanted to take until the beginning of my third year. After ruling out the actuarial route, I set about researching the banking sector. A careers adviser suggested risk management because of my interest in statistics.

HOW DID YOU GET WHERE YOU ARE TODAY?

At the end of my third year I got a Bank of America summer internship, which gave me a great insight into what market risk management entails day-o-day, and how an investment bank works and makes money.

During the internship I picked up key ideas behind risk management and became increasingly comfortable with speaking about technical subjects with colleagues. I was offered a position to start on the graduate programme on graduation but I decided I wanted to take a gap year to travel the world. I was then offered a second internship, with a view to a permanent role the following year. During my second internship I was placed in a slightly different team looking at different financial products, although still within market risk management.

After my gap year I joined the graduate programme. One of the best parts of the training was that it was in New York, with over 400 graduates from around the globe. As well as revising the basics of the banking world, I also made valuable contacts in different areas of the bank, in different parts of the world. This put me in good stead to start in my team in London.

WHAT DOES YOUR JOB INVOLVE?

I work in the structured credit team for market risk management at Bank of America Merrill Lynch, offering innovative financing and investing ideas and solutions to our clients. The risk management team is responsible for monitoring the trading desks' risk positions, setting trading limits and advising on potential new products/deals.

As the most junior person in my team, a lot of my time is spent producing daily risk reports, checking that our internal systems correctly portray the desks' risk positions, signing off data and performing calculations and investigations to analyse whether or not changes need to be made to our estimation methodologies.

I usually get to the office at around 8.30am and finish between 6.30 and 7.30pm. This might sound like long hours, but it is surprising how quickly you adapt, and I always have my weekends off.

WHAT HAS BEEN YOUR BIGGEST CHALLENGE?

The products my trading desk trades are probably the most complex on the market, and there was a mountain of reading I needed to do before I could even comprehend some of the products my colleagues were talking about. I am still trying to understand some of the finer details of the most complex trades, but luckily my team has been very helpful.

WHAT DO YOU LIKE MOST ABOUT YOUR JOB?

There are always new projects going on and we constantly seek to improve our processes and practices, so there is never a dull moment. I also enjoy interacting with the traders and trying to get into their mindset.

JAMES'S TOP TIPS

Think of an internship as a long interview rather than a summer job – take the opportunity to show your potential employer what you can do. If you're applying for a full-time position, make sure you know what you're applying for and that it is what you want to go into. If you don't, the interviewer will see straight through you.

Actuarial trainee

Aviva

NICOLA JACKSON

Route into finance:
A levels – maths, further maths, psychology (2005); BSc mathematics, University of Leeds (2008)

WHY FINANCE?

I chose my degree because I like a challenge and the feeling of achievement when I've been able to solve complex problems. The maths course at Leeds really suited me because there was a lot of choice in what I could study. I opted for a computing module and business modules as well as maths ones.

I have always had an interest in finance, and chose to train as an actuary because I wanted to continue learning while working, and apply the concepts I had learned in my degree to real-life situations.

My degree has certainly helped out with my job as I am using things I learned on a daily basis, especially for the exams I am studying for.

HOW DID YOU GET WHERE YOU ARE TODAY?

At university I wasn't entirely sure what career path I wanted to take, so I decided to get some work experience. I was offered an internship in the summer before my final year, which really helped me to understand what actuaries do and what it would be like to work in this area.

WHAT DOES YOUR JOB INVOLVE?

I currently work in the Bulk Purchase Annuities (BPA) team, which provides valuations of company pension schemes. We can then give the companies the option to buy out their pension scheme if they want to decrease the risk they hold. I try to make our valuation as accurate as possible by reviewing and improving the assumptions we use, for example on inflation, marriage and mortality. This means we can provide the client with an accurate and competitive price for their pension scheme. In my job it is therefore important to be able to communicate results effectively to a wide range of audiences so that they understand your findings.

I work 9am – 5pm most days, but get time off to study every week. I am based in an office in the centre of York, and spend my time working between two different teams, which means I get to meet and work with a lot of different people.

WHAT HAS BEEN YOUR BIGGEST CHALLENGE?

Studying for exams while working has been a big challenge. It's sometimes hard to find the right work-life balance and to motivate myself to study after a day at work. However, I have been assigned a buddy and a mentor to help out with any problems or questions. There are lots of motivating factors, too, such as the pay rise when I have passed an exam, and when something I have studied comes up at work. It makes the studying feel worthwhile and helps link the theory with the practical side of things.

WHAT DO YOU LIKE MOST ABOUT YOUR JOB?

The best part of my job is the people I work with. Everyone is really friendly and the atmosphere at work is always good. Being on the graduate scheme means I have been provided with good learning and development opportunities: we attend a number of training programmes over the course of the scheme. The most recent one involved going to an outdoor activities centre in the middle of the North Yorkshire Moors and doing various activities such as abseiling.

NICOLA'S TOP TIPS

Work hard, but make sure you also have interests outside your studies to make you stand out in an interview. Get some experience under your belt so you have a better idea of the sort of work you will be involved in.

Entry routes

ProgressionSeries

Routes to qualification

There are over 1,000 finance undergraduate courses on the UCAS Course Search. With so much choice, how can you pick the best course for you?

UNDERGRADUATE QUALIFICATIONS

If you're interested in studying finance and/or accounting at university, the first decision you need to make is whether to undertake a single honours degree (ie either finance or accounting) or a combined honours degree (ie finance and accounting together or one of these combined with another subject).

Remember that it is not essential to study a finance or accounting degree to work in these areas, although a finance or accounting degree will demonstrate your interest clearly.

SINGLE HONOURS VS...

Single honours accounting degrees will vary in content and focus from one university to the next. However, some basic principles apply. According to the Quality Assurance Agency for Higher Education, accounting degrees require students 'to study how the design, operation and validation of accounting systems affects, and is affected by, individuals, organisations, markets and society. This study is informed by perspectives from the social sciences … and may include, but is not restricted to, the behavioural, the economic, the political and the sociological.' In addition, a degree course should include study of the operation and design of financial systems, risk, financial structures and financial instruments.

The purpose of undergraduate finance degrees is to give students an in-depth knowledge of the decisions made by companies, investors and financial middlemen, as well as an understanding of complex modern-day financial markets. Studying finance is essential to understanding how financial markets, and the investments traded on these markets, affect the way in which companies operate.

With both finance and accounting single honours degrees, you can normally expect the first year to provide a more general introduction to the subject area, as well as to the methods and techniques employed by various financial and accountancy professionals in their jobs. The following two years allow for more specialisation within the individual subject, depending on where your current academic and future career aspirations lie. For example, you could choose from a wide variety of options such as public-sector accounting, corporate finance, auditing or business studies, or even related areas like business, law and banking.

JOINT HONOURS

Accounting and finance can be studied together, as they complement each other very well in terms of subject matter and skills learnt. For example, you can learn about the stock exchange and financial markets as well as areas such as taxes and auditing, which could be of great use in your future career.

However, there is a vast array of other degree courses you can choose from to combine with your studies. You could either opt for a complementary subject, such as economics, entrepreneurship, computer science, law, marketing, management or business studies, or you could choose something completely different, such as creative writing, divinity, philosophy and even anthropology.

COURSE LENGTH

Whatever your decision, most finance and/or accounting courses last for three years, unless combined, for example, with a language, when you would be expected to spend your second or third year abroad to develop your linguistic skills.

ASSESSMENT

Undergraduate courses are normally graded according to the following structure: first class, upper second, lower second, and third, all of which carry (Hons) afterwards. Anything below this will not be graded as an honours degree.

Universities vary in how they award degree classifications to their students. Some rely on a totally examination-based method, in which you will sit 'finals' at the end of your third (or fourth, if relevant) year. This is often the case with more traditional universities, such as Oxford and Cambridge, although expect smaller examinations, often taken at the start of each term, as a revision aid too. Other universities will combine a mixture of coursework and examinations to arrive at a final degree classification. You might like to think about this when choosing a university; after all, if you worry about your performance in examinations, you might want to consider doing a course where continuous assessment plays a feature in your final grade.

POSTGRADUATE AND PROFESSIONAL QUALIFICATIONS

If you have studied for an undergraduate degree unrelated to finance or accounting and are considering postgraduate study in a related subject, check out the UKPASS website (**www.ukpass.ac.uk**). This offers useful web-based tools to help you research and apply for postgraduate courses.

If, once you have completed your undergraduate degree, you are certain that you want a career in finance or accounting, you may need or want to undertake further study as part of your professional development. The financial advice sector is currently experiencing high levels of change and this also applies to the qualification requirements of its professionals.

The Financial Services Skills Council (FSSC) is the employer-led body that sets performance standards for this sector – find out more about ithem on their website **www.fssc.org.uk**.

Below is an example of the sort of professional qualifications you may need or want to gain as part of your continuous professional development.

PROFESSION	A SAMPLE OF PROFESSIONAL QUALIFICATIONS	MORE INFORMATION
Accountants	Need to complete a training contract (lasting 3–5 years) with an approved firm, involving external tutoring and home study	The Association of Chartered Certified Accountants **www.acca.org.uk**
	OR You can train outside of professional practice with the Chartered Institute of Management Accountants (CIMA) or the Chartered Institute of Public Finance and Accountancy (CIPFA)	The Chartered Institute of Management Accountants **www.cimaglobal.com**
		Chartered Institute of Public Finance and Accountancy **www.cipfa.org.uk**
		Institute of Chartered Accountants of England & Wales **www.icaew.co.uk**
Actuaries	Need to become a Fellow of either the Faculty of Actuaries in Edinburgh or the Faculty and Institute of Actuaries in London and Oxford	The Actuarial Profession **www.actuaries.org.uk**
Retail bankers and financial advisers	Certificate in Financial Planning (Chartered Insurance Institute – ICC)	The Chartered Insurance Institute **www.cii.co.uk**
	Certificate for Financial Advisers (ifs School of Finance)	ifs School of Finance **www.ifslearning.ac.uk**
	Introduction to investment (International Certificate in Financial Advice	Chartered Institute for Securities and Investment **www.cisi.org**
	Certificate in Investment Planning (Chartered Institute of Bankers in Scotland – CIOBS)	The Chartered Institute of Bankers in Scotland **www.ciobs.org.uk**
Pension advisers	Fellow or Associate of the Pensions Management Institute (for pension transfer specialists)	Pensions Management Institute **www.pensions-pmi.org.uk**
	Certificate in Financial Administration (for pensions overseers)	The Chartered Insurance Institute: **www.cii.co.uk**
General business functions	Master of Business Administration (MBA) – a very popular choice among students and employers, the latter of whom will only offer funding if the student chooses one of the partner business schools	TOPMBA **www.topmba.com**
		Association of MBAs **www.mbaworld.com**

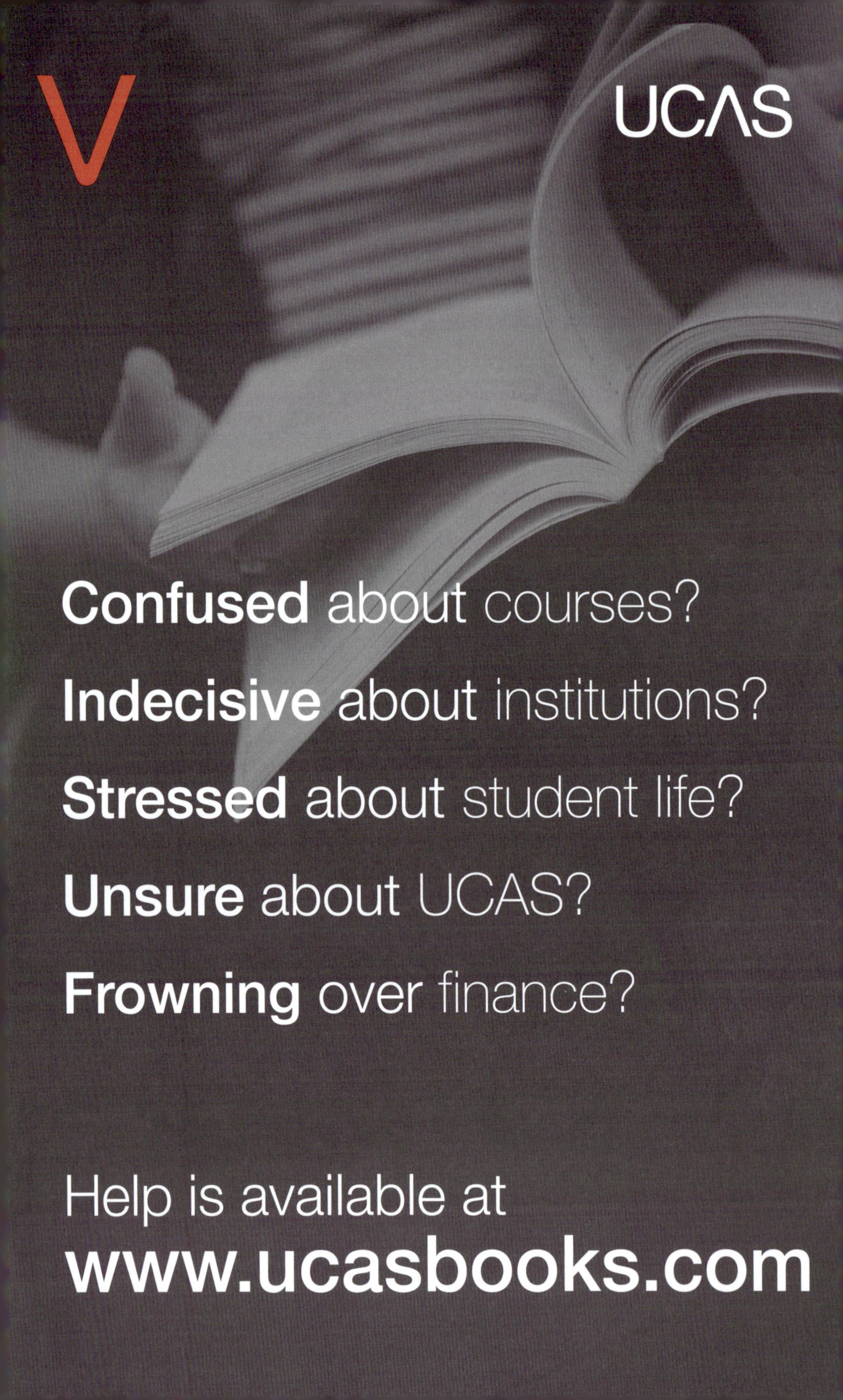
UCAS
Confused about courses?
Indecisive about institutions?
Stressed about student life?
Unsure about UCAS?
Frowning over finance?
Help is available at
www.ucasbooks.com

Applicant
journey
ProgressionSeries

SIX EASY STEPS TO UNIVERSITY AND COLLEGE

STEP 1

1 Choosing courses

Use Course Search at www.ucas.com to find out which courses might suit you and the universities and colleges that offer them.

STEP 2

2 Applying

You can apply for up to five courses using the online application system at www.ucas.com.

STEP 3

3 Offers

You can check the progress of your application using Track at www.ucas.com, which will be updated as we receive decisions from universities and colleges. If you don't receive any offers, or decline all the offers you do receive, you may be able to use Extra, which allows eligible applicants to apply for a new choice.

STEP 4

4 Results

UCAS receives many exam results direct from the awarding bodies – you can check the list at www.ucas.com. If your qualification is listed, you don't need to send your results to UCAS or the universities and colleges. Check Track at www.ucas.com to see if you've got a place on your chosen course.

STEP 5

5 Next steps

Depending on your circumstances, you might use this step. If you have received different grades than expected, or have changed your mind, there may be other options available. You need to look at Track and course vacancies at www.ucas.com.

STEP 6

6 Starting university or college

Make sure you have everything ready, such as accommodation, finances, travel arrangements, books and equipment required for the course.

Choosing courses

1

Step 1 – Planning your application for economics, finance or accountancy

Planning your application is the start of your journey to finding a place at a university or college.

This section will help you decide what course to study and how to choose a university or college where you'll enjoy living and studying. Find out about qualifications, degree options, how they'll assess you, and coping with the cost of higher education.

WHICH SUBJECTS?

The good news is that most A level subjects are acceptable for economics, finance or accounting degrees. However, the more prestigious universities tend to prefer traditional subjects, such as English, maths, languages and sciences, over more modern vocational ones, such as business studies, sports studies, theatre studies or media studies. If an applicant offers a mixture of the two types with more emphasis on traditional subjects, this may be acceptable. It is worth bearing in mind that many universities do not normally consider general studies or key skills as suitable subjects for making an offer, although they may take them into account when looking at your application as a whole.

While A level economics is not normally a prerequisite for economics degrees (some universities such as

Kingston offer a special route for undergraduates without an economics background), mathematics A level is often desired, if not necessary. Check with individual institutions for their entry requirements.

WHICH GRADES?

Economics, finance and accounting courses are mentally demanding and high offers are often the norm to ensure you have the academic ability to cope. These can range from AAB at the most popular and prestigious institutions to CCC elsewhere. Universities will usually ask for at least a GCSE in maths and English, often at grade C or above, as proof of your numeracy and language abilities.

HOW DO I FIND THE BEST COURSE FOR ME?

To find out what courses are on offer, for both single and joint honours, visit **www.ucas.com** and select Course Search.

Applicants are advised to use various sources of information in order to make their choices for higher education, including the Course Search facility and Stamford Test at **www.ucas.com**. League tables might be a component of this research, but applicants should bear in mind that these tables attempt to rank institutions in an overall order, which reflects the interests, preoccupations and decisions of those who have produced and edited them. The ways in which they are compiled vary greatly and you need to look closely at the criteria that have been used.

UCAS CARD

If you're in Year 12, S5 or equivalent and thinking about higher education you can sign up for your free UCAS Card to receive the following benefits.

- Save money on the high street with your UCAS discount card.
- Information about the courses and universities you're interested in.
- Expert help from Giles, the UCAS adviser with all the reminders, hints and tips.
- Free copies of The Independent's 'You Can' magazine delivered to your door.
- Unlimited use of yougofurther.co.uk, the UCAS student network website.

Receive your free UCAS Card and all that goes with it by registering at **www.ucas.com/ucascard.**

Choosing courses

1

Choosing courses

USE COURSE SEARCH AT WWW.UCAS.COM TO FIND OUT WHICH COURSES MIGHT SUIT YOU, AND THE UNIVERSITIES AND COLLEGES THAT OFFER THEM.

Start thinking about what you want to study and where you want to go. Read the section on 'Finding a course' (page 70-71), and see what courses are available where in the chapter on 'Courses' (page 119). Check the entry requirements required for each course meet your academic expectations.

Use the UCAS website – www.ucas.com has lots of advice on how to find a course. Go to the students' section of the website for the best advice or go straight to Course Search to see a list of all the courses available through UCAS. See the section on Entry Profiles on page 72 which explains what they are and how to find them on the UCAS website.

Watch UCAStv – at www.ucas.tv there are videos on 'how to choose your course', 'attending events' as well as case studies and video diaries from students talking about their experience of finding a course at university or college.

Attend UCAS conventions – UCAS conventions are held throughout the country. Universities and colleges have exhibition stands where their staff offer information about their courses and institutions. Details of when the conventions are happening are shown at **www.ucas.com/events/conventions.**

Look at the prospectuses – universities and colleges have prospectuses and course-specific leaflets on their undergraduate courses. Your school or college library may have copies or go to the university's website to download a copy or you can ask them to send one to you.

Go to university and college open days – most institutions offer open days to anyone who wants to attend. See the institution information pages on Course Search and the UCAS Open Days publication for information on when they are taking place.

League tables – these can be helpful but bear in mind that they attempt to rank institutions in an overall order reflecting the views of those that produce them. They may not reflect your views and needs.

Do your research – speak and refer to as many trusted sources as you can find. The section on 'Which area?' on page 26 will help you identify the different areas of economics, finance and accountancy you might want to enter.

1 Choosing courses

Finding a course

Through UCAS you can apply to five courses in total. How do you find out more information to make an informed decision?

How do you narrow down your courses to five? First of all, look up course details in this book or online on www.ucas.com. This will give you an idea of the full range of courses and topics on offer. You may want to study economics, finance or accounting as single subjects, but there are also many courses which also include additional options, such as a modern language (check out the degree subjects studied by our case studies). You'll quickly be able to eliminate institutions that don't offer the right course, or you can choose a 'hit list' of institutions first, and then see what they have to offer.

Once you've made a short(er) list, read the university and college Entry Profiles (see page 72) to find out what particular courses offer. You can then follow this up by looking at university or college websites, and generally finding out as much as you can about the course, department and institution. Don't be afraid to contact them to ask for more information, request their prospectus or arrange an open day visit.

UCAS WEBSITE – www.ucas.com

Whether you want advice about applying to higher education, to check out what courses are available, to find out what qualifications you need, or to monitor the status of your application, www.ucas.com is a great place to start. The UCAS website is one of the most popular websites in the UK and the most heavily used educational one, with over 1.5 million unique users a month. It is popular for good reason. From it, you can use Course Search as a quick and easy way to find out more about the courses you are interested in, including the vital code information you will need to include in your application later on. From Course Search, you can link to the websites of the universities and colleges in the UCAS system. Once you've applied through UCAS, you can use Track to check the progress of your application, including any decisions from universities or colleges, and you can make replies to your offers online.

1 Choosing courses

Entry Profiles

WHAT ARE THEY?

Entry Profiles give potential applicants to higher education specific information to help them make informed decisions about the courses they apply for. Detailed knowledge about the course, formal entry requirements and the qualities and experiences institutions are looking for in their applicants can help ensure that every applicant finds their way onto the right course. Entry Profiles are published on the UCAS website and can be reached using Course Search. They are available for all potential applicants and their advisers to see as they start making important decisions about where to apply. All course providers are asked to contribute Entry Profiles for the UCAS Course Search facility.

WHY USE THEM?

Courses can vary at different universities and colleges, even though they have the same name. Differences in course content, structure, optional modules, and the department's approach to teaching and learning can make the experience of studying any subject very different for students at different institutions, even before the size and location of the institution are taken into account.

It is important that you are fully informed about the courses and the institutions offering them before you apply, and that you know what academic qualifications and personal qualities are being sought in an applicant. Then you can avoid mistakes and make fully informed choices.

HOW DO I USE THE ENTRY PROFILES?

- When you find courses that interest you, search for the Entry Profile through the Course Search at www.ucas.com. Look for the symbol EP after the course title on the results page. This tells you that it has a complete Entry Profile.
- Courses without the EP symbol have academic entry requirements only.

TOP TIP

Don't be afraid to pick up the phone – university and college admissions officers welcome enquiries directly from students, rather than careers officers phoning on your behalf. It shows you're genuinely interested and committed to your own career early on.

Choosing courses

1

Choosing your institution

Different people look for different things from their university or college course, but the checklist on the next page sets out the kinds of factors all prospective students should consider when choosing their university or college. Keep this list in mind on open days, when talking to friends about their experiences at various universities and colleges, or while reading prospectuses and websites.

WHAT TO CONSIDER WHEN CHOOSING YOUR ECONOMICS, FINANCE OR ACCOUNTING COURSE	
Location	Do you want to stay close to home? Would you prefer to study at a city or campus university?
Grades required	Use Course Search on the UCAS website, www.ucas.com, to view entry requirements for courses you are interested in. Also, check out the university website or call up the admissions office. Some universities specify grades required, eg AAB, while others specify points required, eg 340. If they ask for points, it means they're using the UCAS Tariff system, which basically awards points to different types and levels of qualification. For example, an A grade at A level = 120 points; a B grade at A level = 100 points. The full Tariff tables are available on pages 100–105 and at www.ucas.com.
Employer links	Ask the course tutor and university careers office about links with employers such as banks, insurance companies, financial services providers, etc. Find out if the course involves visiting lecturers from the professional side of the industry and where they typically come from.
Graduate prospects	Ask the university department and careers office for their lists of graduate destinations.
Cost	Ask the admissions office about variable tuition fees and financial assistance.
Degree type	Think about whether you want to study finance or accounting on its own (single honours degree) or as a joint honours degree, eg with a language or with another subject such as legal studies or even geography.
Teaching style	How is the course taught? Ask about the number of lectures per week, the amount of seminars and if the university runs a tutorial system.
Course assessment	How is your final degree classification reached? Is it completely exam-based (ie through finals) or is there an element of continuous assessment?
'Fit'	Even if all the above criteria are fulfilled, this one relies on your instinct – visit the university and the individual departments that you are interested in and see if they 'fit' you. Open days can help with this, plus there will be other finance and accounting undergraduates on hand to speak to, and to give you a good idea of the type and level of work the course produces. Also ask about lecturers' own particular interests; many will have personal web pages somewhere on the departmental website.

1 Choosing courses

How will they choose you?

University departments receive thousands of applications each year for only a limited number of places. So how can you make your UCAS application stand out from the others?

ACADEMIC ABILITY

Many economics, finance and accounting degrees (and related areas) are intellectually demanding. Not only will you possibly be learning about the basics of these disciplines for the very first time but you will also be expected to work on them in greater analytical depth than you have ever done before at GCSE and A level (or equivalent). Therefore, in order for admissions tutors to be certain that you have what it takes to cope with the course, you will have to show you have the academic ability to take on new ideas.

SELF-MOTIVATION AND SELF-DISCIPLINE

Studying at university is very different from school and sixth form. In those settings, you will have followed a set course, normally following a study pattern suggested by your teachers. Homework set each night will have ensured that you completed your study regularly and on time.

At university, tutors and lecturers do not have the time to keep tabs on their students in the same way. Whereas at A level your teachers will have helped motivate you to finish your work on time, university tutors will simply hand out reading lists and essay titles or problem sheets in advance and will expect you to complete them on-time without constant reminders.

This can, understandably, be daunting for some people. Certainly, time management and self-motivation are skills you hone at university but it also helps if your referee can write about any instances where you have shown an ability to work well on your own, as this is how you will be studying throughout your undergraduate course.

DEVOTION TO YOUR CHOSEN SUBJECT

You might think that a degree in economics, finance or accounting will be the best way to earn a good salary as a graduate but this desire will not convince admissions tutors that you are devoted to their subject. In fact, it could put them off your application altogether if you cannot show any other commitment to their subject than what you will earn three or four years down the line.

The tutors who select students on to their courses want to see evidence that you have carefully considered what a degree in economics, finance or accounting will involve and why it appeals to you. After all, you don't need an economics, finance or accounting degree to get a job in the financial sector, so why have you chosen to specialise in this field earlier than some of your peers? Only you will know the reasons why you're fascinated by these subject areas and it's your job to convey this enthusiasm to others in your UCAS application.

DO SOME READING

This is related to the above point. A good way to prove to potential admissions tutors that you have an interest in their field is to find out their specialist academic areas and do some reading into these, potentially from books that they have written. Additionally, contact the relevant department and ask for their first-year reading list, if this is not available online. You do not need to read everything on it but if you choose two or three books that most appeal to you and read them in some depth it does show a commitment to both the subject and the relevant university's course.

Be warned, though: don't think that merely mentioning a few key books will automatically get you through. Admissions tutors will know if you're lying, so unless you can make a few valid points about why you enjoyed their books, don't bother: it could do more harm than good.

WORK EXPERIENCE

While relevant work experience is not essential to gain a university place in economics, finance or accounting, if you have had any, do include details in your personal statement (see below). A job working as an office junior in an accounting firm, or perhaps work shadowing in a bank, can give you valuable insight into these sorts of careers, as well as real inspiration to study what it is that drives their businesses. Relevant work experience can be of real interest to admissions tutors so do make sure you give details of anything you learnt during the time and how it has led you to make the decisions you are taking today.

YOUR PERSONAL STATEMENT

Your personal statement can really enhance your application. It is here that you can show evidence of all the above issues – academic attainment, self-discipline, work experience, a desire for your chosen subject. Most universities place much importance on personal statements as this is where your own voice comes through, so make the most of it and use it to your advantage. Be honest but not over-friendly and give well-reasoned statements. And above all make sure it's free from mistakes and easy to read. There's nothing more offputting for an admissions tutor than applications and personal statements that have glaring grammatical and spelling mistakes or are difficult to decipher.

As this is such an important part of your application, it's worth drafting it a few times before sending it to UCAS. Ask your family or friends and teacher to check it, not only for mistakes but also to see if you're leaving anything out that should be in, or equally if there's anything that should come out.

For more hints and tips about your personal statement, see page 90.

OTHER APPLICATION TESTS AND PROCEDURES

Most universities these days do not interview their students, preferring to select from their UCAS applications. However, some do use different procedures.

The University of Oxford and the University of Cambridge have an applications closing date of 15 October, which is earlier than other universities.

You may well be asked to attend an interview and may also need to sit a test or submit some written work.

INTERVIEWS

Once they have sifted through the thousands of applications they receive, some universities will then ask shortlisted candidates for interview. This is normal at Oxford and Cambridge, and not uncommon at other prestigious institutions.

It may also be dependent on the subject you are applying to study: check individual websites for full information on their selection policies.

Interviews may sound daunting but they are actually a very effective way of helping admissions tutors to assess whether a candidate has what it takes to cope with the course and the university environment, and for the applicant to see if they like the course on offer, the tutors and the university as a whole.

Choosing courses

1

The cost of higher education

The information in this section was up-to-date when this book was published. You should visit the websites mentioned in this section for the very latest information.

As a student, you will have to pay for two things:

- tuition fees for your course
- living costs, such as rent, food, books, transport and entertainment.

If that sounds expensive, don't worry. You can get financial help from the Government in the form of loans and grants.

FEES

The amount of tuition fees you have to pay, and the financial assistance you may be entitled to, depends on:

- where you live
- where you want to study
- what you want to study
- your financial circumstances.

STUDENT LOANS

The purpose of a student loan is to help cover the costs of your tuition fees and basic living (rent, bills, food etc). Many other kinds of loan are available to students while they are studying at university or college. Depending on the source of the loan, the interest rate can have a severe impact upon the overall debt at the end of your degree. However, a student loan (or student maintenance loan as it is sometimes known) takes only inflation into account, so the overall amount will only be slightly higher than the figure borrowed. Maintenance loans are available to all citizens who satisfy UK residency requirements.

Remember that a student loan is not a grant: you do have to pay it back once you have left university and are earning over £15,000 a year.

In addition, there are non-repayable grants and bursaries available, depending on your circumstances and the courses and institutions to which you are applying.

USEFUL WEBSITES

There is lots of information available about student finance. Listed below are some websites you may find useful:

UCAS
www.ucas.com/students/studentfinance.

National Union of Students
www.nus.org.uk/money.

If your family lives in England, you should visit **www.direct.gov.uk/studentfinance**.

If your family lives in Wales, you should visit **www.studentfinancewales.co.uk** **www.cyllidmyfyrwyrcymru.co.uk**.

If your family lives in Northern Ireland, you should visit **www.studentfinanceni.co.uk**.

If your family lives in Scotland, you should visit **www.saas.gov.uk**.

If your family lives in the Channel Islands, visit **www.gov.je** for Jersey or **www.gov.gg** for Guernsey.

If your family lives in the Isle of Man, visit **www.gov.im**.

Disabled Students' Allowance

If you have a disablilty or specific learning difficulty you may be able to apply for a Disabled Students' Allowance. To find out more go to the websites above and search on Disabled Student.

Childcare Grant

This is available to students who have dependent children and a low household income. This includes students who are lone parents and students who are married to, or the partners of, other students.

TOP TIP

Before you choose your institution, make sure you find out about the bursaries they offer. Some are likely to be more generous than others, and this may make the difference between a financially comfortable or uncomfortable time.

Choosing courses

1

International students

APPLYING TO STUDY IN THE UK

Deciding to go to university or college in the UK is very exciting. You need to think about what course to do, where to study, and how much it will cost. The decisions you make can have a huge effect on your future but UCAS is here to help.

What is UCAS?

UCAS is the organisation that manages applications to full-time undergraduate courses in the UK. All the UK universities and many colleges use us. We are respected around the world and you can access our website 24 hours a day, seven days a week at **www.ucas.com**.

Whatever your age or qualifications, if you want to apply for any of the 50,000 courses listed at over 300 universities and colleges on the UCAS website, you must apply through UCAS at **www.ucas.com**. If you are unsure, your school, college, adviser, or local British Council office will be able to help. Further advice and a video guide for international students can be found on the non-UK section of the UCAS website at **www.ucas.com/students/wheretostart/nonukstudents**.

What is Apply?

Apply is our secure online application system that you can use anytime and anywhere, giving you the flexibility to fill in your application when it suits you. Each time you log in, you can enter more information and take as long as you wish to change and complete it. Using Apply is the fastest and most efficient method of applying, but students with limited or no internet access should contact the UCAS Customer Service Unit on 0044 330 333 0230 for advice on what to do. By applying through UCAS, you are able to use the one application for up to five choices.

Students may apply on their own or through their school, college, adviser, or local British Council if they are registered with UCAS to use Apply. If you choose to use an education agent's services, check with the British Council to see if they hold a list of certificated or registered agents in your country. Check also on any charges you may need to pay. UCAS charges only the application fee (see below) but agents may charge for additional services.

How much will my application cost?

If you choose to apply to more than one course, university or college you need to pay UCAS £21 GBP when you apply. If you only apply to one course at one university or college, you pay UCAS £11 GBP.

WHAT LEVEL OF ENGLISH?

UCAS provides a list of English language qualifications and grades that are acceptable to most UK universities and colleges, however you are advised to contact the institutions directly as each have their own entry requirement in English. For more information go to **www.ucas.com/students/wheretostart/nonukstudents/englangprof**.

INTERNATIONAL STUDENT FEES

If you study in the UK, your fee status (whether you pay full-cost fees or a subsidised fee rate) will be decided by the UK university or college you plan to attend. Before you decide which university or college to attend, you need to be absolutely certain that you can pay the full cost of:

- your tuition fees (the amount is set by universities and colleges, so contact them for more information – visit their websites where many list their fees)
- the everyday living expenses for you and your family for the whole time that you are in the UK, including accommodation, food, heat, light, clothes, travel
- books and equipment for your course
- travel to and from your country.

You must include everything when you work out how much it will cost. You can get information to help you do this accurately from the international offices at universities and colleges, UKCISA (UK Council for International Student Affairs) and the British Council. There is a useful website tool to help you manage your money at university – **www.studentcalculator.org.uk**.

Scholarships and bursaries are offered at some universities and colleges and you should contact them for more information. In addition, you should check with your local British Council for additional scholarships available to students from your country who want to study in the UK.

LEGAL DOCUMENTS YOU WILL NEED

As you prepare to study in the UK, it is very important to think about the legal documents you will need to enter the country.

Everyone who comes to study in the UK needs a valid passport. If you do not have one, you should apply for one as soon as possible. People from certain countries also need visas before they come into the UK. They are known as 'visa nationals'. You can check if you require a visa to travel to the UK by visiting the UK Border Agency website and selecting "Studying in the UK" So, please check the UK Border Agency website at **www.ukba.homeoffice.gov.uk** for the most up-to-date guidance and information about the United Kingdom's visa requirements.

When you apply for your visa you need to make sure you have the following documents:

- A confirmation of acceptance for studies (CAS) number from the university or college where you are going to study. The institution must be on the UKBA Register of Sponsors in order to accept international students.
- A valid passport.
- Evidence that you have enough money to pay for your course and living costs.
- Certificates for all qualifications you have that are relevant to the course you have been accepted for and for any English language qualifications.

You will also have to give your biometric data.

Do check for further information from your local British Embassy or High Commission. Guidance information for international students is also available from UKCISA and from UKBA.

ADDITIONAL RESOURCES

There are a number of organisations that can provide further guidance and information to you as you prepare to study in the UK:

- British Council
  www.britishcouncil.org
- Education UK (British Council website dealing with educational matters)
  www.educationuk.org
- English UK (British Council accredited website listing English language courses in the UK)
  www.englishuk.com
- UK Border Agency (provides information on visa requirements and applications)
  www.ukba.homeoffice.gov.uk
- UKCISA (UK Council for International Student Affairs)
  www.ukcisa.org.uk
- BIS (Department for Business Innovation and Skills)
  www.bis.gov.uk
- Prepare for success
  www.prepareforsuccess.org.uk.

2 Applying

Step 2 – Applying

Apply for up to five courses using the UCAS online application system at **www.ucas.com**

WHEN TO APPLY

Make a note of these important dates for your diary.

- **Mid-September 2010**
  Opening date for receiving applications.
- **15 October 2010**
  Application deadline for the receipt at UCAS of applications for all courses at the universities of Oxford and Cambridge.
- **15 January 2011**
  Application deadline for the receipt at UCAS of applications for economics, finance and accounting courses, at all other universities and colleges.
- **25 February 2011**
  Start of Extra
- **30 June 2011**
  Final deadline for all applications, including those from outside the UK and EU. Any applications we receive after this date go directly into Clearing.
- **20 September 2011**
  Last date for Clearing applications.

Don't forget…

Universities and colleges guarantee to consider your application if we receive it by the appropriate deadline. If you send it in after the deadline, but by 30 June 2011, universities and colleges will consider it if they want to make more offers.

2 Applying

How to apply

You apply online at **www.ucas.com** through Apply – a secure, web-based application service that is designed for all our applicants, whether they are applying through a UCAS-registered centre or as an individual, anywhere in the world. Apply is:

- easy to access – all you need is an internet connection
- easy to use – you don't have to complete your application all in one go: you can save the sections as you complete them and come back to it later
- easy to monitor – once you've applied, you can use Track to check the progress of your application, including any decisions from universities or colleges. You can also reply to your offers using Track.

Watch the UCAStv guide to applying through UCAS at **www.ucas.tv**.

DEFERRED ENTRY

If you want to apply for deferred entry in 2012, perhaps because you want to take a year out between school or college and higher education, you should check that the university or college will accept a deferred entry application. Occasionally, tutors are not happy to accept students who take a gap year, because it interrupts the flow of their learning. If you apply for deferred entry, you must meet the conditions of any offers by 31 August 2011, unless otherwise agreed by the university or college. If you accept a place for 2012 entry and then change your mind, you cannot reapply through us in the 2012 entry cycle unless you withdraw your original application.

INVISIBILITY OF CHOICES

Universities and colleges cannot see details of the other choices on your application until you reply to any offers or you have not been successful at any of your choices.

You can submit only one UCAS application in each year's application cycle.

APPLYING THROUGH YOUR SCHOOL OR COLLEGE

1 GET SCHOOL OR COLLEGE 'BUZZWORD'

Ask your UCAS application coordinator (may be your sixth form tutor) for your school or college UCAS 'buzzword'. This is a password for the school or college.

2 REGISTER

Go to **www.ucas.com/students/apply** and click on **Register/Log in to use Apply** and then **register**. After you have entered your registration details, the online system will automatically generate a username for you, but you'll have to come up with a password and answers to security questions.

3 COMPLETE SIX SECTIONS

Complete the sections of the application. To access any section, click on the section name at the top of the screen and follow the instructions. The sections are:

Personal details – contact details, residential status, disability status

Additional information – only UK applicants need to complete this section

Choices – which courses you'd like to apply for

Education – your education and qualifications

Employment – for example, work experience, holiday jobs

Personal statement – see page 90.

4 PASS TO REFEREE

Once you've completed all the sections, send your application electronically to your referee (normally your form tutor). They'll check it, approve it and add their reference to it, and will then send it to UCAS on your behalf.

USEFUL INFORMATION ABOUT APPLY

- Important details like date of birth and course codes will be checked by Apply. It will alert you if they are not valid.
- The text for your personal statement and reference can be copied and pasted into your application.
- You can change your application at any time before it is completed and sent to UCAS.
- You can print and preview your application at any time.
- Your school, college or centre can choose different payment methods. For example, they may want us to bill them, or you may be able to pay online by debit or credit card.

NOT APPLYING THROUGH A SCHOOL OR COLLEGE

For example, if you are not currently studying – you can follow the same steps, but, as you can't supply a 'buzzword', you'll just be asked a few extra questions to check you are eligible to apply, and you'll have to supply a reference from someone who knows you well enough to comment on your suitability for higher education. Guidance on choosing a suitable referee is available in Apply and on the UCAS website. If you are not applying through a school, college or other UCAS-registered centre, you should apply online and pay by debit or credit card.

If you have recently left school or college you can ask them to supply your reference online.

2 Applying

Making your application

We want this to run smoothly for you and we also want to process your application as quickly as possible. You can help us to do this by remembering to do the following:

- check the closing dates for applications – see page 86
- start early and allow plenty of time for completing your application – including enough time for your referee to complete the reference section
- read the instructions carefully before you start
- consider what each question is actually asking for
- ask a teacher, parent, friend or careers adviser to review your draft application – particularly the personal statement
- pay special attention to questions that ask you about your interests and experience
- if you have extra information that will not fit on your application, send it direct to your chosen universities or colleges after we have sent you your Welcome letter with your Personal ID – don't send it to us
- keep a copy of the final version of your application, in case you are asked questions on it at an interview.

Applying

2

The personal statement

Next to choosing your courses, this section of your application will take up most of your time. It is of immense importance as many colleges and universities rely solely on the information in the UCAS application, rather than interviews and admissions tests, when selecting students. The personal statement can be the deciding factor in whether or not they offer you a place. If it is an institution that interviews, it could be the deciding factor in whether you get called for interview.

Keep a copy of your personal statement – if you are called for interview, you will almost certainly be asked questions based on it.

Tutors will look carefully at your exam results, actual and predicted, your referee's statement and your own personal statement. Remember, they are looking for reasons to offer you a place – try to give them every opportunity to do so!

A SALES DOCUMENT

The personal statement is your opportunity to sell yourself, so do so. The university or college admissions tutor who reads your personal statement wants to get a rounded picture of you to decide whether you will make an interesting member of the university or college both academically and socially. They want to know more about you than the subjects you are studying at school.

HOW TO IMPRESS

Don't be put off by the blank space. The secret is to cover key areas that admissions tutors always look for. Include things such as hobbies and work experience, especially if they are linked in some way to the type of course you are applying for. You could talk about your career plans and interesting things you have done outside the classroom. Have you belonged to sports teams or orchestras or held positions of responsibility? Maybe you've been a school play stalwart or been involved in community activities. If you left full-time education a while ago, talk about the work you have done and the skills you have gathered or how you have juggled bringing up a family with other activities – that is evidence of time management skills. Whoever you are, make sure you explain what appeals to you about the course you are applying for.

Visit **www.ucas.tv** to view the video to help guide you through the process, and address the most common fears and concerns about writing a personal statement.

WHAT ADMISSIONS TUTORS LOOK FOR

- Your reasons for wanting to take this course.
- Your communication skills – how you express yourself in the personal statement.
- Relevant experience – experience that's related to your choice of course.
- Evidence of your interest in this field.
- Evidence of your teamworking ability.
- Evidence of your skills, for example IT skills, people skills, debating and public speaking.
- Other activities that show your dedication and ability to apply yourself.

WHAT TO TELL THEM

- Why you want to do this subject.
- What experience you already have in this field – for example work experience, school projects, hobbies, voluntary work.
- The skills and qualities you have as a person that would make you a good student, for example anything that shows your dedication, communication ability, academic achievement, initiative.
- Anything that shows you can knuckle down and apply yourself, for example running a marathon or raising money for charity.
- If you're taking a gap year, why and (if possible) what you're going to do during it.
- About your other interests and activities away from studying – to show you're a rounded person.

Offers

3

Step 3 – Offers

Once we have sent your application to your chosen universities and colleges, they will all consider it independently and tell us whether or not they can offer you a place. Some universities and colleges will take longer to make decisions than others. You may be asked to attend an interview, sit an additional test or provide a piece of work such as an essay before a decision can be made.

You may or may not be called for an interview as part of the selection process. Many institutions prefer not to interview people, as it's a very subjective and time-consuming process. However, some interview candidates as a matter of course, and others interview to clarify some aspect of a candidate's application – for example, if you're an international student in the UK, to check your communication skills, or if your grades are borderline.

If you are called for interview, the key areas they are likely to cover will be:

- evidence of your academic ability
- your capacity to study hard
- your commitment to a career in economics, finance or accountancy, best shown by work experience
- your awareness of current issues in the news that may have an impact on your chosen field of study.
- your logic and reasoning ability.

A lot of the interview will be based on information supplied on your application – especially your **personal statement** – see pages 90 and 91 for tips about the personal statement.

Each time a university or college makes a decision about your application we record it and let you know. You can check the progress of your application using Track at **www.ucas.com**. This is our secure online service which gives you access to your application using the same username and password you used when you applied. You can use it to find out if you have been invited for interview or need to provide an additional piece of work, as well as check to see if you have received any offers.

Find out more about how to use Track in the UCAStv video guide at **www.ucas.tv**.

Types of offer

Universities and colleges can make two types of offer: conditional or unconditional. If they want you to pass your exams before they can accept you, they will make a conditional offer. The conditions of the offer may specify the number of UCAS Tariff points, for example 200 points from three A levels, or the grades for your A levels, such as B in English and C in history.

If they want to offer you a place and you already have all the necessary qualifications, they will make you an unconditional offer. This means that if you accept this offer you have a definite place.

However, for either type of offer there may be some non-academic requirements:

- For courses that involve contact with children and vulnerable adults you may need to have criminal record checks and ISA registration before you can start the course.
- For students who are not resident in either the UK or the EU, there may be some financial conditions to meet.

Replying to offers

When you have received decisions for all your choices, you must decide what you want to accept and you do this by using Track. You will be given a deadline by which to decide what to accept.

You can accept up to two offers. If you accept a conditional offer as your firm or preferred choice, you may accept another offer as an insurance or back-up choice. You may accept an unconditional or conditional offer as your insurance choice. If you accept an unconditional offer as your firm or preferred choice, you cannot accept another offer and you will go straight to step 6 (see page 110) on your applicant journey.

When you accept your firm and, if permitted, insurance choice, you must turn down all your other offers.

If you turn down all your offers, you may be able to apply for further courses using Extra (page 95). If you are not eligible to use Extra, you can contact universities and colleges with vacancies in Clearing (page 108). For more information and advice about replying to your offers, watch the UCAStv video guide at **www.ucas.tv**.

What if you have no offers?

If you have applied through UCAS and are not holding any offers, you may be able to add more choices if you have not used all five choices, or apply through Extra for another course.

If you are not eligible for Extra, you can contact universities and colleges with vacancies in Clearing from mid-July 2011 (page 108).

3 Offers

Extra

Extra allows you to make additional choices, one at a time, without having to wait for Clearing in July. It is completely optional and free, and is designed to encourage you to continue researching and choosing courses if you need to. The courses available through Extra will be highlighted on Course Search, at **www.ucas.com**.

Who is eligible?

You will be eligible for Extra if you have already made five choices and:

- you have had unsuccessful or withdrawal decisions from all five of your choices, or
- you have cancelled your outstanding choices and hold no offers, or
- you have received decisions from all five choices and have declined all offers made to you.

How does it work?

We contact you and explain what to do if you are eligible for Extra. If you are eligible you should:

- see a special Extra button on your Track screen
- check on Course Search for courses that are available through Extra; they are shown by the symbol X after the course title.
- choose one that you would like to apply for and enter the details on your Track screen.

When you have chosen a course the university or college will be able to see your application.

What happens next?

We give universities and colleges 21 days to consider your Extra application. During this time, you cannot be considered by another university or college. After 21 days you can refer yourself to a different university or college if you wish, but it is a good idea to ring the one currently considering you before doing so. If you are made an offer, you can choose whether or not to accept it.

If you are currently studying for examinations, any offer that you receive is likely to be an offer conditional on exam grades. If you decide to accept a conditional offer, you will not be able to take any further part in Extra.

If you already have your examination results, it is possible that a university or college may make an unconditional offer.

If you accept an unconditional offer, you will be placed. You cannot then apply to any other universities or colleges in Extra.

If you decide to decline the offer, or the university or college decides they cannot make you an offer, you will be given another opportunity to use Extra, time permitting. Your Extra button on Track will be reactivated.

Once you have accepted an offer in Extra, you are committed to it in the same way as you would be with an offer through the main UCAS system. Conditional offers made through Extra will be treated in the same way as other conditional offers, when your examination results become available.

If your results do not meet the conditions and the university or college decides that they cannot confirm your Extra offer, you will automatically become eligible for Clearing if it is too late for you to be considered by another university or college in Extra.

If you are unsuccessful, decline an offer, or do not receive an offer, or 21 days have elapsed since choosing a course through Extra, you can use Extra to apply for another course.

From 1 October – 30 June

Applicants informed as they become eligible for Extra.

From 25 February – early July

The Extra service is available to eligible applicants through Track at www.ucas.com.

Advice

Do some careful research and seek guidance on your Extra choice of university or college and course. If you applied to high-demand courses and institutions in your original application and were unsuccessful, you could consider related or alternative subjects or perhaps apply for the subject you want in combination with another. Your teachers or careers advisers or the universities and colleges themselves can provide useful guidance. Entry Profiles, which appear with most courses listed on Course Search, are another important source of information. Be flexible, that is the key to success. But you are the only one who knows how flexible you are prepared to be. Remember that even if you decide to take a degree course other than economics, finance or accountancy, you can take the postgraduate route into these professions.

Visit www.ucas.tv to watch the video guide on how to use Extra.

3 Offers

The Tariff

Admission to higher education courses is generally dependent upon an individual's achievement in level 3 qualifications, such as GCE A levels. Did you know that there are currently over 3,000 level 3 qualifications available in the UK alone?

As if the number of qualifications available was not confusing enough, different qualifications can have different grading structures (alphabetical, numerical or a mixture of both). Finding out what qualifications are needed for different higher education courses can be very confusing.

The UCAS Tariff is the system for allocating points to qualifications used for entry to HE. It allows students to use a range of different qualifications to help secure a place on an undergraduate course.

Universities and colleges use the UCAS Tariff to make comparisons between applicants with different qualifications. Tariff points are often used in entry requirements, although other factors are often taken into account. Entry Profiles provide a fuller picture of what admissions tutors are seeking.

The tables on the following pages show the qualifications covered by the UCAS Tariff. There may have been changes to these tables since this book was printed. You should visit **www.ucas.com** to view the most up-to-date tables.

FURTHER INFORMATION?

Although Tariff points can be accumulated in a variety of ways, not all of these will necessarily be acceptable for entry to a particular HE course. The achievement of a points score therefore does not give an automatic entitlement to entry, and many other factors are taken into account in the admissions process.

The Course Search facility at **www.ucas.com** is the best source of reference to find out what qualifications are acceptable for entry to specific courses. Updates to the Tariff, including details on how new qualifications are added, can be found at **www.ucas.com/students/ucas_tariff/.**

HOW DOES THE TARIFF WORK?

- Students can collect Tariff points from a range of different qualifications, eg GCE A level with BTEC Nationals.
- There is no ceiling to the number of points that can be accumulated.
- There is no double counting. Certain qualifications within the Tariff build on qualifications in the same subject. In these cases only the qualification with the higher Tariff score will be counted. This principle applies to:
    - GCE Advanced Subsidiary level and GCE Advanced level
    - Scottish Highers and Advanced Highers
    - Speech, drama and music awards at grades 6, 7 and 8.
- Tariff points for the Advanced Diploma come from the Progression Diploma score plus the relevant Additional and Specialist Learning (ASL) Tariff points. Please see the appropriate qualification in the Tariff tables to calculate the ASL score.
- The Extended Project Tariff points are included within the Tariff points for Progression and Advanced Diplomas. Extended Project points represented in the Tariff only count when the qualification is taken outside of these Diplomas.
- Where the Tariff tables refer to specific awarding organisations, only qualifications from these awarding organisations attract Tariff points. Qualifications with a similar title, but from a different qualification awarding organisation do not attract Tariff points.

HOW DO UNIVERSITIES AND COLLEGES USE THE TARIFF?

The Tariff provides a facility to help universities and colleges when expressing entrance requirements and when making conditional offers. Entry requirements and conditional offers expressed as Tariff points will often require a minimum level of achievement in a specified subject (for example, '300 points to include grade A at A level chemistry', or '260 points including SQA Higher grade B in mathematics').

Use of the Tariff may also vary from department to department at any one institution, and may in some cases be dependent on the programme being offered.

WHAT QUALIFICATIONS ARE INCLUDED IN THE TARIFF?

The following qualifications are included in the UCAS Tariff. See the number on the qualification title to find the relevant section of the Tariff table.

1 AAT NVQ level 3 in Accounting
2 Advanced Diploma
3 Advanced Extension Awards
4 Advanced Placement Programme
5 Asset Languages Advanced Stage
6 ASDAN Community Volunteering qualification
7 British Horse Society Stage 3 Horse Knowledge & Care, Stage 3 Riding and Preliminary Teacher's Certificate
8 BTEC Awards
9 BTEC Certificates and Extended Certificates
10 BTEC Diplomas
11 BTEC National in Early Years
12 BTEC National Award, National Certificate and National Diploma
13 CACHE Award, Certificate and Diploma in Child Care and Education
14 Cambridge Pre-U
15 Certificate of Personal Effectiveness (COPE)
16 CISI Introduction to Securities and Investment
17 Diploma in Fashion Retail
18 Diploma in Foundation Studies (Art & Design; Art, Design & Media)
19 EDI Level 3 Certificate in Accounting, Certificate in Accounting (IAS)
20 Extended Project
21 Free-standing Mathematics qualifications
22 GCE AS, AS Double Award, A level, A level Double Award and A level with additional AS
23 Higher Sports Leader Award
24 Hong Kong Diploma of Secondary Education (from 2012 entry to HE)
25 ifs School of Finance, Certificate and Diploma in Financial Studies
26 International Baccalaureate Diploma
27 International Baccalaureate Certificate
28 iMedia Users (iMedia) Certificate and Diploma
29 IT for Professionals (iPRO) Certificate and Diploma
30 Irish Leaving Certificate - Higher and Ordinary levels
31 Key Skills at level 3 and 4
32 Music examinations at grades 6, 7 and 8
33 OCR Level 3 Certificate in Mathematics for Engineering
34 OCR National Certificate, National Diploma and National Extended Diploma
35 Progression Diploma
36 Scottish Higher and Advanced Higher, National Certificates, Ungraded Higher, National Progression Awards, and Interdisciplinary Project
37 Speech and Drama examinations at grades 6, 7 and 8 and Performance Studies
38 Welsh Baccalaureate Advanced Diploma

Updates on the Tariff, including details on the incorporation of any new qualifications, are posted on **www.ucas.com**.

UCAS TARIFF TABLES

1

AAT NVQ LEVEL 3 IN ACCOUNTING	
GRADE	TARIFF POINTS
PASS	160

2

ADVANCED DIPLOMA

Advanced Diploma = Progression Diploma plus Additional & Specialist Learning (ASL). Please see the appropriate qualification to calculate the ASL score. Please see the Progression Diploma (Table 35) for Tariff scores

3

ADVANCED EXTENSION AWARDS	
GRADE	TARIFF POINTS
DISTINCTION	40
MERIT	20

Points for Advanced Extension Awards are over and above those gained from the A level grade

4

ADVANCED PLACEMENT PROGRAMME (US & CANADA)	
GRADE	TARIFF POINTS
Group A	
5	120
4	90
3	60
Group B	
5	50
4	35
3	20

5

ASSET LANGUAGES ADVANCED STAGE			
GRADE	TARIFF POINTS	GRADE	TARIFF POINTS
Speaking		Listening	
GRADE 12	28	GRADE 12	25
GRADE 11	20	GRADE 11	18
GRADE 10	12	GRADE 10	11
Reading		Writing	
GRADE 12	25	GRADE 12	25
GRADE 11	18	GRADE 11	18
GRADE 10	11	GRADE 10	11

6

ASDAN COMMUNITY VOLUNTEERING QUALIFICATION	
GRADE	TARIFF POINTS
CERTIFICATE	50
AWARD	30

Points for the ASDAN Commmunity Volunteering qualification come into effect for entry into higher education from 2011 onwards

7

BRITISH HORSE SOCIETY	
GRADE	TARIFF POINTS
Stage 3 Horse Knowledge & Care	
PASS	35
Stage 3 Riding	
PASS	35
Preliminary Teacher's Certificate	
PASS	35

Awarded by Equestrian Qualifications (GB) Ltd (EQL) on behalf of British Horse Society

8

BTEC AWARDS (EXCLUDING BTEC NATIONAL QUALIFICATIONS)			
GRADE	TARIFF POINTS		
	Group A	Group B	Group C
DISTINCTION	20	30	40
MERIT	13	20	26
PASS	7	10	13

9

BTEC CERTIFICATES AND EXTENDED CERTIFICATES (EXCLUDING BTEC NATIONAL QUALIFICATIONS)					
GRADE	TARIFF POINTS				
	Group A	Group B	Group C	Group D	Extended Certificates
DISTINCTION	40	60	80	100	60
MERIT	26	40	52	65	40
PASS	13	20	26	35	20

10

BTEC DIPLOMAS (EXCLUDING BTEC NATIONAL QUALIFICATIONS)			
GRADE	TARIFF POINTS		
	Group A	Group B	Group C
DISTINCTION	80	100	120
MERIT	52	65	80
PASS	26	35	40

UCAS TARIFF TABLES

11

BTEC NATIONAL IN EARLY YEARS					
GRADE	TARIFF POINTS	GRADE	TARIFF POINTS	GRADE	TARIFF POINTS
Theory				Practical	
Diploma		Certificate			
DDD	320	DD	200	D	120
DDM	280	DM	160	M	80
DMM	240	MM	120	P	40
MMM	220	MP	80		
MMP	160	PP	40		
MPP	120				
PPP	80				

Points apply to the following qualifications only: BTEC National Diploma in Early Years (100/1279/5); BTEC National Certificate in Early Years (100/1280/1).

12

BTEC NATIONALS					
GRADE	TARIFF POINTS	GRADE	TARIFF POINTS	GRADE	TARIFF POINTS
National Diploma		National Certificate		National Award	
DDD	360	DD	240	D	120
DDM	320	DM	200	M	80
DMM	280	MM	160	P	40
MMM	240	MP	120		
MMP	200	PP	80		
MPP	160				
PPP	120				

13

CACHE AWARD, CERTIFICATE AND DIPLOMA IN CHILD CARE & EDUCATION					
AWARD		CERTIFICATE		DIPLOMA	
GRADE	TARIFF POINTS	GRADE	TARIFF POINTS	GRADE	TARIFF POINTS
A	30	A	110	A	360
B	25	B	90	B	300
C	20	C	70	C	240
D	15	D	55	D	180
E	10	E	35	E	120

14

CAMBRIDGE PRE-U					
GRADE	TARIFF POINTS	GRADE	TARIFF POINTS	GRADE	TARIFF POINTS
Principal Subject		Global Perspectives and Research		Short Course	
D1	TBC	D1	TBC	D1	TBC
D2	145	D2	140	D2	TBC
D3	130	D3	126	D3	60
M1	115	M1	112	M1	53
M2	101	M2	98	M2	46
M3	87	M3	84	M3	39
P1	73	P1	70	P1	32
P2	59	P2	56	P2	26
P3	46	P3	42	P3	20

UCAS TARIFF TABLES

15

CERTIFICATE OF PERSONAL EFFECTIVENESS (COPE)	
GRADE	TARIFF POINTS
PASS	70

Points are awarded for the Certificate of Personal Effectiveness (CoPE) awarded by ASDAN and CCEA

16

CISI INTRODUCTION TO SECURITIES AND INVESTMENT	
GRADE	TARIFF POINTS
PASS WITH DISTINCITON	60
PASS WITH MERIT	40
PASS	20

Points for the CISI Introduction to Securities and Investment come into effect into higher education from 2011 onwards

17

DIPLOMA IN FASHION RETAIL	
GRADE	TARIFF POINTS
DISTINCTION	160
MERIT	120
PASS	80

Awarded by ABC Awards

18

DIPLOMA IN FOUNDATION STUDIES (ART & DESIGN, AND ART, DESIGN & MEDIA)	
GRADE	TARIFF POINTS
DISTINCTION	285
MERIT	225
PASS	165

Points are awarded for Edexcel Level 3 BTEC Diploma in Foundation Studies (Art & Design) and Level 3 Diploma in Foundation Studies (Art, Design & Media) awarded by ABC Awards and WJEC

19

EDI LEVEL 3 CERTIFICATE IN ACCOUNTING AND CERTIFICATE IN ACCOUNTING (IAS)	
GRADE	TARIFF POINTS
DISTINCTION	120
MERIT	90
PASS	70

20

EXTENDED PROJECT (STAND ALONE)	
GRADE	TARIFF POINTS
A*	70
A	60
B	50
C	40
D	30
E	20

Points for the Extended Project cannot be counted if taken as part of Progression/Advanced Diploma

21

FREE-STANDING MATHEMATICS	
GRADE	TARIFF POINTS
A	20
B	17
C	13
D	10
E	7

Covers free-standing Mathematics - Additional Maths, Using and Applying Statistics, Working with Algebraic and Graphical Techniques, Modelling with Calculus

22

GCE

GRADE	TARIFF POINTS	GRADE	TARIFF POINTS	GRADE	TARIFF POINTS	GRADE	TARIFF POINTS	GRADE	TARIFF POINTS
GCE Double Award		A level with additional AS (9 units)		GCE A level		GCE AS		GCE AS Double Award	
A*A*	280	A*A	200	A*	140	A	60	AA	120
A*A	260	AA	180	A	120	B	50	AB	110
AA	240	AB	170	B	100	C	40	BB	100
AB	220	BB	150	C	80	D	30	BC	90
BB	200	BC	140	D	60	E	20	CC	80
BC	180	CC	120	E	40			CD	70
CC	160	CD	110					DD	60
CD	140	DD	90					DE	50
DD	120	DE	80					EE	40
DE	100	EE	60						
EE	80								

UCAS TARIFF TABLES

23

HIGHER SPORTS LEADER AWARD	
GRADE	TARIFF POINTS
PASS	30

24

HONG KONG DIPLOMA OF SECONDARY EDUCATION					
GRADE	TARIFF POINTS	GRADE	TARIFF POINTS	GRADE	TARIFF POINTS
All subjects except mathematics		Mathematics compulsory component		Mathematics optional components	
5**	No value	5**	No value	5**	No value
5*	130	5*	60	5*	70
5	120	5	45	5	60
4	80	4	35	4	50
3	40	3	25	3	40

Points come into effect for entry to higher education from 2012 onwards.
No value for 5** pending receipt of candidate evidence (post 2012)

25

IFS SCHOOL OF FINANCE			
GRADE	TARIFF POINTS	GRADE	TARIFF POINTS
Certificate in Financial Studies (CeFS)		Diploma in Financial Studies (DipFS)	
A	60	A	60
B	50	B	50
C	40	C	40
D	30	D	30
E	20	E	20

Completion of both qualifications will result in a maximum of 120 UCAS Tariff points

26

INTERNATIONAL BACCALAUREATE (IB) DIPLOMA			
GRADE	TARIFF POINTS	GRADE	TARIFF POINTS
45	720	34	479
44	698	33	457
43	676	32	435
42	654	31	413
41	632	30	392
40	611	29	370
39	589	28	348
38	567	27	326
37	545	26	304
36	523	25	282
35	501	24	260

27

INTERNATIONAL BACCALAUREATE (IB) CERTIFICATE					
GRADE	TARIFF POINTS	GRADE	TARIFF POINTS	GRADE	TARIFF POINTS
Higher Level		Standard Level		Core	
7	130	7	70	3	120
6	110	6	59	2	80
5	80	5	43	1	40
4	50	4	27	0	10
3	20	3	11		

28

iMEDIA USERS (iMEDIA)	
GRADE	TARIFF POINTS
DIPLOMA	66
CERTIFICATE	40

Awarded by OCR

UCAS TARIFF TABLES

29

IT PROFESSIONALS (iPRO)	
GRADE	TARIFF POINTS
DIPLOMA	100
CERTIFICATE	80

Awarded by OCR

30

IRISH LEAVING CERTIFICATE			
GRADE	TARIFF POINTS	GRADE	TARIFF POINTS
Higher		Ordinary	
A1	90	A1	39
A2	77	A2	26
B1	71	B1	20
B2	64	B2	14
B3	58	B3	7
C1	52		
C2	45		
C3	39		
D1	33		
D2	26		
D3	20		

31

KEY SKILLS	
GRADE	TARIFF POINTS
LEVEL 4	30
LEVEL 3	20

32

MUSIC EXAMINATIONS					
GRADE	TARIFF POINTS	GRADE	TARIFF POINTS	GRADE	TARIFF POINTS
Practical					
Grade 8		Grade 7		Grade 6	
DISTINCTION	75	DISTINCTION	60	DISTINCTION	45
MERIT	70	MERIT	55	MERIT	40
PASS	55	PASS	40	PASS	25
Theory					
Grade 8		Grade 7		Grade 6	
DISTINCTION	30	DISTINCTION	20	DISTINCTION	15
MERIT	25	MERIT	15	MERIT	10
PASS	20	PASS	10	PASS	5

Points shown are for the ABRSM, Guildhall, LCMM, Rockschool and Trinity College London Advanced level music examinations

33

OCR LEVEL 3 CERTIFICATE IN MATHEMATICS FOR ENGINEERING	
GRADE	TARIFF POINTS
A*	TBC
A	90
B	75
C	60
D	45
E	30

Points come into effect for entry to higher education from 2011 onwards

34

OCR NATIONALS					
GRADE	TARIFF POINTS	GRADE	TARIFF POINTS	GRADE	TARIFF POINTS
National Extended Diploma		National Diploma		National Certificate	
D1	360	D	240	D	120
D2/M1	320	M1	200	M	80
M2	280	M2/P1	160	P	40
M3	240	P2	120		
P1	200	P3	80		
P2	160				
P3	120				

35

PROGRESSION DIPLOMA	
GRADE	TARIFF POINTS
A*	350
A	300
B	250
C	200
D	150
E	100

Advanced Diploma = Progression Diploma plus Additional & Specialist Learning (ASL). Please see the appropriate qualification to calculate the ASL score.

UCAS TARIFF TABLES

36

SCOTTISH QUALIFICATIONS

GRADE	TARIFF POINTS
Advanced Higher	
A	130
B	110
C	90
D	72
Ungraded Higher	
PASS	45

GRADE	TARIFF POINTS
Higher	
A	80
B	65
C	50
D	36
NPA PC Passport	
PASS	45
Core Skills	
HIGHER	20

GRADE	TARIFF POINTS
Scottish Interdisciplinary Project	
A	65
B	55
C	45

GROUP	TARIFF POINTS
Scottish National Certificates	
C	125
B	100
A	75

Points for Scottish National Certificates come into effect for entry into higher education from 2011 onwards.

37

SPEECH AND DRAMA EXAMINATIONS

GRADE	TARIFF POINTS
PCertLAM	
DISTINCTION	90
MERIT	80
PASS	60

GRADE	TARIFF POINTS
Grade 8	
DISTINCTION	65
MERIT	60
PASS	45

GRADE	TARIFF POINTS
Grade 7	
DISTINCTION	55
MERIT	50
PASS	35

GRADE	TARIFF POINTS
Grade 6	
DISTINCTION	40
MERIT	35
PASS	20

Points shown are for ESB, LAMDA, LCMM and Trinity Guildhall Advanced level speech and drama examinations accredited in the National Qualifications Framework and LAMDA'S Certificates in Communication and Certificate in Performance accredited on the Qualifications and Credit framework (QCF). A full list of the subjects covered is available on the UCAS website.

38

WELSH BACCALAUREATE CORE

GRADE	TARIFF POINTS
PASS	120

These points are for the Core and are awarded only when a candidate achieves the Welsh Baccalaureate Advanced Diploma

Results

4

Step 4 – Results

We receive many exam results direct from the exam boards – check the list at www.ucas.com. If your qualification is listed, you don't need to send your results to us or the universities and colleges. Check Track at www.ucas.com to see if you've got a place on your chosen course.

If your qualification is listed, we send your results to the universities and colleges that you have accepted as your firm and insurance choices. If your qualification is not listed, you must send your exam results to the universities and colleges where you are holding offers.

You should arrange your holidays so that you are at home when your exam results are published because, if there are any issues to discuss, admissions tutors will want to speak to you in person.

After you have received your exam results check Track to find out if you have a place on your chosen course.

If you have met all the conditions for your firm choice, the university or college will confirm that you have a place. Sometimes, they may still confirm you have a place even if you have not quite met all the offer conditions; or they may offer you a place on a similar course.

If you have not met the conditions of your firm choice and the university or college has not confirmed your place, but you have met all the conditions of your insurance offer, the university or college will confirm that you have a place.

When a university or college tells us that you have a place, we send you confirmation by letter.

WHAT IF YOU DON'T HAVE A PLACE?

If you have not met the conditions of either your firm or insurance choice, and your chosen universities or colleges have not confirmed your place, you are eligible for Clearing. In Clearing you can apply for courses that still have vacancies. Clearing operates from mid-July to late September 2011 (page 108).

BETTER RESULTS THAN EXPECTED?

If you obtain exam results that meet and exceed the conditions of the offer for your firm choice, you can for a short period use a process called Adjustment to look for an alternative place, whilst still keeping your original firm choice. See page 109 for information about Adjustment.

5 Next steps

Step 5 – Next steps

CLEARING

If you find yourself in Clearing, you will need to

Find a course you like – do your research thoroughly and quickly. You could consider related or alternative subjects or perhaps apply for the subject you want in combination with another. Your teachers or careers advisers or the universities and colleges themselves can provide useful guidance. If your results are reasonable, and you are flexible about where and what you want to study, you have every chance of finding a place on a suitable course.

Talk to the institutions – don't be afraid to call them. Prepare notes on what you will say to them about:

- why you want to study the course
- why you want to study at their institution
- what relevant employment or activities you have done that relate to the course
- your grades

and have ready your:

- Personal ID
- Clearing number.

Getting an offer – don't be pressured into doing something you don't like but once you find a course you will enjoy, stick with it.

ADJUSTMENT

If your results meet and exceed your conditional firm offer, you can adjust your place

You may decide to research alternative institutions and courses. Talk to your school or college adviser first. If you find a course that you think you may be qualified for and which has places available, you need to talk to the new institution to adjust your place.

There are no published vacancies in Adjustment so you'll need to talk to the institutions – have all your information ready before you call:

- full details of your exam results
- why you want to change your course
- why you want to study at their institution
- what relevant employment or activities you have done that relate to the course
- your Personal ID.

You may be able to adjust to a deferred entry place if there are no places left and if your results meet the course entry requirements – you do not need to withdraw and reapply. Be aware that you have only five calendar days (including weekends) to consider changing your course in these circumstances – you must complete both your research and your negotiation within this time.

More information about Clearing and Adjustment is available at www.ucas.com.

IF YOU ARE STILL WITHOUT A PLACE TO STUDY:

You could re-sit your exams and try again next year, find employment, decide to do a further education course or apply for a part-time course and a part-time job. Seek advice from your school or college or careers office.

6 Starting university or college

Step 6 – Starting university or college

Make sure you have everything ready, such as accommodation, finances, travel arrangements, books and equipment required for the course.

Congratulations! Now you have your place at university or college you will need to make plans on how to get there, where to live and how to finance it.

Where to live - Unless you are planning to live at home, your university or college will usually provide you with guidance on how to find somewhere to live. The earlier you contact them the better your chance of finding a suitable range of options to choose from.

Student finance - You will need to budget for living costs, accommodation, travel, books and tuition fees. Tuition fees vary depending on the course and university you choose, and are shown on Course Search at **www.ucas.com**. Help is available from some universities and colleges in the form of bursaries and scholarships. Details of these bursaries and scholarships can also be found on Course Search.

yougofurther.co.uk - The UCAS student network allows you to make friends with other students who are going to the same university or college and could be on the same course. yougo allows you to talk to UCAS online as well as to the universities and colleges on their profile pages. yougo is your direct route to the information you need.

The UCAS student network
Meet people before you go
Going to university is a big step but fear not, you're not alone.
Join yougofurther online at
yougofurther.co.uk
yougo further
brought to you by UCAS

Useful contacts

For information relating to the UCAS application process, please contact the UCAS Customer Service Unit on 0871 468 0 468 or on 0044 871 468 0 468 from outside the UK. Calls from BT landlines within the UK will cost no more than 9p per minute. The cost of calls from mobiles and other networks may vary.

If you have hearing difficulties, you can call the Text Relay service on 18001 0871 468 0 468 (outside the UK 0044 151 494 1260). Calls are charged at normal rates.

CAREERS ADVICE

Connexions Direct is for you if you live in England, are aged 13 to 19 and want advice on getting to where you want to be in life.

Connexions personal advisers can give you information, advice and practical help with all sorts of things, like choosing subjects at school or mapping out your future career options. They can help you with anything that might be affecting you at school, college, work or in your personal or family life.

For where to find your local office, look at **www.connexions-direct.com**.

Careers Scotland provides a starting point for anyone looking for careers information, advice or guidance. **www.careers-scotland.org.uk**.

Careers Wales – Wales' national all-age careers guidance service.
www.careerswales.com
www.gyrfacymru.com.

Northern Ireland Careers Service website for the new, all-age careers guidance service in Northern Ireland. **www.careersserviceni.com**.

Learndirect – Not sure what job you want? Need help to decide which course to do? Give learndirect a call on 0800 101 901 or, for Scotland, 0808 100 9000.
www.learndirect.co.uk.
www.learndirectscotland.com.

YEAR OUT

For useful information on taking a year out, see **www.gap-year.com**.

The Year Out Group website is packed with information and guidance for young people and their parents and advisers.
www.yearoutgroup.org.

STUDENTS WITH DISABILITIES

If you have a disability or specific learning difficulty, you are strongly encouraged to make early direct contact with individual institutions before submitting your application. Most universities and colleges have disability coordinators or advisers. You can find their contact details and further advice at the Skill: National Bureau for Students with Disabilities' website – **www.skill.org.uk**.

For information about the Disabled Students' Allowance, see page 80.

Essential reading

UCAS has brought together the best books and resources you need to make the important decisions regarding entry to higher education. With guidance on choosing courses, finding the right institution, information about student finance, admissions tests, gap years and lots more, you can find the most trusted guides at www.ucasbooks.com.

The publications listed on the following pages are available through www.ucasbooks.com or from UCAS Publication Services unless otherwise stated.

UCAS Publication Services

UCAS Publication Services
PO Box 130
Cheltenham
Gloucestershire GL52 3ZF

f: 01242 544 806
e: publicationservices@ucas.ac.uk
// www.ucasbooks.com

NEED HELP COMPLETING YOUR APPLICATION?

How to Complete your UCAS Application 2011

A must for anyone applying through UCAS. Contains advice on the preparation needed, a step-by-step guide to filling out the UCAS application, information on the UCAS process and useful tips for completing the personal statement.
Published by Trotman
Price £12.99

Insider's Guide to Applying to University

Full of honest insights, this is a thorough guide to the application process. It reveals advice from careers advisers and current students, guidance on making sense of university information and choosing courses. Also includes tips for the personal statement, interviews, admissions tests, UCAS Extra and Clearing.
Published by Trotman
Price £12.99

How to Write a Winning UCAS Personal Statement

The personal statement is your chance to stand out from the crowd. Based on information from admissions tutors, this book will help you sell yourself. It includes specific guidance for over 30 popular subjects, common mistakes to avoid, information on what admissions tutors look for, and much more.
Published by Trotman
Price £12.99

CHOOSING COURSES

Progression Series 2011 entry

The 'Progression to…' titles are designed to help you access good quality, useful information on some of the most competitive subject areas. The books cover advice on applying through UCAS, routes to qualifications, course details, job prospects, case studies and career advice.

Progression to…
Art and Design
Economics, Finance and Accountancy
Engineering and Mathematics
Health and Social Care
Law
Media and Performing Arts
Medicine, Dentistry and Optometry
Psychology
Sports Science and Physiotherapy
Teaching and Education
Published by UCAS
Price £15.99 each

UCAS Parent Guide

Free of charge.
Order online at **www.ucas.com/parents**.

Open Days 2010

Attending open days, taster courses and higher education conventions is an important part of the application process. This publication makes planning attendance at these events quick and easy.
Published annually by UCAS.
Price £3.50

'Getting into...' guides

Clear and concise guides to help applicants secure places. They include qualifications required, advice on applying, tests, interviews and case studies. The guides give an honest view and discuss current issues and careers.

Getting into Business and Management Courses
Getting into Oxford and Cambridge
Getting into US and Canadian Universities
Getting into Veterinary School
Published by Trotman
Price £12.99 each

Choosing Your Degree Course & University

With so many universities and courses to choose from, it is not an easy decision for students embarking on their journey to higher education. This guide will offer expert guidance on the questions students need to ask when considering the opportunities available.
Published by Trotman
Price £24.99

Degree Course Descriptions

Providing details of the nature of degree courses, the descriptions in this book are written by heads of departments and senior lecturers at major universities. Each description contains an overview of the course area, details of course structures, career opportunities and more.
Published by COA
Price £12.99

CHOOSING WHERE TO STUDY

The Virgin 2011 Guide to British Universities

An insider's guide to choosing a university or college. Written by students and using independent statistics, this guide evaluates what you get from a higher education institution.
Published by Virgin
Price £15.99

Times Good University Guide 2011

How do you find the best university for the subject you wish to study? You need a guide that evaluates the quality of what is available, giving facts, figures and comparative assessments of universities. The rankings provide hard data, analysed, interpreted and presented by a team of experts.
Published by Harper Collins
Price £16.99

Guardian University Guide 2011

Packed with no-nonsense advice, this book takes prospective students through every process they will encounter: from applications to interviews, accommodation to finances. The Guardian subject ratings are based on the UCAS entry Tariffs so that students can judge for themselves which are the best universities available to them.
Published by The Guardian
Price £16.99

Which Uni?

One person's perfect uni might be hell for someone else. Picking the right one will give you the best chance of future happiness, academic success and brighter job prospects. This guide is packed with tables from a variety of sources, rating universities on everything from the quality of teaching to the make-up of the student population and much more.
Published by Trotman
Price £14.99

Getting into the UK's Best Universities and Courses

This book is for those who set their goals high and dream of studying on a highly regarded course at a good university. It provides information on selecting the best courses for a subject, the application and personal statement, interviews, results day, timescales for applications and much more.
Published by Trotman
Price £12.99

FINANCIAL INFORMATION

Student Finance

All students need to know about tuition fees, loans, grants, bursaries and much more. Covering all forms of income and expenditure, this comprehensive guide is produced in association with UCAS and offers great value for money.
Published by Constable Robinson
Price: £7.99

The Essential Guide to Paying for University

Parents and students alike are increasingly concerned about the rising cost of university education. However, there are strategies that can help, and there are many bursaries that go unclaimed every year. This guide covers the cost of university, funding available to help, and how parents and students can plan and budget.
Published by Kogan Page
Price £9.99

University Scholarships, Awards & Bursaries

Students embarking on HE courses face an increasingly challenging financial situation. This book enables applicants and current students to find the support that may help them make ends meet. Packed with information on virtually all awards available.
Published by Trotman
Price £22.99

CAREERS PLANNING

A-Z of Careers and Jobs

It is vital to be well informed about career decisions and this guide will help you make the right choice. It provides full details of the wide range of opportunities on the market, the personal qualities and skills needed for each job, entry qualifications and training, realistic salary expectations and useful contact details.
Published by Kogan Page
Price £14.99

The Careers Directory

An indispensable resource for anyone seeking careers information, covering over 350 careers. It presents up-to-date information in an innovative double-page format. Ideal for students in years 10 to 13 who are considering their futures and for other careers professionals.
Published by COA
Price £14.99

DEFERRING ENTRY

Your Gap Year

The essential book for all young people planning a gap year before continuing with their education. This up-to-date guide provides essential information on specialist gap year programes, as well as the vast range of jobs and voluntary opportunities available to young people around the world.
Published by Crimson Publishing
Price £12.99

Gap Year Guidebook 2010

This thorough and easy-to-use guide contains everything you need to know before taking a gap year. It includes real-life traveller tips, hundreds of contact details, realistic advice on everything from preparing, learning and working abroad, coping with coming home and much more.
Published by John Catt Education
Price £12.95

Summer Jobs Worldwide 2010

This unique and specialist guide contains over 40,000 jobs for all ages. No other book includes such a variety and wealth of summer work opportunities in Britain and aboard. Anything from horse trainer in Iceland, to a guide for nature walks in Peru, to a yoga centre helper in Greece, to an animal keeper for London Zoo, can be found.
Published by Crimson Publishing
Price £14.99

Please note all publications incur a postage and packing charge. All information was correct at the time of printing.

For a full list of publications, please visit www.ucasbooks.com.

Courses
ProgressionSeries

Courses

Keen to get started on your career in economics, finance or accountancy? This section contains details of the various courses available at UK institutions.

EXPLAINING THE LIST OF COURSES

We list the universities and colleges by their UCAS institution codes. Within each institution, courses are listed first by award type (such as BA, BSc, FdA, HND, MA and many others), then alphabetically by course title.

You might find some courses showing an award type '(Mod)', which indicates a combined degree that might be modular in design. A small number of courses have award type '(FYr)'. This indicates a 12-month foundation course, after which students can choose to apply for a degree course. In either case, you should contact the university or college for further details.

Generally speaking, when a course comprises two or more subjects, the word used to connect the subjects indicates the make-up of the award: 'Subject A and Subject B' is a joint award, where both subjects carry equal weight; 'Subject A with Subject B' is a major/minor award, where Subject A accounts for at least 60% of your study. If the title shows 'Subject A/Subject B', it may indicate that students can decide on the weighting of the subjects at the end of the first year. You should check with the university or college for full details.

Each entry in the UCAS sections shows the UCAS course code and the duration of the course. Where known, the entry contains details of the minimum qualification requirements for the course, as supplied to UCAS by the universities and colleges. Bear in mind that possessing the minimum qualifications does not guarantee acceptance to the course: there may be far more applicants than places. You may be asked to attend an interview, present a portfolio or sit an admissions test.

Before applying for any course, you are advised to contact the university or college to check any changes in entry requirements and to see if any new courses have come on stream since the data was approved for publication. To make this easy, each institution's entry starts with their address, email, phone and fax details, as well as their website address. You will also find it useful to check the Entry Profiles section of Course Search at **www.ucas.com**.

LIST OF COURSES

The list of courses in this section has been divided into the following subject categories

ECONOMICS

A20 THE UNIVERSITY OF ABERDEEN

UNIVERSITY OFFICE
KING'S COLLEGE
ABERDEEN AB24 3FX
t: +44 (0) 1224 273504 f: +44 (0) 1224 272034
e: sras@abdn.ac.uk
// www.abdn.ac.uk/sras

L100 MA Economics
Duration: 4FT Hon
Entry Requirements: ***GCE:*** BBB. ***SQAH:*** BBBB. ***IB:*** 30. ***BTEC ND:*** MMM.

A30 UNIVERSITY OF ABERTAY DUNDEE

BELL STREET
DUNDEE DD1 1HG
t: 01382 308080 f: 01382 308081
e: sro@abertay.ac.uk
// www.abertay.ac.uk

N100 BA Business Studies option - Economics
Duration: 4SW Hon
Entry Requirements: ***GCE:*** DDD. ***SQAH:*** BBC. ***IB:*** 24. ***BTEC NC:*** DM. ***BTEC ND:*** MMP.

A40 ABERYSTWYTH UNIVERSITY

WELCOME CENTRE, ABERYSTWYTH UNIVERSITY
PENGLAIS CAMPUS
ABERYSTWYTH
CEREDIGION SY23 3FB
t: 01970 622021 f: 01970 627410
e: ug-admissions@aber.ac.uk
// www.aber.ac.uk

L113 BScEcon Business Economics
Duration: 3FT Hon
Entry Requirements: ***GCE:*** 280. ***IB:*** 27.

L100 BScEcon Economics
Duration: 3FT Hon
Entry Requirements: ***GCE:*** 280. ***IB:*** 27.

A60 ANGLIA RUSKIN UNIVERSITY

BISHOP HALL LANE
CHELMSFORD
ESSEX CM1 1SQ
t: 0845 271 3333 f: 01245 251789
e: answers@anglia.ac.uk
// www.anglia.ac.uk

L100 BSc Business Economics
Duration: 3FT Hon
Entry Requirements: ***GCE:*** 200. ***SQAH:*** BBCC. ***SQAAH:*** CC. ***IB:*** 24.

B06 BANGOR UNIVERSITY

BANGOR
GWYNEDD LL57 2DG
t: 01248 382016/2017 f: 01248 370451
e: admissions@bangor.ac.uk
// www.bangor.ac.uk

L114 BA Business Economics
Duration: 3FT Hon
Entry Requirements: ***GCE:*** 260-300. ***IB:*** 28.

L190 BSc Business Economics
Duration: 3FT Hon
Entry Requirements: ***GCE:*** 260-300. ***IB:*** 28.

B16 UNIVERSITY OF BATH

CLAVERTON DOWN
BATH BA2 7AY
t: 01225 383019 f: 01225 386366
e: admissions@bath.ac.uk
// www.bath.ac.uk

L100 BSc Economics
Duration: 3FT Hon
Entry Requirements: ***GCE:*** AAA. ***SQAAH:*** AAB. ***IB:*** 38. ***BTEC NC:*** DD. ***BTEC ND:*** DDD.

L101 BSc Economics (4 year sandwich)
Duration: 4SW Hon
Entry Requirements: ***GCE:*** AAA-AAB. ***SQAAH:*** AAB. ***IB:*** 38. ***BTEC NC:*** DD. ***BTEC ND:*** DDD.

B32 THE UNIVERSITY OF BIRMINGHAM

EDGBASTON
BIRMINGHAM B15 2TT
t: 0121 415 8900 f: 0121 414 7159
e: admissions@bham.ac.uk
// www.bham.ac.uk

L150 BA Political Economy
Duration: 3FT Hon
Entry Requirements: ***GCE:*** AAB-ABB. ***SQAH:*** AAABB-AABBB. ***SQAAH:*** ABB-AA.

L100 BSc Economics
Duration: 3FT Hon
Entry Requirements: ***GCE:*** AAB. ***SQAH:*** AAABB. ***SQAAH:*** AAB-ABB.

B56 THE UNIVERSITY OF BRADFORD

RICHMOND ROAD
BRADFORD
WEST YORKSHIRE BD7 1DP
t: 0800 073 1225 f: 01274 235585
e: course-enquiries@bradford.ac.uk
// www.bradford.ac.uk

L101 BSc Business Economics

Duration: 3FT Hon
Entry Requirements: ***GCE:*** 240-260. ***IB:*** 28.

L100 BSc Economics

Duration: 3FT Hon
Entry Requirements: ***GCE:*** 240-260. ***IB:*** 28.

L111 BSc Financial Economics

Duration: 3FT Hon
Entry Requirements: ***GCE:*** 240-260. ***IB:*** 28.

L160 BSc International Economics

Duration: 3FT Hon
Entry Requirements: ***GCE:*** 240-260. ***IB:*** 28.

B78 UNIVERSITY OF BRISTOL

UNDERGRADUATE ADMISSIONS OFFICE
SENATE HOUSE
TYNDALL AVENUE
BRISTOL BS8 1TH
t: 0117 928 9000 f: 0117 925 1424
e: ug-admissions@bristol.ac.uk
// www.bristol.ac.uk

L100 BSc Economics

Duration: 3FT Hon
Entry Requirements: ***GCE:*** A*AA-ABB. ***SQAH:*** AAAAA-AAABB. ***SQAAH:*** AA. ***BTEC ND:*** DDD.

L140 BSc Economics and Econometrics

Duration: 3FT Hon
Entry Requirements: ***GCE:*** A*AA-ABB. ***SQAH:*** AAAAA-AAABB. ***SQAAH:*** AA. ***BTEC ND:*** DDD.

L101 BSc Economics with Study in Continental Europe (4 years)

Duration: 4FT Hon
Entry Requirements: ***GCE:*** A*AA-ABB. ***SQAH:*** AAAAA-AAABB. ***SQAAH:*** AA. ***BTEC ND:*** DDD.

B80 UNIVERSITY OF THE WEST OF ENGLAND, BRISTOL

FRENCHAY CAMPUS
COLDHARBOUR LANE
BRISTOL BS16 1QY
t: +44 (0)117 32 83333 f: +44 (0)117 32 82810
e: admissions@uwe.ac.uk
// www.uwe.ac.uk

L100 BA Economics

Duration: 3FT/4SW Hon
Entry Requirements: ***GCE:*** 280-340.

B84 BRUNEL UNIVERSITY

UXBRIDGE
MIDDLESEX UB8 3PH
t: 01895 265265 f: 01895 269790
e: admissions@brunel.ac.uk
// www.brunel.ac.uk

L113 BSc Business Economics

Duration: 3FT Hon
Entry Requirements: ***GCE:*** 280-320. ***IB:*** 32. ***BTEC NC:*** DM. ***BTEC ND:*** DDM.

L111 BSc Business Economics (4 year Thick SW)

Duration: 4SW Hon
Entry Requirements: ***GCE:*** 280-320. ***IB:*** 32. ***BTEC NC:*** DM. ***BTEC ND:*** DDM.

L101 BSc Economics

Duration: 3FT Hon
Entry Requirements: ***GCE:*** 280-320. ***IB:*** 32. ***BTEC NC:*** DM. ***BTEC ND:*** DDM.

L106 BSc Economics (4 year Thick SW)

Duration: 4SW Hon
Entry Requirements: ***GCE:*** 280-320. ***IB:*** 32. ***BTEC NC:*** DM. ***BTEC ND:*** DDM.

B90 THE UNIVERSITY OF BUCKINGHAM

YEOMANRY HOUSE
HUNTER STREET
BUCKINGHAM MK18 1EG
t: 01280 820313 f: 01280 822245
e: info@buckingham.ac.uk
// www.buckingham.ac.uk

L112 BScEcon Business Economics

Duration: 2FT Hon
Entry Requirements: ***GCE:*** 240. ***IB:*** 26. ***BTEC NC:*** DD. ***BTEC ND:*** MMM.

L100 BScEcon Economics

Duration: 2FT/3FT Hon
Entry Requirements: ***GCE:*** 240. ***IB:*** 26. ***BTEC NC:*** DD. ***BTEC ND:*** MMM.

C05 UNIVERSITY OF CAMBRIDGE

CAMBRIDGE ADMISSIONS OFFICE
FITZWILLIAM HOUSE
32 TRUMPINGTON STREET
CAMBRIDGE CB2 1QY
t: 01223 333 308 f: 01223 746 868
e: admissions@cam.ac.uk
// www.cam.ac.uk/admissions/undergraduate/

L100 BA Economics

Duration: 3FT Hon

Entry Requirements: ***GCE:*** A*AA. ***SQAAH:*** AAA-AAB. Interview required.

C15 CARDIFF UNIVERSITY

PO BOX 927
30-36 NEWPORT ROAD
CARDIFF CF24 0DE
t: 029 2087 9999 f: 029 2087 6138
e: admissions@cardiff.ac.uk
// www.cardiff.ac.uk

L160 BSc Economics with a European Language (4 years)

Duration: 4FT Hon

Entry Requirements: ***GCE:*** AAB. ***SQAH:*** AAABB. ***SQAAH:*** AAB. ***IB:*** 35. ***BTEC ND:*** DDD. ***OCR NED:*** D2

L114 BScEcon Business Economics

Duration: 3FT Hon

Entry Requirements: ***GCE:*** AAB. ***SQAH:*** AAABB. ***SQAAH:*** AAB. ***IB:*** 35. ***BTEC ND:*** DDD. ***OCR NED:*** D2

L100 BScEcon Economics

Duration: 3FT Hon

Entry Requirements: ***GCE:*** AAB. ***SQAH:*** AAABB. ***SQAAH:*** AAB. ***IB:*** 35. ***BTEC ND:*** DDD. ***OCR NED:*** D2

C20 UNIVERSITY OF WALES INSTITUTE, CARDIFF

PO BOX 377
LLANDAFF CAMPUS
WESTERN AVENUE
CARDIFF CF5 2SG
t: 029 2041 6070 f: 029 2041 6286
e: admissions@uwic.ac.uk
// www.uwic.ac.uk

L100 BSc Economics

Duration: 3FT Hon

Entry Requirements: ***GCE:*** 240. ***IB:*** 24. ***BTEC NC:*** DD. ***BTEC ND:*** MMM. ***OCR ND:*** D ***OCR NED:*** M3

C30 UNIVERSITY OF CENTRAL LANCASHIRE

PRESTON
LANCS PR1 2HE
t: 01772 201201 f: 01772 894954
e: uadmissions@uclan.ac.uk
// www.uclan.ac.uk

L110 BA Business Economics

Duration: 3FT Hon

Entry Requirements: ***GCE:*** 240-280. ***SQAH:*** AABB-BBBB. ***IB:*** 28. ***BTEC NC:*** DD. ***OCR ND:*** D

L100 BA Economics

Duration: 3FT Hon

Entry Requirements: ***GCE:*** 240-280. ***SQAH:*** AABB-BBBB. ***IB:*** 28. ***BTEC NC:*** DD. ***OCR ND:*** D

L101 BSc Economics

Duration: 3FT Hon

Entry Requirements: ***GCE:*** 240-280. ***SQAH:*** AABB-BBBB. ***IB:*** 28. ***BTEC NC:*** DD. ***OCR ND:*** D

C55 UNIVERSITY OF CHESTER

PARKGATE ROAD
CHESTER CH1 4BJ
t: 01244 511000 f: 01244 511300
e: enquiries@chester.ac.uk
// www.chester.ac.uk

L100 BSc Economics

Duration: 3FT Hon

Entry Requirements: ***GCE:*** 220-260. ***SQAH:*** BBBB. ***IB:*** 24. ***BTEC NC:*** DM. ***BTEC ND:*** MMM.

C60 CITY UNIVERSITY

NORTHAMPTON SQUARE
LONDON EC1V 0HB
t: 020 7040 5060 f: 020 7040 8995
e: ugadmissions@city.ac.uk
// www.city.ac.uk

L100 BSc Economics

Duration: 3FT Hon

Entry Requirements: ***GCE:*** ABB. ***SQAH:*** BBBBC. ***IB:*** 34.

L111 BSc Financial Economics

Duration: 3FT Hon

Entry Requirements: ***GCE:*** ABB. ***SQAH:*** BBBBB. ***IB:*** 34.

L190 BSc International Foundation Programme (Economics routes)

Duration: 4FT Hon

Entry Requirements: Contact the institution for details.

C85 COVENTRY UNIVERSITY
THE STUDENT CENTRE
COVENTRY UNIVERSITY
1 GULSON ROAD
COVENTRY CV1 2JH
t: 024 7615 2222 f: 024 7615 2223
e: studentenquiries@coventry.ac.uk
// www.coventry.ac.uk

L112 BA Business Economics
Duration: 3FT/4SW Hon
Entry Requirements: ***GCE:*** 260-320. ***IB:*** 30. Interview required.

L100 BA Economics
Duration: 3FT Hon
Entry Requirements: ***GCE:*** 260-320. ***IB:*** 30. Interview required.

L111 BA Financial Economics
Duration: 3FT Hon
Entry Requirements: ***GCE:*** 260-320. ***IB:*** 30. Interview required.

D39 UNIVERSITY OF DERBY
KEDLESTON ROAD
DERBY DE22 1GB
t: 08701 202330 f: 01332 597724
e: askadmissions@derby.ac.uk
// www.derby.ac.uk

L160 BA International Trade (Top-up)
Duration: 1FT Hon
Entry Requirements: HND required.

D65 UNIVERSITY OF DUNDEE
DUNDEE DD1 4HN
t: 01382 383838 f: 01382 388150
e: ContactUs@dundee.ac.uk
// www.dundee.ac.uk/admissions/undergraduate/

L101 BSc Economics
Duration: 4FT Hon
Entry Requirements: ***GCE:*** BCC. ***SQAH:*** BBBB. ***IB:*** 30. ***BTEC ND:*** DMM.

L111 BSc Financial Economics
Duration: 4FT Hon
Entry Requirements: ***GCE:*** BCC. ***SQAH:*** BBBB. ***IB:*** 30. ***BTEC ND:*** DMM.

L100 MA Economics
Duration: 4FT Hon
Entry Requirements: ***GCE:*** BCC. ***SQAH:*** BBBB. ***IB:*** 30. ***BTEC ND:*** DMM.

L114 MA Financial Economics
Duration: 4FT Hon
Entry Requirements: ***GCE:*** BCC. ***SQAH:*** BBBB. ***IB:*** 30. ***BTEC ND:*** DMM.

D86 DURHAM UNIVERSITY
DURHAM UNIVERSITY
UNIVERSITY OFFICE
DURHAM DH1 3HP
t: 0191 334 2000 f: 0191 334 6055
e: admissions@durham.ac.uk
// www.durham.ac.uk

L112 BA Business Economics
Duration: 3FT Hon
Entry Requirements: ***GCE:*** AAA. ***SQAAH:*** AAA. ***IB:*** 37.

L100 BA Economics
Duration: 3FT Hon
Entry Requirements: ***GCE:*** AAA. ***SQAAH:*** AAA. ***IB:*** 37.

L101 BA Economics with Foundation
Duration: 4FT Hon
Entry Requirements: Contact the institution for details.

E14 UNIVERSITY OF EAST ANGLIA
NORWICH NR4 7TJ
t: 01603 591515 f: 01603 458596
e: admissions@uea.ac.uk
// www.uea.ac.uk

L111 BSc Business Economics
Duration: 3FT Hon
Entry Requirements: ***GCE:*** ABB-BBB. ***SQAH:*** AAAB. ***SQAAH:*** ABB. ***IB:*** 32. ***BTEC NC:*** DD. ***BTEC ND:*** DDM. ***OCR ND:*** M1 ***OCR NED:*** D2

L100 BSc Economics
Duration: 3FT Hon
Entry Requirements: ***GCE:*** ABB-BBB. ***SQAH:*** AAAB. ***SQAAH:*** ABB. ***IB:*** 32. ***BTEC NC:*** DD. ***BTEC ND:*** DDM. ***OCR ND:*** M1 ***OCR NED:*** D2

E28 UNIVERSITY OF EAST LONDON
DOCKLANDS CAMPUS
UNIVERSITY WAY
LONDON E16 2RD
t: 020 8223 3333 f: 020 8223 2978
e: study@uel.ac.uk
// www.uel.ac.uk

L190 BSc Business Economics
Duration: 3FT Hon
Entry Requirements: ***GCE:*** 200. ***IB:*** 24. ***BTEC NC:*** DM. ***BTEC ND:*** MMP.

E56 THE UNIVERSITY OF EDINBURGH

STUDENT RECRUITMENT & ADMISSIONS
57 GEORGE SQUARE
EDINBURGH EH8 9JU
t: 0131 650 4360 f: 0131 651 1236
e: sra.enquiries@ed.ac.uk
// www.ed.ac.uk/studying/undergraduate/

L100 MA Economics

Duration: 4FT Hon
Entry Requirements: ***GCE:*** AAA-BBB. ***SQAH:*** AABB-BBBB. ***IB:*** 34.

E70 THE UNIVERSITY OF ESSEX

WIVENHOE PARK
COLCHESTER
ESSEX CO4 3SQ
t: 01206 873666 f: 01206 873423
e: admit@essex.ac.uk
// www.essex.ac.uk

L100 BA Economics

Duration: 3FT Hon
Entry Requirements: ***GCE:*** 320. ***SQAH:*** AAAB. ***IB:*** 34. ***BTEC NC:*** DD. ***BTEC ND:*** DDM.

L106 BA Economics (International Exchange)

Duration: 4FT Hon
Entry Requirements: ***GCE:*** 320. ***SQAH:*** AAAB. ***IB:*** 34. ***BTEC NC:*** DD. ***BTEC ND:*** DDM.

L102 BA Economics (four-year)

Duration: 4FT Hon
Entry Requirements: ***GCE:*** 180. ***SQAH:*** CCCD. ***IB:*** 24. ***BTEC NC:*** DM. ***BTEC ND:*** MMP.

L111 BA Financial Economics

Duration: 3FT Hon
Entry Requirements: ***GCE:*** 320. ***SQAH:*** AAAB. ***IB:*** 34. ***BTEC NC:*** DD. ***BTEC ND:*** DDM.

L195 BA Financial Economics (International Exchange)

Duration: 4FT Hon
Entry Requirements: ***GCE:*** 320. ***SQAH:*** AAAB. ***IB:*** 34. ***BTEC NC:*** DD. ***BTEC ND:*** DDM.

L118 BA Financial Economics (four-year)

Duration: 4FT Hon
Entry Requirements: ***GCE:*** 180. ***SQAH:*** CCCD. ***IB:*** 24. ***BTEC NC:*** DM. ***BTEC ND:*** MMP.

L115 BA International Economics

Duration: 3FT Hon
Entry Requirements: ***GCE:*** 320. ***SQAH:*** AAAB. ***IB:*** 34. ***BTEC NC:*** DD. ***BTEC ND:*** DDM.

L163 BA International Economics (International Exchange)

Duration: 4FT Hon
Entry Requirements: ***GCE:*** 320. ***SQAH:*** AAAB. ***IB:*** 34. ***BTEC NC:*** DD. ***BTEC ND:*** DDM.

L160 BA International Economics (four-year)

Duration: 4FT Hon
Entry Requirements: ***GCE:*** 180. ***SQAH:*** CCCD. ***IB:*** 24. ***BTEC NC:*** DM. ***BTEC ND:*** MMP.

L108 BA Management Economics

Duration: 3FT Hon
Entry Requirements: ***GCE:*** 320. ***SQAH:*** AAAB. ***IB:*** 34. ***BTEC NC:*** DD. ***BTEC ND:*** DDM.

L192 BA Management Economics (International Exchange)

Duration: 4FT Hon
Entry Requirements: ***GCE:*** 320. ***SQAH:*** AAAB. ***IB:*** 34. ***BTEC NC:*** DD. ***BTEC ND:*** DDM.

L190 BA Management Economics (four-year)

Duration: 4FT Hon
Entry Requirements: ***GCE:*** 180. ***SQAH:*** CCCD. ***IB:*** 24. ***BTEC NC:*** DM. ***BTEC ND:*** MMP.

L101 BSc Economics

Duration: 3FT Hon
Entry Requirements: ***GCE:*** 320. ***SQAH:*** AAAB. ***IB:*** 34. ***BTEC NC:*** DD. ***BTEC ND:*** DDM.

L107 BSc Economics (International Exchange)

Duration: 4FT Hon
Entry Requirements: ***GCE:*** 320. ***SQAH:*** AAAB. ***IB:*** 34. ***BTEC NC:*** DD. ***BTEC ND:*** DDM.

L103 BSc Economics (four-year)

Duration: 4FT Hon
Entry Requirements: ***GCE:*** 180. ***SQAH:*** CCCD. ***IB:*** 24. ***BTEC NC:*** DM. ***BTEC ND:*** MMP.

L114 BSc Financial Economics

Duration: 3FT Hon
Entry Requirements: ***GCE:*** 320. ***SQAH:*** AAAB. ***IB:*** 34. ***BTEC NC:*** DD. ***BTEC ND:*** DDM.

L194 BSc Financial Economics (International Exchange)

Duration: 4FT Hon
Entry Requirements: ***GCE:*** 320. ***SQAH:*** AAAB. ***IB:*** 34. ***BTEC NC:*** DD. ***BTEC ND:*** DDM.

L117 BSc Financial Economics (four-year)

Duration: 4FT Hon
Entry Requirements: ***GCE:*** 180. ***SQAH:*** CCCD. ***IB:*** 24. ***BTEC NC:*** DM. ***BTEC ND:*** MMP.

L116 BSc International Economics
Duration: 3FT Hon
Entry Requirements: ***GCE:*** 320. ***SQAH:*** AAAB. ***IB:*** 34. ***BTEC NC:*** DD. ***BTEC ND:*** DDM.

L162 BSc International Economics (International Exchange)
Duration: 4FT Hon
Entry Requirements: ***GCE:*** 320. ***SQAH:*** AAAB. ***IB:*** 34. ***BTEC NC:*** DD. ***BTEC ND:*** DDM.

L161 BSc International Economics (four-year)
Duration: 4FT Hon
Entry Requirements: ***GCE:*** 180. ***SQAH:*** CCCD. ***IB:*** 24. ***BTEC NC:*** DM. ***BTEC ND:*** MMP.

L109 BSc Management Economics
Duration: 3FT Hon
Entry Requirements: ***GCE:*** 320. ***SQAH:*** AAAB. ***IB:*** 34. ***BTEC NC:*** DD. ***BTEC ND:*** DDM.

L193 BSc Management Economics (International Exchange)
Duration: 4FT Hon
Entry Requirements: ***GCE:*** 320. ***SQAH:*** AAAB. ***IB:*** 34. ***BTEC NC:*** DD. ***BTEC ND:*** DDM.

L191 BSc Management Economics (four-year)
Duration: 4FT Hon
Entry Requirements: ***GCE:*** 180. ***SQAH:*** CCCD. ***IB:*** 24. ***BTEC NC:*** DM. ***BTEC ND:*** MMP.

E84 UNIVERSITY OF EXETER
LAVER BUILDING
NORTH PARK ROAD
EXETER
DEVON EX4 4QE
t: 01392 263855 f: 01392 263857/262479
e: admissions@exeter.ac.uk
// www.exeter.ac.uk/admissions

L112 BA Business Economics
Duration: 3FT Hon
Entry Requirements: ***GCE:*** AAA-AAB. ***SQAH:*** AAAAB-AAABB. ***SQAAH:*** AAB-ABB. ***BTEC ND:*** DDD.

L115 BA Business Economics with European Study (4 years)
Duration: 4FT Hon
Entry Requirements: ***GCE:*** AAA-AAB. ***SQAH:*** AAAAB-AAABB. ***SQAAH:*** AAB-ABB. ***BTEC ND:*** DDD.

L192 BA Business Economics with Industrial Experience (4 years)
Duration: 4FT Hon
Entry Requirements: ***GCE:*** AAA-AAB. ***SQAH:*** AAAAB-AAABB. ***SQAAH:*** AAB-ABB. ***BTEC ND:*** DDD.

L194 BA Business Economics with International Study (4 years)
Duration: 4FT Hon
Entry Requirements: ***GCE:*** AAA-AAB. ***SQAH:*** AAAAB-AAABB. ***SQAAH:*** AAB-ABB. ***BTEC ND:*** DDD.

L100 BA Economics
Duration: 3FT Hon
Entry Requirements: ***GCE:*** AAA-AAB. ***SQAH:*** AAAAB-AAABB. ***SQAAH:*** AAB-ABB. ***BTEC ND:*** DDD.

L195 BA Economics with Econometrics with International Study (4 years)
Duration: 4FT Hon
Entry Requirements: ***GCE:*** AAA-AAB. ***SQAH:*** AAAAB-AAABB. ***SQAAH:*** AAB-ABB. ***BTEC ND:*** DDD.

L101 BA Economics with European Study (4 years)
Duration: 4FT Hon
Entry Requirements: ***GCE:*** AAA-AAB. ***SQAH:*** AAAAB-AAABB. ***SQAAH:*** AAB-ABB. ***BTEC ND:*** DDD.

L102 BA Economics with Industrial Experience (4 years)
Duration: 4FT Hon
Entry Requirements: ***GCE:*** AAA-AAB. ***SQAH:*** AAAAB-AAABB. ***SQAAH:*** AAB-ABB. ***BTEC ND:*** DDD.

L103 BA Economics with International Study (4 years)
Duration: 4FT Hon
Entry Requirements: ***GCE:*** AAA-AAB. ***SQAH:*** AAAAB-AAABB. ***SQAAH:*** AAB-ABB. ***BTEC ND:*** DDD.

G28 UNIVERSITY OF GLASGOW
THE UNIVERSITY OF GLASGOW
THE FRASER BUILDING
65 HILLHEAD STREET
GLASGOW G12 8QF
t: 0141 330 6062 f: 0141 330 2961
e: ugenquiries@gla.ac.uk (UK/EU undergrad enquiries only)
// www.glasgow.ac.uk

L112 MA Business Economics
Duration: 4FT Hon
Entry Requirements: ***GCE:*** AAB. ***SQAH:*** AAAB-AABB. ***IB:*** 34.

L110 MA Business Economics/Economics
Duration: 4FT Hon
Entry Requirements: ***GCE:*** AAB. ***SQAH:*** AAAB-AABB. ***IB:*** 34.

L150 MA Economics
Duration: 4FT Hon
Entry Requirements: ***GCE:*** AAB. ***SQAH:*** AAAB-AABB. ***IB:*** 34.

L148 MA Economics/Statistics
Duration: 4FT Hon
Entry Requirements: ***GCE:*** AAB. ***SQAH:*** AAAB-AABB. ***IB:*** 34.

G70 UNIVERSITY OF GREENWICH
GREENWICH CAMPUS
OLD ROYAL NAVAL COLLEGE
PARK ROW
LONDON SE10 9LS
t: 0800 005 006 f: 020 8331 8145
e: courseinfo@gre.ac.uk
// www.gre.ac.uk

L112 BA Business Economics
Duration: 3FT Hon
Entry Requirements: ***GCE:*** 180. ***IB:*** 24.

L100 BSc Economics
Duration: 3FT Hon
Entry Requirements: ***GCE:*** 180. ***IB:*** 24.

H24 HERIOT-WATT UNIVERSITY, EDINBURGH
EDINBURGH CAMPUS
EDINBURGH EH14 4AS
t: 0131 449 5111 f: 0131 451 3630
e: ugadmissions@hw.ac.uk
// www.hw.ac.uk

L100 MA Economics
Duration: 4FT Hon
Entry Requirements: ***GCE:*** ABC-BBB. ***SQAH:*** AAAB-BBBBC. ***SQAAH:*** BB. ***IB:*** 29.

H36 UNIVERSITY OF HERTFORDSHIRE
UNIVERSITY ADMISSIONS SERVICE
COLLEGE LANE
HATFIELD
HERTS AL10 9AB
t: 01707 284800 f: 01707 284870
// www.herts.ac.uk

L112 BA Business Economics
Duration: 3FT/4SW Hon
Entry Requirements: ***GCE:*** 260.

L101 BA Economics
Duration: 3FT/4SW Hon
Entry Requirements: ***GCE:*** 240.

H72 THE UNIVERSITY OF HULL
THE UNIVERSITY OF HULL
COTTINGHAM ROAD
HULL HU6 7RX
t: 01482 466100 f: 01482 442290
e: admissions@hull.ac.uk
// www.hull.ac.uk

L112 BA Business Economics
Duration: 3FT Hon
Entry Requirements: ***GCE:*** 280. ***IB:*** 28.

L160 BA Business Economics (International) (4 years)
Duration: 4FT Hon
Entry Requirements: ***GCE:*** 280. ***IB:*** 28.

L101 BA Business Economics (with Professional Experience) (4 years)
Duration: 4FT Hon
Entry Requirements: ***GCE:*** 280. ***IB:*** 28.

L100 BScEcon Economics
Duration: 3FT Hon
Entry Requirements: ***GCE:*** 280. ***IB:*** 28.

L161 BScEcon Economics (International) (4 years)
Duration: 4FT Hon
Entry Requirements: ***GCE:*** 280. ***IB:*** 28.

L102 BScEcon Economics (with Professional Experience) (4 years)
Duration: 4FT Hon
Entry Requirements: ***GCE:*** 280. ***IB:*** 28.

K24 THE UNIVERSITY OF KENT
INFORMATION, RECRUITMENT & ADMISSIONS
REGISTRY
UNIVERSITY OF KENT
CANTERBURY, KENT CT2 7NZ
t: 01227 827272 f: 01227 827077
e: information@kent.ac.uk
// www.kent.ac.uk

L100 BSc Economics
Duration: 3FT Hon
Entry Requirements: ***GCE:*** 320. ***IB:*** 34. ***BTEC NC:*** DD. ***BTEC ND:*** DDM. ***OCR ND:*** D ***OCR NED:*** D2

L141 BSc Economics with Econometrics
Duration: 3FT Hon
Entry Requirements: ***GCE:*** 320. ***IB:*** 34. ***BTEC NC:*** DD. ***BTEC ND:*** MMM. ***OCR ND:*** M1 ***OCR NED:*** M3

L102 BSc Economics with a Year in Industry
Duration: 4SW Hon
Entry Requirements: ***GCE:*** 320. ***IB:*** 34. ***BTEC NC:*** DD. ***BTEC ND:*** DDM. ***OCR ND:*** D ***OCR NED:*** D2

L171 BSc European Economics (4 years)
Duration: 4FT Hon
Entry Requirements: ***GCE:*** 320. ***IB:*** 34. ***BTEC NC:*** DD. ***BTEC ND:*** DDM. ***OCR ND:*** D ***OCR NED:*** D2

L176 BSc European Economics (French) (4 years)
Duration: 4FT Hon
Entry Requirements: ***GCE:*** 320. ***IB:*** 34. ***BTEC NC:*** DD. ***BTEC ND:*** DDM. ***OCR ND:*** D ***OCR NED:*** D2

L174 BSc European Economics (German) (4 years)
Duration: 4FT Hon
Entry Requirements: ***GCE:*** 320. ***IB:*** 34. ***BTEC NC:*** DD. ***BTEC ND:*** DMM. ***OCR ND:*** M1 ***OCR NED:*** M3

L177 BSc European Economics (Spanish) (4 years)
Duration: 4FT Hon
Entry Requirements: ***GCE:*** 320. ***IB:*** 34. ***BTEC NC:*** DD. ***BTEC ND:*** DDM. ***OCR ND:*** D ***OCR NED:*** D2

L111 BSc Financial Economics
Duration: 3FT Hon
Entry Requirements: ***GCE:*** 320. ***IB:*** 34. ***BTEC NC:*** DD. ***BTEC ND:*** DDM. ***OCR ND:*** D ***OCR NED:*** D2

L142 BSc Financial Economics (with Econometrics)
Duration: 3FT Hon
Entry Requirements: ***GCE:*** 320. ***IB:*** 34. ***BTEC NC:*** DD. ***BTEC ND:*** MMM. ***OCR ND:*** M1 ***OCR NED:*** M3

K84 KINGSTON UNIVERSITY
STUDENT INFORMATION & ADVICE CENTRE
COOPER HOUSE
40-46 SURBITON ROAD
KINGSTON UPON THAMES KT1 2HX
t: 0844 8552177 f: 020 8547 7080
e: aps@kingston.ac.uk
// www.kingston.ac.uk

L110 BA Applied Economics
Duration: 3FT Hon
Entry Requirements: ***GCE:*** 260.

L100 BSc Economics
Duration: 3FT Hon
Entry Requirements: ***GCE:*** 260. ***IB:*** 24.

L111 BSc Financial Economics
Duration: 3FT Hon
Entry Requirements: ***GCE:*** 280. ***IB:*** 30.

L14 LANCASTER UNIVERSITY
THE UNIVERSITY
LANCASTER
LANCASHIRE LA1 4YW
t: 01524 592029 f: 01524 846243
e: ugadmissions@lancaster.ac.uk
// www.lancs.ac.uk

L102 BA Business Economics
Duration: 3FT Hon
Entry Requirements: ***GCE:*** AAB. ***SQAH:*** ABBBB. ***SQAAH:*** AAB. ***IB:*** 34. ***BTEC ND:*** DDM.

L103 BA Business Economics (Study Abroad)
Duration: 3FT Hon
Entry Requirements: ***GCE:*** AAA. ***SQAH:*** AAABB. ***SQAAH:*** AAA. ***IB:*** 36. ***BTEC ND:*** DDD.

L100 BSc Economics
Duration: 3FT Hon
Entry Requirements: ***GCE:*** AAB. ***SQAH:*** ABBBB. ***SQAAH:*** AAB. ***IB:*** 34.

L101 BSc Economics (Study Abroad)
Duration: 3FT Hon
Entry Requirements: ***GCE:*** AAA. ***SQAH:*** AAABB. ***SQAAH:*** AAA. ***IB:*** 36. ***BTEC ND:*** DDD.

L23 UNIVERSITY OF LEEDS
THE UNIVERSITY OF LEEDS
LEEDS LS2 9JT
t: 0113 343 3999
e: admissions@adm.leeds.ac.uk
// www.leeds.ac.uk

L112 BSc Business Economics
Duration: 3FT Hon
Entry Requirements: ***GCE:*** AAB. ***SQAH:*** AAAAB. ***SQAAH:*** AAB. ***IB:*** 34.

L100 BSc Economics
Duration: 3FT Hon
Entry Requirements: ***GCE:*** AAB. ***SQAH:*** AAAAB. ***SQAAH:*** AAB. ***IB:*** 34.

L27 LEEDS METROPOLITAN UNIVERSITY
COURSE ENQUIRIES OFFICE
CIVIC QUARTER
LEEDS LS1 3HE
t: 0113 81 23113 f: 0113 81 23129
e: https://experience.leedsmet.ac.uk/leeds/index.do
// www.leedsmet.ac.uk

L110 BA Economics for Business
Duration: 3FT/4SW Hon
Entry Requirements: ***GCE:*** 220. ***IB:*** 28.

L34 UNIVERSITY OF LEICESTER

UNIVERSITY ROAD
LEICESTER LE1 7RH
t: 0116 252 5281 f: 0116 252 2447
e: admissions@le.ac.uk
// www.le.ac.uk

L112 BA Business Economics

Duration: 3FT Hon

Entry Requirements: ***GCE:*** ABB. ***SQAH:*** AABBB. ***SQAAH:*** ABB. ***IB:*** 32. ***BTEC ND:*** DDM.

L100 BA Economics

Duration: 3FT Hon

Entry Requirements: ***GCE:*** ABB. ***SQAH:*** AABBB. ***SQAAH:*** ABB. ***IB:*** 32. ***BTEC ND:*** DDM.

L111 BA Financial Economics

Duration: 3FT Hon

Entry Requirements: ***GCE:*** ABB. ***SQAH:*** AABBB. ***SQAAH:*** ABB. ***IB:*** 32. ***BTEC ND:*** DDM.

L115 BSc Financial Economics

Duration: 3FT Hon

Entry Requirements: ***GCE:*** ABB. ***SQAH:*** AABBB. ***SQAAH:*** ABB. ***IB:*** 32. ***BTEC ND:*** DDM.

L113 BScEcon Business Economics

Duration: 3FT Hon

Entry Requirements: ***GCE:*** ABB. ***SQAH:*** AABBB. ***SQAAH:*** ABB. ***IB:*** 32. ***BTEC ND:*** DDM.

L102 BScEcon Economics

Duration: 3FT Hon

Entry Requirements: ***GCE:*** ABB. ***SQAH:*** AABBB. ***SQAAH:*** ABB. ***IB:*** 32. ***BTEC ND:*** DDM.

L41 THE UNIVERSITY OF LIVERPOOL

THE FOUNDATION BUILDING
BROWNLOW HILL
LIVERPOOL L69 7ZX
t: 0151 794 2000 f: 0151 708 6502
e: ugrecruitment@liv.ac.uk
// www.liv.ac.uk

L100 BSc Economics

Duration: 3FT Hon

Entry Requirements: ***GCE:*** BBB. ***SQAH:*** AABBB. ***SQAAH:*** ABB. ***IB:*** 33. ***BTEC ND:*** DDM. ***OCR ND:*** D ***OCR NED:*** M1

L68 LONDON METROPOLITAN UNIVERSITY

166-220 HOLLOWAY ROAD
LONDON N7 8DB
t: 020 7133 4200
e: admissions@londonmet.ac.uk
// www.londonmet.ac.uk

L103 BA Business Economics

Duration: 3FT Hon

Entry Requirements: ***GCE:*** 240. ***IB:*** 28.

L102 BA Business Economics & Finance

Duration: 3FT Hon

Entry Requirements: ***GCE:*** 240. ***IB:*** 28.

L101 BA Economic Studies

Duration: 3FT Hon

Entry Requirements: ***GCE:*** 240. ***IB:*** 28.

L100 BA Economics

Duration: 3FT Hon

Entry Requirements: ***GCE:*** 240. ***IB:*** 28.

L160 BA International Economics

Duration: 3FT Hon

Entry Requirements: ***GCE:*** 240. ***IB:*** 28.

L111 BSc Financial Economics

Duration: 3FT Hon

Entry Requirements: ***GCE:*** 240. ***IB:*** 28.

L72 LONDON SCHOOL OF ECONOMICS AND POLITICAL SCIENCE (UNIVERSITY OF LONDON)

HOUGHTON STREET
LONDON WC2A 2AE
t: 020 7955 7125/7769 f: 020 7955 6001
e: ug-admissions@lse.ac.uk
// www.lse.ac.uk

L140 BSc Econometrics & Mathematical Economics

Duration: 3FT Hon

Entry Requirements: ***GCE:*** A*AA. ***SQAH:*** AAAAA. ***SQAAH:*** AAA. ***IB:*** 38.

L101 BSc Economics

Duration: 3FT Hon

Entry Requirements: ***GCE:*** A*AA. ***SQAH:*** AAAAA. ***SQAAH:*** AAA. ***IB:*** 38.

L79 LOUGHBOROUGH UNIVERSITY
LOUGHBOROUGH
LEICESTERSHIRE LE11 3TU
t: 01509 223522 f: 01509 223905
e: admissions@lboro.ac.uk
// www.lboro.ac.uk

L100 BSc Economics
Duration: 3FT Hon
Entry Requirements: ***GCE:*** AAB. ***SQAH:*** AABBB. ***SQAAH:*** AB. ***IB:*** 34. ***BTEC ND:*** DDM.

L115 BSc International Economics
Duration: 3FT Hon
Entry Requirements: ***GCE:*** AAB. ***SQAH:*** AABBB. ***SQAAH:*** AB. ***IB:*** 34. ***BTEC ND:*** DDM.

M20 THE UNIVERSITY OF MANCHESTER
OXFORD ROAD
MANCHESTER M13 9PL
t: 0161 275 2077 f: 0161 275 2106
e: ug-admissions@manchester.ac.uk
// www.manchester.ac.uk

L100 BAEcon Economics
Duration: 3FT Hon
Entry Requirements: ***GCE:*** ABB. ***SQAH:*** AABBB. ***SQAAH:*** ABB. ***IB:*** 34. ***BTEC ND:*** DDM. Interview required.

L102 BEconSc Economics
Duration: 3FT Hon
Entry Requirements: ***GCE:*** AAB. ***SQAH:*** AABBB. ***SQAAH:*** AAB. ***IB:*** 35. Interview required.

M40 THE MANCHESTER METROPOLITAN UNIVERSITY
ADMISSIONS OFFICE
ALL SAINTS (GMS)
ALL SAINTS
MANCHESTER M15 6BH
t: 0161 247 2000
// www.mmu.ac.uk

L112 BA Business Economics
Duration: 3FT Hon
Entry Requirements: ***GCE:*** 240. ***SQAH:*** BBBB. ***SQAAH:*** CCC. ***IB:*** 27.

L114 BA Business Economics (Foundation)
Duration: 4FT Hon
Entry Requirements: ***GCE:*** 60.

L100 BA Economics
Duration: 3FT Hon
Entry Requirements: ***GCE:*** 240. ***SQAH:*** BBBB. ***SQAAH:*** CCC. ***IB:*** 27.

L101 BSc Economics
Duration: 3FT Hon
Entry Requirements: ***GCE:*** 240. ***SQAH:*** BBBB. ***SQAAH:*** CCC. ***IB:*** 27.

L170 BSc Trading Standards
Duration: 3FT Hon
Entry Requirements: ***GCE:*** 240. ***IB:*** 27. Interview required.

L175 BSc Trading Standards (Foundation)
Duration: 4FT/5SW Hon
Entry Requirements: ***GCE:*** 60.

L176 BSc Trading Standards (Sandwich)
Duration: 4SW Hon
Entry Requirements: ***GCE:*** 240. ***IB:*** 27. Interview required.

M80 MIDDLESEX UNIVERSITY
MIDDLESEX UNIVERSITY
THE BURROUGHS
LONDON NW4 4BT
t: 020 8411 5555 f: 020 8411 5649
e: enquiries@mdx.ac.uk
// www.mdx.ac.uk

L160 BA International Development
Duration: 3FT Hon
Entry Requirements: Contact the institution for details.

L110 BSc Business Economics
Duration: 3FT/4SW Hon
Entry Requirements: ***GCE:*** 200-300. ***IB:*** 28.

N21 NEWCASTLE UNIVERSITY
KING'S GATE
NEWCASTLE UPON TYNE NE1 7RU
t: 0191 208 3333 f: 0191 222 6143
e: enquiries@ncl.ac.uk
// www.ncl.ac.uk

L100 BA Economics
Duration: 3FT Hon
Entry Requirements: ***GCE:*** AAB. ***SQAH:*** AAABB. ***IB:*** 34. ***BTEC ND:*** DDM.

L161 BA Financial and Business Economics
Duration: 3FT Hon
Entry Requirements: ***GCE:*** AAB. ***SQAH:*** AAABB. ***IB:*** 34. ***BTEC ND:*** DDM.

N84 THE UNIVERSITY OF NOTTINGHAM

THE ADMISSIONS OFFICE
THE UNIVERSITY OF NOTTINGHAM
UNIVERSITY PARK
NOTTINGHAM NG7 2RD
t: 0115 951 5151 f: 0115 951 4668
// www.nottingham.ac.uk

L1N2 BA Industrial Economics
Duration: 3FT Hon
Entry Requirements: ***GCE:*** AAB. ***SQAAH:*** AAB. ***IB:*** 34. ***BTEC ND:*** DDM.

L1N3 BA Industrial Economics with Insurance
Duration: 3FT Hon
Entry Requirements: ***GCE:*** AAB. ***SQAAH:*** AAB. ***IB:*** 34. ***BTEC ND:*** DDM.

L100 BA/BSc Economics
Duration: 3FT Hon
Entry Requirements: ***GCE:*** AAA-AABB. ***SQAAH:*** AAA. ***IB:*** 38.

L140 BSc Economics and Econometrics
Duration: 3FT Hon
Entry Requirements: ***GCE:*** AAA-AABB. ***SQAAH:*** AAA. ***IB:*** 38.

N91 NOTTINGHAM TRENT UNIVERSITY

DRYDEN CENTRE
BURTON STREET
NOTTINGHAM NG1 4BU
t: +44 (0) 115 848 4200 f: +44 (0) 115 848 8869
e: ask.ntu@ntu.ac.uk
// www.ntu.ac.uk/

L101 BA Business Economics
Duration: 3FT Hon
Entry Requirements: ***GCE:*** 280. ***IB:*** 25. ***BTEC ND:*** DMM.

L100 BA Economics
Duration: 3FT Hon
Entry Requirements: ***GCE:*** 280. ***IB:*** 25. ***BTEC ND:*** DMM.

P60 UNIVERSITY OF PLYMOUTH

DRAKE CIRCUS
PLYMOUTH PL4 8AA
t: 01752 588037 f: 01752 588050
e: admissions@plymouth.ac.uk
// www.plymouth.ac.uk

L112 BSc Business Economics
Duration: 3FT/4SW Hon
Entry Requirements: ***GCE:*** 240. ***IB:*** 26. ***BTEC NC:*** DD. ***BTEC ND:*** MMM.

L101 BSc Economics
Duration: 3FT/4SW Hon
Entry Requirements: ***GCE:*** 240. ***IB:*** 26. ***BTEC NC:*** DD. ***BTEC ND:*** MMM.

L111 BSc Financial Economics
Duration: 3FT/4SW Hon
Entry Requirements: ***GCE:*** 240. ***IB:*** 26.

L160 BSc International Business Economics
Duration: 3FT/4SW Hon
Entry Requirements: ***GCE:*** 240. ***IB:*** 26.

P80 UNIVERSITY OF PORTSMOUTH

ACADEMIC REGISTRY
UNIVERSITY HOUSE
WINSTON CHURCHILL AVENUE
PORTSMOUTH PO1 2UP
t: 023 9284 8484 f: 023 9284 3082
e: admissions@port.ac.uk
// www.port.ac.uk

L110 BA Applied Economics
Duration: 3FT/4SW Hon
Entry Requirements: ***GCE:*** 220-280. ***IB:*** 24. ***BTEC NC:*** DD. ***BTEC ND:*** DMM.

L112 BSc Business Economics
Duration: 3FT/4SW Hon
Entry Requirements: ***GCE:*** 260-300. ***IB:*** 24. ***BTEC ND:*** DMM.

L100 BSc Economics
Duration: 3FT/4SW Hon
Entry Requirements: ***GCE:*** 260-300. ***IB:*** 24. ***BTEC ND:*** DMM.

Q50 QUEEN MARY, UNIVERSITY OF LONDON

MILE END ROAD
LONDON E1 4NS
t: 020 7882 5555 f: 020 7882 5500
e: admissions@qmul.ac.uk
// www.qmul.ac.uk

L100 BScEcon Economics
Duration: 3FT Hon
Entry Requirements: ***GCE:*** AAB. ***SQAAH:*** AAB. ***IB:*** 36.

Q75 QUEEN'S UNIVERSITY BELFAST

UNIVERSITY ROAD
BELFAST BT7 1NN
t: 028 9097 3838 f: 028 9097 2828
e: admissions@qub.ac.uk
// www.qub.ac.uk

L110 BSc Business Economics
Duration: 3FT Hon
Entry Requirements: ***GCE:*** BBB-BBCb. ***SQAH:*** BBBBB. ***SQAAH:*** BBB. ***IB:*** 32.

L100 BSc Economics
Duration: 3FT Hon
Entry Requirements: ***GCE:*** BBB-BBCb. ***SQAH:*** BBBBB. ***SQAAH:*** BBB. ***IB:*** 32.

R12 THE UNIVERSITY OF READING

THE UNIVERSITY OF READING
PO BOX 217
READING RG6 6AH
t: 0118 378 8619 f: 0118 378 8924
e: student.recruitment@reading.ac.uk
// www.reading.ac.uk

L114 BA Business Economics

Duration: 3FT Hon

Entry Requirements: ***GCE:*** 320-340.

L101 BA Economics

Duration: 3FT Hon

Entry Requirements: ***GCE:*** 320-340.

L113 BSc Business Economics

Duration: 3FT Hon

Entry Requirements: ***GCE:*** 320-340.

L100 BSc Economics

Duration: 3FT Hon

Entry Requirements: ***GCE:*** 320-340.

L140 BSc Economics and Econometrics

Duration: 3FT Hon

Entry Requirements: ***GCE:*** 320-340.

R20 RICHMOND, THE AMERICAN INTERNATIONAL UNIVERSITY IN LONDON

QUEENS ROAD
RICHMOND
SURREY TW10 6JP
t: 020 8332 9000 f: 020 8332 1596
e: enroll@richmond.ac.uk
// www.richmond.ac.uk

L100 BA Economics

Duration: 3FT/4FT Hon

Entry Requirements: ***GCE:*** 260. ***IB:*** 33.

R72 ROYAL HOLLOWAY, UNIVERSITY OF LONDON

ROYAL HOLLOWAY, UNIVERSITY OF LONDON
EGHAM
SURREY TW20 0EX
t: 01784 434455 f: 01784 473662
e: Admissions@rhul.ac.uk
// www.rhul.ac.uk

L101 BSc Economics

Duration: 3FT Hon

Entry Requirements: ***GCE:*** AAA-ABB. ***SQAH:*** AAAAA-AABBB. ***SQAAH:*** AAA-ABB. ***IB:*** 32. ***BTEC NC:*** DM. ***BTEC ND:*** DDM.

L111 BSc Financial and Business Economics

Duration: 3FT Hon

Entry Requirements: ***GCE:*** AAA-ABB. ***SQAH:*** AAAAA-AABBB. ***SQAAH:*** AAA-ABB. ***IB:*** 32. ***BTEC NC:*** DM. ***BTEC ND:*** DDM.

S09 SCHOOL OF ORIENTAL AND AFRICAN STUDIES (UNIVERSITY OF LONDON)

THORNHAUGH STREET
RUSSELL SQUARE
LONDON WC1H 0XG
t: 020 7074 5106 f: 020 7898 4039
e: undergradadmissions@soas.ac.uk
// www.soas.ac.uk

L170 BSc Development Economics

Duration: 3FT Hon

Entry Requirements: Contact the institution for details.

L100 BSc Economics

Duration: 3FT Hon

Entry Requirements: Contact the institution for details.

S18 THE UNIVERSITY OF SHEFFIELD

9 NORTHUMBERLAND ROAD
SHEFFIELD S10 2TT
t: 0114 222 1299 f: 0114 222 8032
e: ask@sheffield.ac.uk
// www.sheffield.ac.uk

L100 BA Economics

Duration: 3FT Hon

Entry Requirements: ***GCE:*** ABB. ***SQAH:*** AAAB. ***SQAAH:*** ABB. ***IB:*** 33. ***BTEC ND:*** DDM.

L101 BSc Economics

Duration: 3FT Hon

Entry Requirements: ***GCE:*** AAB. ***SQAH:*** AAAA. ***SQAAH:*** AAB. ***IB:*** 34. ***BTEC NC:*** DD.

S21 SHEFFIELD HALLAM UNIVERSITY

CITY CAMPUS
HOWARD STREET
SHEFFIELD S1 1WB
t: 0114 225 5555 f: 0114 225 2167
e: admissions@shu.ac.uk
// www.shu.ac.uk

L100 BA Business Economics

Duration: 3FT/4SW Hon

Entry Requirements: ***GCE:*** 240.

S27 UNIVERSITY OF SOUTHAMPTON

HIGHFIELD
SOUTHAMPTON SO17 1BJ
t: 023 8059 4732 f: 023 8059 3037
e: admissions@soton.ac.uk
// www.southampton.ac.uk

L100 BSc Economics

Duration: 3FT Hon

Entry Requirements: ***GCE:*** AAB. ***IB:*** 34. ***BTEC NC:*** DD. ***BTEC ND:*** DDD.

L112 BSc Economics and Management Sciences
Duration: 3FT Hon
Entry Requirements: ***GCE:*** AAB. ***IB:*** 34. ***BTEC NC:*** DD. ***BTEC ND:*** DDD.

L101 MEcon Master of Economics
Duration: 4FT Hon
Entry Requirements: ***GCE:*** AAB. ***IB:*** 34. ***BTEC NC:*** DD. ***BTEC ND:*** DDD.

S36 UNIVERSITY OF ST ANDREWS
ST KATHARINE'S WEST
16 THE SCORES
ST ANDREWS
FIFE KY16 9AX
t: 01334 462150 f: 01334 463330
e: admissions@st-andrews.ac.uk
// www.st-and.ac.uk

L112 BSc Applied Economics
Duration: 4FT Hon
Entry Requirements: ***GCE:*** AAA. ***SQAH:*** AAAA. ***IB:*** 38.

L102 BSc Economics (Science)
Duration: 4FT Hon
Entry Requirements: ***GCE:*** AAA. ***SQAH:*** AAAA. ***IB:*** 38.

L161 BSc Financial Economics
Duration: 4FT Hon
Entry Requirements: ***GCE:*** AAA. ***SQAH:*** AAAA. ***IB:*** 38.

L110 MA Applied Economics
Duration: 4FT Hon
Entry Requirements: ***GCE:*** AAA. ***SQAH:*** AAAA. ***IB:*** 38.

L100 MA Economics
Duration: 4FT Hon
Entry Requirements: ***GCE:*** AAA. ***SQAH:*** AAAA. ***IB:*** 38.

L111 MA Financial Economics
Duration: 4FT Hon
Entry Requirements: ***GCE:*** AAA. ***SQAH:*** AAAA. ***IB:*** 38.

S72 STAFFORDSHIRE UNIVERSITY
COLLEGE ROAD
STOKE ON TRENT ST4 2DE
t: 01782 292753 f: 01782 292740
e: admissions@staffs.ac.uk
// www.staffs.ac.uk

L190 BA Business Economics
Duration: 3FT/4SW Hon
Entry Requirements: ***GCE:*** BCC-BB. ***IB:*** 24. ***BTEC NC:*** DM. ***BTEC ND:*** MMM.

S75 THE UNIVERSITY OF STIRLING
STIRLING FK9 4LA
t: 01786 467044 f: 01786 466800
e: admissions@stir.ac.uk
// www.stir.ac.uk

L100 BA Economics
Duration: 4FT Hon
Entry Requirements: ***GCE:*** BCC. ***SQAH:*** BBBB. ***SQAAH:*** AAA-CCC. ***IB:*** 30. ***BTEC ND:*** MMM.

S78 THE UNIVERSITY OF STRATHCLYDE
GLASGOW G1 1XQ
t: 0141 552 4400 f: 0141 552 0775
// www.strath.ac.uk

L100 BA Economics
Duration: 4FT Hon
Entry Requirements: ***GCE:*** ABB. ***SQAH:*** AABB-ABBBC. ***IB:*** 34.

S85 UNIVERSITY OF SURREY
STAG HILL
GUILDFORD
SURREY GU2 7XH
t: +44(0)1483 689305 f: +44(0)1483 689388
e: admissions@surrey.ac.uk
// www.surrey.ac.uk

L111 BSc Business Economics with Finance (3 or 4 years)
Duration: 3FT/4SW Hon
Entry Requirements: ***GCE:*** ABB. ***SQAH:*** BBBBB. ***SQAAH:*** BBB. ***IB:*** 30.

L100 BSc Economics (3 or 4 years)
Duration: 3FT/4SW Hon
Entry Requirements: ***GCE:*** ABB. ***SQAH:*** BBBBB. ***SQAAH:*** BBB. ***IB:*** 32.

S90 UNIVERSITY OF SUSSEX
UNDERGRADUATE ADMISSIONS
SUSSEX HOUSE
UNIVERSITY OF SUSSEX
BRIGHTON BN1 9RH
t: 01273 678416 f: 01273 678545
e: ug.applicants@sussex.ac.uk
// www.sussex.ac.uk

L100 BA Economics
Duration: 3FT Hon
Entry Requirements: ***GCE:*** ABB-BBB. ***SQAH:*** AABBB-ABBBB.

L102 BSc Economics
Duration: 3FT Hon
Entry Requirements: ***GCE:*** ABB-BBB. ***SQAH:*** AABBB-ABBBB.

S93 SWANSEA UNIVERSITY

SINGLETON PARK
SWANSEA SA2 8PP
t: 01792 295111 f: 01792 295110
e: admissions@swansea.ac.uk
// www.swansea.ac.uk

L115 BA Business Economics with a year abroad

Duration: 4FT Hon
Entry Requirements: ***GCE:*** AAB. ***IB:*** 34.

L104 BA Economics

Duration: 3FT Hon
Entry Requirements: ***GCE:*** ABB. ***IB:*** 33. ***BTEC ND:*** DDM.

L105 BA Economics with a Year Abroad

Duration: 4FT Hon
Entry Requirements: ***GCE:*** AAB. ***IB:*** 34.

L112 BSc Business Economics

Duration: 3FT Hon
Entry Requirements: ***GCE:*** ABB. ***IB:*** 33. ***BTEC ND:*** DDM.

L114 BSc Business Economics with a year abroad

Duration: 4FT Hon
Entry Requirements: ***GCE:*** AAB. ***IB:*** 34.

L100 BSc Economics

Duration: 3FT Hon
Entry Requirements: ***GCE:*** ABB. ***IB:*** 33. ***BTEC ND:*** DDM.

L101 BSc Economics With A Year Abroad

Duration: 4FT Hon
Entry Requirements: ***GCE:*** AAB. ***IB:*** 34.

L111 BSc Financial Economics

Duration: 3FT Hon
Entry Requirements: ***GCE:*** ABB. ***IB:*** 33. ***BTEC ND:*** DDM.

L160 BSc International Business Economics

Duration: 3FT Hon
Entry Requirements: ***GCE:*** ABB. ***IB:*** 33. ***BTEC ND:*** DDM.

L113 BScEcon Business Economics

Duration: 3FT Hon
Entry Requirements: ***GCE:*** ABB. ***IB:*** 33. ***BTEC ND:*** DDM.

U20 UNIVERSITY OF ULSTER

COLERAINE
CO. LONDONDERRY
NORTHERN IRELAND BT52 1SA
t: 028 7032 4221 f: 028 7032 4908
e: online@ulster.ac.uk
// www.ulster.ac.uk

L191 BSc Business Economics

Duration: 4SW Hon
Entry Requirements: ***GCE:*** 260. ***IB:*** 24. ***BTEC ND:*** DMM.

L100 BSc Economics

Duration: 4SW Hon
Entry Requirements: ***GCE:*** 240. ***IB:*** 24. ***BTEC NC:*** MM. ***BTEC ND:*** MMM.

U40 UNIVERSITY OF THE WEST OF SCOTLAND

PAISLEY CAMPUS
RENFREWSHIRE
SCOTLAND PA1 2BE
t: 0141 848 3727 f: 0141 848 3623
e: admissions@uws.ac.uk
// www.uws.ac.uk

L110 BA Business Economics

Duration: 3FT/4FT Ord/Hon
Entry Requirements: ***SQAH:*** BBCC.

U80 UNIVERSITY COLLEGE LONDON (UNIVERSITY OF LONDON)

GOWER STREET
LONDON WC1E 6BT
t: 020 7679 3000 f: 020 7679 3001
// www.ucl.ac.uk

L101 BSc (Econ) Economics (International Programme)

Duration: 4FT Hon
Entry Requirements: ***GCE:*** A*AAe. ***SQAAH:*** AAA. ***IB:*** 39.

L100 BScEcon Economics

Duration: 3FT Hon
Entry Requirements: ***GCE:*** A*AAe. ***SQAAH:*** AAA. ***IB:*** 39.

W20 THE UNIVERSITY OF WARWICK

COVENTRY CV4 8UW
t: 024 7652 3723 f: 024 7652 4649
e: ugadmissions@warwick.ac.uk
// www.warwick.ac.uk

L100 BSc Economics

Duration: 3FT Hon
Entry Requirements: ***GCE:*** A*AAb -AAAb. ***SQAAH:*** AA. ***IB:*** 38.

L112 BSc Economics and Industrial Organization
Duration: 3FT Hon
Entry Requirements: ***GCE:*** A*AAb -AAAb. ***SQAAH:*** AA. ***IB:*** 38.

W50 UNIVERSITY OF WESTMINSTER
101 NEW CAVENDISH STREET
LONDON W1W 6XH
t: 020 7915 5511 f: 020 7911 5788
e: course-enquiries@westminster.ac.uk
// www.westminster.ac.uk

L114 BSc Business Economics
Duration: 3FT/4SW Hon
Entry Requirements: ***GCE:*** BBB. ***SQAH:*** BBBBB. ***SQAAH:*** BBB. ***IB:*** 28.

Y50 THE UNIVERSITY OF YORK
ADMISSIONS AND UK/EU STUDENT RECRUITMENT
UNIVERSITY OF YORK
HESLINGTON
YORK YO10 5DD
t: 01904 433533 f: 01904 433538
e: admissions@york.ac.uk
// www.york.ac.uk

L144 BA/BSc Economics/Econometrics (Equal)
Duration: 3FT Hon
Entry Requirements: ***GCE:*** AAB. ***SQAH:*** AAAAB. ***SQAAH:*** AB. ***IB:*** 34. ***BTEC ND:*** DDD.

L100 BSc Economics
Duration: 3FT Hon
Entry Requirements: ***GCE:*** AAB. ***SQAH:*** AAAAB. ***SQAAH:*** AB. ***IB:*** 34. ***BTEC ND:*** DDD.

L112 BSc Economics and Finance
Duration: 3FT Hon
Entry Requirements: ***GCE:*** AAB. ***SQAH:*** AAAAB. ***SQAAH:*** AB. ***IB:*** 34. ***BTEC ND:*** DDD.

FINANCE

A20 THE UNIVERSITY OF ABERDEEN
UNIVERSITY OFFICE
KING'S COLLEGE
ABERDEEN AB24 3FX
t: +44 (0) 1224 273504 f: +44 (0) 1224 272034
e: sras@abdn.ac.uk
// www.abdn.ac.uk/sras

N300 MA Finance
Duration: 4FT Hon
Entry Requirements: ***GCE:*** BBB. ***SQAH:*** BBBB. ***IB:*** 30. ***BTEC ND:*** MMM.

A30 UNIVERSITY OF ABERTAY DUNDEE
BELL STREET
DUNDEE DD1 1HG
t: 01382 308080 f: 01382 308081
e: sro@abertay.ac.uk
// www.abertay.ac.uk

N100 BA Business Studies option - Finance
Duration: 4SW Hon
Entry Requirements: ***GCE:*** DDD. ***SQAH:*** BBC. ***IB:*** 24. ***BTEC NC:*** DM. ***BTEC ND:*** MMP.

A80 ASTON UNIVERSITY, BIRMINGHAM
ASTON TRIANGLE
BIRMINGHAM B4 7ET
t: 0121 204 4444 f: 0121 204 3696
e: admissions@aston.ac.uk
// www.aston.ac.uk

N300 BSc Finance
Duration: 4SW Hon
Entry Requirements: ***GCE:*** 320-340. ***SQAH:*** AAAAB-AAABB. ***SQAAH:*** AAB-ABB. ***IB:*** 34. ***BTEC ND:*** DDM. ***OCR NED:*** D2

B06 BANGOR UNIVERSITY
BANGOR
GWYNEDD LL57 2DG
t: 01248 382016/2017 f: 01248 370451
e: admissions@bangor.ac.uk
// www.bangor.ac.uk

N322 BA Banking and Finance
Duration: 3FT Hon
Entry Requirements: ***GCE:*** 260-300. ***IB:*** 28.

B22 UNIVERSITY OF BEDFORDSHIRE

PARK SQUARE
LUTON
BEDS LU1 3JU
t: 01582 489286 f: 01582 489323
e: admissions@beds.ac.uk
// www.beds.ac.uk

N300 BA Business Studies (Finance)
Duration: 3FT Hon
Entry Requirements: ***Foundation:*** Pass. ***GCE:*** 200. ***SQAH:*** BCC. ***SQAAH:*** BCC. ***IB:*** 24. ***BTEC NC:*** MM. ***BTEC ND:*** MPP. ***OCR ND:*** M1 ***OCR NED:*** P1

N390 BSc International Finance
Duration: 3FT Hon
Entry Requirements: ***Foundation:*** Pass. ***GCE:*** 200. ***SQAH:*** BCC. ***SQAAH:*** BCC. ***IB:*** 24. ***BTEC NC:*** MM. ***BTEC ND:*** MPP. ***OCR ND:*** M1 ***OCR NED:*** P1

B25 BIRMINGHAM CITY UNIVERSITY

CITY NORTH CAMPUS
PERRY BARR
BIRMINGHAM B42 2SU
t: 0121 331 5595 f: 0121 331 7994
e: choices@bcu.ac.uk
// www.bcu.ac.uk/courses/choices/contact-choices

N390 BA International Finance (1 year top-up)
Duration: 1FT Hon
Entry Requirements: Interview required.

B32 THE UNIVERSITY OF BIRMINGHAM

EDGBASTON
BIRMINGHAM B15 2TT
t: 0121 415 8900 f: 0121 414 7159
e: admissions@bham.ac.uk
// www.bham.ac.uk

N300 BSc Money, Banking and Finance
Duration: 3FT Hon
Entry Requirements: ***GCE:*** AAB. ***SQAH:*** AAABB. ***SQAAH:*** AAB-ABB.

B40 BLACKBURN COLLEGE

FEILDEN STREET
BLACKBURN BB2 1LH
t: 01254 292594 f: 01254 679647
e: he-admissions@blackburn.ac.uk
// www.blackburn.ac.uk

N300 BA Financial Services
Duration: 1FT Hon
Entry Requirements: Contact the institution for details.

N340 BA Financial Services Management
Duration: 1FT Hon
Entry Requirements: Contact the institution for details.

B50 BOURNEMOUTH UNIVERSITY

TALBOT CAMPUS
FERN BARROW
POOLE
DORSET BH12 5BB
t: 01202 524111
// www.bournemouth.ac.uk

N390 BA International Finance (Top Up)
Duration: 1FT Hon
Entry Requirements: Contact the institution for details.

B56 THE UNIVERSITY OF BRADFORD

RICHMOND ROAD
BRADFORD
WEST YORKSHIRE BD7 1DP
t: 0800 073 1225 f: 01274 235585
e: course-enquiries@bradford.ac.uk
// www.bradford.ac.uk

N390 BSc Financial Planning
Duration: 4SW Hon
Entry Requirements: Contact the institution for details.

B60 BRADFORD COLLEGE: AN ASSOCIATE COLLEGE OF LEEDS METROPOLITAN UNIVERSITY

GREAT HORTON ROAD
BRADFORD
WEST YORKSHIRE BD7 1AY
t: 01274 433333 f: 01274 433241
e: admissions@bradfordcollege.ac.uk
// www.bradfordcollege.ac.uk

N300 BA Financial Services
Duration: 3FT Hon
Entry Requirements: ***GCE:*** 100-140. ***BTEC NC:*** MM. ***BTEC ND:*** MPP.

C10 CANTERBURY CHRIST CHURCH UNIVERSITY

NORTH HOLMES ROAD
CANTERBURY
KENT CT1 1QU
t: 01227 782900 f: 01227 782888
e: admissions@canterbury.ac.uk
// www.canterbury.ac.uk

N300 BSc Business Finance
Duration: 3FT Hon
Entry Requirements: ***GCE:*** 240. ***IB:*** 24.

C15 CARDIFF UNIVERSITY

PO BOX 927
30-36 NEWPORT ROAD
CARDIFF CF24 0DE
t: 029 2087 9999 f: 029 2087 6138
e: admissions@cardiff.ac.uk
// www.cardiff.ac.uk

N300 BScEcon Banking and Finance

Duration: 3FT Hon

Entry Requirements: ***GCE:*** AAB. ***SQAH:*** AAABB. ***SQAAH:*** AAB. ***IB:*** 35. ***BTEC ND:*** DDD. ***OCR NED:*** D2

C60 CITY UNIVERSITY

NORTHAMPTON SQUARE
LONDON EC1V 0HB
t: 020 7040 5060 f: 020 7040 8995
e: ugadmissions@city.ac.uk
// www.city.ac.uk

N302 BSc Banking and International Finance (3 years or 4 year SW)

Duration: 3FT Hon

Entry Requirements: ***GCE:*** AAB. ***SQAH:*** AAA-BB. ***IB:*** 35. ***BTEC ND:*** DDM.

N390 BSc Investment and Financial Risk Management (3 years or 4 year SW)

Duration: 3FT/4SW Hon

Entry Requirements: ***GCE:*** AAB. ***SQAH:*** AAA-BB. ***IB:*** 35. ***BTEC ND:*** DDM.

N391 BSc Real Estate Finance and Investment (3 years or 4 year SW)

Duration: 3FT/4SW Hon

Entry Requirements: ***GCE:*** AAB. ***SQAH:*** AAA-BB. ***IB:*** 35. ***BTEC ND:*** DDM.

C85 COVENTRY UNIVERSITY

THE STUDENT CENTRE
COVENTRY UNIVERSITY
1 GULSON ROAD
COVENTRY CV1 2JH
t: 024 7615 2222 f: 024 7615 2223
e: studentenquiries@coventry.ac.uk
// www.coventry.ac.uk

N341 BA Finance and Investment

Duration: 3FT/4SW Hon

Entry Requirements: ***GCE:*** 260-320. ***IB:*** 30.

D26 DE MONTFORT UNIVERSITY

THE GATEWAY
LEICESTER LE1 9BH
t: 0116 255 1551 f: 0116 250 6204
e: enquiries@dmu.ac.uk
// www.dmu.ac.uk

N340 BA Financial Management

Duration: 3FT Hon

Entry Requirements: ***GCE:*** 280. ***IB:*** 24. Interview required.

D39 UNIVERSITY OF DERBY

KEDLESTON ROAD
DERBY DE22 1GB
t: 08701 202330 f: 01332 597724
e: askadmissions@derby.ac.uk
// www.derby.ac.uk

N300 BA Financial Markets (Top-up)

Duration: 1FT Hon

Entry Requirements: HND required.

D65 UNIVERSITY OF DUNDEE

DUNDEE DD1 4HN
t: 01382 383838 f: 01382 388150
e: ContactUs@dundee.ac.uk
// www.dundee.ac.uk/admissions/undergraduate/

N300 BFin Finance

Duration: 4FT Hon

Entry Requirements: ***GCE:*** BCC. ***SQAH:*** BBBB. ***IB:*** 30. ***BTEC ND:*** DMM.

N390 BIFin International Finance

Duration: 4FT Hon

Entry Requirements: ***GCE:*** BCC. ***SQAH:*** BBBB. ***IB:*** 30. ***BTEC ND:*** DMM.

D86 DURHAM UNIVERSITY

DURHAM UNIVERSITY
UNIVERSITY OFFICE
DURHAM DH1 3HP
t: 0191 334 2000 f: 0191 334 6055
e: admissions@durham.ac.uk
// www.durham.ac.uk

N390 BA Business Finance with Foundation

Duration: 4FT Hon

Entry Requirements: Interview required.

E14 UNIVERSITY OF EAST ANGLIA

NORWICH NR4 7TJ
t: 01603 591515 f: 01603 458596
e: admissions@uea.ac.uk
// www.uea.ac.uk

N323 BSc Actuarial Science with a Year in Industry

Duration: 4FT Hon
Entry Requirements: ***GCE:*** AAB-AAC. ***SQAH:*** AABB. ***SQAAH:*** AAB. ***IB:*** 33.

E28 UNIVERSITY OF EAST LONDON

DOCKLANDS CAMPUS
UNIVERSITY WAY
LONDON E16 2RD
t: 020 8223 3333 f: 020 8223 2978
e: study@uel.ac.uk
// www.uel.ac.uk

N390 BA Business Finance

Duration: 3FT Hon
Entry Requirements: ***GCE:*** 200. ***IB:*** 24. ***BTEC NC:*** DM. ***BTEC ND:*** MMP.

N300 BSc Finance, Money and Banking

Duration: 3FT Hon
Entry Requirements: ***GCE:*** 200. ***IB:*** 24. ***BTEC NC:*** DM. ***BTEC ND:*** MMP. ***OCR ND:*** M1 ***OCR NED:*** P1

E59 EDINBURGH NAPIER UNIVERSITY

CRAIGLOCKHART CAMPUS
EDINBURGH EH14 1DJ
t: +44 (0)8452 60 60 40 f: 0131 455 6464
e: info@napier.ac.uk
// www.napier.ac.uk

N340 BA Financial Services Management

Duration: 3FT/4FT Ord/Hon
Entry Requirements: ***GCE:*** 230.

E70 THE UNIVERSITY OF ESSEX

WIVENHOE PARK
COLCHESTER
ESSEX CO4 3SQ
t: 01206 873666 f: 01206 873423
e: admit@essex.ac.uk
// www.essex.ac.uk

N300 BSc Finance

Duration: 3FT Hon
Entry Requirements: ***GCE:*** 320. ***SQAH:*** AAAB. ***IB:*** 34. ***BTEC NC:*** DD. ***BTEC ND:*** DDM. ***OCR ND:*** D

N301 BSc Finance (four-year)

Duration: 4FT Hon
Entry Requirements: ***GCE:*** 180. ***SQAH:*** CCCD. ***IB:*** 24. ***BTEC NC:*** DM. ***BTEC ND:*** MMP.

N340 BSc Financial Management

Duration: 3FT Hon
Entry Requirements: ***GCE:*** 320. ***SQAH:*** AAAB. ***IB:*** 34. ***BTEC NC:*** DD. ***BTEC ND:*** DDM. ***OCR ND:*** D

N341 BSc Financial Management (four-year)

Duration: 4FT Hon
Entry Requirements: ***GCE:*** 180. ***SQAH:*** CCCD. ***IB:*** 24. ***BTEC NC:*** DM. ***BTEC ND:*** MMP.

E78 EUROPEAN SCHOOL OF ECONOMICS

8/9 GROSVENOR PLACE
BELGRAVIA
LONDON SW1X 7SH
t: 020 7245 6148 f: 020 7245 6164
e: e.ovies@eselondon.ac.uk
// www.eselondon.ac.uk

N390 BA International Finance

Duration: 4FT/3FT Hon
Entry Requirements: ***GCE:*** 200. ***IB:*** 26.

G70 UNIVERSITY OF GREENWICH

GREENWICH CAMPUS
OLD ROYAL NAVAL COLLEGE
PARK ROW
LONDON SE10 9LS
t: 0800 005 006 f: 020 8331 8145
e: courseinfo@gre.ac.uk
// www.gre.ac.uk

N390 BSc Financial Mathematics

Duration: 3FT Hon
Entry Requirements: ***GCE:*** 200. ***IB:*** 24.

H36 UNIVERSITY OF HERTFORDSHIRE

UNIVERSITY ADMISSIONS SERVICE
COLLEGE LANE
HATFIELD
HERTS AL10 9AB
t: 01707 284800 f: 01707 284870
// www.herts.ac.uk

N300 BA Finance

Duration: 3FT/4SW Hon
Entry Requirements: ***GCE:*** 220-260.

H72 THE UNIVERSITY OF HULL

THE UNIVERSITY OF HULL
COTTINGHAM ROAD
HULL HU6 7RX
t: 01482 466100 f: 01482 442290
e: admissions@hull.ac.uk
// www.hull.ac.uk

N340 BSc Financial Management

Duration: 3FT Hon

Entry Requirements: ***GCE:*** 280. ***IB:*** 28.

N341 BSc Financial Management (International) (4 years)

Duration: 4FT Hon

Entry Requirements: ***GCE:*** 280. ***IB:*** 28.

N342 BSc Financial Management (with Professional Experience) (4 years)

Duration: 4FT Hon

Entry Requirements: ***GCE:*** 280. ***IB:*** 28.

K12 KEELE UNIVERSITY

STAFFS ST5 5BG
t: 01782 734005 f: 01782 632343
e: undergraduate@keele.ac.uk
// www.keele.ac.uk

N323 BSc Actuarial Science

Duration: 3FT Hon

Entry Requirements: ***GCE:*** AAB. ***SQAAH:*** AAB.

K24 THE UNIVERSITY OF KENT

INFORMATION, RECRUITMENT & ADMISSIONS
REGISTRY
UNIVERSITY OF KENT
CANTERBURY, KENT CT2 7NZ
t: 01227 827272 f: 01227 827077
e: information@kent.ac.uk
// www.kent.ac.uk

N323 BSc Actuarial Science

Duration: 3FT Hon

Entry Requirements: ***GCE:*** 340-360. ***IB:*** 36. ***BTEC NC:*** DM. ***BTEC ND:*** MMM. ***OCR ND:*** D ***OCR NED:*** M3

N324 BSc Actuarial Science with a year in Industry

Duration: 4FT Hon

Entry Requirements: ***GCE:*** 340-360. ***IB:*** 36. ***BTEC NC:*** DM. ***BTEC ND:*** MMM. ***OCR ND:*** D ***OCR NED:*** M3

L14 LANCASTER UNIVERSITY

THE UNIVERSITY
LANCASTER
LANCASHIRE LA1 4YW
t: 01524 592029 f: 01524 846243
e: ugadmissions@lancaster.ac.uk
// www.lancs.ac.uk

N300 BSc Finance

Duration: 3FT Hon

Entry Requirements: ***GCE:*** AAB. ***SQAH:*** ABBBB. ***SQAAH:*** AAB. ***IB:*** 34.

L21 LEEDS CITY COLLEGE

PARK LANE HOUSE
PARK LANE CAMPUS
LEEDS CITY COLLEGE
LEEDS LS3 1AA
t: 0113 216 2406 f: 0113 216 2401
e: helen.middleton@leedscitycollege.ac.uk
// www.leedscitycollege.ac.uk

N340 FdA Financial Services

Duration: 2FT Fdg

Entry Requirements: Contact the institution for details.

L41 THE UNIVERSITY OF LIVERPOOL

THE FOUNDATION BUILDING
BROWNLOW HILL
LIVERPOOL L69 7ZX
t: 0151 794 2000 f: 0151 708 6502
e: ugrecruitment@liv.ac.uk
// www.liv.ac.uk

N300 BSc e-Finance

Duration: 3FT Hon

Entry Requirements: ***GCE:*** ABB. ***SQAAH:*** ABB. ***IB:*** 33. ***BTEC ND:*** DDD.

L62 THE LONDON COLLEGE, UCK

VICTORIA GARDENS
NOTTING HILL GATE
LONDON W11 3PE
t: 020 7243 4000 f: 020 7243 1484
e: admissions@lcuck.ac.uk
// www.lcuck.ac.uk

193N HNC Business Finance

Duration: 1FT/2SW HNC

Entry Requirements: ***BTEC NC:*** PP. ***BTEC ND:*** PPP.

093N HND Business Finance

Duration: 2FT/3SW HND

Entry Requirements: ***BTEC NC:*** PP. ***BTEC ND:*** PPP.

L68 LONDON METROPOLITAN UNIVERSITY

166-220 HOLLOWAY ROAD
LONDON N7 8DB
t: 020 7133 4200
e: admissions@londonmet.ac.uk
// www.londonmet.ac.uk

N300 BA Banking & Finance

Duration: 4SW Hon

Entry Requirements: ***GCE:*** 240. ***IB:*** 28.

N340 BA Financial Services

Duration: 3FT Hon

Entry Requirements: ***GCE:*** 240. ***IB:*** 28.

N390 BA International Financial Services (1 year Top-up)

Duration: 1FT Hon

Entry Requirements: HND required.

N301 BSc Finance

Duration: 3FT Hon

Entry Requirements: ***GCE:*** 240. ***IB:*** 28.

L72 LONDON SCHOOL OF ECONOMICS AND POLITICAL SCIENCE (UNIVERSITY OF LONDON)

HOUGHTON STREET
LONDON WC2A 2AE
t: 020 7955 7125/7769 f: 020 7955 6001
e: ug-admissions@lse.ac.uk
// www.lse.ac.uk

N321 BSc Actuarial Science

Duration: 3FT Hon

Entry Requirements: ***GCE:*** AAA. ***SQAH:*** AAAAA. ***SQAAH:*** AAA. ***IB:*** 38.

L79 LOUGHBOROUGH UNIVERSITY

LOUGHBOROUGH
LEICESTERSHIRE LE11 3TU
t: 01509 223522 f: 01509 223905
e: admissions@lboro.ac.uk
// www.lboro.ac.uk

N301 BSc Banking Finance and Management (4 year SW)

Duration: 4SW Hon

Entry Requirements: ***GCE:*** AAB. ***IB:*** 36. ***BTEC ND:*** DDM.

M20 THE UNIVERSITY OF MANCHESTER

OXFORD ROAD
MANCHESTER M13 9PL
t: 0161 275 2077 f: 0161 275 2106
e: ug-admissions@manchester.ac.uk
// www.manchester.ac.uk

N300 BAEcon Finance

Duration: 3FT Hon

Entry Requirements: ***GCE:*** AAB. ***SQAH:*** AAAAB. ***SQAAH:*** AAB. ***IB:*** 35. ***BTEC ND:*** DDM. Interview required.

M40 THE MANCHESTER METROPOLITAN UNIVERSITY

ADMISSIONS OFFICE
ALL SAINTS (GMS)
ALL SAINTS
MANCHESTER M15 6BH
t: 0161 247 2000
// www.mmu.ac.uk

N300 BA Financial Studies

Duration: 1FT Hon

Entry Requirements: Contact the institution for details.

M80 MIDDLESEX UNIVERSITY

MIDDLESEX UNIVERSITY
THE BURROUGHS
LONDON NW4 4BT
t: 020 8411 5555 f: 020 8411 5649
e: enquiries@mdx.ac.uk
// www.mdx.ac.uk

N300 BSc Money Banking and Finance

Duration: 3FT/4SW Hon

Entry Requirements: ***GCE:*** 200-300. ***IB:*** 28.

N38 UNIVERSITY OF NORTHAMPTON

PARK CAMPUS
BOUGHTON GREEN ROAD
NORTHAMPTON NN2 7AL
t: 0800 358 2232 f: 01604 722083
e: admissions@northampton.ac.uk
// www.northampton.ac.uk

N390 BSc Financial Services Management

Duration: 3FT Hon

Entry Requirements: ***GCE:*** 220-260. ***SQAH:*** ABB-BBBC. ***IB:*** 24.

N391 BSc Financial Services Management (4 year extended)

Duration: 4FT Hon

Entry Requirements: ***GCE:*** 220-260. ***SQAH:*** ABB-BBBC. ***IB:*** 24.

N82 NORWICH CITY COLLEGE OF FURTHER AND HIGHER EDUCATION (AN ASSOCIATE COLLEGE OF UEA)
IPSWICH ROAD
NORWICH
NORFOLK NR2 2LJ
t: 01603 773005 f: 01603 773301
e: admissions@ccn.ac.uk
// www.ccn.ac.uk

N322 FdA Financial Services - Insurance
Duration: 2.5FT Fdg
Entry Requirements: Contact the institution for details.

N340 FdA Financial Services - Retail
Duration: 2FT Fdg
Entry Requirements: Contact the institution for details.

P60 UNIVERSITY OF PLYMOUTH
DRAKE CIRCUS
PLYMOUTH PL4 8AA
t: 01752 588037 f: 01752 588050
e: admissions@plymouth.ac.uk
// www.plymouth.ac.uk

N304 BA International Finance
Duration: 1FT Hon
Entry Requirements: Contact the institution for details.

N302 BA International Financial Services
Duration: 4SW Hon
Entry Requirements: ***GCE:*** 240. ***IB:*** 26. ***BTEC NC:*** DD. ***BTEC ND:*** MMM.

N303 FdA Financial Services
Duration: 2FT Fdg
Entry Requirements: ***GCE:*** 60. ***BTEC NC:*** PP. ***BTEC ND:*** PPP. ***OCR ND:*** P ***OCR NED:*** M

P80 UNIVERSITY OF PORTSMOUTH
ACADEMIC REGISTRY
UNIVERSITY HOUSE
WINSTON CHURCHILL AVENUE
PORTSMOUTH PO1 2UP
t: 023 9284 8484 f: 023 9284 3082
e: admissions@port.ac.uk
// www.port.ac.uk

N350 BA International Finance and Trade
Duration: 3FT/4SW Hon
Entry Requirements: ***GCE:*** 280. ***IB:*** 25. ***BTEC ND:*** DMM.

N300 BSc Finance
Duration: 3FT/4SW Hon
Entry Requirements: ***GCE:*** 280. ***IB:*** 25. ***BTEC ND:*** DMM.

Q75 QUEEN'S UNIVERSITY BELFAST
UNIVERSITY ROAD
BELFAST BT7 1NN
t: 028 9097 3838 f: 028 9097 2828
e: admissions@qub.ac.uk
// www.qub.ac.uk

N300 BSc Finance (4 year Sandwich)
Duration: 4SW Hon
Entry Requirements: ***GCE:*** ABB-BBBb. ***SQAH:*** ABBBB. ***SQAAH:*** ABB. ***IB:*** 32.

R12 THE UNIVERSITY OF READING
THE UNIVERSITY OF READING
PO BOX 217
READING RG6 6AH
t: 0118 378 8619 f: 0118 378 8924
e: student.recruitment@reading.ac.uk
// www.reading.ac.uk

N380 BSc Investment and Finance in Property
Duration: 3FT Hon
Entry Requirements: ***GCE:*** 340.

R18 REGENTS BUSINESS SCHOOL, LONDON (REGENTS COLLEGE)
INNER CIRCLE, REGENT'S COLLEGE
REGENT'S PARK
LONDON NW1 4NS
t: +44(0)20 7487 7505 f: +44(0)20 7487 7425
e: rbsl@regents.ac.uk
// www.RBSLondon.ac.uk

N342 BA Global Financial Management
Duration: 3FT Hon
Entry Requirements: ***SQAH:*** BBCC. ***SQAAH:*** CC.

N340 BA Global Financial Management (Int FND)
Duration: 4FT Hon
Entry Requirements: Contact the institution for details.

S21 SHEFFIELD HALLAM UNIVERSITY
CITY CAMPUS
HOWARD STREET
SHEFFIELD S1 1WB
t: 0114 225 5555 f: 0114 225 2167
e: admissions@shu.ac.uk
// www.shu.ac.uk

N300 BA Business and Financial Services
Duration: 3FT/4SW Hon
Entry Requirements: ***GCE:*** 240.

S72 STAFFORDSHIRE UNIVERSITY
COLLEGE ROAD
STOKE ON TRENT ST4 2DE
t: 01782 292753 f: 01782 292740
e: admissions@staffs.ac.uk
// www.staffs.ac.uk

N300 BA Finance
Duration: 3FT/4SW Hon
Entry Requirements: ***GCE:*** BCC-BB. ***IB:*** 24. ***BTEC NC:*** DM. ***BTEC ND:*** MMM. Interview required.

S75 THE UNIVERSITY OF STIRLING
STIRLING FK9 4LA
t: 01786 467044 f: 01786 466800
e: admissions@stir.ac.uk
// www.stir.ac.uk

N300 BA Finance
Duration: 4FT Hon
Entry Requirements: ***GCE:*** CCC. ***SQAH:*** BBBB. ***SQAAH:*** AAA-CCC. ***IB:*** 30. ***BTEC ND:*** DMM.

S78 THE UNIVERSITY OF STRATHCLYDE
GLASGOW G1 1XQ
t: 0141 552 4400 f: 0141 552 0775
// www.strath.ac.uk

N300 BA Finance
Duration: 4FT Hon
Entry Requirements: ***GCE:*** ABB. ***SQAH:*** AABB-ABBBC. ***IB:*** 34.

S85 UNIVERSITY OF SURREY
STAG HILL
GUILDFORD
SURREY GU2 7XH
t: +44(0)1483 689305 f: +44(0)1483 689388
e: admissions@surrey.ac.uk
// www.surrey.ac.uk

N300 BSc Financial Mathematics (3 years)
Duration: 3FT Hon
Entry Requirements: ***GCE:*** 340. Interview required.

N301 BSc Financial Mathematics (4 years)
Duration: 4SW Hon
Entry Requirements: ***GCE:*** 340. Interview required.

T20 TEESSIDE UNIVERSITY
MIDDLESBROUGH TS1 3BA
t: 01642 218121 f: 01642 384201
e: registry@tees.ac.uk
// www.tees.ac.uk

N390 BA Business Finance
Duration: 3FT/4SW Hon
Entry Requirements: ***GCE:*** 240. ***BTEC NC:*** DD. ***BTEC ND:*** MMM. ***OCR ND:*** D ***OCR NED:*** M3

U20 UNIVERSITY OF ULSTER
COLERAINE
CO. LONDONDERRY
NORTHERN IRELAND BT52 1SA
t: 028 7032 4221 f: 028 7032 4908
e: online@ulster.ac.uk
// www.ulster.ac.uk

N321 BSc Finance and Investment Analysis
Duration: 4SW Hon
Entry Requirements: ***GCE:*** 300. ***IB:*** 25. ***BTEC ND:*** DDM.

N300 BSc Financial Services
Duration: 3FT/4SW Hon
Entry Requirements: ***GCE:*** 240. ***IB:*** 24. ***BTEC NC:*** MM. ***BTEC ND:*** MMM.

W80 UNIVERSITY OF WORCESTER
HENWICK GROVE
WORCESTER WR2 6AJ
t: 01905 855111 f: 01905 857542
e: admissions@worc.ac.uk
// www.worcester.ac.uk

N390 BA International Finance
Duration: 1FT Hon
Entry Requirements: HND required.

ACCOUNTANCY

A20 THE UNIVERSITY OF ABERDEEN
UNIVERSITY OFFICE
KING'S COLLEGE
ABERDEEN AB24 3FX
t: +44 (0) 1224 273504 f: +44 (0) 1224 272034
e: sras@abdn.ac.uk
// www.abdn.ac.uk/sras

N400 MA Accountancy
Duration: 4FT Hon
Entry Requirements: ***GCE:*** BBB. ***SQAH:*** BBBB. ***IB:*** 30. ***BTEC ND:*** MMM.

A40 ABERYSTWYTH UNIVERSITY
WELCOME CENTRE, ABERYSTWYTH UNIVERSITY
PENGLAIS CAMPUS
ABERYSTWYTH
CEREDIGION SY23 3FB
t: 01970 622021 f: 01970 627410
e: ug-admissions@aber.ac.uk
// www.aber.ac.uk

N400 BScEcon Accounting & Finance
Duration: 3FT Hon
Entry Requirements: ***GCE:*** 280. ***IB:*** 27.

A80 ASTON UNIVERSITY, BIRMINGHAM
ASTON TRIANGLE
BIRMINGHAM B4 7ET
t: 0121 204 4444 f: 0121 204 3696
e: admissions@aston.ac.uk
// www.aston.ac.uk

N420 BSc Accounting for Management
Duration: 4SW Hon
Entry Requirements: ***GCE:*** 320-340. ***SQAH:*** AAAAB-AAABB. ***SQAAH:*** AAB-ABB. ***IB:*** 34. ***BTEC ND:*** DDM. ***OCR NED:*** D2

B06 BANGOR UNIVERSITY
BANGOR
GWYNEDD LL57 2DG
t: 01248 382016/2017 f: 01248 370451
e: admissions@bangor.ac.uk
// www.bangor.ac.uk

N400 BA Accounting and Finance
Duration: 3FT Hon
Entry Requirements: ***GCE:*** 260-300. ***IB:*** 28.

B22 UNIVERSITY OF BEDFORDSHIRE
PARK SQUARE
LUTON
BEDS LU1 3JU
t: 01582 489286 f: 01582 489323
e: admissions@beds.ac.uk
// www.beds.ac.uk

N403 BA Accounting
Duration: 4SW Hon
Entry Requirements: Contact the institution for details.

N420 BA Accounting
Duration: 3FT Hon
Entry Requirements: ***GCE:*** 160-240. ***SQAH:*** BCC. ***SQAAH:*** BB. ***IB:*** 30.

N400 BA Extended Degree of Higher Education - Accounting
Duration: 4FT Hon
Entry Requirements: Contact the institution for details.

B25 BIRMINGHAM CITY UNIVERSITY
CITY NORTH CAMPUS
PERRY BARR
BIRMINGHAM B42 2SU
t: 0121 331 5595 f: 0121 331 7994
e: choices@bcu.ac.uk
// www.bcu.ac.uk/courses/choices/contact-choices

N400 BA Accountancy
Duration: 3FT/4SW Hon
Entry Requirements: ***GCE:*** 280. ***IB:*** 32. ***BTEC NC:*** DD. ***BTEC ND:*** MMM. Interview required.

B40 BLACKBURN COLLEGE
FEILDEN STREET
BLACKBURN BB2 1LH
t: 01254 292594 f: 01254 679647
e: he-admissions@blackburn.ac.uk
// www.blackburn.ac.uk

N400 BA Business Accounting
Duration: 3FT Hon
Entry Requirements: ***GCE:*** 120.

N401 FdA Accounting
Duration: 2FT Fdg
Entry Requirements: ***GCE:*** 80.

B41 BLACKPOOL AND THE FYLDE COLLEGE AN ASSOCIATE COLLEGE OF LANCASTER UNIVERSITY
ASHFIELD ROAD
BISPHAM
BLACKPOOL
LANCS FY2 0HB
t: 01253 504346 f: 01253 356127
e: admissions@blackpool.ac.uk
// www.blackpool.ac.uk

N400 FdA Accounting
Duration: 2FT Fdg
Entry Requirements: Interview required.

B44 THE UNIVERSITY OF BOLTON
DEANE ROAD
BOLTON BL3 5AB
t: 01204 900600 f: 01204 399074
e: enquiries@bolton.ac.uk
// www.bolton.ac.uk

N400 BA Accountancy
Duration: 3FT Hon
Entry Requirements: ***GCE:*** 260. ***IB:*** 24. ***BTEC ND:*** DMM.

B50 BOURNEMOUTH UNIVERSITY
TALBOT CAMPUS
FERN BARROW
POOLE
DORSET BH12 5BB
t: 01202 524111
// www.bournemouth.ac.uk

N420 BA Accounting and Finance
Duration: 3FT Hon
Entry Requirements: ***GCE:*** 320. ***IB:*** 32. ***BTEC ND:*** DDM.

B54 BPP COLLEGE OF PROFESSIONAL STUDIES
68-70 RED LION STREET
LONDON WC1R 4NY
t: +44 (0) 845 077 5566 f: +44 (0) 20 7404 1389
e: admissions@bpp.com
// www.bpp.com/courses/degree-programmes.aspx

N400 BSc Professional Accounting
Duration: 3FT Hon
Entry Requirements: Contact the institution for details.

N401 BSc Professional Accounting (2yrs)
Duration: 2FT Hon
Entry Requirements: Contact the institution for details.

B56 THE UNIVERSITY OF BRADFORD
RICHMOND ROAD
BRADFORD
WEST YORKSHIRE BD7 1DP
t: 0800 073 1225 f: 01274 235585
e: course-enquiries@bradford.ac.uk
// www.bradford.ac.uk

N420 BSc Accounting and Finance
Duration: 3FT Hon
Entry Requirements: ***GCE:*** 240. ***IB:*** 24.

N421 BSc Accounting and Finance (4 years)
Duration: 4SW Hon
Entry Requirements: ***GCE:*** 240. ***IB:*** 24.

B60 BRADFORD COLLEGE: AN ASSOCIATE COLLEGE OF LEEDS METROPOLITAN UNIVERSITY
GREAT HORTON ROAD
BRADFORD
WEST YORKSHIRE BD7 1AY
t: 01274 433333 f: 01274 433241
e: admissions@bradfordcollege.ac.uk
// www.bradfordcollege.ac.uk

N410 BA Accountancy
Duration: 3FT Hon
Entry Requirements: ***GCE:*** 180. ***BTEC NC:*** MM. ***BTEC ND:*** MPP.

B72 UNIVERSITY OF BRIGHTON
MITHRAS HOUSE
LEWES ROAD
BRIGHTON BN2 4AT
t: 01273 644644 f: 01273 642607
e: admissions@brighton.ac.uk
// www.brighton.ac.uk

N410 BA Accountancy Studies
Duration: 3FT Hon
Entry Requirements: ***GCE:*** BBC. ***IB:*** 30. ***BTEC ND:*** DMM.

N420 BA Accounting and Finance
Duration: 3FT/4SW Hon
Entry Requirements: ***GCE:*** BBC. ***IB:*** 30. ***BTEC ND:*** DMM.

B80 UNIVERSITY OF THE WEST OF ENGLAND, BRISTOL
FRENCHAY CAMPUS
COLDHARBOUR LANE
BRISTOL BS16 1QY
t: +44 (0)117 32 83333 f: +44 (0)117 32 82810
e: admissions@uwe.ac.uk
// www.uwe.ac.uk

N420 BA Accounting and Finance
Duration: 3FT/4SW Hon
Entry Requirements: ***GCE:*** 280-340.

C15 CARDIFF UNIVERSITY
PO BOX 927
30-36 NEWPORT ROAD
CARDIFF CF24 0DE
t: 029 2087 9999 f: 029 2087 6138
e: admissions@cardiff.ac.uk
// www.cardiff.ac.uk

N400 BSc Accounting
Duration: 3FT Hon
Entry Requirements: ***GCE:*** AAB. ***SQAH:*** AAABB. ***SQAAH:*** AAB. ***IB:*** 35. ***BTEC ND:*** DDD. ***OCR NED:*** D2

N490 BSc Accounting and Finance

Duration: 3FT Hon

Entry Requirements: ***GCE:*** AAB. ***SQAH:*** AAABB. ***SQAAH:*** AAB. ***IB:*** 35. ***BTEC ND:*** DDD. ***OCR NED:*** D2

N410 BSc Accounting with a European Language (4 years)

Duration: 4FT Hon

Entry Requirements: ***GCE:*** AAB. ***SQAH:*** AAABB. ***SQAAH:*** AAB. ***IB:*** 35. ***BTEC ND:*** DDD. ***OCR NED:*** D2

C20 UNIVERSITY OF WALES INSTITUTE, CARDIFF

PO BOX 377
LLANDAFF CAMPUS
WESTERN AVENUE
CARDIFF CF5 2SG
t: 029 2041 6070 f: 029 2041 6286
e: admissions@uwic.ac.uk
// www.uwic.ac.uk

N400 BA Accounting

Duration: 3FT Hon

Entry Requirements: ***GCE:*** 240. ***IB:*** 24. ***BTEC NC:*** DD. ***BTEC ND:*** MMM. ***OCR ND:*** D ***OCR NED:*** M3

C30 UNIVERSITY OF CENTRAL LANCASHIRE

PRESTON
LANCS PR1 2HE
t: 01772 201201 f: 01772 894954
e: uadmissions@uclan.ac.uk
// www.uclan.ac.uk

N400 BA Accounting

Duration: 3FT Hon

Entry Requirements: ***GCE:*** 260-280. ***SQAH:*** AABB-BBBB. ***IB:*** 28. ***BTEC NC:*** DD. ***OCR ND:*** D

N420 BA Accounting and Financial Studies

Duration: 3FT Hon

Entry Requirements: ***GCE:*** 260-280. ***SQAH:*** AABB-BBBB. ***IB:*** 28. ***BTEC NC:*** DD. ***OCR ND:*** D

N421 BA Accounting and Financial Studies (Year 2 entry)

Duration: 2FT Hon

Entry Requirements: ***GCE:*** 260-280. ***SQAH:*** AABB-BBBB. ***IB:*** 28. ***BTEC NC:*** DD. ***OCR ND:*** D

C85 COVENTRY UNIVERSITY

THE STUDENT CENTRE
COVENTRY UNIVERSITY
1 GULSON ROAD
COVENTRY CV1 2JH
t: 024 7615 2222 f: 024 7615 2223
e: studentenquiries@coventry.ac.uk
// www.coventry.ac.uk

N410 BA Accountancy

Duration: 3FT/4SW Hon

Entry Requirements: ***GCE:*** 300. ***IB:*** 30. ***BTEC ND:*** DDM. ***OCR NED:*** M1

D26 DE MONTFORT UNIVERSITY

THE GATEWAY
LEICESTER LE1 9BH
t: 0116 255 1551 f: 0116 250 6204
e: enquiries@dmu.ac.uk
// www.dmu.ac.uk

N420 BA Accounting and Finance

Duration: 3FT/4SW Hon

Entry Requirements: ***GCE:*** 280. ***IB:*** 24. Interview required.

D39 UNIVERSITY OF DERBY

KEDLESTON ROAD
DERBY DE22 1GB
t: 08701 202330 f: 01332 597724
e: askadmissions@derby.ac.uk
// www.derby.ac.uk

N400 BA Accounting and Finance

Duration: 3FT/4SW Hon

Entry Requirements: ***Foundation:*** Distinction. ***GCE:*** 240. ***IB:*** 26. ***BTEC NC:*** DD. ***BTEC ND:*** MMM. ***OCR ND:*** D ***OCR NED:*** M3

D65 UNIVERSITY OF DUNDEE

DUNDEE DD1 4HN
t: 01382 383838 f: 01382 388150
e: ContactUs@dundee.ac.uk
// www.dundee.ac.uk/admissions/undergraduate/

N400 BAcc Accountancy

Duration: 4FT Hon

Entry Requirements: ***GCE:*** BCC. ***SQAH:*** BBBB. ***IB:*** 30. ***BTEC ND:*** DMM.

N410 BAcc Accountancy

Duration: 3FT Ord

Entry Requirements: ***GCE:*** BCC. ***SQAH:*** BBBB. ***IB:*** 30. ***BTEC ND:*** DMM.

N490 BIAcc International Accountancy

Duration: 4FT Hon

Entry Requirements: ***GCE:*** BCC. ***SQAH:*** BBBB. ***IB:*** 30. ***BTEC ND:*** DMM.

D86 DURHAM UNIVERSITY

DURHAM UNIVERSITY
UNIVERSITY OFFICE
DURHAM DH1 3HP
t: 0191 334 2000 f: 0191 334 6055
e: admissions@durham.ac.uk
// www.durham.ac.uk

N420 BA Business Finance

Duration: 3FT Hon

Entry Requirements: ***GCE:*** ABB. ***SQAH:*** AABBB. ***SQAAH:*** ABB. ***IB:*** 34.

E14 UNIVERSITY OF EAST ANGLIA

NORWICH NR4 7TJ
t: 01603 591515 f: 01603 458596
e: admissions@uea.ac.uk
// www.uea.ac.uk

N400 BSc Accounting and Finance

Duration: 3FT Hon

Entry Requirements: ***GCE:*** BBB. ***SQAH:*** ABBBB. ***SQAAH:*** BBB. ***IB:*** 31. ***BTEC NC:*** DD. ***BTEC ND:*** DDM. ***OCR ND:*** M1 ***OCR NED:*** M1

E28 UNIVERSITY OF EAST LONDON

DOCKLANDS CAMPUS
UNIVERSITY WAY
LONDON E16 2RD
t: 020 8223 3333 f: 020 8223 2978
e: study@uel.ac.uk
// www.uel.ac.uk

N400 BA Accounting

Duration: 3FT Hon

Entry Requirements: ***GCE:*** 200. ***IB:*** 24. ***BTEC NC:*** DM. ***BTEC ND:*** MMP.

N420 BA Accounting and Finance

Duration: 3FT Hon

Entry Requirements: ***GCE:*** 200. ***IB:*** 24. ***BTEC NC:*** DM. ***BTEC ND:*** MMP.

E42 EDGE HILL UNIVERSITY

ORMSKIRK
LANCASHIRE L39 4QP
t: 0800 195 5063 f: 01695 584355
e: enquiries@edgehill.ac.uk
// www.edgehill.ac.uk

N410 BSc Accountancy

Duration: 3FT Hon

Entry Requirements: ***GCE:*** 280. ***IB:*** 24. ***BTEC NC:*** DM. ***BTEC ND:*** MMP. ***OCR ND:*** D ***OCR NED:*** M2

E59 EDINBURGH NAPIER UNIVERSITY

CRAIGLOCKHART CAMPUS
EDINBURGH EH14 1DJ
t: +44 (0)8452 60 60 40 f: 0131 455 6464
e: info@napier.ac.uk
// www.napier.ac.uk

N400 BA Accounting

Duration: 3FT/4FT Deg/Hon

Entry Requirements: ***GCE:*** 230.

E70 THE UNIVERSITY OF ESSEX

WIVENHOE PARK
COLCHESTER
ESSEX CO4 3SQ
t: 01206 873666 f: 01206 873423
e: admit@essex.ac.uk
// www.essex.ac.uk

N400 BA Accounting

Duration: 3FT Hon

Entry Requirements: ***GCE:*** 320. ***SQAH:*** AAAB. ***IB:*** 34. ***BTEC NC:*** DD. ***BTEC ND:*** DDM. ***OCR ND:*** D

N420 BA Accounting & Finance

Duration: 3FT Hon

Entry Requirements: ***GCE:*** 320. ***SQAH:*** AAAB. ***IB:*** 34. ***BTEC NC:*** DD. ***BTEC ND:*** DDM. ***OCR ND:*** D

N401 BA Accounting (four-year)

Duration: 4FT Hon

Entry Requirements: ***GCE:*** 180. ***SQAH:*** CCCD. ***IB:*** 24. ***BTEC NC:*** DM. ***BTEC ND:*** MMP.

E84 UNIVERSITY OF EXETER

LAVER BUILDING
NORTH PARK ROAD
EXETER
DEVON EX4 4QE
t: 01392 263855 f: 01392 263857/262479
e: admissions@exeter.ac.uk
// www.exeter.ac.uk/admissions

N422 BA Accounting and Finance

Duration: 3FT Hon

Entry Requirements: ***GCE:*** AAA-AAB. ***SQAH:*** AAAAB-AAABB. ***SQAAH:*** AAB-ABB. ***BTEC ND:*** DDD.

N423 BA Accounting and Finance with European Study (4 years)

Duration: 4FT Hon

Entry Requirements: ***GCE:*** AAA-AAB. ***SQAH:*** AAAAB-AAABB. ***SQAAH:*** AAB-ABB. ***BTEC ND:*** DDD.

G14 UNIVERSITY OF GLAMORGAN, CARDIFF AND PONTYPRIDD

ENQUIRIES AND ADMISSIONS UNIT
PONTYPRIDD CF37 1DL
t: 0800 716925 f: 01443 654050
e: enquiries@glam.ac.uk
// www.glam.ac.uk

N420 BA Accounting & Finance

Duration: 3FT/4SW Hon
Entry Requirements: ***GCE:*** 240-280. ***IB:*** 24. ***BTEC NC:*** DD. ***BTEC ND:*** MMM.

N490 BA Forensic Accounting

Duration: 3FT Hon
Entry Requirements: ***GCE:*** 240-280.

N401 BA International Accounting

Duration: 3FT/4SW Hon
Entry Requirements: ***GCE:*** 240-280. ***IB:*** 26. ***BTEC NC:*** DD. ***BTEC ND:*** MMM.

004N HND Accounting

Duration: 2FT HND
Entry Requirements: ***GCE:*** 100-140. ***BTEC NC:*** PP. ***BTEC ND:*** PPP.

G28 UNIVERSITY OF GLASGOW

THE UNIVERSITY OF GLASGOW
THE FRASER BUILDING
65 HILLHEAD STREET
GLASGOW G12 8QF
t: 0141 330 6062 f: 0141 330 2961
e: ugenquiries@gla.ac.uk (UK/EU undergrad enquiries only)
// www.glasgow.ac.uk

N400 BAcc Accountancy

Duration: 4FT Hon
Entry Requirements: ***GCE:*** AAB. ***SQAH:*** AAABB. ***IB:*** 34.

N401 BAcc Accountancy with International Accounting

Duration: 4FT Hon
Entry Requirements: ***GCE:*** AAB. ***SQAH:*** AAABB. ***IB:*** 34.

G42 GLASGOW CALEDONIAN UNIVERSITY

CITY CAMPUS
COWCADDENS ROAD
GLASGOW G4 0BA
t: 0141 331 3000 f: 0141 331 3449
e: admissions@gcu.ac.uk
// www.gcu.ac.uk

N400 BA Accountancy

Duration: 4FT Hon
Entry Requirements: ***GCE:*** CCC. ***SQAH:*** BBBB-BBBC. ***IB:*** 24.

G50 THE UNIVERSITY OF GLOUCESTERSHIRE

HARDWICK CAMPUS
ST PAUL'S ROAD
CHELTENHAM GL50 4BS
t: 01242 714501 f: 01242 543334
e: admissions@glos.ac.uk
// www.glos.ac.uk

N400 BA Accounting & Financial Management Studies

Duration: 3FT Hon
Entry Requirements: ***GCE:*** 280-300.

G70 UNIVERSITY OF GREENWICH

GREENWICH CAMPUS
OLD ROYAL NAVAL COLLEGE
PARK ROW
LONDON SE10 9LS
t: 0800 005 006 f: 020 8331 8145
e: courseinfo@gre.ac.uk
// www.gre.ac.uk

N400 BA Accounting and Finance

Duration: 3FT Hon
Entry Requirements: ***GCE:*** 220-260. ***IB:*** 30.

H36 UNIVERSITY OF HERTFORDSHIRE

UNIVERSITY ADMISSIONS SERVICE
COLLEGE LANE
HATFIELD
HERTS AL10 9AB
t: 01707 284800 f: 01707 284870
// www.herts.ac.uk

N400 BA Accounting

Duration: 3FT/4SW Hon
Entry Requirements: ***GCE:*** 280.

H49 UHI MILLENNIUM INSTITUTE

UHI EXECUTIVE OFFICE
NESS WALK
INVERNESS
SCOTLAND IV3 5SQ
t: 01463 279000 f: 01463 279001
e: info@uhi.ac.uk
// www.uhi.ac.uk

104N HNC Accounting

Duration: 1FT HNC
Entry Requirements: ***SQAH:*** C.

004N HND Accounting

Duration: 2FT HND
Entry Requirements: ***SQAH:*** CC.

H50 HOLBORN COLLEGE

WOOLWICH ROAD
LONDON SE7 8LN
t: 020 8317 6000 f: 020 8317 6001
e: admissions@holborncollege.ac.uk
// www.holborncollege.ac.uk

N400 BA (Hons) Accountancy

Duration: 3FT Hon

Entry Requirements: Contact the institution for details.

H60 THE UNIVERSITY OF HUDDERSFIELD

QUEENSGATE
HUDDERSFIELD HD1 3DH
t: 01484 473969 f: 01484 472765
e: admissionsandrecords@hud.ac.uk
// www.hud.ac.uk

N410 BA Accountancy

Duration: 3FT/4SW Hon

Entry Requirements: ***GCE:*** 300. ***SQAH:*** BBCC. ***IB:*** 28.

N420 BA Accountancy and Finance

Duration: 3FT/4SW Hon

Entry Requirements: ***GCE:*** 300. ***SQAH:*** BBCC. ***IB:*** 28.

N414 BA International Accountancy (Top-up)

Duration: 1FT Hon

Entry Requirements: HND required.

H72 THE UNIVERSITY OF HULL

THE UNIVERSITY OF HULL
COTTINGHAM ROAD
HULL HU6 7RX
t: 01482 466100 f: 01482 442290
e: admissions@hull.ac.uk
// www.hull.ac.uk

N400 BSc Accounting

Duration: 3FT Hon

Entry Requirements: ***GCE:*** 280. ***IB:*** 28.

N401 BSc Accounting (International) (4 years)

Duration: 4FT Hon

Entry Requirements: ***GCE:*** 280. ***IB:*** 28.

N402 BSc Accounting (with Professional Experience) (4 years)

Duration: 4SW Hon

Entry Requirements: ***GCE:*** 280. ***IB:*** 28.

K24 THE UNIVERSITY OF KENT

INFORMATION, RECRUITMENT & ADMISSIONS
REGISTRY
UNIVERSITY OF KENT
CANTERBURY, KENT CT2 7NZ
t: 01227 827272 f: 01227 827077
e: information@kent.ac.uk
// www.kent.ac.uk

N400 BA Accounting & Finance

Duration: 3FT Hon

Entry Requirements: ***GCE:*** 300. ***IB:*** 33. ***BTEC NC:*** DD. ***BTEC ND:*** DMM. ***OCR ND:*** D

N402 BA Accounting & Finance with German (4 years)

Duration: 4FT Hon

Entry Requirements: ***GCE:*** 300. ***IB:*** 33. ***BTEC NC:*** DD. ***BTEC ND:*** DMM. ***OCR ND:*** D

N403 BA British & French Accounting and Finance (4 years)

Duration: 4FT Hon

Entry Requirements: ***GCE:*** 300. ***IB:*** 33. ***BTEC NC:*** DD. ***BTEC ND:*** DMM. ***OCR ND:*** D

N404 BSc Accounting & Finance with a year in Industry

Duration: 4SW Hon

Entry Requirements: ***GCE:*** 300. ***IB:*** 33. ***BTEC NC:*** DD. ***BTEC ND:*** DMM. ***OCR ND:*** D

K84 KINGSTON UNIVERSITY

STUDENT INFORMATION & ADVICE CENTRE
COOPER HOUSE
40-46 SURBITON ROAD
KINGSTON UPON THAMES KT1 2HX
t: 0844 8552177 f: 020 8547 7080
e: aps@kingston.ac.uk
// www.kingston.ac.uk

N420 BA Accounting & Finance

Duration: 3FT Hon

Entry Requirements: ***GCE:*** 320. ***IB:*** 27. ***BTEC ND:*** DDM.

L14 LANCASTER UNIVERSITY
THE UNIVERSITY
LANCASTER
LANCASHIRE LA1 4YW
t: 01524 592029 f: 01524 846243
e: ugadmissions@lancaster.ac.uk
// www.lancs.ac.uk

N400 BA/BSc Accounting and Finance
Duration: 3FT Hon
Entry Requirements: ***GCE:*** AAB. ***SQAH:*** ABBBB. ***SQAAH:*** AAB. ***IB:*** 34. ***BTEC ND:*** DDM.

L23 UNIVERSITY OF LEEDS
THE UNIVERSITY OF LEEDS
LEEDS LS2 9JT
t: 0113 343 3999
e: admissions@adm.leeds.ac.uk
// www.leeds.ac.uk

N420 BSc Accounting & Finance
Duration: 3FT Hon
Entry Requirements: ***GCE:*** AAB. ***SQAH:*** AAAAB. ***SQAAH:*** AAB. ***IB:*** 35.

L27 LEEDS METROPOLITAN UNIVERSITY
COURSE ENQUIRIES OFFICE
CIVIC QUARTER
LEEDS LS1 3HE
t: 0113 81 23113 f: 0113 81 23129
e: https://experience.leedsmet.ac.uk/leeds/index.do
// www.leedsmet.ac.uk

N420 BA Accounting and Finance
Duration: 3FT/4SW Hon
Entry Requirements: ***GCE:*** 220. ***IB:*** 28.

L41 THE UNIVERSITY OF LIVERPOOL
THE FOUNDATION BUILDING
BROWNLOW HILL
LIVERPOOL L69 7ZX
t: 0151 794 2000 f: 0151 708 6502
e: ugrecruitment@liv.ac.uk
// www.liv.ac.uk

N400 BA Accounting
Duration: 3FT Hon
Entry Requirements: ***GCE:*** ABB. ***SQAH:*** AABBB. ***SQAAH:*** ABB. ***IB:*** 33. ***BTEC ND:*** DDM. ***OCR ND:*** D ***OCR NED:*** M1

L46 LIVERPOOL HOPE UNIVERSITY
HOPE PARK
LIVERPOOL L16 9JD
t: 0151 291 3295 f: 0151 291 2050
e: admission@hope.ac.uk
// www.hope.ac.uk

N400 BA Accounting
Duration: 3FT Hon
Entry Requirements: ***GCE:*** 260. ***IB:*** 25.

L51 LIVERPOOL JOHN MOORES UNIVERSITY
ROSCOE COURT
4 RODNEY STREET
LIVERPOOL L1 2TZ
t: 0151 231 5090 f: 0151 231 3462
e: courses@ljmu.ac.uk
// www.ljmu.ac.uk

N420 BA Accounting and Finance
Duration: 3FT Hon
Entry Requirements: ***GCE:*** 260. ***IB:*** 24.

L68 LONDON METROPOLITAN UNIVERSITY
166-220 HOLLOWAY ROAD
LONDON N7 8DB
t: 020 7133 4200
e: admissions@londonmet.ac.uk
// www.londonmet.ac.uk

N400 BA Accounting and Finance
Duration: 3FT Hon
Entry Requirements: ***GCE:*** 240. ***IB:*** 28.

L75 LONDON SOUTH BANK UNIVERSITY
103 BOROUGH ROAD
LONDON SE1 0AA
t: 020 7815 7815 f: 020 7815 8273
e: enquiry@lsbu.ac.uk
// www.lsbu.ac.uk

N420 BA Accounting and Finance
Duration: 3FT Hon
Entry Requirements: ***GCE:*** 160. ***IB:*** 24. ***BTEC NC:*** MM. ***BTEC ND:*** MPP.

N400 FdA Accounting
Duration: 2FT Fdg
Entry Requirements: ***GCE:*** 80.

M20 THE UNIVERSITY OF MANCHESTER
OXFORD ROAD
MANCHESTER M13 9PL
t: 0161 275 2077 f: 0161 275 2106
e: ug-admissions@manchester.ac.uk
// www.manchester.ac.uk

N420 BAEcon Accounting
Duration: 3FT Hon
Entry Requirements: ***GCE:*** AAB. ***SQAH:*** AAAAB. ***SQAAH:*** AAB. ***IB:*** 35. ***BTEC ND:*** DDM. Interview required.

N400 BSc Accounting
Duration: 3FT/4FT Hon
Entry Requirements: ***GCE:*** AAA. ***SQAAH:*** AAA. ***IB:*** 37. ***BTEC ND:*** DDD.

M40 THE MANCHESTER METROPOLITAN UNIVERSITY
ADMISSIONS OFFICE
ALL SAINTS (GMS)
ALL SAINTS
MANCHESTER M15 6BH
t: 0161 247 2000
// www.mmu.ac.uk

N420 BA Accounting and Finance
Duration: 3FT Hon
Entry Requirements: ***GCE:*** 240. ***IB:*** 28.

N423 BA Accounting and Finance (Foundation)
Duration: 4FT/5SW Hon
Entry Requirements: ***GCE:*** 120. ***IB:*** 24.

M80 MIDDLESEX UNIVERSITY
MIDDLESEX UNIVERSITY
THE BURROUGHS
LONDON NW4 4BT
t: 020 8411 5555 f: 020 8411 5649
e: enquiries@mdx.ac.uk
// www.mdx.ac.uk

N420 BA Accounting and Finance
Duration: 3FT/4SW Hon
Entry Requirements: ***GCE:*** 200-300. ***IB:*** 28.

N490 BA Business Accounting
Duration: 3FT Hon
Entry Requirements: ***GCE:*** 200-300. ***IB:*** 28.

N21 NEWCASTLE UNIVERSITY
KING'S GATE
NEWCASTLE UPON TYNE NE1 7RU
t: 0191 208 3333 f: 0191 222 6143
e: enquiries@ncl.ac.uk
// www.ncl.ac.uk

N400 BA Accounting and Finance
Duration: 3FT Hon
Entry Requirements: ***GCE:*** AAB. ***SQAH:*** AAABB. ***IB:*** 34. ***BTEC ND:*** DDM.

N37 UNIVERSITY OF WALES, NEWPORT
CAERLEON CAMPUS
LODGE ROAD
CAERLEON
NEWPORT NP18 3QT
t: 01633 432030 f: 01633 432850
e: admissions@newport.ac.uk
// www.newport.ac.uk

N401 BSc Accounting
Duration: 3FT Hon
Entry Requirements: ***GCE:*** 240. ***IB:*** 24.

N38 UNIVERSITY OF NORTHAMPTON
PARK CAMPUS
BOUGHTON GREEN ROAD
NORTHAMPTON NN2 7AL
t: 0800 358 2232 f: 01604 722083
e: admissions@northampton.ac.uk
// www.northampton.ac.uk

N420 BA Accounting and Finance
Duration: 3FT Hon
Entry Requirements: ***GCE:*** 220-260. ***SQAH:*** ABB-BBBC. ***IB:*** 24.

N491 BA International Accounting (top-up)
Duration: 1FT Hon
Entry Requirements: HND required.

N77 NORTHUMBRIA UNIVERSITY
TRINITY BUILDING
NORTHUMBERLAND ROAD
NEWCASTLE UPON TYNE NE1 8ST
t: 0191 243 7420 f: 0191 227 4561
e: er.admissions@northumbria.ac.uk
// www.northumbria.ac.uk

N400 BA Accounting
Duration: 3FT Hon
Entry Requirements: ***GCE:*** 300. ***SQAH:*** BBBBC. ***SQAAH:*** BBC. ***IB:*** 26. ***BTEC ND:*** DDM. ***OCR NED:*** D2

N420 BA Accounting and Finance (Top-up)
Duration: 1FT Hon
Entry Requirements: HND required.

P60 UNIVERSITY OF PLYMOUTH
DRAKE CIRCUS
PLYMOUTH PL4 8AA
t: 01752 588037 f: 01752 588050
e: admissions@plymouth.ac.uk
// www.plymouth.ac.uk

N420 BA Accounting and Finance
Duration: 3FT/4SW Hon
Entry Requirements: ***GCE:*** 240.

N401 FdA Accounting and Finance
Duration: 2FT Fdg
Entry Requirements: ***GCE:*** 60. ***IB:*** 24. ***BTEC NC:*** PP. ***BTEC ND:*** PPP. ***OCR ND:*** P ***OCR NED:*** P

P80 UNIVERSITY OF PORTSMOUTH
ACADEMIC REGISTRY
UNIVERSITY HOUSE
WINSTON CHURCHILL AVENUE
PORTSMOUTH PO1 2UP
t: 023 9284 8484 f: 023 9284 3082
e: admissions@port.ac.uk
// www.port.ac.uk

N420 BA Accountancy Studies
Duration: 2FT Hon
Entry Requirements: Contact the institution for details.

N400 BA Accounting
Duration: 3FT/4SW Hon
Entry Requirements: ***GCE:*** 300. ***IB:*** 26. ***BTEC ND:*** DDM.

Q75 QUEEN'S UNIVERSITY BELFAST
UNIVERSITY ROAD
BELFAST BT7 1NN
t: 028 9097 3838 f: 028 9097 2828
e: admissions@qub.ac.uk
// www.qub.ac.uk

N400 BSc Accounting
Duration: 3FT Hon
Entry Requirements: ***GCE:*** AAB-ABBa. ***SQAH:*** AAAA-AAABB. ***SQAAH:*** AAB. ***IB:*** 34.

R36 THE ROBERT GORDON UNIVERSITY
ROBERT GORDON UNIVERSITY
SCHOOLHILL
ABERDEEN
SCOTLAND AB10 1FR
t: 01224 26 27 28 f: 01224 262147
e: admissions@rgu.ac.uk
// www.rgu.ac.uk

N420 BA Accounting and Finance
Duration: 4FT Hon
Entry Requirements: ***GCE:*** CCC. ***SQAH:*** BBCC. ***IB:*** 26. ***BTEC ND:*** MMM.

S03 THE UNIVERSITY OF SALFORD
SALFORD M5 4WT
t: 0161 295 4545 f: 0161 295 3126
e: ugadmissions-exrel@salford.ac.uk
// www.salford.ac.uk

N401 DipHE Accounting
Duration: 2FT Dip
Entry Requirements: ***GCE:*** 80. ***BTEC NC:*** PP. ***BTEC ND:*** PPP.

S18 THE UNIVERSITY OF SHEFFIELD
9 NORTHUMBERLAND ROAD
SHEFFIELD S10 2TT
t: 0114 222 1299 f: 0114 222 8032
e: ask@sheffield.ac.uk
// www.sheffield.ac.uk

N420 BA Accounting & Financial Management
Duration: 3FT Hon
Entry Requirements: ***GCE:*** ABB. ***SQAH:*** AAAB. ***SQAAH:*** ABB. ***IB:*** 33. ***BTEC ND:*** DDM.

S21 SHEFFIELD HALLAM UNIVERSITY
CITY CAMPUS
HOWARD STREET
SHEFFIELD S1 1WB
t: 0114 225 5555 f: 0114 225 2167
e: admissions@shu.ac.uk
// www.shu.ac.uk

N400 BA Accounting
Duration: 3FT/4SW Hon
Entry Requirements: ***GCE:*** 240.

N420 BA Accounting and Financial Management
Duration: 3FT/4SW Hon
Entry Requirements: ***GCE:*** 240.

N490 BA Forensic Accounting
Duration: 3FT/4SW Hon
Entry Requirements: ***GCE:*** 240.

S30 SOUTHAMPTON SOLENT UNIVERSITY
EAST PARK TERRACE
SOUTHAMPTON
HAMPSHIRE SO14 0RT
t: +44 (0) 23 8031 9039 f: + 44 (0)23 8022 2259
e: admissions@solent.ac.uk or ask@solent.ac.uk
// www.solent.ac.uk/

N400 BA Accountancy
Duration: 3FT Hon
Entry Requirements: ***GCE:*** 220. ***BTEC NC:*** MM. ***BTEC ND:*** PPP.

S72 STAFFORDSHIRE UNIVERSITY
COLLEGE ROAD
STOKE ON TRENT ST4 2DE
t: 01782 292753 f: 01782 292740
e: admissions@staffs.ac.uk
// www.staffs.ac.uk

N490 BA Forensic Accounting
Duration: 3FT Hon
Entry Requirements: ***GCE:*** BBC-BB. ***IB:*** 24.

S75 THE UNIVERSITY OF STIRLING
STIRLING FK9 4LA
t: 01786 467044 f: 01786 466800
e: admissions@stir.ac.uk
// www.stir.ac.uk

N400 BAcc Accountancy
Duration: 4FT Hon
Entry Requirements: ***GCE:*** CCC. ***SQAH:*** BBBB. ***SQAAH:*** AAA-CCC. ***IB:*** 30. ***BTEC ND:*** DMM.

S78 THE UNIVERSITY OF STRATHCLYDE
GLASGOW G1 1XQ
t: 0141 552 4400 f: 0141 552 0775
// www.strath.ac.uk

N400 BA Accounting
Duration: 4FT Hon
Entry Requirements: ***GCE:*** AAB. ***SQAH:*** AAAA-AAABB. ***IB:*** 36.

S96 SWANSEA METROPOLITAN UNIVERSITY
MOUNT PLEASANT CAMPUS
SWANSEA SA1 6ED
t: 01792 481000 f: 01792 481061
e: gemma.garbutt@smu.ac.uk
// www.smu.ac.uk

N400 BA Accounting
Duration: 3FT/4SW Hon
Entry Requirements: ***GCE:*** 160-360. ***IB:*** 24.

T20 TEESSIDE UNIVERSITY
MIDDLESBROUGH TS1 3BA
t: 01642 218121 f: 01642 384201
e: registry@tees.ac.uk
// www.tees.ac.uk

N420 BA Accounting & Finance
Duration: 3FT/4SW Hon
Entry Requirements: ***GCE:*** 240. ***IB:*** 30. ***BTEC NC:*** DD. ***BTEC ND:*** MMM. ***OCR ND:*** D ***OCR NED:*** M3

T40 THAMES VALLEY UNIVERSITY
ST MARY'S ROAD
EALING
LONDON W5 5RF
t: 0800 036 8888 f: 020 8566 1353
e: learning.advice@tvu.ac.uk
// www.tvu.ac.uk

N420 BA Accounting and Finance
Duration: 3FT Hon
Entry Requirements: ***GCE:*** 200.

U20 UNIVERSITY OF ULSTER
COLERAINE
CO. LONDONDERRY
NORTHERN IRELAND BT52 1SA
t: 028 7032 4221 f: 028 7032 4908
e: online@ulster.ac.uk
// www.ulster.ac.uk

N400 BSc Accounting
Duration: 3FT Hon
Entry Requirements: ***GCE:*** 340. ***IB:*** 33. ***BTEC ND:*** DDM.

U40 UNIVERSITY OF THE WEST OF SCOTLAND
PAISLEY CAMPUS
RENFREWSHIRE
SCOTLAND PA1 2BE
t: 0141 848 3727 f: 0141 848 3623
e: admissions@uws.ac.uk
// www.uws.ac.uk

N400 BAcc Accounting
Duration: 3FT/4FT/5SW Ord/Hon
Entry Requirements: ***GCE:*** CC. ***SQAH:*** BBCC. ***BTEC NC:*** PP.

W75 UNIVERSITY OF WOLVERHAMPTON

ADMISSIONS UNIT
MX207, CAMP STREET
WOLVERHAMPTON
WEST MIDLANDS WV1 1AD
t: 01902 321000 f: 01902 321896
e: admissions@wlv.ac.uk
// www.wlv.ac.uk

N400 BA Accounting and Finance (3 years)

Duration: 3SW Hon

Entry Requirements: ***GCE:*** 220. ***IB:*** 28. ***BTEC NC:*** DD. ***BTEC ND:*** MMM.

N490 FdA Business Accounting

Duration: 2FT Fdg

Entry Requirements: Contact the institution for details.

W80 UNIVERSITY OF WORCESTER

HENWICK GROVE
WORCESTER WR2 6AJ
t: 01905 855111 f: 01905 857542
e: admissions@worc.ac.uk
// www.worcester.ac.uk

N400 BA Accounting

Duration: 3FT/4SW Hon

Entry Requirements: ***GCE:*** 280. ***IB:*** 25. ***BTEC NC:*** DD. ***BTEC ND:*** MMM. ***OCR ND:*** D ***OCR NED:*** M3

ECONOMICS AND ACCOUNTANCY/ACCOUNTANCY AND ECONOMICS

A20 THE UNIVERSITY OF ABERDEEN

UNIVERSITY OFFICE
KING'S COLLEGE
ABERDEEN AB24 3FX
t: +44 (0) 1224 273504 f: +44 (0) 1224 272034
e: sras@abdn.ac.uk
// www.abdn.ac.uk/sras

NL41 MA Accountancy and Economics

Duration: 4FT Hon

Entry Requirements: ***GCE:*** BBB. ***SQAH:*** BBBB. ***IB:*** 30. ***BTEC ND:*** MMM.

A40 ABERYSTWYTH UNIVERSITY

WELCOME CENTRE, ABERYSTWYTH UNIVERSITY
PENGLAIS CAMPUS
ABERYSTWYTH
CEREDIGION SY23 3FB
t: 01970 622021 f: 01970 627410
e: ug-admissions@aber.ac.uk
// www.aber.ac.uk

LN14 BScEcon Accounting & Finance/Economics

Duration: 3FT Hon

Entry Requirements: ***GCE:*** 280. ***IB:*** 27.

B06 BANGOR UNIVERSITY

BANGOR
GWYNEDD LL57 2DG
t: 01248 382016/2017 f: 01248 370451
e: admissions@bangor.ac.uk
// www.bangor.ac.uk

LN14 BA Economics/Accounting

Duration: 3FT Hon

Entry Requirements: ***GCE:*** 260-300. ***IB:*** 28.

NL41 BSc Accounting and Economics

Duration: 3FT Hon

Entry Requirements: ***GCE:*** 260-300. ***IB:*** 28.

B25 BIRMINGHAM CITY UNIVERSITY

CITY NORTH CAMPUS
PERRY BARR
BIRMINGHAM B42 2SU
t: 0121 331 5595 f: 0121 331 7994
e: choices@bcu.ac.uk
// www.bcu.ac.uk/courses/choices/contact-choices

NL41 BA Accountancy and Economics

Duration: 3FT/4SW Hon

Entry Requirements: ***GCE:*** 260. ***IB:*** 30. ***BTEC NC:*** DD. ***BTEC ND:*** DMM. ***OCR ND:*** D ***OCR NED:*** M3 Interview required. Portfolio required.

B78 UNIVERSITY OF BRISTOL

UNDERGRADUATE ADMISSIONS OFFICE
SENATE HOUSE
TYNDALL AVENUE
BRISTOL BS8 1TH
t: 0117 928 9000 f: 0117 925 1424
e: ug-admissions@bristol.ac.uk
// www.bristol.ac.uk

LN14 BSc Economics and Accounting

Duration: 3FT Hon

Entry Requirements: ***GCE:*** AAA-ABB. ***SQAH:*** AAAAA-AAABB. ***SQAAH:*** AAA-ABB.

B84 BRUNEL UNIVERSITY

UXBRIDGE
MIDDLESEX UB8 3PH
t: 01895 265265 f: 01895 269790
e: admissions@brunel.ac.uk
// www.brunel.ac.uk

LN14 BSc Economics and Accounting

Duration: 3FT Hon

Entry Requirements: Contact the institution for details.

NL41 BSc Economics and Accounting (Thick SW)

Duration: 4SW Hon

Entry Requirements: Contact the institution for details.

C15 CARDIFF UNIVERSITY

PO BOX 927
30-36 NEWPORT ROAD
CARDIFF CF24 0DE
t: 029 2087 9999 f: 029 2087 6138
e: admissions@cardiff.ac.uk
// www.cardiff.ac.uk

LN14 BScEcon Accounting and Economics

Duration: 3FT Hon

Entry Requirements: ***GCE:*** AAB. ***SQAH:*** AAABB. ***SQAAH:*** AAB. ***IB:*** 35. ***BTEC ND:*** DDD. ***OCR NED:*** D2

C30 UNIVERSITY OF CENTRAL LANCASHIRE

PRESTON
LANCS PR1 2HE
t: 01772 201201 f: 01772 894954
e: uadmissions@uclan.ac.uk
// www.uclan.ac.uk

LNC4 BA Accounting and Economics

Duration: 3FT Hon

Entry Requirements: ***GCE:*** 240-280. ***SQAH:*** AABB-BBBB. ***IB:*** 28. ***BTEC NC:*** DD. ***OCR ND:*** D

LN14 BA Economics and Accounting

Duration: 3FT Hon

Entry Requirements: ***GCE:*** 240-280. ***SQAH:*** AABB-BBBB. ***IB:*** 28. ***BTEC NC:*** DD. ***OCR ND:*** D

C60 CITY UNIVERSITY

NORTHAMPTON SQUARE
LONDON EC1V 0HB
t: 020 7040 5060 f: 020 7040 8995
e: ugadmissions@city.ac.uk
// www.city.ac.uk

LN14 BSc Economics/Accountancy

Duration: 3FT Hon

Entry Requirements: ***GCE:*** ABB. ***SQAH:*** BBBBB. ***IB:*** 34.

C85 COVENTRY UNIVERSITY

THE STUDENT CENTRE
COVENTRY UNIVERSITY
1 GULSON ROAD
COVENTRY CV1 2JH
t: 024 7615 2222 f: 024 7615 2223
e: studentenquiries@coventry.ac.uk
// www.coventry.ac.uk

NLK1 BA Accounting and Economics

Duration: 3FT Hon

Entry Requirements: ***GCE:*** 260-280. ***IB:*** 29. ***BTEC ND:*** DMM. ***OCR NED:*** M2 Interview required.

E14 UNIVERSITY OF EAST ANGLIA

NORWICH NR4 7TJ
t: 01603 591515 f: 01603 458596
e: admissions@uea.ac.uk
// www.uea.ac.uk

NL41 BSc Business Finance and Economics

Duration: 3FT Hon

Entry Requirements: ***GCE:*** ABB-BBB. ***SQAH:*** AAAB. ***SQAAH:*** ABB. ***IB:*** 32. ***BTEC NC:*** DD. ***BTEC ND:*** DDM. ***OCR ND:*** M1 ***OCR NED:*** D2

L1N4 BSc Economics with Accountancy

Duration: 3FT Hon

Entry Requirements: ***GCE:*** ABB-BBB. ***SQAH:*** AABB. ***SQAAH:*** BBB. ***IB:*** 31. ***BTEC NC:*** DD. ***BTEC ND:*** DDM.

E28 UNIVERSITY OF EAST LONDON

DOCKLANDS CAMPUS
UNIVERSITY WAY
LONDON E16 2RD
t: 020 8223 3333 f: 020 8223 2978
e: study@uel.ac.uk
// www.uel.ac.uk

LN14 BA Accounting/Business Economics

Duration: 3FT Hon

Entry Requirements: ***GCE:*** 200. ***IB:*** 24. ***BTEC NC:*** DM. ***BTEC ND:*** MMP. ***OCR ND:*** M1 ***OCR NED:*** P1

L1N4 BA Business Economics with Accounting

Duration: 3FT Hon

Entry Requirements: ***GCE:*** 200. ***IB:*** 24. ***BTEC NC:*** DM. ***BTEC ND:*** MMP. ***OCR ND:*** M1 ***OCR NED:*** P1

E56 THE UNIVERSITY OF EDINBURGH

STUDENT RECRUITMENT & ADMISSIONS
57 GEORGE SQUARE
EDINBURGH EH8 9JU
t: 0131 650 4360 f: 0131 651 1236
e: sra.enquiries@ed.ac.uk
// www.ed.ac.uk/studying/undergraduate/

LN14 MA Economics and Accounting

Duration: 4FT Hon

Entry Requirements: ***GCE:*** AAA-BBB. ***SQAH:*** AABB-BBBB. ***IB:*** 34.

E59 EDINBURGH NAPIER UNIVERSITY

CRAIGLOCKHART CAMPUS
EDINBURGH EH14 1DJ
t: +44 (0)8452 60 60 40 f: 0131 455 6464
e: info@napier.ac.uk
// www.napier.ac.uk

N4L1 BA Accounting with Economics

Duration: 3FT/4FT Ord/Hon

Entry Requirements: ***GCE:*** 230.

E70 THE UNIVERSITY OF ESSEX

WIVENHOE PARK
COLCHESTER
ESSEX CO4 3SQ
t: 01206 873666 f: 01206 873423
e: admit@essex.ac.uk
// www.essex.ac.uk

NL41 BA Accounting with Economics

Duration: 3FT Hon

Entry Requirements: ***GCE:*** 320. ***SQAH:*** AAAB. ***IB:*** 34. ***BTEC NC:*** DD. ***BTEC ND:*** DDM. ***OCR ND:*** D

N4L1 BA Accounting with Economics (four-year)

Duration: 4FT Hon

Entry Requirements: ***GCE:*** 180. ***SQAH:*** CCCD. ***IB:*** 24. ***BTEC NC:*** DM. ***BTEC ND:*** MMP.

G28 UNIVERSITY OF GLASGOW

THE UNIVERSITY OF GLASGOW
THE FRASER BUILDING
65 HILLHEAD STREET
GLASGOW G12 8QF
t: 0141 330 6062 f: 0141 330 2961
e: ugenquiries@gla.ac.uk (UK/EU undergrad enquiries only)
// www.glasgow.ac.uk

LN14 BAcc Accountancy/Economics

Duration: 4FT Hon

Entry Requirements: ***GCE:*** AAB. ***SQAH:*** AAABB. ***IB:*** 34.

H24 HERIOT-WATT UNIVERSITY, EDINBURGH

EDINBURGH CAMPUS
EDINBURGH EH14 4AS
t: 0131 449 5111 f: 0131 451 3630
e: ugadmissions@hw.ac.uk
// www.hw.ac.uk

LN14 MA Economics and Accountancy

Duration: 4FT Hon

Entry Requirements: ***GCE:*** ABC-BBB. ***SQAH:*** AAAB-BBBBC. ***SQAAH:*** BB. ***IB:*** 29.

H36 UNIVERSITY OF HERTFORDSHIRE

UNIVERSITY ADMISSIONS SERVICE
COLLEGE LANE
HATFIELD
HERTS AL10 9AB
t: 01707 284800 f: 01707 284870
// www.herts.ac.uk

NL41 BA Accounting/Economics

Duration: 3FT/4SW Hon

Entry Requirements: ***GCE:*** 260.

H72 THE UNIVERSITY OF HULL

THE UNIVERSITY OF HULL
COTTINGHAM ROAD
HULL HU6 7RX
t: 01482 466100 f: 01482 442290
e: admissions@hull.ac.uk
// www.hull.ac.uk

LN14 BSc Accounting and Business Economics

Duration: 3FT Hon

Entry Requirements: ***GCE:*** 280. ***IB:*** 28.

LNC4 BSc Accounting and Business Economics (International) (4 years)

Duration: 4FT Hon

Entry Requirements: ***GCE:*** 280. ***IB:*** 28.

LND4 BSc Accounting and Business Economics (with Professional Experience) (4 years)

Duration: 4FT Hon

Entry Requirements: ***GCE:*** 280. ***IB:*** 28.

NL41 BSc Accounting and Economics

Duration: 3FT Hon

Entry Requirements: ***GCE:*** 280. ***IB:*** 28.

NL4C BSc Accounting and Economics (International) (4 years)

Duration: 4FT Hon

Entry Requirements: ***GCE:*** 280. ***IB:*** 28.

NLK1 BSc Accounting and Economics (with Professional Experience) (4 years)

Duration: 4FT Hon

Entry Requirements: ***GCE:*** 280. ***IB:*** 28.

K24 THE UNIVERSITY OF KENT

INFORMATION, RECRUITMENT & ADMISSIONS REGISTRY
UNIVERSITY OF KENT
CANTERBURY, KENT CT2 7NZ
t: 01227 827272 f: 01227 827077
e: information@kent.ac.uk
// www.kent.ac.uk

LN14 BA Accounting & Finance and Economics

Duration: 3FT Hon

Entry Requirements: ***GCE:*** 300. ***IB:*** 33. ***BTEC NC:*** DD. ***BTEC ND:*** DMM. ***OCR ND:*** D

L14 LANCASTER UNIVERSITY

THE UNIVERSITY
LANCASTER
LANCASHIRE LA1 4YW
t: 01524 592029 f: 01524 846243
e: ugadmissions@lancaster.ac.uk
// www.lancs.ac.uk

NL41 BA Accounting and Economics

Duration: 3FT Hon

Entry Requirements: ***GCE:*** AAB. ***SQAH:*** ABBBB. ***SQAAH:*** AAB. ***IB:*** 34. ***BTEC ND:*** DDM.

L68 LONDON METROPOLITAN UNIVERSITY

166-220 HOLLOWAY ROAD
LONDON N7 8DB
t: 020 7133 4200
e: admissions@londonmet.ac.uk
// www.londonmet.ac.uk

LN14 BA Accounting and Economics

Duration: 3FT Hon

Entry Requirements: ***GCE:*** 240. ***IB:*** 28.

NL4C BA/BSc Accounting Information Systems and Business Economics

Duration: 3FT Hon

Entry Requirements: ***GCE:*** 240. ***IB:*** 28.

L79 LOUGHBOROUGH UNIVERSITY

LOUGHBOROUGH
LEICESTERSHIRE LE11 3TU
t: 01509 223522 f: 01509 223905
e: admissions@lboro.ac.uk
// www.lboro.ac.uk

L1NK BSc Business Economics and Finance

Duration: 3FT Hon

Entry Requirements: ***GCE:*** AAB. ***SQAH:*** AABBB. ***SQAAH:*** AB. ***IB:*** 34. ***BTEC ND:*** DDM.

L1N4 BSc Economics with Accounting

Duration: 3FT Hon

Entry Requirements: ***GCE:*** AAB. ***SQAH:*** AABBB. ***SQAAH:*** AB. ***IB:*** 34. ***BTEC ND:*** DDM.

M20 THE UNIVERSITY OF MANCHESTER

OXFORD ROAD
MANCHESTER M13 9PL
t: 0161 275 2077 f: 0161 275 2106
e: ug-admissions@manchester.ac.uk
// www.manchester.ac.uk

NL41 BAEcon Accounting and Economics

Duration: 3FT Hon

Entry Requirements: ***GCE:*** AAB. ***SQAH:*** AAAAB. ***SQAAH:*** AAB. ***IB:*** 35. ***BTEC ND:*** DDM. Interview required.

M80 MIDDLESEX UNIVERSITY

MIDDLESEX UNIVERSITY
THE BURROUGHS
LONDON NW4 4BT
t: 020 8411 5555 f: 020 8411 5649
e: enquiries@mdx.ac.uk
// www.mdx.ac.uk

NL41 BSc Accounting and Business Economics

Duration: 3FT Hon

Entry Requirements: ***GCE:*** 200-300. ***IB:*** 28.

N37 UNIVERSITY OF WALES, NEWPORT
CAERLEON CAMPUS
LODGE ROAD
CAERLEON
NEWPORT NP18 3QT
t: 01633 432030 f: 01633 432850
e: admissions@newport.ac.uk
// www.newport.ac.uk

LN14 BSc Accounting and Economics
Duration: 3FT Hon
Entry Requirements: ***GCE:*** 240. ***IB:*** 24.

N38 UNIVERSITY OF NORTHAMPTON
PARK CAMPUS
BOUGHTON GREEN ROAD
NORTHAMPTON NN2 7AL
t: 0800 358 2232 f: 01604 722083
e: admissions@northampton.ac.uk
// www.northampton.ac.uk

N4L1 BA Accounting/Economics
Duration: 3FT Hon
Entry Requirements: ***GCE:*** 220-260. ***SQAH:*** ABB-BBBC. ***IB:*** 24.

L1N4 BA Economics/Accounting
Duration: 3FT Hon
Entry Requirements: ***GCE:*** 220-260. ***SQAH:*** ABB-BBBC. ***IB:*** 24.

P60 UNIVERSITY OF PLYMOUTH
DRAKE CIRCUS
PLYMOUTH PL4 8AA
t: 01752 588037 f: 01752 588050
e: admissions@plymouth.ac.uk
// www.plymouth.ac.uk

L1NK BSc Business Economics with Accounting
Duration: 3FT/4SW Hon
Entry Requirements: ***GCE:*** 240. ***IB:*** 26. ***BTEC NC:*** DD. ***BTEC ND:*** MMM.

Q75 QUEEN'S UNIVERSITY BELFAST
UNIVERSITY ROAD
BELFAST BT7 1NN
t: 028 9097 3838 f: 028 9097 2828
e: admissions@qub.ac.uk
// www.qub.ac.uk

LN14 BSc Economics and Accounting
Duration: 3FT Hon
Entry Requirements: ***GCE:*** ABB-BBBb. ***SQAH:*** ABBBB. ***SQAAH:*** ABB. ***IB:*** 33.

R12 THE UNIVERSITY OF READING
THE UNIVERSITY OF READING
PO BOX 217
READING RG6 6AH
t: 0118 378 8619 f: 0118 378 8924
e: student.recruitment@reading.ac.uk
// www.reading.ac.uk

NL41 BA Accounting and Economics
Duration: 3FT Hon
Entry Requirements: ***GCE:*** AAB. ***SQAH:*** AAAAB. ***SQAAH:*** AAB.

LN14 BSc Accounting and Economics
Duration: 3FT Hon
Entry Requirements: ***GCE:*** AAB. ***SQAH:*** AAAAB. ***SQAAH:*** AAB.

S18 THE UNIVERSITY OF SHEFFIELD
9 NORTHUMBERLAND ROAD
SHEFFIELD S10 2TT
t: 0114 222 1299 f: 0114 222 8032
e: ask@sheffield.ac.uk
// www.sheffield.ac.uk

NL41 BA Accounting & Financial Management and Economics
Duration: 3FT Hon
Entry Requirements: ***GCE:*** ABB. ***SQAH:*** AAAB. ***SQAAH:*** ABB. ***IB:*** 33. ***BTEC ND:*** DDM.

S27 UNIVERSITY OF SOUTHAMPTON
HIGHFIELD
SOUTHAMPTON SO17 1BJ
t: 023 8059 4732 f: 023 8059 3037
e: admissions@soton.ac.uk
// www.southampton.ac.uk

NL41 BSc Accounting and Economics
Duration: 3FT Hon
Entry Requirements: ***GCE:*** AAB. ***IB:*** 34. ***BTEC NC:*** DD. ***BTEC ND:*** DDD.

S72 STAFFORDSHIRE UNIVERSITY
COLLEGE ROAD
STOKE ON TRENT ST4 2DE
t: 01782 292753 f: 01782 292740
e: admissions@staffs.ac.uk
// www.staffs.ac.uk

LN1K BA Accounting and Economics
Duration: 3FT/4SW Hon
Entry Requirements: ***GCE:*** BCC-BB. ***IB:*** 24. Interview required.

S75 THE UNIVERSITY OF STIRLING

STIRLING FK9 4LA
t: 01786 467044 f: 01786 466800
e: admissions@stir.ac.uk
// www.stir.ac.uk

LN14 BAcc Accountancy and Economics

Duration: 4FT Hon

Entry Requirements: ***GCE:*** BCC. ***SQAH:*** BBBB. ***SQAAH:*** AAA-CCC. ***IB:*** 30. ***BTEC ND:*** DMM.

S78 THE UNIVERSITY OF STRATHCLYDE

GLASGOW G1 1XQ
t: 0141 552 4400 f: 0141 552 0775
// www.strath.ac.uk

NL41 BA Accounting and Economics

Duration: 4FT Hon

Entry Requirements: ***GCE:*** AAB. ***SQAH:*** AAAA-AAABB. ***IB:*** 36.

S93 SWANSEA UNIVERSITY

SINGLETON PARK
SWANSEA SA2 8PP
t: 01792 295111 f: 01792 295110
e: admissions@swansea.ac.uk
// www.swansea.ac.uk

L1N4 BA Business Economics with Accounting

Duration: 3FT Hon

Entry Requirements: ***GCE:*** ABB. ***IB:*** 33. ***BTEC ND:*** DDM.

L1NK BSc Financial Economics with Accounting

Duration: 3FT Hon

Entry Requirements: ***GCE:*** ABB. ***IB:*** 33. ***BTEC ND:*** DDM.

U20 UNIVERSITY OF ULSTER

COLERAINE
CO. LONDONDERRY
NORTHERN IRELAND BT52 1SA
t: 028 7032 4221 f: 028 7032 4908
e: online@ulster.ac.uk
// www.ulster.ac.uk

L1N4 BSc Economics with Accountancy Studies

Duration: 4SW Hon

Entry Requirements: ***GCE:*** 240. ***IB:*** 24. ***BTEC NC:*** MM. ***BTEC ND:*** MMM.

FINANCE AND ECONOMICS/ECONOMICS AND FINANCE

A20 THE UNIVERSITY OF ABERDEEN

UNIVERSITY OFFICE
KING'S COLLEGE
ABERDEEN AB24 3FX
t: +44 (0) 1224 273504 f: +44 (0) 1224 272034
e: sras@abdn.ac.uk
// www.abdn.ac.uk/sras

LN13 MA Economics and Finance

Duration: 4FT Hon

Entry Requirements: ***GCE:*** BBB. ***SQAH:*** BBBB. ***IB:*** 30. ***BTEC ND:*** MMM.

B25 BIRMINGHAM CITY UNIVERSITY

CITY NORTH CAMPUS
PERRY BARR
BIRMINGHAM B42 2SU
t: 0121 331 5595 f: 0121 331 7994
e: choices@bcu.ac.uk
// www.bcu.ac.uk/courses/choices/contact-choices

LN13 BA Economics and Finance

Duration: 3FT/4SW Hon

Entry Requirements: ***GCE:*** 260. ***IB:*** 30. ***BTEC NC:*** DD. ***BTEC ND:*** DMM. ***OCR ND:*** D ***OCR NED:*** M3 Interview required. Portfolio required.

B50 BOURNEMOUTH UNIVERSITY

TALBOT CAMPUS
FERN BARROW
POOLE
DORSET BH12 5BB
t: 01202 524111
// www.bournemouth.ac.uk

NL31 BA Finance and Economics

Duration: 3FT/4SW Hon

Entry Requirements: ***GCE:*** 320. ***IB:*** 32. ***BTEC ND:*** DDM.

B72 UNIVERSITY OF BRIGHTON

MITHRAS HOUSE
LEWES ROAD
BRIGHTON BN2 4AT
t: 01273 644644 f: 01273 642607
e: admissions@brighton.ac.uk
// www.brighton.ac.uk

LN13 BSc Economics and Finance

Duration: 3FT/4SW Hon

Entry Requirements: ***GCE:*** BBC. ***IB:*** 30. ***BTEC ND:*** DMM.

B78 UNIVERSITY OF BRISTOL
UNDERGRADUATE ADMISSIONS OFFICE
SENATE HOUSE
TYNDALL AVENUE
BRISTOL BS8 1TH
t: 0117 928 9000 f: 0117 925 1424
e: ug-admissions@bristol.ac.uk
// www.bristol.ac.uk

LN13 BSc Economics and Finance
Duration: 3FT Hon
Entry Requirements: ***GCE:*** A*AA-ABB. ***SQAH:*** AAAAA-AAABB. ***SQAAH:*** AA. ***BTEC ND:*** DDD.

B80 UNIVERSITY OF THE WEST OF ENGLAND, BRISTOL
FRENCHAY CAMPUS
COLDHARBOUR LANE
BRISTOL BS16 1QY
t: +44 (0)117 32 83333 f: +44 (0)117 32 82810
e: admissions@uwe.ac.uk
// www.uwe.ac.uk

LN13 BA Economics of Money, Banking and Finance
Duration: 3FT/4SW Hon
Entry Requirements: ***GCE:*** 280-340.

B84 BRUNEL UNIVERSITY
UXBRIDGE
MIDDLESEX UB8 3PH
t: 01895 265265 f: 01895 269790
e: admissions@brunel.ac.uk
// www.brunel.ac.uk

LND3 BSc Economics and Business Finance
Duration: 3FT Hon
Entry Requirements: ***GCE:*** 280-320. ***IB:*** 32. ***BTEC NC:*** DM. ***BTEC ND:*** DDM.

LNC3 BSc Economics and Business Finance (4 year Thick SW)
Duration: 4SW Hon
Entry Requirements: ***GCE:*** 280-320. ***IB:*** 32. ***BTEC NC:*** DM. ***BTEC ND:*** DDM.

C15 CARDIFF UNIVERSITY
PO BOX 927
30-36 NEWPORT ROAD
CARDIFF CF24 0DE
t: 029 2087 9999 f: 029 2087 6138
e: admissions@cardiff.ac.uk
// www.cardiff.ac.uk

LN13 BSc Econ Economics and Finance
Duration: 3FT Hon
Entry Requirements: ***GCE:*** AAB. ***SQAH:*** AAABB. ***SQAAH:*** AAB. ***IB:*** 35. ***BTEC ND:*** DDD. ***OCR NED:*** D2

D26 DE MONTFORT UNIVERSITY
THE GATEWAY
LEICESTER LE1 9BH
t: 0116 255 1551 f: 0116 250 6204
e: enquiries@dmu.ac.uk
// www.dmu.ac.uk

LN13 BSc Economics and Finance
Duration: 3FT/4SW Hon
Entry Requirements: ***GCE:*** 280. ***IB:*** 24. Interview required.

E56 THE UNIVERSITY OF EDINBURGH
STUDENT RECRUITMENT & ADMISSIONS
57 GEORGE SQUARE
EDINBURGH EH8 9JU
t: 0131 650 4360 f: 0131 651 1236
e: sra.enquiries@ed.ac.uk
// www.ed.ac.uk/studying/undergraduate/

L1N3 MA Economics with Finance
Duration: 4FT Hon
Entry Requirements: ***GCE:*** AAA-BBB. ***SQAH:*** AABB-BBBB. ***IB:*** 34.

E84 UNIVERSITY OF EXETER
LAVER BUILDING
NORTH PARK ROAD
EXETER
DEVON EX4 4QE
t: 01392 263855 f: 01392 263857/262479
e: admissions@exeter.ac.uk
// www.exeter.ac.uk/admissions

LN13 BA Economics and Finance
Duration: 3FT Hon
Entry Requirements: ***GCE:*** AAA-AAB. ***SQAH:*** AAAAB-AAABB. ***SQAAH:*** AAB-ABB. ***BTEC ND:*** DDD.

LNC3 BA Economics and Finance with European Study (4 years)
Duration: 4FT Hon
Entry Requirements: ***GCE:*** AAA-AAB. ***SQAH:*** AAAAB-AAABB. ***SQAAH:*** AAB-ABB. ***BTEC ND:*** DDD.

LND3 BA Economics and Finance with Industrial Experience (4 years)

Duration: 4FT Hon

Entry Requirements: ***GCE:*** AAA-AAB. ***SQAH:*** AAAAB-AAABB. ***SQAAH:*** AAB-ABB. ***BTEC ND:*** DDD.

LN1J BA Economics and Finance with International Study (4 years)

Duration: 4FT Hon

Entry Requirements: ***GCE:*** AAA-AAB. ***SQAH:*** AAAAB-AAABB. ***SQAAH:*** AAB-ABB. ***BTEC ND:*** DDD.

G70 UNIVERSITY OF GREENWICH

GREENWICH CAMPUS
OLD ROYAL NAVAL COLLEGE
PARK ROW
LONDON SE10 9LS
t: 0800 005 006 f: 020 8331 8145
e: courseinfo@gre.ac.uk
// www.gre.ac.uk

L1NH BSc Economics with Banking

Duration: 3FT Hon

Entry Requirements: ***GCE:*** 180. ***IB:*** 24.

H24 HERIOT-WATT UNIVERSITY, EDINBURGH

EDINBURGH CAMPUS
EDINBURGH EH14 4AS
t: 0131 449 5111 f: 0131 451 3630
e: ugadmissions@hw.ac.uk
// www.hw.ac.uk

LN13 MA Economics and Finance

Duration: 4FT Hon

Entry Requirements: ***GCE:*** ABC-BBB. ***SQAH:*** AAAB-BBBBC. ***SQAAH:*** BB. ***IB:*** 29.

H36 UNIVERSITY OF HERTFORDSHIRE

UNIVERSITY ADMISSIONS SERVICE
COLLEGE LANE
HATFIELD
HERTS AL10 9AB
t: 01707 284800 f: 01707 284870
// www.herts.ac.uk

L1N3 BA Economics with Finance

Duration: 3FT/4SW Hon

Entry Requirements: ***GCE:*** 260.

H72 THE UNIVERSITY OF HULL

THE UNIVERSITY OF HULL
COTTINGHAM ROAD
HULL HU6 7RX
t: 01482 466100 f: 01482 442290
e: admissions@hull.ac.uk
// www.hull.ac.uk

LN13 BA Business Economics and Financial Management

Duration: 3FT Hon

Entry Requirements: ***GCE:*** 280. ***IB:*** 28.

LN1H BA Business Economics and Financial Management (International) (4 years)

Duration: 4FT Hon

Entry Requirements: ***GCE:*** 280. ***IB:*** 28.

LNC3 BA Business Economics and Financial Management (with Prof Experience) (4 years)

Duration: 4FT Hon

Entry Requirements: ***GCE:*** 280. ***IB:*** 28.

NL31 BSc Financial Management and Economics

Duration: 3FT Hon

Entry Requirements: ***GCE:*** 280. ***IB:*** 28.

NL3C BSc Financial Management and Economics (International) (4 years)

Duration: 4FT Hon

Entry Requirements: ***GCE:*** 280. ***IB:*** 28.

NLH1 BSc Financial Management and Economics (with Professional Experience) (4 years)

Duration: 4FT Hon

Entry Requirements: ***GCE:*** 280. ***IB:*** 28.

K12 KEELE UNIVERSITY

STAFFS ST5 5BG
t: 01782 734005 f: 01782 632343
e: undergraduate@keele.ac.uk
// www.keele.ac.uk

LNC3 BA Business Economics

Duration: 3FT Hon

Entry Requirements: ***GCE:*** 300-360. ***BTEC ND:*** DDM.

LN13 BA Economics and Finance

Duration: 3FT Hon

Entry Requirements: ***GCE:*** 280-340.

L14 LANCASTER UNIVERSITY
THE UNIVERSITY
LANCASTER
LANCASHIRE LA1 4YW
t: 01524 592029 f: 01524 846243
e: ugadmissions@lancaster.ac.uk
// www.lancs.ac.uk

NL31 BSc Finance and Economics
Duration: 3FT Hon
Entry Requirements: ***GCE:*** AAB. ***SQAH:*** ABBBB. ***SQAAH:*** AAB. ***IB:*** 34.

L34 UNIVERSITY OF LEICESTER
UNIVERSITY ROAD
LEICESTER LE1 7RH
t: 0116 252 5281 f: 0116 252 2447
e: admissions@le.ac.uk
// www.le.ac.uk

LN13 BA Banking and Finance
Duration: 3FT Hon
Entry Requirements: ***GCE:*** ABB. ***SQAH:*** AABBB. ***SQAAH:*** ABB. ***IB:*** 32. ***BTEC ND:*** DDM.

NL31 BSc Banking and Finance
Duration: 3FT Hon
Entry Requirements: ***GCE:*** ABB. ***SQAH:*** AABBB. ***SQAAH:*** ABB. ***IB:*** 32. ***BTEC ND:*** DDM.

L68 LONDON METROPOLITAN UNIVERSITY
166-220 HOLLOWAY ROAD
LONDON N7 8DB
t: 020 7133 4200
e: admissions@londonmet.ac.uk
// www.londonmet.ac.uk

NL3C BA Banking and Business Economics
Duration: 3FT Hon
Entry Requirements: ***GCE:*** 240. ***IB:*** 28.

LNC3 BA Business Economics and Financial Services
Duration: 3FT Hon
Entry Requirements: ***GCE:*** 240. ***IB:*** 28.

LN1H BA Economics and Financial Services
Duration: 3FT Hon
Entry Requirements: ***GCE:*** 240. ***IB:*** 28.

NL31 BA/BSc Banking and Financial Economics
Duration: 3FT Hon
Entry Requirements: ***GCE:*** 240. ***IB:*** 28.

LND3 BSc International Economics & Finance
Duration: 3FT Hon
Entry Requirements: ***GCE:*** 240. ***IB:*** 28.

M20 THE UNIVERSITY OF MANCHESTER
OXFORD ROAD
MANCHESTER M13 9PL
t: 0161 275 2077 f: 0161 275 2106
e: ug-admissions@manchester.ac.uk
// www.manchester.ac.uk

LN13 BA Economics and Finance
Duration: 3FT Hon
Entry Requirements: ***GCE:*** AAB. ***SQAH:*** AAAAB. ***SQAAH:*** AAB. ***IB:*** 35. ***BTEC ND:*** DDM. Interview required.

M40 THE MANCHESTER METROPOLITAN UNIVERSITY
ADMISSIONS OFFICE
ALL SAINTS (GMS)
ALL SAINTS
MANCHESTER M15 6BH
t: 0161 247 2000
// www.mmu.ac.uk

LN13 BSc Economics and Finance
Duration: 3FT Hon
Entry Requirements: ***GCE:*** 240. ***SQAH:*** BBBB. ***SQAAH:*** CCC. ***IB:*** 27.

N91 NOTTINGHAM TRENT UNIVERSITY
DRYDEN CENTRE
BURTON STREET
NOTTINGHAM NG1 4BU
t: +44 (0) 115 848 4200 f: +44 (0) 115 848 8869
e: ask.ntu@ntu.ac.uk
// www.ntu.ac.uk/

LN13 BA Economics, Finance and Banking
Duration: 4SW Hon
Entry Requirements: ***GCE:*** 280. ***IB:*** 25. ***BTEC ND:*** DMM.

LN1H BA Economics, Finance and Banking
Duration: 3FT Hon
Entry Requirements: ***GCE:*** 280. ***IB:*** 25. ***BTEC ND:*** DMM.

P80 UNIVERSITY OF PORTSMOUTH
ACADEMIC REGISTRY
UNIVERSITY HOUSE
WINSTON CHURCHILL AVENUE
PORTSMOUTH PO1 2UP
t: 023 9284 8484 f: 023 9284 3082
e: admissions@port.ac.uk
// www.port.ac.uk

LN13 BSc Economics, Finance and Banking
Duration: 3FT/4SW Hon
Entry Requirements: ***GCE:*** 260-300. ***IB:*** 24. ***BTEC ND:*** DMM.

Q50 QUEEN MARY, UNIVERSITY OF LONDON

MILE END ROAD
LONDON E1 4NS
t: 020 7882 5555 f: 020 7882 5500
e: admissions@qmul.ac.uk
// www.qmul.ac.uk

LN13 BScEcon Economics and Finance

Duration: 3FT Hon

Entry Requirements: ***GCE:*** AAB. ***SQAAH:*** AAB. ***IB:*** 36.

Q75 QUEEN'S UNIVERSITY BELFAST

UNIVERSITY ROAD
BELFAST BT7 1NN
t: 028 9097 3838 f: 028 9097 2828
e: admissions@qub.ac.uk
// www.qub.ac.uk

L1N3 BSc Economics with Finance

Duration: 3FT Hon

Entry Requirements: ***GCE:*** BBB-BBCb. ***SQAH:*** BBBBB. ***SQAAH:*** BBB. ***IB:*** 32.

S18 THE UNIVERSITY OF SHEFFIELD

9 NORTHUMBERLAND ROAD
SHEFFIELD S10 2TT
t: 0114 222 1299 f: 0114 222 8032
e: ask@sheffield.ac.uk
// www.sheffield.ac.uk

L1N3 BSc Economics with Finance

Duration: 3FT Hon

Entry Requirements: ***GCE:*** ABB. ***SQAH:*** AAAB. ***SQAAH:*** ABB. ***IB:*** 33. ***BTEC ND:*** DDM.

S27 UNIVERSITY OF SOUTHAMPTON

HIGHFIELD
SOUTHAMPTON SO17 1BJ
t: 023 8059 4732 f: 023 8059 3037
e: admissions@soton.ac.uk
// www.southampton.ac.uk

L1N3 BSc Economics and Actuarial Science

Duration: 3FT Hon

Entry Requirements: ***GCE:*** AAB. ***IB:*** 34. ***BTEC NC:*** DD. ***BTEC ND:*** DDD.

L1NH BSc Economics and Finance

Duration: 3FT Hon

Entry Requirements: ***GCE:*** AAB. ***IB:*** 34. ***BTEC NC:*** DD. ***BTEC ND:*** DDD.

S75 THE UNIVERSITY OF STIRLING

STIRLING FK9 4LA
t: 01786 467044 f: 01786 466800
e: admissions@stir.ac.uk
// www.stir.ac.uk

LN13 BA Economics and Finance

Duration: 4FT Hon

Entry Requirements: ***GCE:*** BCC. ***SQAH:*** BBBB. ***SQAAH:*** AAA-CCC. ***IB:*** 30. ***BTEC ND:*** MMM.

S78 THE UNIVERSITY OF STRATHCLYDE

GLASGOW G1 1XQ
t: 0141 552 4400 f: 0141 552 0775
// www.strath.ac.uk

LN13 BA Economics and Finance

Duration: 4FT Hon

Entry Requirements: ***GCE:*** ABB. ***SQAH:*** AABB-ABBBC. ***IB:*** 34.

Y50 THE UNIVERSITY OF YORK

ADMISSIONS AND UK/EU STUDENT RECRUITMENT
UNIVERSITY OF YORK
HESLINGTON
YORK YO10 5DD
t: 01904 433533 f: 01904 433538
e: admissions@york.ac.uk
// www.york.ac.uk

L124 BA/BSc Economics, Econometrics and Finance

Duration: 3FT Hon

Entry Requirements: ***GCE:*** AAB. ***SQAH:*** AAAAB. ***SQAAH:*** AB. ***IB:*** 34. ***BTEC ND:*** DDD.

ACCOUNTANCY AND FINANCE/FINANCE AND ACCOUNTANCY

A20 THE UNIVERSITY OF ABERDEEN

UNIVERSITY OFFICE
KING'S COLLEGE
ABERDEEN AB24 3FX
t: +44 (0) 1224 273504 f: +44 (0) 1224 272034
e: sras@abdn.ac.uk
// www.abdn.ac.uk/sras

NN34 MA Accountancy and Finance

Duration: 4FT Hon

Entry Requirements: ***GCE:*** BBB. ***SQAH:*** BBBB. ***IB:*** 30. ***BTEC ND:*** MMM.

A30 UNIVERSITY OF ABERTAY DUNDEE
BELL STREET
DUNDEE DD1 1HG
t: 01382 308080 f: 01382 308081
e: sro@abertay.ac.uk
// www.abertay.ac.uk

N4N3 BA Accounting with Finance
Duration: 3FT Hon
Entry Requirements: Contact the institution for details.

A60 ANGLIA RUSKIN UNIVERSITY
BISHOP HALL LANE
CHELMSFORD
ESSEX CM1 1SQ
t: 0845 271 3333 f: 01245 251789
e: answers@anglia.ac.uk
// www.anglia.ac.uk

N421 BA Accounting and Finance
Duration: 3FT Hon
Entry Requirements: ***GCE:*** 200. ***SQAH:*** BCCC. ***SQAAH:*** CC. ***IB:*** 24.

B06 BANGOR UNIVERSITY
BANGOR
GWYNEDD LL57 2DG
t: 01248 382016/2017 f: 01248 370451
e: admissions@bangor.ac.uk
// www.bangor.ac.uk

NN34 BA Banking/Accounting
Duration: 3FT Hon
Entry Requirements: ***GCE:*** 260-300. ***IB:*** 28.

NN43 BSc Accounting and Banking
Duration: 3FT Hon
Entry Requirements: ***GCE:*** 260-300. ***IB:*** 28.

NN4H BSc Accounting and Finance
Duration: 3FT Hon
Entry Requirements: ***GCE:*** 260-300. ***IB:*** 28.

B16 UNIVERSITY OF BATH
CLAVERTON DOWN
BATH BA2 7AY
t: 01225 383019 f: 01225 386366
e: admissions@bath.ac.uk
// www.bath.ac.uk

NN34 BSc Accounting and Finance
Duration: 3FT Hon
Entry Requirements: ***GCE:*** AAA-AAB. ***SQAAH:*** AAA. ***IB:*** 36.

NN43 BSc Accounting and Finance (4 year sandwich)
Duration: 4SW Hon
Entry Requirements: ***GCE:*** AAA-AAB. ***SQAAH:*** AAA. ***IB:*** 36.

B25 BIRMINGHAM CITY UNIVERSITY
CITY NORTH CAMPUS
PERRY BARR
BIRMINGHAM B42 2SU
t: 0121 331 5595 f: 0121 331 7994
e: choices@bcu.ac.uk
// www.bcu.ac.uk/courses/choices/contact-choices

NN43 BA Accounting and Finance
Duration: 3FT/4SW Hon
Entry Requirements: ***GCE:*** 260. ***IB:*** 30. ***BTEC NC:*** DM. ***BTEC ND:*** MMP. Interview required.

B32 THE UNIVERSITY OF BIRMINGHAM
EDGBASTON
BIRMINGHAM B15 2TT
t: 0121 415 8900 f: 0121 414 7159
e: admissions@bham.ac.uk
// www.bham.ac.uk

N400 BSc Accounting and Finance
Duration: 3FT Hon
Entry Requirements: ***GCE:*** AAB-ABB. ***SQAAH:*** AAB-ABB. ***BTEC NC:*** DD. ***BTEC ND:*** DDD.

B50 BOURNEMOUTH UNIVERSITY
TALBOT CAMPUS
FERN BARROW
POOLE
DORSET BH12 5BB
t: 01202 524111
// www.bournemouth.ac.uk

NN43 BA Accounting and Taxation
Duration: 3FT/4SW Hon
Entry Requirements: ***GCE:*** 320. ***IB:*** 32. ***BTEC ND:*** DDM.

B78 UNIVERSITY OF BRISTOL
UNDERGRADUATE ADMISSIONS OFFICE
SENATE HOUSE
TYNDALL AVENUE
BRISTOL BS8 1TH
t: 0117 928 9000 f: 0117 925 1424
e: ug-admissions@bristol.ac.uk
// www.bristol.ac.uk

NN43 BSc Accounting and Finance
Duration: 3FT Hon
Entry Requirements: ***GCE:*** AAA-ABB. ***SQAH:*** AAAAA-AAABB. ***SQAAH:*** AAA-ABB.

NN34 BSc Accounting and Finance with Study in Continental Europe
Duration: 4FT Hon
Entry Requirements: ***GCE:*** AAA-ABB. ***SQAH:*** AAAAA-AAABB. ***SQAAH:*** AAA-ABB.

B84 BRUNEL UNIVERSITY

UXBRIDGE
MIDDLESEX UB8 3PH
t: 01895 265265 f: 01895 269790
e: admissions@brunel.ac.uk
// www.brunel.ac.uk

NN34 BSc Finance and Accounting

Duration: 3FT Hon

Entry Requirements: ***GCE:*** 280-320. ***IB:*** 32. ***BTEC NC:*** DM. ***BTEC ND:*** DDM.

NN3K BSc Finance and Accounting (4 year Thick SW)

Duration: 4SW Hon

Entry Requirements: ***GCE:*** 280-320. ***IB:*** 32. ***BTEC NC:*** DM. ***BTEC ND:*** DDM.

B90 THE UNIVERSITY OF BUCKINGHAM

YEOMANRY HOUSE
HUNTER STREET
BUCKINGHAM MK18 1EG
t: 01280 820313 f: 01280 822245
e: info@buckingham.ac.uk
// www.buckingham.ac.uk

NN43 BSc Accounting and Financial Management

Duration: 2FT Hon

Entry Requirements: ***GCE:*** 240. ***IB:*** 26. ***BTEC NC:*** DD. ***BTEC ND:*** MMM.

B94 BUCKINGHAMSHIRE NEW UNIVERSITY

QUEEN ALEXANDRA ROAD
HIGH WYCOMBE
BUCKS HP11 2JZ
t: 0800 0565 660 f: 01494 605023
e: admissions@bucks.ac.uk
// www.bucks.ac.uk

NN43 BA Accounting and Finance

Duration: 3FT Hon

Entry Requirements: ***GCE:*** 200-240.

C10 CANTERBURY CHRIST CHURCH UNIVERSITY

NORTH HOLMES ROAD
CANTERBURY
KENT CT1 1QU
t: 01227 782900 f: 01227 782888
e: admissions@canterbury.ac.uk
// www.canterbury.ac.uk

NN43 BSc Accounting and Finance

Duration: 3FT Hon

Entry Requirements: ***GCE:*** 240. ***IB:*** 24.

NN4H BSc Accounting and Finance 'International only'

Duration: 4FT Hon

Entry Requirements: Interview required.

C20 UNIVERSITY OF WALES INSTITUTE, CARDIFF

PO BOX 377
LLANDAFF CAMPUS
WESTERN AVENUE
CARDIFF CF5 2SG
t: 029 2041 6070 f: 029 2041 6286
e: admissions@uwic.ac.uk
// www.uwic.ac.uk

NN43 BA Accounting & Finance

Duration: 3FT Hon

Entry Requirements: ***GCE:*** 240. ***IB:*** 24. ***BTEC NC:*** DD. ***BTEC ND:*** MMM. ***OCR ND:*** D ***OCR NED:*** M3

C30 UNIVERSITY OF CENTRAL LANCASHIRE

PRESTON
LANCS PR1 2HE
t: 01772 201201 f: 01772 894954
e: uadmissions@uclan.ac.uk
// www.uclan.ac.uk

NN43 FdA Accounting and Financial Studies

Duration: 2FT Fdg

Entry Requirements: ***GCE:*** 80-120.

C55 UNIVERSITY OF CHESTER

PARKGATE ROAD
CHESTER CH1 4BJ
t: 01244 511000 f: 01244 511300
e: enquiries@chester.ac.uk
// www.chester.ac.uk

NN4H BSc Accounting and Finance (3 year)

Duration: 3FT Hon

Entry Requirements: ***GCE:*** 220-260. ***SQAH:*** BBBB. ***IB:*** 24. ***BTEC NC:*** DM. ***BTEC ND:*** MMM.

NN4J BSc Accounting and Finance (4 year)

Duration: 4FT Hon

Entry Requirements: ***GCE:*** 220-260. ***SQAH:*** BBBB. ***IB:*** 24. ***BTEC NC:*** DM. ***BTEC ND:*** MMM.

C58 UNIVERSITY OF CHICHESTER

BISHOP OTTER CAMPUS
COLLEGE LANE
CHICHESTER
WEST SUSSEX PO19 6PE
t: 01243 816002 f: 01243 816161
e: admissions@chi.ac.uk
// www.chiuni.ac.uk

NN43 BA Accounting and Finance

Duration: 3FT Hon
Entry Requirements: ***GCE:*** CCC. ***SQAAH:*** CCC. ***IB:*** 28. ***BTEC ND:*** MMM.

NN4H BA Accounting and Finance - Professional Placement

Duration: 4SW Hon
Entry Requirements: ***GCE:*** CCC. ***SQAAH:*** CCC. ***IB:*** 28. ***BTEC ND:*** MMM.

C60 CITY UNIVERSITY

NORTHAMPTON SQUARE
LONDON EC1V 0HB
t: 020 7040 5060 f: 020 7040 8995
e: ugadmissions@city.ac.uk
// www.city.ac.uk

NN43 BSc Accounting and Finance

Duration: 3FT Hon
Entry Requirements: ***GCE:*** AAA. ***IB:*** 35. ***BTEC ND:*** DDD.

C85 COVENTRY UNIVERSITY

THE STUDENT CENTRE
COVENTRY UNIVERSITY
1 GULSON ROAD
COVENTRY CV1 2JH
t: 024 7615 2222 f: 024 7615 2223
e: studentenquiries@coventry.ac.uk
// www.coventry.ac.uk

NN34 BA Accounting and Finance

Duration: 3FT Hon
Entry Requirements: ***GCE:*** 280. ***IB:*** 29. ***BTEC ND:*** DMM. ***OCR NED:*** M2

C99 UNIVERSITY OF CUMBRIA

FUSEHILL STREET
CARLISLE
CUMBRIA CA1 2HH
t: 01228 616234 f: 01228 616235
// www.cumbria.ac.uk

NN34 BA Accounting & Finance Top Up

Duration: 1FT Hon
Entry Requirements: Contact the institution for details.

NN43 BA Accounting and Finance

Duration: 3FT Hon
Entry Requirements: ***Foundation:*** Distinction. ***GCE:*** 240. ***IB:*** 28. ***BTEC NC:*** DD. ***BTEC ND:*** MMM. ***OCR ND:*** D

D86 DURHAM UNIVERSITY

DURHAM UNIVERSITY
UNIVERSITY OFFICE
DURHAM DH1 3HP
t: 0191 334 2000 f: 0191 334 6055
e: admissions@durham.ac.uk
// www.durham.ac.uk

NN43 BA Accounting and Finance

Duration: 3FT Hon
Entry Requirements: ***GCE:*** ABB. ***SQAH:*** AABBB. ***SQAAH:*** ABB. ***IB:*** 34.

NN4H BA Accounting and Finance with Foundation

Duration: 4FT Hon
Entry Requirements: Interview required.

E56 THE UNIVERSITY OF EDINBURGH

STUDENT RECRUITMENT & ADMISSIONS
57 GEORGE SQUARE
EDINBURGH EH8 9JU
t: 0131 650 4360 f: 0131 651 1236
e: sra.enquiries@ed.ac.uk
// www.ed.ac.uk/studying/undergraduate/

NN43 MA Accounting and Finance

Duration: 4FT Hon
Entry Requirements: ***GCE:*** AAA-BBB. ***SQAH:*** AABB-BBBB. ***IB:*** 34.

E59 EDINBURGH NAPIER UNIVERSITY

CRAIGLOCKHART CAMPUS
EDINBURGH EH14 1DJ
t: +44 (0)8452 60 60 40 f: 0131 455 6464
e: info@napier.ac.uk
// www.napier.ac.uk

NN43 BA Accounting and Finance

Duration: 1FT/2FT Ord/Hon
Entry Requirements: Contact the institution for details.

N4N3 BA Accounting with Corporate Finance

Duration: 3FT/4FT Ord/Hon
Entry Requirements: ***GCE:*** 230.

E70 THE UNIVERSITY OF ESSEX

WIVENHOE PARK
COLCHESTER
ESSEX CO4 3SQ
t: 01206 873666 f: 01206 873423
e: admit@essex.ac.uk
// www.essex.ac.uk

NN43 BA Accounting and Finance (four-year)
Duration: 4FT Hon
Entry Requirements: ***GCE:*** 180. ***SQAH:*** CCCD. ***IB:*** 24. ***BTEC NC:*** DM. ***BTEC ND:*** MMP.

E84 UNIVERSITY OF EXETER

LAVER BUILDING
NORTH PARK ROAD
EXETER
DEVON EX4 4QE
t: 01392 263855 f: 01392 263857/262479
e: admissions@exeter.ac.uk
// www.exeter.ac.uk/admissions

NN43 BA Accounting and Finance with Industrial Experience (4 years)
Duration: 4FT Hon
Entry Requirements: ***GCE:*** AAA-AAB. ***SQAH:*** AAAAB-AAABB. ***SQAAH:*** AAB-ABB. ***BTEC ND:*** DDD.

NN4H BA Accounting and Finance with International Study (4 years)
Duration: 4FT Hon
Entry Requirements: ***GCE:*** AAA-AAB. ***SQAH:*** AAAAB-AAABB. ***SQAAH:*** AAB-ABB. ***BTEC ND:*** DDD.

G28 UNIVERSITY OF GLASGOW

THE UNIVERSITY OF GLASGOW
THE FRASER BUILDING
65 HILLHEAD STREET
GLASGOW G12 8QF
t: 0141 330 6062 f: 0141 330 2961
e: ugenquiries@gla.ac.uk (UK/EU undergrad enquiries only)
// www.glasgow.ac.uk

N4N3 BAcc Accountancy with Finance
Duration: 4FT Hon
Entry Requirements: ***GCE:*** AAB. ***SQAH:*** AAABB. ***IB:*** 34.

G50 THE UNIVERSITY OF GLOUCESTERSHIRE

HARDWICK CAMPUS
ST PAUL'S ROAD
CHELTENHAM GL50 4BS
t: 01242 714501 f: 01242 543334
e: admissions@glos.ac.uk
// www.glos.ac.uk

NN34 BA Accounting & Financial Management
Duration: 3FT/4SW Hon
Entry Requirements: ***GCE:*** 280-300.

G70 UNIVERSITY OF GREENWICH

GREENWICH CAMPUS
OLD ROYAL NAVAL COLLEGE
PARK ROW
LONDON SE10 9LS
t: 0800 005 006 f: 020 8331 8145
e: courseinfo@gre.ac.uk
// www.gre.ac.uk

NN43 BA Accounting and Financial Information Systems
Duration: 3FT Hon
Entry Requirements: ***GCE:*** 180. ***IB:*** 24.

NN4H BA Accounting, Audit and Assurance
Duration: 3FT/4SW Hon
Entry Requirements: ***GCE:*** 220-260.

G74 GREENWICH SCHOOL OF MANAGEMENT

MERIDIAN HOUSE
ROYAL HILL
GREENWICH
LONDON SE10 8RD
t: +44(0)20 8516 7800 f: +44(0)20 8516 7801
e: san@greenwich-college.ac.uk
// www.greenwich-college.ac.uk

NN43 BSc Accounting and Finance
Duration: 2FT Hon
Entry Requirements: Contact the institution for details.

H24 HERIOT-WATT UNIVERSITY, EDINBURGH

EDINBURGH CAMPUS
EDINBURGH EH14 4AS
t: 0131 449 5111 f: 0131 451 3630
e: ugadmissions@hw.ac.uk
// www.hw.ac.uk

NN34 MA Accountancy and Finance

Duration: 4FT Hon
Entry Requirements: ***GCE:*** ABC-BBB. ***SQAH:*** AAAB-BBBBC. ***SQAAH:*** BB. ***IB:*** 29.

H36 UNIVERSITY OF HERTFORDSHIRE

UNIVERSITY ADMISSIONS SERVICE
COLLEGE LANE
HATFIELD
HERTS AL10 9AB
t: 01707 284800 f: 01707 284870
// www.herts.ac.uk

NN43 BA Accounting and Finance

Duration: 3FT/4SW Hon
Entry Requirements: ***GCE:*** 280.

N4N3 BA Accounting with Finance

Duration: 3FT/4SW Hon
Entry Requirements: ***GCE:*** 260.

H60 THE UNIVERSITY OF HUDDERSFIELD

QUEENSGATE
HUDDERSFIELD HD1 3DH
t: 01484 473969 f: 01484 472765
e: admissionsandrecords@hud.ac.uk
// www.hud.ac.uk

N4N3 BA Accountancy with Financial Services

Duration: 3FT/4SW Hon
Entry Requirements: ***GCE:*** 300. ***SQAH:*** BBCC. ***IB:*** 28.

H72 THE UNIVERSITY OF HULL

THE UNIVERSITY OF HULL
COTTINGHAM ROAD
HULL HU6 7RX
t: 01482 466100 f: 01482 442290
e: admissions@hull.ac.uk
// www.hull.ac.uk

NN43 BSc Accounting and Financial Management

Duration: 3FT Hon
Entry Requirements: ***GCE:*** 280. ***IB:*** 28.

NN4H BSc Accounting and Financial Management (International) (4 years)

Duration: 4FT Hon
Entry Requirements: ***GCE:*** 280. ***IB:*** 28.

NN4J BSc Accounting and Financial Management (with Professional Experience) (4 years)

Duration: 4FT Hon
Entry Requirements: ***GCE:*** 280. ***IB:*** 28.

K12 KEELE UNIVERSITY

STAFFS ST5 5BG
t: 01782 734005 f: 01782 632343
e: undergraduate@keele.ac.uk
// www.keele.ac.uk

NN34 BA Accounting & Finance

Duration: 3FT Hon
Entry Requirements: ***GCE:*** 320-360.

K24 THE UNIVERSITY OF KENT

INFORMATION, RECRUITMENT & ADMISSIONS REGISTRY
UNIVERSITY OF KENT
CANTERBURY, KENT CT2 7NZ
t: 01227 827272 f: 01227 827077
e: information@kent.ac.uk
// www.kent.ac.uk

N405 BA Accounting & Finance with an optional deferred subject

Duration: 3FT Hon
Entry Requirements: ***GCE:*** 300. ***IB:*** 33. ***BTEC NC:*** DD. ***BTEC ND:*** DMM. ***OCR ND:*** D

K84 KINGSTON UNIVERSITY

STUDENT INFORMATION & ADVICE CENTRE
COOPER HOUSE
40-46 SURBITON ROAD
KINGSTON UPON THAMES KT1 2HX
t: 0844 8552177 f: 020 8547 7080
e: aps@kingston.ac.uk
// www.kingston.ac.uk

NN43 BA Accounting & Finance

Duration: 4SW Hon
Entry Requirements: ***GCE:*** 320. ***IB:*** 27. ***BTEC ND:*** DDM.

NN4H BA Accounting and Finance

Duration: 4FT Hon
Entry Requirements: ***GCE:*** 320. ***SQAH:*** BBBBB. ***SQAAH:*** BBB. ***IB:*** 27. ***BTEC ND:*** DDM.

L14 LANCASTER UNIVERSITY
THE UNIVERSITY
LANCASTER
LANCASHIRE LA1 4YW
t: 01524 592029 f: 01524 846243
e: ugadmissions@lancaster.ac.uk
// www.lancs.ac.uk

NN43 BSc Accounting, Auditing and Finance
Duration: 4SW Hon
Entry Requirements: ***GCE:*** AAA. ***SQAH:*** AAABB. ***SQAAH:*** AAA. ***IB:*** 36. ***BTEC ND:*** DDD. Admissions Test required.

L39 UNIVERSITY OF LINCOLN
ADMISSIONS
BRAYFORD POOL
LINCOLN LN6 7TS
t: 01522 886097 f: 01522 886146
e: admissions@lincoln.ac.uk
// www.lincoln.ac.uk

N400 BA Accountancy and Finance
Duration: 3FT Hon
Entry Requirements: ***GCE:*** 260.

L53 COLEG LLANDRILLO CYMRU
LLANDUDNO ROAD
RHOS-ON-SEA
COLWYN BAY
NORTH WALES LL28 4HZ
t: 01492 542338/339 f: 01492 543052
e: degrees@llandrillo.ac.uk
// www.llandrillo.ac.uk

NN43 FdA Accounting and Finance
Duration: 2FT Fdg
Entry Requirements: Contact the institution for details.

L68 LONDON METROPOLITAN UNIVERSITY
166-220 HOLLOWAY ROAD
LONDON N7 8DB
t: 020 7133 4200
e: admissions@londonmet.ac.uk
// www.londonmet.ac.uk

NN43 BA Accounting and Banking
Duration: 3FT Hon
Entry Requirements: ***GCE:*** 240. ***IB:*** 28.

L72 LONDON SCHOOL OF ECONOMICS AND POLITICAL SCIENCE (UNIVERSITY OF LONDON)
HOUGHTON STREET
LONDON WC2A 2AE
t: 020 7955 7125/7769 f: 020 7955 6001
e: ug-admissions@lse.ac.uk
// www.lse.ac.uk

NN34 BSc Accounting & Finance
Duration: 3FT Hon
Entry Requirements: ***GCE:*** AAB. ***SQAH:*** AAAAA-AAAAB. ***SQAAH:*** AAA-AAB. ***IB:*** 37.

L75 LONDON SOUTH BANK UNIVERSITY
103 BOROUGH ROAD
LONDON SE1 0AA
t: 020 7815 7815 f: 020 7815 8273
e: enquiry@lsbu.ac.uk
// www.lsbu.ac.uk

NN43 BSc International Accounting and Finance
Duration: 1FT Hon
Entry Requirements: Contact the institution for details.

L79 LOUGHBOROUGH UNIVERSITY
LOUGHBOROUGH
LEICESTERSHIRE LE11 3TU
t: 01509 223522 f: 01509 223905
e: admissions@lboro.ac.uk
// www.lboro.ac.uk

NN34 BSc Accounting and Financial Management (4 year SW)
Duration: 4SW Hon
Entry Requirements: ***GCE:*** AAB. ***IB:*** 36. ***BTEC ND:*** DDM.

M10 THE MANCHESTER COLLEGE
OPENSHAW CAMPUS
ASHTON OLD ROAD
OPENSHAW
MANCHESTER M11 2WH
t: 0800 068 8585 f: 0161 920 4103
e: enquiries@themanchestercollege.ac.uk
// www.themanchestercollege.ac.uk

NN43 BA Accounting and Finance
Duration: 1FT Hon
Entry Requirements: HND required.

M20 THE UNIVERSITY OF MANCHESTER

OXFORD ROAD
MANCHESTER M13 9PL
t: 0161 275 2077 f: 0161 275 2106
e: ug-admissions@manchester.ac.uk
// www.manchester.ac.uk

NN43 BA Accounting and Finance

Duration: 3FT Hon

Entry Requirements: ***GCE:*** AAB. ***SQAH:*** AAAAB. ***SQAAH:*** AAB. ***IB:*** 35. ***BTEC ND:*** DDM. Interview required.

M40 THE MANCHESTER METROPOLITAN UNIVERSITY

ADMISSIONS OFFICE
ALL SAINTS (GMS)
ALL SAINTS
MANCHESTER M15 6BH
t: 0161 247 2000
// www.mmu.ac.uk

NN34 BA Accounting and Finance (Sandwich)

Duration: 4SW Hon

Entry Requirements: ***GCE:*** 240. ***IB:*** 28.

N84 THE UNIVERSITY OF NOTTINGHAM

THE ADMISSIONS OFFICE
THE UNIVERSITY OF NOTTINGHAM
UNIVERSITY PARK
NOTTINGHAM NG7 2RD
t: 0115 951 5151 f: 0115 951 4668
// www.nottingham.ac.uk

NN34 BA Finance, Accounting and Management

Duration: 3FT Hon

Entry Requirements: ***GCE:*** AAB. ***SQAAH:*** AAB. ***IB:*** 34. ***BTEC ND:*** DDM.

N91 NOTTINGHAM TRENT UNIVERSITY

DRYDEN CENTRE
BURTON STREET
NOTTINGHAM NG1 4BU
t: +44 (0) 115 848 4200 f: +44 (0) 115 848 8869
e: ask.ntu@ntu.ac.uk
// www.ntu.ac.uk/

NN43 BA Accounting & Finance

Duration: 4SW Hon

Entry Requirements: ***GCE:*** 280. ***IB:*** 25. ***BTEC ND:*** DMM. ***OCR NED:*** M1

NN4H BA Accounting & Finance

Duration: 3FT Hon

Entry Requirements: ***GCE:*** 280. ***IB:*** 25. ***BTEC ND:*** DMM.

O66 OXFORD BROOKES UNIVERSITY

ADMISSIONS OFFICE
HEADINGTON CAMPUS
GIPSY LANE
OXFORD OX3 0BP
t: 01865 483040 f: 01865 483983
e: admissions@brookes.ac.uk
// www.brookes.ac.uk

NN43 BSc Accounting and Finance

Duration: 3FT/4SW Hon

Entry Requirements: ***GCE:*** BBC.

P56 UNIVERSITY CENTRE PETERBOROUGH

PARK CRESCENT
PETERBOROUGH PE1 4DZ
t: 0845 196 5754 f: 01733 767986
e: ucp@peterborough.ac.uk
// www.anglia.ac.uk/ucp

NN43 BSc Accounting and Finance

Duration: 3FT Hon

Entry Requirements: Contact the institution for details.

P80 UNIVERSITY OF PORTSMOUTH

ACADEMIC REGISTRY
UNIVERSITY HOUSE
WINSTON CHURCHILL AVENUE
PORTSMOUTH PO1 2UP
t: 023 9284 8484 f: 023 9284 3082
e: admissions@port.ac.uk
// www.port.ac.uk

NN34 BA Accountancy and Financial Management

Duration: 2FT Hon

Entry Requirements: Contact the institution for details.

N4N3 BA Accounting with Finance

Duration: 3FT/4SW Hon

Entry Requirements: ***GCE:*** 280. ***IB:*** 25. ***BTEC ND:*** DMM.

S03 THE UNIVERSITY OF SALFORD

SALFORD M5 4WT
t: 0161 295 4545 f: 0161 295 3126
e: ugadmissions-exrel@salford.ac.uk
// www.salford.ac.uk

NN34 BSc Finance and Accounting

Duration: 3FT Hon

Entry Requirements: ***GCE:*** 260. ***IB:*** 28. ***BTEC NC:*** DD. ***BTEC ND:*** DMM.

S27 UNIVERSITY OF SOUTHAMPTON

HIGHFIELD
SOUTHAMPTON SO17 1BJ
t: 023 8059 4732 f: 023 8059 3037
e: admissions@soton.ac.uk
// www.southampton.ac.uk

N400 BSc Accounting and Finance

Duration: 3FT Hon

Entry Requirements: ***GCE:*** AAB. ***SQAH:*** AAABB. ***SQAAH:*** AB. ***IB:*** 34. ***BTEC NC:*** DD. ***BTEC ND:*** DDD.

S30 SOUTHAMPTON SOLENT UNIVERSITY

EAST PARK TERRACE
SOUTHAMPTON
HAMPSHIRE SO14 0RT
t: +44 (0) 23 8031 9039 f: + 44 (0)23 8022 2259
e: admissions@solent.ac.uk or ask@solent.ac.uk
// www.solent.ac.uk/

NN34 BA Accountancy and Finance

Duration: 3FT Hon

Entry Requirements: ***GCE:*** 200.

NN3K BA Accountancy and Finance (with foundation)

Duration: 4FT Hon

Entry Requirements: ***GCE:*** 80.

S72 STAFFORDSHIRE UNIVERSITY

COLLEGE ROAD
STOKE ON TRENT ST4 2DE
t: 01782 292753 f: 01782 292740
e: admissions@staffs.ac.uk
// www.staffs.ac.uk

NN43 BA Accounting and Finance

Duration: 3FT Hon

Entry Requirements: ***GCE:*** BCC-BB. ***IB:*** 24. Interview required.

NN34 BA Accounting and Finance (2 year award)

Duration: 2FT Hon

Entry Requirements: ***GCE:*** BCC-BB. ***IB:*** 24. Interview required.

S75 THE UNIVERSITY OF STIRLING

STIRLING FK9 4LA
t: 01786 467044 f: 01786 466800
e: admissions@stir.ac.uk
// www.stir.ac.uk

NN43 BAcc Accountancy and Finance

Duration: 4FT Hon

Entry Requirements: ***GCE:*** CCC. ***SQAH:*** BBBB. ***SQAAH:*** AAA-CCC. ***IB:*** 30. ***BTEC ND:*** DMM.

S78 THE UNIVERSITY OF STRATHCLYDE

GLASGOW G1 1XQ
t: 0141 552 4400 f: 0141 552 0775
// www.strath.ac.uk

NN43 BA Accounting and Finance

Duration: 4FT Hon

Entry Requirements: ***GCE:*** AAB. ***SQAH:*** AAAA-AAABB. ***IB:*** 36.

S84 UNIVERSITY OF SUNDERLAND

STUDENT HELPLINE
THE STUDENT GATEWAY
CHESTER ROAD
SUNDERLAND SR1 3SD
t: 0191 515 3000 f: 0191 515 3805
e: student-helpline@sunderland.ac.uk
// www.sunderland.ac.uk

NN43 BA Accounting and Financial Management

Duration: 1FT Hon

Entry Requirements: Contact the institution for details.

S85 UNIVERSITY OF SURREY

STAG HILL
GUILDFORD
SURREY GU2 7XH
t: +44(0)1483 689305 f: +44(0)1483 689388
e: admissions@surrey.ac.uk
// www.surrey.ac.uk

NN34 BSc Accounting and Financial Management (3 or 4 years)

Duration: 3FT/4SW Hon

Entry Requirements: ***GCE:*** 340. ***SQAH:*** AAAB. ***BTEC ND:*** DDM. Interview required.

S90 UNIVERSITY OF SUSSEX

UNDERGRADUATE ADMISSIONS
SUSSEX HOUSE
UNIVERSITY OF SUSSEX
BRIGHTON BN1 9RH
t: 01273 678416 f: 01273 678545
e: ug.applicants@sussex.ac.uk
// www.sussex.ac.uk

NN43 BSc Accounting and Finance

Duration: 3FT Hon

Entry Requirements: ***GCE:*** ABB. ***SQAH:*** AABBB. ***IB:*** 34.

NN4H BSc Accounting and Finance (with a professional placement year) (4 years)

Duration: 4FT Hon

Entry Requirements: ***GCE:*** ABB. ***SQAH:*** AABBB. ***IB:*** 34.

S93 SWANSEA UNIVERSITY
SINGLETON PARK
SWANSEA SA2 8PP
t: 01792 295111 f: 01792 295110
e: admissions@swansea.ac.uk
// www.swansea.ac.uk

NN43 BSc Accounting and Finance
Duration: 3FT Hon
Entry Requirements: ***GCE:*** ABB. ***BTEC ND:*** DDM.

NN4H BSc Accounting and Finance with a year abroad
Duration: 4FT Hon
Entry Requirements: ***GCE:*** ABB. ***BTEC ND:*** DDM.

T40 THAMES VALLEY UNIVERSITY
ST MARY'S ROAD
EALING
LONDON W5 5RF
t: 0800 036 8888 f: 020 8566 1353
e: learning.advice@tvu.ac.uk
// www.tvu.ac.uk

NN34 BA Accounting and Finance (with foundation year)
Duration: 4FT Hon
Entry Requirements: Contact the institution for details.

NN3K BA Accounting and Finance with Sandwich Year
Duration: 3FT Hon
Entry Requirements: ***GCE:*** 200.

U20 UNIVERSITY OF ULSTER
COLERAINE
CO. LONDONDERRY
NORTHERN IRELAND BT52 1SA
t: 028 7032 4221 f: 028 7032 4908
e: online@ulster.ac.uk
// www.ulster.ac.uk

NN43 BSc Accounting and Managerial Finance
Duration: 4SW Hon
Entry Requirements: ***GCE:*** 340. ***IB:*** 33. ***BTEC ND:*** DDM.

W20 THE UNIVERSITY OF WARWICK
COVENTRY CV4 8UW
t: 024 7652 3723 f: 024 7652 4649
e: ugadmissions@warwick.ac.uk
// www.warwick.ac.uk

NN34 BSc Accounting and Finance
Duration: 3FT Hon
Entry Requirements: ***GCE:*** AAAb-AABb. ***SQAAH:*** AA. ***IB:*** 36.

W76 UNIVERSITY OF WINCHESTER
WINCHESTER
HANTS SO22 4NR
t: 01962 827234 f: 01962 827288
e: course.enquiries@winchester.ac.uk
// www.winchester.ac.uk

NN34 BA Accounting & Finance
Duration: 3FT Hon
Entry Requirements: ***Foundation:*** Distinction. ***GCE:*** 260-300. ***IB:*** 25. ***BTEC NC:*** DD. ***BTEC ND:*** DMM. ***OCR ND:*** D ***OCR NED:*** M2

BANKING COMBINATIONS

B06 BANGOR UNIVERSITY
BANGOR
GWYNEDD LL57 2DG
t: 01248 382016/2017 f: 01248 370451
e: admissions@bangor.ac.uk
// www.bangor.ac.uk

NR33 BA Banking/Italian (4 years)
Duration: 4FT Hon
Entry Requirements: ***GCE:*** 240-260. ***IB:*** 28.

NR34 BA Banking/Spanish (4 years)
Duration: 4FT Hon
Entry Requirements: ***GCE:*** 240-260. ***IB:*** 28.

NR31 BA French/Banking (4 years)
Duration: 4FT Hon
Entry Requirements: ***GCE:*** 240-260. ***IB:*** 28.

NR32 BA German/Banking (4 years)
Duration: 4FT Hon
Entry Requirements: ***GCE:*** 240-260. ***IB:*** 28.

N2N3 BA Management with Banking & Finance
Duration: 3FT Hon
Entry Requirements: ***GCE:*** 260-300. ***IB:*** 28.

N391 BSc Banking and Finance
Duration: 3FT Hon
Entry Requirements: ***GCE:*** 260-300. ***IB:*** 28.

N2NH BSc Management with Banking & Finance
Duration: 3FT Hon
Entry Requirements: ***GCE:*** 260-300. ***IB:*** 28.

B32 THE UNIVERSITY OF BIRMINGHAM
EDGBASTON
BIRMINGHAM B15 2TT
t: 0121 415 8900 f: 0121 414 7159
e: admissions@bham.ac.uk
// www.bham.ac.uk

N3R1 BSc Money, Banking & Finance with French (4 years)
Duration: 4FT Hon
Entry Requirements: ***GCE:*** AAB. ***SQAH:*** AAABB. ***SQAAH:*** AAB-ABB.

N3R2 BSc Money, Banking & Finance with German (4 years)
Duration: 4FT Hon
Entry Requirements: ***GCE:*** AAB. ***SQAH:*** AAABB. ***SQAAH:*** AAB-ABB.

N3R3 BSc Money, Banking & Finance with Italian (4 years)
Duration: 4FT Hon
Entry Requirements: ***GCE:*** AAB. ***SQAH:*** AAABB. ***SQAAH:*** AAB-ABB.

N3R5 BSc Money, Banking & Finance with Portuguese (4 years)
Duration: 4FT Hon
Entry Requirements: ***GCE:*** AAB. ***SQAH:*** AAABB. ***SQAAH:*** AAB-ABB.

N3R4 BSc Money, Banking & Finance with Spanish (4 years)
Duration: 4FT Hon
Entry Requirements: ***GCE:*** AAB. ***SQAH:*** AAABB. ***SQAAH:*** AAB-ABB.

C15 CARDIFF UNIVERSITY
PO BOX 927
30-36 NEWPORT ROAD
CARDIFF CF24 0DE
t: 029 2087 9999 f: 029 2087 6138
e: admissions@cardiff.ac.uk
// www.cardiff.ac.uk

N3R9 BSc Banking and Finance with a European Language (4 years)
Duration: 4FT Hon
Entry Requirements: ***GCE:*** AAB. ***SQAH:*** AAABB. ***SQAAH:*** AAB. ***IB:*** 35. ***BTEC ND:*** DDD. ***OCR NED:*** D2

E28 UNIVERSITY OF EAST LONDON
DOCKLANDS CAMPUS
UNIVERSITY WAY
LONDON E16 2RD
t: 020 8223 3333 f: 020 8223 2978
e: study@uel.ac.uk
// www.uel.ac.uk

N3N8 BSc Finance, Money & Banking with International Tourism Management
Duration: 3FT Hon
Entry Requirements: Contact the institution for details.

N3GC BSc Finance, Money & Banking with Mathematics
Duration: 3FT Hon
Entry Requirements: Contact the institution for details.

NN38 BSc/BA Finance, Money & Banking and International Tourism Management
Duration: 3FT Hon
Entry Requirements: Contact the institution for details.

E70 THE UNIVERSITY OF ESSEX
WIVENHOE PARK
COLCHESTER
ESSEX CO4 3SQ
t: 01206 873666 f: 01206 873423
e: admit@essex.ac.uk
// www.essex.ac.uk

N390 BSc Banking and Finance
Duration: 3FT Hon
Entry Requirements: ***GCE:*** 320. ***SQAH:*** AAAB. ***IB:*** 34. ***BTEC NC:*** DD. ***BTEC ND:*** DDM. ***OCR ND:*** D

L68 LONDON METROPOLITAN UNIVERSITY
166-220 HOLLOWAY ROAD
LONDON N7 8DB
t: 020 7133 4200
e: admissions@londonmet.ac.uk
// www.londonmet.ac.uk

NN31 BA Banking and Business
Duration: 3FT Hon
Entry Requirements: ***GCE:*** 240. ***IB:*** 28.

NM31 BA Banking and Law
Duration: 3FT Hon
Entry Requirements: ***GCE:*** 240. ***IB:*** 28.

N310 BA European Banking & Finance
Duration: 4SW Hon
Entry Requirements: ***GCE:*** 240. ***IB:*** 28.

R12 THE UNIVERSITY OF READING

THE UNIVERSITY OF READING
PO BOX 217
READING RG6 6AH
t: 0118 378 8619 f: 0118 378 8924
e: student.recruitment@reading.ac.uk
// www.reading.ac.uk

N302 BSc Finance and Investment Banking

Duration: 3FT Hon
Entry Requirements: ***GCE:*** 340-360. ***BTEC NC:*** DD. ***BTEC ND:*** DDD. ***OCR ND:*** D ***OCR NED:*** D1

S21 SHEFFIELD HALLAM UNIVERSITY

CITY CAMPUS
HOWARD STREET
SHEFFIELD S1 1WB
t: 0114 225 5555 f: 0114 225 2167
e: admissions@shu.ac.uk
// www.shu.ac.uk

N302 BA Banking and Financial Management

Duration: 3FT/4SW Hon
Entry Requirements: ***GCE:*** 240.

S75 THE UNIVERSITY OF STIRLING

STIRLING FK9 4LA
t: 01786 467044 f: 01786 466800
e: admissions@stir.ac.uk
// www.stir.ac.uk

N310 BA Money, Banking and Finance

Duration: 4FT Hon
Entry Requirements: ***GCE:*** BCC. ***SQAH:*** BBBB. ***SQAAH:*** AAA-CCC. ***IB:*** 30. ***BTEC ND:*** MMM.

BUSINESS COMBINATIONS

A30 UNIVERSITY OF ABERTAY DUNDEE

BELL STREET
DUNDEE DD1 1HG
t: 01382 308080 f: 01382 308081
e: sro@abertay.ac.uk
// www.abertay.ac.uk

NN13 BA Finance & Business

Duration: 4FT Hon
Entry Requirements: ***GCE:*** DDD. ***SQAH:*** BBC. ***IB:*** 24. ***BTEC NC:*** DM. ***BTEC ND:*** MMP.

A40 ABERYSTWYTH UNIVERSITY

WELCOME CENTRE, ABERYSTWYTH UNIVERSITY
PENGLAIS CAMPUS
ABERYSTWYTH
CEREDIGION SY23 3FB
t: 01970 622021 f: 01970 627410
e: ug-admissions@aber.ac.uk
// www.aber.ac.uk

G5N4 BSc Business Information Technology with Accounting & Finance

Duration: 3FT Hon
Entry Requirements: ***GCE:*** 200. ***IB:*** 24.

L1G4 BScEcon Business Economics with Computer Science

Duration: 3FT Hon
Entry Requirements: ***GCE:*** 280. ***IB:*** 27.

N310 BScEcon Business Finance

Duration: 3FT Hon
Entry Requirements: ***GCE:*** 280. ***IB:*** 27.

A80 ASTON UNIVERSITY, BIRMINGHAM

ASTON TRIANGLE
BIRMINGHAM B4 7ET
t: 0121 204 4444 f: 0121 204 3696
e: admissions@aston.ac.uk
// www.aston.ac.uk

NG45 BSc Business Computing and IT

Duration: 4SW Hon
Entry Requirements: ***GCE:*** 320-340. ***SQAH:*** AAAAB-AAABB. ***SQAAH:*** AAB-ABB. ***IB:*** 34. ***BTEC ND:*** DDM. ***OCR NED:*** D2

LNC1 BSc International Business and Economics

Duration: 4SW Hon
Entry Requirements: ***GCE:*** 320-340. ***SQAH:*** AAAAB-AAABB. ***SQAAH:*** AAB-ABB. ***IB:*** 34. ***BTEC ND:*** DDM. ***OCR NED:*** D2

B06 BANGOR UNIVERSITY

BANGOR
GWYNEDD LL57 2DG
t: 01248 382016/2017 f: 01248 370451
e: admissions@bangor.ac.uk
// www.bangor.ac.uk

NN13 BA Business Studies and Finance

Duration: 3FT Hon
Entry Requirements: ***GCE:*** 260-300. ***IB:*** 28.

NN1H BSc Business Studies and Finance

Duration: 3FT Hon
Entry Requirements: ***GCE:*** 260-300. ***IB:*** 28.

B25 BIRMINGHAM CITY UNIVERSITY

CITY NORTH CAMPUS
PERRY BARR
BIRMINGHAM B42 2SU
t: 0121 331 5595 f: 0121 331 7994
e: choices@bcu.ac.uk
// www.bcu.ac.uk/courses/choices/contact-choices

NN41 BA Accountancy and Business

Duration: 3FT/4SW Hon

Entry Requirements: ***GCE:*** 260. ***IB:*** 30. ***BTEC NC:*** DM. ***BTEC ND:*** MMP. Interview required.

MN24 BA Accountancy and Business Law

Duration: 3FT/4SW Hon

Entry Requirements: ***GCE:*** 260. ***IB:*** 30. ***BTEC NC:*** DD. ***BTEC ND:*** DMM. ***OCR ND:*** D ***OCR NED:*** M3 Interview required. Portfolio required.

MN23 BA Business Law and Finance

Duration: 3FT/4SW Hon

Entry Requirements: ***GCE:*** 260. ***IB:*** 30. ***BTEC NC:*** DD. ***BTEC ND:*** DMM. ***OCR ND:*** D ***OCR NED:*** M3 Interview required. Portfolio required.

NL11 BA Business and Economics

Duration: 3FT/4SW Hon

Entry Requirements: ***GCE:*** 260. ***IB:*** 30. ***BTEC NC:*** DD. ***BTEC ND:*** DMM. ***OCR ND:*** D ***OCR NED:*** M3 Interview required. Portfolio required.

NN13 BA Business and Finance

Duration: 3FT/4SW Hon

Entry Requirements: ***GCE:*** 260. ***IB:*** 30. ***BTEC NC:*** DD. ***BTEC ND:*** DMM. ***OCR ND:*** D ***OCR NED:*** M3 Interview required. Portfolio required.

B44 THE UNIVERSITY OF BOLTON

DEANE ROAD
BOLTON BL3 5AB
t: 01204 900600 f: 01204 399074
e: enquiries@bolton.ac.uk
// www.bolton.ac.uk

NN14 BA Accountancy and Business Management

Duration: 3FT Hon

Entry Requirements: ***GCE:*** 260. ***IB:*** 24. ***BTEC ND:*** DMM.

B50 BOURNEMOUTH UNIVERSITY

TALBOT CAMPUS
FERN BARROW
POOLE
DORSET BH12 5BB
t: 01202 524111
// www.bournemouth.ac.uk

NN41 BA Accounting and Business

Duration: 3FT/4SW Hon

Entry Requirements: ***GCE:*** 320. ***IB:*** 32. ***BTEC ND:*** DDM.

NN13 BA Finance and Business

Duration: 4SW Hon

Entry Requirements: ***GCE:*** 320. ***IB:*** 32. ***BTEC ND:*** DDM.

B56 THE UNIVERSITY OF BRADFORD

RICHMOND ROAD
BRADFORD
WEST YORKSHIRE BD7 1DP
t: 0800 073 1225 f: 01274 235585
e: course-enquiries@bradford.ac.uk
// www.bradford.ac.uk

NL11 BSc International Business Economics

Duration: 1FT Hon

Entry Requirements: Contact the institution for details.

B72 UNIVERSITY OF BRIGHTON

MITHRAS HOUSE
LEWES ROAD
BRIGHTON BN2 4AT
t: 01273 644644 f: 01273 642607
e: admissions@brighton.ac.uk
// www.brighton.ac.uk

N2N3 BA Business Management with Finance

Duration: 3FT/4SW Hon

Entry Requirements: ***GCE:*** BBC. ***IB:*** 30. ***BTEC ND:*** DMM.

B80 UNIVERSITY OF THE WEST OF ENGLAND, BRISTOL

FRENCHAY CAMPUS
COLDHARBOUR LANE
BRISTOL BS16 1QY
t: +44 (0)117 32 83333 f: +44 (0)117 32 82810
e: admissions@uwe.ac.uk
// www.uwe.ac.uk

N1N4 BA Business Studies with Accounting & Finance

Duration: 3FT/4SW Hon

Entry Requirements: ***GCE:*** 280-340.

N1L1 BA Business Studies with Economics

Duration: 3FT Hon

Entry Requirements: ***GCE:*** 280-340.

N1N3 FdA Business with Financial Management
Duration: 2FT Fdg
Entry Requirements: ***GCE:*** 80-120.

B84 BRUNEL UNIVERSITY
UXBRIDGE
MIDDLESEX UB8 3PH
t: 01895 265265 f: 01895 269790
e: admissions@brunel.ac.uk
// www.brunel.ac.uk

NN14 BSc Business and Management (Accounting)
Duration: 3FT Hon
Entry Requirements: ***GCE:*** 300-350. ***IB:*** 33. ***BTEC ND:*** DDD. ***OCR NED:*** D1

N2NL BSc Business and Management (Accounting) (4 year Thick SW)
Duration: 4FT Hon
Entry Requirements: ***GCE:*** 300-350. ***IB:*** 33. ***BTEC ND:*** DDD. ***OCR NED:*** D1

B90 THE UNIVERSITY OF BUCKINGHAM
YEOMANRY HOUSE
HUNTER STREET
BUCKINGHAM MK18 1EG
t: 01280 820313 f: 01280 822245
e: info@buckingham.ac.uk
// www.buckingham.ac.uk

L1P5 BSc Economics with Business Journalism
Duration: 2FT Hon
Entry Requirements: ***GCE:*** 240. ***IB:*** 26. ***BTEC NC:*** DD. ***BTEC ND:*** MMM.

LM11 BSc Economics, Business and Law
Duration: 2FT Hon
Entry Requirements: ***GCE:*** 240. ***IB:*** 26. ***BTEC NC:*** DD. ***BTEC ND:*** MMM.

M1N3 LLB Law with Business Finance
Duration: 2FT Hon
Entry Requirements: ***GCE:*** 300. ***IB:*** 28. ***BTEC NC:*** DD. ***BTEC ND:*** DMM. ***OCR NED:*** M2 Interview required.

B94 BUCKINGHAMSHIRE NEW UNIVERSITY
QUEEN ALEXANDRA ROAD
HIGH WYCOMBE
BUCKS HP11 2JZ
t: 0800 0565 660 f: 01494 605023
e: admissions@bucks.ac.uk
// www.bucks.ac.uk

NN13 BA Business and Finance
Duration: 3FT Hon
Entry Requirements: ***GCE:*** 200-240.

C10 CANTERBURY CHRIST CHURCH UNIVERSITY
NORTH HOLMES ROAD
CANTERBURY
KENT CT1 1QU
t: 01227 782900 f: 01227 782888
e: admissions@canterbury.ac.uk
// www.canterbury.ac.uk

N1NL BSc Business Studies with Accounting 'International Only'
Duration: 4FT Hon
Entry Requirements: Interview required.

C15 CARDIFF UNIVERSITY
PO BOX 927
30-36 NEWPORT ROAD
CARDIFF CF24 0DE
t: 029 2087 9999 f: 029 2087 6138
e: admissions@cardiff.ac.uk
// www.cardiff.ac.uk

L1R9 BSc Business Economics with a European Language
Duration: 4FT Hon
Entry Requirements: ***GCE:*** AAB. ***SQAH:*** AAABB. ***SQAAH:*** AAB. ***IB:*** 35. ***BTEC ND:*** DDD. ***OCR NED:*** D2

NN23 BSc Business Management and Finance
Duration: 3FT Hon
Entry Requirements: ***GCE:*** AAB. ***SQAH:*** AAABB. ***SQAAH:*** AAB. ***IB:*** 35. ***BTEC ND:*** DDD. ***OCR NED:*** D2

C20 UNIVERSITY OF WALES INSTITUTE, CARDIFF

PO BOX 377
LLANDAFF CAMPUS
WESTERN AVENUE
CARDIFF CF5 2SG
t: 029 2041 6070 f: 029 2041 6286
e: admissions@uwic.ac.uk
// www.uwic.ac.uk

N1L1 BA Business & Management Studies with Economics

Duration: 3FT Hon

Entry Requirements: ***GCE:*** 240. ***IB:*** 24. ***BTEC NC:*** DD. ***BTEC ND:*** MMM. ***OCR ND:*** D ***OCR NED:*** M3

N1N3 BA Business & Management Studies with Finance

Duration: 3FT Hon

Entry Requirements: ***GCE:*** 240. ***IB:*** 24. ***BTEC NC:*** DD. ***BTEC ND:*** MMM. ***OCR ND:*** D ***OCR NED:*** M3

3N1N HND Business & Management Studies with Finance

Duration: 2FT HND

Entry Requirements: ***GCE:*** 120. ***IB:*** 24. ***BTEC NC:*** MP. ***BTEC ND:*** PPP. ***OCR ND:*** P2 ***OCR NED:*** P3

C30 UNIVERSITY OF CENTRAL LANCASHIRE

PRESTON
LANCS PR1 2HE
t: 01772 201201 f: 01772 894954
e: uadmissions@uclan.ac.uk
// www.uclan.ac.uk

NN14 BA Accounting and Business

Duration: 3FT Hon

Entry Requirements: ***GCE:*** 240-280. ***SQAH:*** AABB-BBBB. ***IB:*** 28. ***BTEC NC:*** DD. ***OCR ND:*** D

NNF4 BA Accounting and International Business

Duration: 3FT Hon

Entry Requirements: ***GCE:*** 240-280. ***SQAH:*** AABB-BBBB. ***IB:*** 28. ***BTEC NC:*** DD. ***OCR ND:*** D

NNC3 BA Business (Foundation Entry) - January start

Duration: 4FT Hon

Entry Requirements: Contact the institution for details.

NNC4 BA Business and Accounting

Duration: 3FT Hon

Entry Requirements: ***GCE:*** 240-280. ***SQAH:*** AABB-BBBB. ***IB:*** 28. ***BTEC NC:*** DD. ***OCR ND:*** D

NN41 BA International Business and Accounting

Duration: 3FT Hon

Entry Requirements: ***GCE:*** 240-280. ***SQAH:*** AABB-BBBB. ***IB:*** 28. ***BTEC NC:*** DD. ***OCR ND:*** D

NL21 BA International Business and Economics

Duration: 3FT Hon

Entry Requirements: ***GCE:*** 240-280. ***SQAH:*** AABB-BBBB. ***IB:*** 28. ***BTEC NC:*** DD. ***OCR ND:*** D

C55 UNIVERSITY OF CHESTER

PARKGATE ROAD
CHESTER CH1 4BJ
t: 01244 511000 f: 01244 511300
e: enquiries@chester.ac.uk
// www.chester.ac.uk

N1L1 BA Business with Economics

Duration: 3FT Hon

Entry Requirements: ***GCE:*** 240. ***SQAH:*** BBBB. ***IB:*** 24. ***BTEC NC:*** DM. ***BTEC ND:*** MMM.

LN11 BA Economics and Business

Duration: 3FT Hon

Entry Requirements: ***GCE:*** 240. ***SQAH:*** BBBB. ***IB:*** 24. ***BTEC NC:*** DM. ***BTEC ND:*** MMM.

LN1C BA Economics and International Business

Duration: 3FT Hon

Entry Requirements: ***GCE:*** 240. ***SQAH:*** BBBB. ***IB:*** 24. ***BTEC NC:*** DM. ***BTEC ND:*** MMM.

N1LC BA International Business with Economics

Duration: 3FT Hon

Entry Requirements: ***GCE:*** 240. ***SQAH:*** BBBB. ***IB:*** 24. ***BTEC NC:*** DM. ***BTEC ND:*** MMM.

L1N1 BSc Economics with Business

Duration: 3FT Hon

Entry Requirements: ***GCE:*** 240. ***SQAH:*** BBBB. ***IB:*** 24. ***BTEC NC:*** DM. ***BTEC ND:*** MMM.

L1NC BSc Economics with International Business

Duration: 3FT Hon

Entry Requirements: ***GCE:*** 240. ***SQAH:*** BBBB. ***IB:*** 24. ***BTEC NC:*** DM. ***BTEC ND:*** MMM.

C58 UNIVERSITY OF CHICHESTER
BISHOP OTTER CAMPUS
COLLEGE LANE
CHICHESTER
WEST SUSSEX PO19 6PE
t: 01243 816002 f: 01243 816161
e: admissions@chi.ac.uk
// www.chiuni.ac.uk

NN13 BA Business Studies and Finance
Duration: 3FT Hon
Entry Requirements: ***GCE:*** CCC. ***SQAAH:*** CCC. ***IB:*** 28. ***BTEC ND:*** MMM.

NN1H BA Business Studies and Finance - Placement
Duration: 4FT Hon
Entry Requirements: ***GCE:*** CCC. ***SQAAH:*** CCC. ***IB:*** 28. ***BTEC ND:*** MMM.

GN54 BA IT Management for Business and Accounting & Finance
Duration: 3FT Hon
Entry Requirements: ***GCE:*** CCC. ***SQAAH:*** CCC. ***IB:*** 28. ***BTEC ND:*** MMM.

GN53 BA IT Management for Business and Finance - Placement
Duration: 4SW Hon
Entry Requirements: ***GCE:*** CCC. ***SQAAH:*** CCC. ***IB:*** 28. ***BTEC ND:*** MMM.

C85 COVENTRY UNIVERSITY
THE STUDENT CENTRE
COVENTRY UNIVERSITY
1 GULSON ROAD
COVENTRY CV1 2JH
t: 024 7615 2222 f: 024 7615 2223
e: studentenquiries@coventry.ac.uk
// www.coventry.ac.uk

NN14 BA Business and Accounting
Duration: 3FT Hon
Entry Requirements: ***GCE:*** 260-280. ***IB:*** 29. ***BTEC ND:*** DMM. ***OCR NED:*** M2

LN1C BA Business and Economics
Duration: 3FT Hon
Entry Requirements: ***GCE:*** 260-280. ***IB:*** 29. ***BTEC ND:*** DMM. ***OCR NED:*** M2

D26 DE MONTFORT UNIVERSITY
THE GATEWAY
LEICESTER LE1 9BH
t: 0116 255 1551 f: 0116 250 6204
e: enquiries@dmu.ac.uk
// www.dmu.ac.uk

NN14 BA Accounting and Business
Duration: 3FT/4SW Hon
Entry Requirements: ***GCE:*** 240. ***IB:*** 24. ***BTEC NC:*** DD. ***BTEC ND:*** MMM. ***OCR ND:*** D ***OCR NED:*** M3 Interview required.

NL21 BA Business Management and Economics
Duration: 3FT/4SW Hon
Entry Requirements: ***GCE:*** 280. ***IB:*** 24. Interview required.

NN31 BA Business and Finance
Duration: 3FT/4SW Hon
Entry Requirements: ***GCE:*** 280. ***IB:*** 24. Interview required.

D39 UNIVERSITY OF DERBY
KEDLESTON ROAD
DERBY DE22 1GB
t: 08701 202330 f: 01332 597724
e: askadmissions@derby.ac.uk
// www.derby.ac.uk

NN24 BA Accounting and Business Management
Duration: 3FT Hon
Entry Requirements: ***Foundation:*** Merit. ***GCE:*** 180-240. ***IB:*** 26. ***BTEC NC:*** DM. ***BTEC ND:*** MMP.

NN13 BA Business (Finance)
Duration: 3FT Hon
Entry Requirements: ***Foundation:*** Distinction. ***GCE:*** 240. ***IB:*** 26. ***BTEC NC:*** DD. ***BTEC ND:*** MMM. ***OCR ND:*** D ***OCR NED:*** M3

D65 UNIVERSITY OF DUNDEE
DUNDEE DD1 4HN
t: 01382 383838 f: 01382 388150
e: ContactUs@dundee.ac.uk
// www.dundee.ac.uk/admissions/undergraduate/

L1N5 BSc Business Economics with Marketing
Duration: 4FT Hon
Entry Requirements: ***GCE:*** BCC. ***SQAH:*** BBBB. ***IB:*** 30. ***BTEC ND:*** DMM.

N1N3 BSc International Business with Financial Management
Duration: 4FT Hon
Entry Requirements: ***GCE:*** BCC. ***SQAH:*** BBBB. ***IB:*** 30. ***BTEC ND:*** DMM.

TLN0 MA American Studies and Business Economics with Marketing

Duration: 4FT Hon

Entry Requirements: ***GCE:*** BCC. ***SQAH:*** BBBB. ***IB:*** 30. ***BTEC ND:*** DMM.

LN15 MA Business Economics with Marketing

Duration: 4FT Hon

Entry Requirements: ***GCE:*** BCC. ***SQAH:*** BBBB. ***IB:*** 30. ***BTEC ND:*** DMM.

LNR0 MA Business Economics with Marketing and European Studies

Duration: 4FT Hon

Entry Requirements: ***GCE:*** BCC. ***SQAH:*** BBBB. ***IB:*** 30. ***BTEC ND:*** DMM.

LLN0 MA Business Economics with Marketing and Geography

Duration: 4FT Hon

Entry Requirements: ***GCE:*** BCC. ***SQAH:*** BBBB. ***IB:*** 30. ***BTEC ND:*** DMM.

LNV0 MA Business Economics with Marketing and History

Duration: 4FT Hon

Entry Requirements: ***GCE:*** BCC. ***SQAH:*** BBBB. ***IB:*** 30. ***BTEC ND:*** DMM.

LNG0 MA Business Economics with Marketing and Mathematics

Duration: 4FT Hon

Entry Requirements: ***GCE:*** BCC. ***SQAH:*** BBBB. ***IB:*** 30. ***BTEC ND:*** DMM.

LON0 MA Business Economics with Marketing and Politics

Duration: 4FT Hon

Entry Requirements: ***GCE:*** BCC. ***SQAH:*** BBBB. ***IB:*** 30. ***BTEC ND:*** DMM.

LNC0 MA Business Economics with Marketing and Psychology

Duration: 4FT Hon

Entry Requirements: ***GCE:*** BCC. ***SQAH:*** BBBB. ***IB:*** 30. ***BTEC ND:*** DMM.

LRN0 MA Business Economics with Marketing with French

Duration: 4FT Hon

Entry Requirements: ***GCE:*** BCC. ***SQAH:*** BBBB. ***IB:*** 30. ***BTEC ND:*** DMM.

RLN0 MA Business Economics with Marketing with German

Duration: 4FT Hon

Entry Requirements: ***GCE:*** BCC. ***SQAH:*** BBBB. ***IB:*** 30. ***BTEC ND:*** DMM.

RNL0 MA Business Economics with Marketing with Spanish

Duration: 4FT Hon

Entry Requirements: ***GCE:*** BCC. ***SQAH:*** BBBB. ***IB:*** 30. ***BTEC ND:*** DMM.

NN1H MA International Business and Finance

Duration: 4FT Hon

Entry Requirements: ***GCE:*** BCC. ***SQAH:*** BBBB. ***IB:*** 30. ***BTEC ND:*** DMM.

E14 UNIVERSITY OF EAST ANGLIA

NORWICH NR4 7TJ
t: 01603 591515 f: 01603 458596
e: admissions@uea.ac.uk
// www.uea.ac.uk

GN54 BSc Business Information Systems

Duration: 3FT Hon

Entry Requirements: ***GCE:*** BBB. ***SQAH:*** AABB. ***IB:*** 31. ***BTEC ND:*** DDM.

E28 UNIVERSITY OF EAST LONDON

DOCKLANDS CAMPUS
UNIVERSITY WAY
LONDON E16 2RD
t: 020 8223 3333 f: 020 8223 2978
e: study@uel.ac.uk
// www.uel.ac.uk

L1Q3 BA Business Economics with English Language

Duration: 3FT Hon

Entry Requirements: ***GCE:*** 200. ***IB:*** 24. ***BTEC NC:*** DM. ***BTEC ND:*** MMP.

L1L2 BA Business Economics with International Politics

Duration: 3FT Hon

Entry Requirements: ***GCE:*** 200. ***IB:*** 24. ***BTEC NC:*** DM. ***BTEC ND:*** MMP.

L1G1 BA Business Economics with Mathematics

Duration: 3FT Hon

Entry Requirements: Contact the institution for details.

L1L9 BA Business Economics with Third World Development

Duration: 3FT Hon

Entry Requirements: ***GCE:*** 200. ***IB:*** 24. ***BTEC NC:*** DM. ***BTEC ND:*** MMP.

LP13 BA Business Economics/Film Studies

Duration: 3FT Hon

Entry Requirements: ***GCE:*** 200. ***IB:*** 24. ***BTEC NC:*** DM. ***BTEC ND:*** MMP.

LV11 BA Business Economics/History
Duration: 3FT Hon
Entry Requirements: ***GCE:*** 200. ***IB:*** 24. ***BTEC NC:*** DM. ***BTEC ND:*** MMP.

LL12 BA Business Economics/International Politics
Duration: 3FT Hon
Entry Requirements: ***GCE:*** 200. ***IB:*** 24. ***BTEC NC:*** DM. ***BTEC ND:*** MMP.

PL31 BA Business Economics/Media Studies
Duration: 3FT Hon
Entry Requirements: ***GCE:*** 200. ***IB:*** 24. ***BTEC NC:*** DM. ***BTEC ND:*** MMP.

LLC3 BA Business Economics/Sociology
Duration: 3FT Hon
Entry Requirements: ***GCE:*** 200. ***IB:*** 24. ***BTEC NC:*** DM. ***BTEC ND:*** MMP.

LL19 BA Business Economics/Third World Development
Duration: 3FT Hon
Entry Requirements: ***GCE:*** 200. ***IB:*** 24. ***BTEC NC:*** DM. ***BTEC ND:*** MMP.

NW3P BA Business Finance and Moving Image
Duration: 3FT Hon
Entry Requirements: Contact the institution for details.

NW33 BA Business Finance/Music Culture
Duration: 3FT Hon
Entry Requirements: ***GCE:*** 200. ***IB:*** 24. ***BTEC NC:*** DM. ***BTEC ND:*** MMP. ***OCR ND:*** M1 ***OCR NED:*** P1

L2L1 BA International Politics with Business Economics
Duration: 3FT Hon
Entry Requirements: ***GCE:*** 200. ***IB:*** 24. ***BTEC NC:*** DM. ***BTEC ND:*** MMP.

L3L1 BA Sociology with Business Economics
Duration: 3FT Hon
Entry Requirements: ***GCE:*** 200. ***IB:*** 24. ***BTEC NC:*** DM. ***BTEC ND:*** MMP.

G5NL BA/BSc Accounting/Business Information Systems
Duration: 3FT Hon
Entry Requirements: ***GCE:*** 200. ***IB:*** 24. ***BTEC NC:*** DM. ***BTEC ND:*** MMP. ***OCR ND:*** M1 ***OCR NED:*** P1

G5L1 BA/BSc Business Economics/Information Technology
Duration: 3FT Hon
Entry Requirements: ***GCE:*** 200. ***IB:*** 24. ***BTEC NC:*** DM. ***BTEC ND:*** MMP. ***OCR ND:*** M1 ***OCR NED:*** P1

GN53 BA/BSc Business Finance/Business Information Systems
Duration: 3FT Hon
Entry Requirements: ***GCE:*** 200. ***IB:*** 24. ***BTEC NC:*** DM. ***BTEC ND:*** MMP. ***OCR ND:*** M1 ***OCR NED:*** P1

GL51 BA/BSc Business Information Systems/Business Economics
Duration: 3FT Hon
Entry Requirements: ***GCE:*** 200. ***IB:*** 24. ***BTEC NC:*** DM. ***BTEC ND:*** MMP. ***OCR ND:*** M1 ***OCR NED:*** P1

N3G5 BSc Business Finance with Business Information Systems
Duration: 3FT Hon
Entry Requirements: ***GCE:*** 200. ***IB:*** 24. ***BTEC NC:*** DM. ***BTEC ND:*** MMP. ***OCR ND:*** M1 ***OCR NED:*** P1

N3GM BSc Business Finance with Information Technology
Duration: 3FT Hon
Entry Requirements: ***GCE:*** 200. ***IB:*** 24. ***BTEC NC:*** DM. ***BTEC ND:*** MMP. ***OCR ND:*** M1 ***OCR NED:*** P1

N3G1 BSc Business Finance with Mathematics
Duration: 3FT Hon
Entry Requirements: Contact the institution for details.

H6N3 BSc Electrical & Electronic Engineering with Business Finance
Duration: 3FT Hon
Entry Requirements: ***GCE:*** 220. ***IB:*** 26.

B9N3 BSc Health Studies with Business Finance
Duration: 3FT Hon
Entry Requirements: ***GCE:*** 200. ***IB:*** 24. ***BTEC NC:*** DM. ***BTEC ND:*** MMP. ***OCR ND:*** M1 ***OCR NED:*** P1

G5N3 BSc Information Security Systems with Business Finance
Duration: 3FT Hon
Entry Requirements: ***GCE:*** 200. ***IB:*** 24. ***BTEC NC:*** DM. ***BTEC ND:*** MMP. ***OCR ND:*** M1 ***OCR NED:*** P1

E42 EDGE HILL UNIVERSITY
ORMSKIRK
LANCASHIRE L39 4QP
t: 0800 195 5063 f: 01695 584355
e: enquiries@edgehill.ac.uk
// www.edgehill.ac.uk

NN24 BSc Business and Management (Accounting)
Duration: 3FT Hon
Entry Requirements: ***GCE:*** 280. ***IB:*** 24. ***BTEC NC:*** DM. ***BTEC ND:*** MMP. ***OCR ND:*** D ***OCR NED:*** M2

E56 THE UNIVERSITY OF EDINBURGH

STUDENT RECRUITMENT & ADMISSIONS
57 GEORGE SQUARE
EDINBURGH EH8 9JU
t: 0131 650 4360 f: 0131 651 1236
e: sra.enquiries@ed.ac.uk
// www.ed.ac.uk/studying/undergraduate/

NN14 MA Business Studies and Accounting

Duration: 4FT Hon

Entry Requirements: ***GCE:*** AAA-BBB. ***SQAH:*** AABB-BBBB. ***IB:*** 34.

NL11 MA Business Studies and Economics

Duration: 4FT Hon

Entry Requirements: ***GCE:*** AAA-BBB. ***SQAH:*** AABB-BBBB. ***IB:*** 34.

E59 EDINBURGH NAPIER UNIVERSITY

CRAIGLOCKHART CAMPUS
EDINBURGH EH14 1DJ
t: +44 (0)8452 60 60 40 f: 0131 455 6464
e: info@napier.ac.uk
// www.napier.ac.uk

N2N4 BA Business Management with Accounting

Duration: 3FT/4FT Ord/Hon

Entry Requirements: ***GCE:*** 230.

N2L1 BA Business Management with Economics

Duration: 3FT Hon

Entry Requirements: ***GCE:*** 230.

N2N3 BA Business Management with Finance

Duration: 3FT/4FT Ord/Hon

Entry Requirements: ***GCE:*** 230.

N2NH BA Business Management with Financial Services

Duration: 3FT/4FT Ord/Hon

Entry Requirements: ***GCE:*** 230.

N1N3 BA Business Studies with Finance

Duration: 3FT/4FT/5SW Ord/Hon/

Entry Requirements: ***GCE:*** 230.

E77 EUROPEAN BUSINESS SCHOOL, LONDON

INNER CIRCLE
REGENT'S PARK
LONDON NW1 4NS
t: +44 (0)20 7487 7505 f: +44 (0)20 7487 7425
e: ebsl@regents.ac.uk
// www.ebslondon.ac.uk

N1L1 BA International Business with Economics and languages

Duration: 3FT/4FT Hon

Entry Requirements: ***SQAH:*** BBCC. ***SQAAH:*** CC.

N1LC BA International Business with Economics and two languages

Duration: 3FT/4FT Hon

Entry Requirements: ***SQAH:*** BBCC. ***SQAAH:*** CC.

N1N3 BA International Business with Finance and one language

Duration: 3FT/4FT Hon

Entry Requirements: ***SQAH:*** BBCC. ***SQAAH:*** CC.

N1NH BA International Business with Finance and two languages

Duration: 3FT/4FT Hon

Entry Requirements: ***SQAH:*** BBCC. ***SQAAH:*** CC.

E84 UNIVERSITY OF EXETER

LAVER BUILDING
NORTH PARK ROAD
EXETER
DEVON EX4 4QE
t: 01392 263855 f: 01392 263857/262479
e: admissions@exeter.ac.uk
// www.exeter.ac.uk/admissions

NN41 BA Business and Accounting

Duration: 3FT Hon

Entry Requirements: ***GCE:*** AAA-AAB. ***SQAH:*** AAAAB-AAABB. ***SQAAH:*** AAB-ABB. ***BTEC ND:*** DDD.

NN4C BA Business and Accounting with European Study (4 years)

Duration: 4FT Hon

Entry Requirements: ***GCE:*** AAA-AAB. ***SQAH:*** AAAAB-AAABB. ***SQAAH:*** AAB-ABB. ***BTEC ND:*** DDD.

NND4 BA Business and Accounting with Industrial Experience (4 years)

Duration: 4FT Hon

Entry Requirements: ***GCE:*** AAA-AAB. ***SQAH:*** AAAAB-AAABB. ***SQAAH:*** AAB-ABB. ***BTEC ND:*** DDD.

NN1L BA Business and Accounting with International Study (4 years)

Duration: 4FT Hon

Entry Requirements: ***GCE:*** AAA-AAB. ***SQAH:*** AAAAB-AAABB. ***SQAAH:*** AAB-ABB. ***BTEC ND:*** DDD.

F66 FARNBOROUGH COLLEGE OF TECHNOLOGY

BOUNDARY ROAD
FARNBOROUGH
HAMPSHIRE GU14 6SB
t: 01252 407028 f: 01252 407041
e: admissions@farn-ct.ac.uk
// www.farn-ct.ac.uk

NN41 FdA Accounting and Business

Duration: 2FT Fdg

Entry Requirements: ***GCE:*** 40-100. ***BTEC NC:*** PP. ***BTEC ND:*** PPP.

G14 UNIVERSITY OF GLAMORGAN, CARDIFF AND PONTYPRIDD

ENQUIRIES AND ADMISSIONS UNIT
PONTYPRIDD CF37 1DL
t: 0800 716925 f: 01443 654050
e: enquiries@glam.ac.uk
// www.glam.ac.uk

NN1L BA Business and International Accounting

Duration: 1FT Hon

Entry Requirements: HND required.

NN14 FdA Business and Accounting

Duration: 2FT Fdg

Entry Requirements: ***GCE:*** 80-140. ***BTEC NC:*** PP. ***BTEC ND:*** PPP.

G28 UNIVERSITY OF GLASGOW

THE UNIVERSITY OF GLASGOW
THE FRASER BUILDING
65 HILLHEAD STREET
GLASGOW G12 8QF
t: 0141 330 6062 f: 0141 330 2961
e: ugenquiries@gla.ac.uk (UK/EU undergrad enquiries only)
// www.glasgow.ac.uk

GL4C BSc Computing Science and Business Economics

Duration: 4FT Hon

Entry Requirements: ***GCE:*** ABB. ***SQAH:*** ABBB. ***IB:*** 32.

LN16 MA Archaeology/Business Economics

Duration: 4FT Hon

Entry Requirements: ***GCE:*** AAB. ***SQAH:*** AAAB-AABB. ***IB:*** 34.

LNC2 MA Business Economics/Business & Management

Duration: 4FT Hon

Entry Requirements: ***GCE:*** AAB. ***SQAH:*** AAAB-AABB. ***IB:*** 34.

LG14 MA Business Economics/Computing Science

Duration: 4FT Hon

Entry Requirements: ***GCE:*** AAB. ***SQAH:*** AAAB-AABB. ***IB:*** 34.

LV13 MA Business Economics/Economic & Social History

Duration: 4FT Hon

Entry Requirements: ***GCE:*** AAB. ***SQAH:*** AAAB-AABB. ***IB:*** 34.

LLC7 MA Business Economics/Geography

Duration: 4FT Hon

Entry Requirements: ***GCE:*** AAB. ***SQAH:*** AAAB-AABB. ***IB:*** 34.

LG11 MA Business Economics/Mathematics

Duration: 4FT Hon

Entry Requirements: ***GCE:*** AAB. ***SQAH:*** AAAB-AABB. ***IB:*** 34.

LV15 MA Business Economics/Philosophy

Duration: 4FT Hon

Entry Requirements: ***GCE:*** AAB. ***SQAH:*** AAAB-AABB. ***IB:*** 34.

LLC2 MA Business Economics/Politics

Duration: 4FT Hon

Entry Requirements: ***GCE:*** AAB. ***SQAH:*** AAAB-AABB. ***IB:*** 34.

LC18 MA Business Economics/Psychology

Duration: 4FT Hon

Entry Requirements: ***GCE:*** AAB. ***SQAH:*** AAAB-AABB. ***IB:*** 34.

LLC4 MA Business Economics/Public Policy

Duration: 4FT Hon

Entry Requirements: ***GCE:*** AAB. ***SQAH:*** AAAB-AABB. ***IB:*** 34.

LVD2 MA Business Economics/Scottish History

Duration: 4FT Hon

Entry Requirements: ***GCE:*** AAB. ***SQAH:*** AAAB-AABB. ***IB:*** 34.

LGC3 MA Business Economics/Statistics

Duration: 4FT Hon

Entry Requirements: ***GCE:*** AAB. ***SQAH:*** AAAB-AABB. ***IB:*** 34.

RL71 MA Central & East European Studies/Business Economics

Duration: 4FT Hon

Entry Requirements: ***GCE:*** AAB. ***SQAH:*** AAAB-AABB. ***IB:*** 34.

LN12 MA Economics/Business & Management

Duration: 4FT Hon

Entry Requirements: ***GCE:*** AAB. ***SQAH:*** AAAB-AABB. ***IB:*** 34.

LLP1 MA Sociology & Anthropology/Business Economics
Duration: 4FT Hon
Entry Requirements: ***GCE:*** AAB. ***SQAH:*** AAAB-AABB. ***IB:*** 34.

G50 THE UNIVERSITY OF GLOUCESTERSHIRE
HARDWICK CAMPUS
ST PAUL'S ROAD
CHELTENHAM GL50 4BS
t: 01242 714501 f: 01242 543334
e: admissions@glos.ac.uk
// www.glos.ac.uk

NNF3 BA Business Management and Accounting & Financial Management
Duration: 3FT/4SW Hon
Entry Requirements: ***GCE:*** 280-300.

GNMK BA/BSc Business Information Technology and Accounting & Financial Management
Duration: 3FT/4SW Hon
Entry Requirements: ***GCE:*** 280-300.

N4N2 FdA Accounting with Business Management
Duration: 2FT Fdg
Entry Requirements: ***GCE:*** 120.

G53 GLYNDWR UNIVERSITY
PLAS COCH
MOLD ROAD
WREXHAM LL11 2AW
t: 01978 293439 f: 01978 290008
e: sid@glyndwr.ac.uk
// www.glyndwr.ac.uk

NN14 BA Business Accounting
Duration: 3FT Hon
Entry Requirements: ***GCE:*** 200.

N2N4 FdA Business Management with Accounting
Duration: 2FT Fdg
Entry Requirements: ***GCE:*** 100.

G70 UNIVERSITY OF GREENWICH
GREENWICH CAMPUS
OLD ROYAL NAVAL COLLEGE
PARK ROW
LONDON SE10 9LS
t: 0800 005 006 f: 020 8331 8145
e: courseinfo@gre.ac.uk
// www.gre.ac.uk

N1NK BA Business Administration with Accounting & Finance (BITE)
Duration: 3FT Hon
Entry Requirements: Contact the institution for details.

N1NJ BA Business with Finance
Duration: 3FT Hon
Entry Requirements: ***GCE:*** 180. ***IB:*** 24.

N1NL FdA Business Administration with Accounting & Finance (BITE)
Duration: 2FT Fdg
Entry Requirements: Contact the institution for details.

4N1N HND Business with Accounting
Duration: 2FT HND
Entry Requirements: Contact the institution for details.

3N9N HND Business with Finance
Duration: 2FT HND
Entry Requirements: Contact the institution for details.

G80 GRIMSBY INSTITUTE OF FURTHER AND HIGHER EDUCATION
NUNS CORNER
GRIMSBY
NE LINCOLNSHIRE DN34 5BQ
t: 0800 328 3631 f: 01472 315506/879924
e: headmissions@grimsby.ac.uk
// www.grimsby.ac.uk

N2N3 BA Business Management with Finance
Duration: 3FT Hon
Entry Requirements: ***GCE:*** 120-240. ***BTEC NC:*** MP. ***BTEC ND:*** PPP. Interview required. Portfolio required.

N1N4 BA Business with Accounting Management
Duration: 3FT Hon
Entry Requirements: Contact the institution for details.

H24 HERIOT-WATT UNIVERSITY, EDINBURGH

EDINBURGH CAMPUS
EDINBURGH EH14 4AS
t: 0131 449 5111 f: 0131 451 3630
e: ugadmissions@hw.ac.uk
// www.hw.ac.uk

NM32 MA Accountancy and Business Law
Duration: 4FT Hon
Entry Requirements: ***GCE:*** ABC-BBB. ***SQAH:*** AAAB-BBBBC. ***SQAAH:*** BB. ***IB:*** 29.

NN23 MA Business and Finance
Duration: 4FT Hon
Entry Requirements: ***GCE:*** ABC-BBB. ***SQAH:*** AAAB-BBBBC. ***SQAAH:*** BB. ***IB:*** 29.

LM12 MA Economics and Business Law
Duration: 4FT Hon
Entry Requirements: ***GCE:*** ABC-BBB. ***SQAH:*** AAAB-BBBBC. ***SQAAH:*** BB. ***IB:*** 29.

LN12 MA Economics and Business Management
Duration: 4FT Hon
Entry Requirements: ***GCE:*** ABC-BBB. ***SQAH:*** AAAB-BBBBC. ***SQAAH:*** BB. ***IB:*** 29.

NMH2 MA Finance and Business Law
Duration: 4FT Hon
Entry Requirements: ***GCE:*** ABC-BBB. ***SQAH:*** AAAB-BBBBC. ***SQAAH:*** BB. ***IB:*** 29.

H36 UNIVERSITY OF HERTFORDSHIRE

UNIVERSITY ADMISSIONS SERVICE
COLLEGE LANE
HATFIELD
HERTS AL10 9AB
t: 01707 284800 f: 01707 284870
// www.herts.ac.uk

NN4D BA Accounting/Business
Duration: 3FT/4SW Hon
Entry Requirements: ***GCE:*** 260.

NN13 BA Business with Finance
Duration: 3FT/4SW Hon
Entry Requirements: ***GCE:*** 260.

N1L1 BA Business/Economics
Duration: 3FT/4SW Hon
Entry Requirements: ***GCE:*** 260.

NN41 BA/BSc Business Joint Honours (Open Programme)
Duration: 3FT/4SW Hon
Entry Requirements: ***GCE:*** 260.

N1N3 FdA Business with Finance
Duration: 2FT Fdg
Entry Requirements: ***GCE:*** 80.

H54 HOPWOOD HALL COLLEGE

ROCHDALE ROAD
MIDDLETON
MANCHESTER M24 6XH
t: 0161 643 7560 f: 0161 643 2114
e: admissions@hopwood.ac.uk
// www.hopwood.ac.uk

31NN HND Business and Finance
Duration: 2FT HND
Entry Requirements: ***GCE:*** 40. Interview required.

H60 THE UNIVERSITY OF HUDDERSFIELD

QUEENSGATE
HUDDERSFIELD HD1 3DH
t: 01484 473969 f: 01484 472765
e: admissionsandrecords@hud.ac.uk
// www.hud.ac.uk

N4N1 BA Accountancy with Small Businesses
Duration: 3FT/4SW Hon
Entry Requirements: ***GCE:*** 300. ***SQAH:*** BBCC. ***IB:*** 28.

N1N3 BA Business Studies with Financial Services
Duration: 3FT/4SW Hon
Entry Requirements: ***GCE:*** 300. ***SQAH:*** BBBB. ***IB:*** 26.

N1NH BA Business with Financial Services (Top up)
Duration: 1FT Hon
Entry Requirements: HND required.

NN13 FdA Business Development and Finance
Duration: 2FT Fdg
Entry Requirements: Contact the institution for details.

H72 THE UNIVERSITY OF HULL

THE UNIVERSITY OF HULL
COTTINGHAM ROAD
HULL HU6 7RX
t: 01482 466100 f: 01482 442290
e: admissions@hull.ac.uk
// www.hull.ac.uk

LJ19 BA Business Economics and Logistics
Duration: 3FT Hon
Entry Requirements: ***GCE:*** 280. ***IB:*** 28.

LJD9 BA Business Economics and Logistics (International) (4 years)
Duration: 4FT Hon
Entry Requirements: ***GCE:*** 280. ***ID:*** 20.

LJC9 BA Business Economics and Logistics (with Professional Experience) (4 years)
Duration: 4FT Hon
Entry Requirements: ***GCE:*** 280. ***IB:*** 28.

NN14 BA Business and Accounting
Duration: 3FT Hon
Entry Requirements: ***GCE:*** 280. ***IB:*** 28.

NNC4 BA Business and Accounting (International) (4 years)
Duration: 4FT Hon
Entry Requirements: ***GCE:*** 280. ***IB:*** 28.

NND4 BA Business and Accounting (with Professional Experience) (4 years)
Duration: 4FT Hon
Entry Requirements: ***GCE:*** 280. ***IB:*** 28.

NL11 BA Business and Business Economics
Duration: 3FT Hon
Entry Requirements: ***GCE:*** 280. ***IB:*** 28.

NLC1 BA Business and Business Economics (International) (4 years)
Duration: 4FT Hon
Entry Requirements: ***GCE:*** 280. ***IB:*** 28.

NL1C BA Business and Business Economics (with Professional Experience) (4 years)
Duration: 4FT Hon
Entry Requirements: ***GCE:*** 280. ***IB:*** 28.

LN1C BA Business and Economics
Duration: 3FT Hon
Entry Requirements: ***GCE:*** 280. ***IB:*** 28.

LNC1 BA Business and Economics (International) (4 years)
Duration: 4FT Hon
Entry Requirements: ***GCE:*** 280. ***IB:*** 28.

LND1 BA Business and Economics (with Professional Experience) (4 years)
Duration: 4FT Hon
Entry Requirements: ***GCE:*** 280. ***IB:*** 28.

NN13 BA Business and Financial Management
Duration: 3FT Hon
Entry Requirements: ***GCE:*** 280. ***IB:*** 28.

NNC3 BA Business and Financial Management (International) (4 years)
Duration: 4FT Hon
Entry Requirements: ***GCE:*** 280. ***IB:*** 28.

NND3 BA Business and Financial Management (with Professional Experience) (4 years)
Duration: 4FT Hon
Entry Requirements: ***GCE:*** 280. ***IB:*** 28.

LN12 BA Management and Business Economics
Duration: 3FT Hon
Entry Requirements: ***GCE:*** 280. ***IB:*** 28.

LND2 BA Management and Business Economics (International) (4 years)
Duration: 4FT Hon
Entry Requirements: ***GCE:*** 280. ***IB:*** 28.

LNCF BA Management and Business Economics (with Professional Experience) (4 years)
Duration: 4FT Hon
Entry Requirements: ***GCE:*** 280. ***IB:*** 28.

NL51 BA Marketing and Business Economics
Duration: 3FT Hon
Entry Requirements: ***GCE:*** 280. ***IB:*** 28.

NLM1 BA Marketing and Business Economics (International) (4 years)
Duration: 4FT Hon
Entry Requirements: ***GCE:*** 280. ***IB:*** 28.

NL5D BA Marketing and Business Economics (with Professional Experience) (4 years)
Duration: 4FT Hon
Entry Requirements: ***GCE:*** 280. ***IB:*** 28.

L192 BSc (Econ) Economics and Business Economics
Duration: 3FT Hon
Entry Requirements: ***GCE:*** 280. ***IB:*** 28.

L193 BSc(Econ) Economics and Business Economics (International) (4 years)
Duration: 4FT Hon
Entry Requirements: ***GCE:*** 280. ***IB:*** 28.

L194 BSc(Econ) Economics and Business Economics (with Professional Experience) (4 years)
Duration: 4FT Hon
Entry Requirements: ***GCE:*** 280. ***IB:*** 28.

K12 KEELE UNIVERSITY

STAFFS ST5 5BG
t: 01782 734005 f: 01782 632343
e: undergraduate@keele.ac.uk
// www.keele.ac.uk

NN42 BA Accounting and Business Management

Duration: 3FT Hon
Entry Requirements: ***GCE:*** 320-340.

NN41 BA Accounting and International Business

Duration: 3FT Hon
Entry Requirements: ***GCE:*** 320-340.

L1L3 BA Business Economics with Social Science Foundation Year

Duration: 4FT Hon
Entry Requirements: ***GCE:*** 160.

LN19 BA Business Management and Economics

Duration: 3FT Hon
Entry Requirements: ***GCE:*** 280-340.

NN39 BA Business Management and Finance

Duration: 3FT Hon
Entry Requirements: ***GCE:*** 280-340.

LN11 BA Economics and International Business

Duration: 3FT Hon
Entry Requirements: ***GCE:*** 280-340.

NN31 BA Finance and International Business

Duration: 3FT Hon
Entry Requirements: ***GCE:*** 280-340.

K15 KENSINGTON COLLEGE OF BUSINESS

WESLEY HOUSE
4 WILD COURT
HOLBORN
LONDON WC2B 4AU
t: 020 7404 6330 f: 020 7404 6708
e: kcb@kensingtoncoll.ac.uk
// www.kensingtoncoll.ac.uk

NN14 FdA Business and Accounts

Duration: 2FT Fdg
Entry Requirements: Contact the institution for details.

K24 THE UNIVERSITY OF KENT

INFORMATION, RECRUITMENT & ADMISSIONS REGISTRY
UNIVERSITY OF KENT
CANTERBURY, KENT CT2 7NZ
t: 01227 827272 f: 01227 827077
e: information@kent.ac.uk
// www.kent.ac.uk

NN42 BA Accounting & Finance and Business Administration

Duration: 3FT Hon
Entry Requirements: ***GCE:*** 300. ***IB:*** 33. ***BTEC NC:*** DD. ***BTEC ND:*** DMM. ***OCR ND:*** D

N4N1 BA Accounting & Finance with French Business Studies (4 years)

Duration: 4FT Hon
Entry Requirements: ***GCE:*** 300. ***IB:*** 33. ***BTEC NC:*** DD. ***BTEC ND:*** DMM. ***OCR ND:*** D

LN11 BA Business and Economics

Duration: 3FT Hon
Entry Requirements: ***GCE:*** 320. ***IB:*** 34. ***BTEC NC:*** DD. ***BTEC ND:*** DDM. ***OCR ND:*** D ***OCR NED:*** D2

3N1N HND Business (Finance)

Duration: 2FT HND
Entry Requirements: ***GCE:*** 80. ***SQAH:*** BC. ***SQAAH:*** C. ***IB:*** 24. ***BTEC NC:*** MM. ***BTEC ND:*** MMP. ***OCR ND:*** M2 ***OCR NED:*** M3

K84 KINGSTON UNIVERSITY

STUDENT INFORMATION & ADVICE CENTRE
COOPER HOUSE
40-46 SURBITON ROAD
KINGSTON UPON THAMES KT1 2HX
t: 0844 8552177 f: 020 8547 7080
e: aps@kingston.ac.uk
// www.kingston.ac.uk

NL11 BA Business and Economics (Applied)

Duration: 3FT Hon
Entry Requirements: ***GCE:*** 280-360. ***IB:*** 25.

N1N4 BA Business with Accounting

Duration: 3FT/4SW Hon/Ord
Entry Requirements: ***GCE:*** 280. ***SQAH:*** BBCCC. ***SQAAH:*** BCC. ***IB:*** 25. ***BTEC ND:*** DMM.

N1NK BA Business with Accounting

Duration: 4SW Hon
Entry Requirements: ***GCE:*** 280. ***SQAH:*** BBCCC. ***SQAAH:*** BCC. ***IB:*** 25. ***BTEC ND:*** DMM.

N1NL BA Business with Accounting with year abroad

Duration: 4FT Hon
Entry Requirements: ***GCE:*** 280. ***SQAH:*** BBCCC. ***SQAAH:*** BCC. ***IB:*** 25. ***BTEC ND:*** DMM.

L1NC BA Economics (Applied) with Business
Duration: 3FT Hon
Entry Requirements: ***GCE:*** 280-360. ***IB:*** 25.

L1N1 BSc Business Economics
Duration: 3FT Hon
Entry Requirements: ***GCE:*** 260. ***IB:*** 24.

L23 UNIVERSITY OF LEEDS
THE UNIVERSITY OF LEEDS
LEEDS LS2 9JT
t: 0113 343 3999
e: admissions@adm.leeds.ac.uk
// www.leeds.ac.uk

L111 BSc Business & Financial Economics
Duration: 3FT Hon
Entry Requirements: ***GCE:*** AAB. ***SQAH:*** AAAAB. ***SQAAH:*** AAB. ***IB:*** 34.

LN11 BSc International Business and Economics
Duration: 3FT Hon
Entry Requirements: ***GCE:*** AAB. ***SQAH:*** AAAAB. ***SQAAH:*** AAB. ***IB:*** 34.

NN13 BSc International Business and Finance
Duration: 3FT Hon
Entry Requirements: ***GCE:*** AAB. ***SQAH:*** AAAAB. ***SQAAH:*** AAB. ***IB:*** 34.

L24 LEEDS TRINITY UNIVERSITY COLLEGE (FORMERLY LEEDS TRINITY AND ALL SAINTS)
BROWNBERRIE LANE
HORSFORTH
LEEDS LS18 5HD
t: 0113 283 7150 f: 0113 283 7222
e: enquiries@leedstrinity.ac.uk
// www.leedstrinity.ac.uk

NN13 BA Business and Finance
Duration: 3FT Hon
Entry Requirements: ***GCE:*** 200. ***IB:*** 24. ***BTEC NC:*** DM. ***BTEC ND:*** MMP.

L39 UNIVERSITY OF LINCOLN
ADMISSIONS
BRAYFORD POOL
LINCOLN LN6 7TS
t: 01522 886097 f: 01522 886146
e: admissions@lincoln.ac.uk
// www.lincoln.ac.uk

NN13 BA Business and Finance
Duration: 3FT Hon
Entry Requirements: ***GCE:*** 260.

NN41 BA/BSc Business and Accountancy
Duration: 3FT Hon
Entry Requirements: ***GCE:*** 260.

L41 THE UNIVERSITY OF LIVERPOOL
THE FOUNDATION BUILDING
BROWNLOW HILL
LIVERPOOL L69 7ZX
t: 0151 794 2000 f: 0151 708 6502
e: ugrecruitment@liv.ac.uk
// www.liv.ac.uk

LN11 BA Business Economics
Duration: 3FT Hon
Entry Requirements: ***GCE:*** ABB. ***SQAH:*** AABBB. ***SQAAH:*** ABB. ***IB:*** 33. ***BTEC ND:*** DDM.

L51 LIVERPOOL JOHN MOORES UNIVERSITY
ROSCOE COURT
4 RODNEY STREET
LIVERPOOL L1 2TZ
t: 0151 231 5090 f: 0151 231 3462
e: courses@ljmu.ac.uk
// www.ljmu.ac.uk

LN11 BA Business and Economics
Duration: 3FT Hon
Entry Requirements: ***GCE:*** 240. ***IB:*** 26.

L68 LONDON METROPOLITAN UNIVERSITY
166-220 HOLLOWAY ROAD
LONDON N7 8DB
t: 020 7133 4200
e: admissions@londonmet.ac.uk
// www.londonmet.ac.uk

NN41 BA Accounting and Business
Duration: 3FT Hon
Entry Requirements: ***GCE:*** 240. ***IB:*** 28.

LLCF BA Business Economics and International Relations
Duration: 3FT Hon
Entry Requirements: ***GCE:*** 240. ***IB:*** 28.

NL11 BA Business and Economics
Duration: 3FT Hon
Entry Requirements: ***GCE:*** 240. ***IB:*** 28.

NN1H BA Business and Taxation
Duration: 3FT Hon
Entry Requirements: ***GCE:*** 240. ***IB:*** 28.

LN1C BA Economics and International Business
Duration: 3FT Hon
Entry Requirements: ***GCE:*** 240. ***IB:*** 28.

NN4C BA/BSc Accounting Information Systems and Business
Duration: 3FT Hon
Entry Requirements: ***GCE:*** 240. ***IB:*** 28.

GN54 BA/BSc Accounting and Business Information Technology
Duration: 3FT Hon
Entry Requirements: ***GCE:*** 240. ***IB:*** 28.

L75 LONDON SOUTH BANK UNIVERSITY
103 BOROUGH ROAD
LONDON SE1 0AA
t: 020 7815 7815 f: 020 7815 8273
e: enquiry@lsbu.ac.uk
// www.lsbu.ac.uk

N4G5 BA Accounting with Business Information Technology
Duration: 3FT Hon
Entry Requirements: ***GCE:*** 160. ***IB:*** 24. ***BTEC NC:*** MM. ***BTEC ND:*** MPP.

GN54 BSc Business Information Technology and Accounting
Duration: 3FT Hon
Entry Requirements: ***GCE:*** 160. ***IB:*** 24. ***BTEC NC:*** MM. ***BTEC ND:*** MPP.

G5N4 BSc Business Information Technology with Accounting
Duration: 3FT Hon
Entry Requirements: ***GCE:*** 160. ***IB:*** 24. ***BTEC NC:*** MM. ***BTEC ND:*** MPP.

M10 THE MANCHESTER COLLEGE
OPENSHAW CAMPUS
ASHTON OLD ROAD
OPENSHAW
MANCHESTER M11 2WH
t: 0800 068 8585 f: 0161 920 4103
e: enquiries@themanchestercollege.ac.uk
// www.themanchestercollege.ac.uk

NN13 FdA Business and Finance
Duration: 2FT Fdg
Entry Requirements: ***GCE:*** 100.

13NN HND Business and Finance
Duration: 2FT HND
Entry Requirements: ***GCE:*** 100.

M20 THE UNIVERSITY OF MANCHESTER
OXFORD ROAD
MANCHESTER M13 9PL
t: 0161 275 2077 f: 0161 275 2106
e: ug-admissions@manchester.ac.uk
// www.manchester.ac.uk

NL11 BA Business Studies and Economics
Duration: 3FT Hon
Entry Requirements: ***GCE:*** ABB. ***SQAH:*** AABBB. ***SQAAH:*** ABB. ***IB:*** 34. ***BTEC ND:*** DDM. Interview required.

M40 THE MANCHESTER METROPOLITAN UNIVERSITY
ADMISSIONS OFFICE
ALL SAINTS (GMS)
ALL SAINTS
MANCHESTER M15 6BH
t: 0161 247 2000
// www.mmu.ac.uk

N2N3 BA Business Management with Financial Management
Duration: 3FT Hon
Entry Requirements: ***GCE:*** 240.

LN11 BA/BSc Business Economics/Business Enterprise
Duration: 3FT Hon
Entry Requirements: ***GCE:*** 240. ***IB:*** 27.

LP13 BA/BSc Business Economics/Cultural Studies
Duration: 3FT Hon
Entry Requirements: ***GCE:*** 240. ***IB:*** 27.

LW16 BA/BSc Business Economics/European Film
Duration: 3FT Hon
Entry Requirements: ***GCE:*** 240. ***IB:*** 27.

LRC9 BA/BSc Business Economics/European Studies
Duration: 3FT Hon
Entry Requirements: ***GCE:*** 220. ***IB:*** 26.

LL17 BA/BSc Business Economics/Geography
Duration: 3FT Hon
Entry Requirements: ***GCE:*** 260. ***IB:*** 28.

LVC1 BA/BSc Business Economics/History
Duration: 3FT Hon
Entry Requirements: ***GCE:*** 220. ***IB:*** 26.

LN16 BA/BSc Business Economics/Human Resource Management
Duration: 3FT Hon
Entry Requirements: ***GCE:*** 240. ***IB:*** 27.

LNC1 BA/BSc Business Economics/International Business
Duration: 3FT Hon
Entry Requirements: ***GCE:*** 240. ***IB:*** 27.

LLC2 BA/BSc Business Economics/International Politics
Duration: 3FT Hon
Entry Requirements: ***GCE:*** 220. ***IB:*** 26.

LR1X BA/BSc Business Economics/Language(s)
Duration: 3FT/4FT Hon
Entry Requirements: ***GCE:*** 240. ***IB:*** 27.

LQ11 BA/BSc Business Economics/Linguistics
Duration: 3FT Hon
Entry Requirements: ***GCE:*** 240. ***IB:*** 27.

LJ19 BA/BSc Business Economics/Logistics
Duration: 3FT Hon
Entry Requirements: ***GCE:*** 240. ***IB:*** 27.

LVC5 BA/BSc Business Economics/Philosophy
Duration: 3FT Hon
Entry Requirements: ***GCE:*** 220. ***IB:*** 26.

LLD2 BA/BSc Business Economics/Politics
Duration: 3FT Hon
Entry Requirements: ***GCE:*** 220. ***IB:*** 26.

LN1G BA/BSc Business Economics/Project Management
Duration: 3FT Hon
Entry Requirements: ***GCE:*** 240. ***IB:*** 27.

LND2 BA/BSc Business Economics/Public Management Studies
Duration: 3FT Hon
Entry Requirements: ***GCE:*** 220. ***IB:*** 26.

LVC3 BA/BSc Business Economics/Social History
Duration: 3FT Hon
Entry Requirements: ***GCE:*** 220. ***IB:*** 26.

LX1C BA/BSc Business Economics/Teaching English as a Foreign Language
Duration: 3FT Hon
Entry Requirements: ***GCE:*** 240. ***IB:*** 27.

LN18 BA/BSc Business Economics/Tourism
Duration: 3FT Hon
Entry Requirements: ***GCE:*** 240. ***IB:*** 27.

NL1C BA/BSc Business/Business Economics
Duration: 3FT Hon
Entry Requirements: ***GCE:*** 240. ***IB:*** 27.

NL1D BA/BSc Business/Economics
Duration: 3FT Hon
Entry Requirements: ***GCE:*** 240. ***IB:*** 27.

LN1C BA/BSc Economics/Business Enterprise
Duration: 3FT Hon
Entry Requirements: ***GCE:*** 240. ***IB:*** 27.

LN1D BA/BSc Economics/International Business
Duration: 3FT Hon
Entry Requirements: ***GCE:*** 240. ***IB:*** 27.

CL11 BSc Biology/Business Economics
Duration: 3FT Hon
Entry Requirements: ***GCE:*** 220. ***IB:*** 26.

FLC1 BSc Business Economics/Chemistry
Duration: 3FT Hon
Entry Requirements: ***GCE:*** 220. ***IB:*** 26.

LG14 BSc Business Economics/Computer Music Technology
Duration: 3FT Hon
Entry Requirements: ***GCE:*** 220. ***IB:*** 26.

GLK1 BSc Business Economics/Computing
Duration: 3FT Hon
Entry Requirements: ***GCE:*** 220. ***IB:*** 26.

LM19 BSc Business Economics/Criminology
Duration: 3FT Hon
Entry Requirements: ***GCE:*** 240. ***IB:*** 27.

LG1K BSc Business Economics/Digital Media
Duration: 3FT Hon
Entry Requirements: ***GCE:*** 220. ***IB:*** 26.

LP11 BSc Business Economics/Information & Communications
Duration: 3FT Hon
Entry Requirements: ***GCE:*** 220. ***IB:*** 26.

LP1C BSc Business Economics/Information Management
Duration: 3FT Hon
Entry Requirements: ***GCE:*** 220. ***IB:*** 26.

LN12 BSc Business Economics/Management Systems
Duration: 3FT Hon
Entry Requirements: ***GCE:*** 240. ***IB:*** 27.

GLD1 BSc Business Economics/Mathematics
Duration: 3FT Hon
Entry Requirements: ***GCE:*** 220. ***IB:*** 26.

HLP1 BSc Business Economics/Multimedia Technology
Duration: 3FT Hon
Entry Requirements: ***GCE:*** 220. ***IB:*** 26.

LC1V BSc Business Economics/Psychology
Duration: 3FT Hon
Entry Requirements: ***GCE:*** 280. ***IB:*** 29.

LLC3 BSc Business Economics/Sociology
Duration: 3FT Hon
Entry Requirements: ***GCE:*** 240. ***IB:*** 27.

NN13 BSc Business/Financial Management
Duration: 3FT Hon
Entry Requirements: ***GCE:*** 260. ***BTEC ND:*** MMM.

M80 MIDDLESEX UNIVERSITY
MIDDLESEX UNIVERSITY
THE BURROUGHS
LONDON NW4 4BT
t: 020 8411 5555 f: 020 8411 5649
e: enquiries@mdx.ac.uk
// www.mdx.ac.uk

NL11 BA Business and Business Economics
Duration: 3FT Hon
Entry Requirements: ***GCE:*** 200-300. ***IB:*** 28.

LG13 BSc Business Economics and Statistics
Duration: 3FT Hon
Entry Requirements: ***GCE:*** 200-300. ***IB:*** 28.

N21 NEWCASTLE UNIVERSITY
KING'S GATE
NEWCASTLE UPON TYNE NE1 7RU
t: 0191 208 3333 f: 0191 222 6143
e: enquiries@ncl.ac.uk
// www.ncl.ac.uk

NN14 BA Business Accounting and Finance (includes business placement) (4 years)
Duration: 4FT Hon
Entry Requirements: ***GCE:*** AAA-AAB. ***SQAH:*** AAAAA-AAABB.
Interview required.

LN12 BA Economics and Business Management
Duration: 3FT/4SW Hon
Entry Requirements: ***GCE:*** AAB. ***SQAH:*** AAABB. ***IB:*** 34. ***BTEC ND:*** DDM.

N37 UNIVERSITY OF WALES, NEWPORT
CAERLEON CAMPUS
LODGE ROAD
CAERLEON
NEWPORT NP18 3QT
t: 01633 432030 f: 01633 432850
e: admissions@newport.ac.uk
// www.newport.ac.uk

NN14 BA Business and Accounting
Duration: 3FT Hon
Entry Requirements: ***GCE:*** 240. ***IB:*** 24.

NL11 BA Business and Economics
Duration: 3FT Hon
Entry Requirements: ***GCE:*** 240. ***IB:*** 24.

N38 UNIVERSITY OF NORTHAMPTON
PARK CAMPUS
BOUGHTON GREEN ROAD
NORTHAMPTON NN2 7AL
t: 0800 358 2232 f: 01604 722083
e: admissions@northampton.ac.uk
// www.northampton.ac.uk

N4N1 BA Accounting/Business
Duration: 3FT Hon
Entry Requirements: ***GCE:*** 220-260. ***SQAH:*** ABB-BBBC. ***IB:*** 24.

N4G5 BA Accounting/Business Computing Systems
Duration: 3FT Hon
Entry Requirements: ***GCE:*** 220-260. ***SQAH:*** ABB-BBBC. ***IB:*** 24.

NN13 BA Business Entrepreneurship
Duration: 3FT Hon
Entry Requirements: ***GCE:*** 220-260. ***SQAH:*** ABB-BBBC. ***IB:*** 24.

N1LC BA Business Entrepreneurship/Economics
Duration: 3FT Hon
Entry Requirements: ***GCE:*** 220-260. ***SQAH:*** ABB-BBBC. ***IB:*** 24.

N1N4 BA Business/Accounting
Duration: 3FT Hon
Entry Requirements: ***GCE:*** 220-260. ***SQAH:*** ABB-BBBC. ***IB:*** 24.

N1L1 BA Business/Economics
Duration: 3FT Hon
Entry Requirements: ***GCE:*** 220-260. ***SQAH:*** ABB-BBBC. ***IB:*** 24.

L1N1 BA Economics/Business
Duration: 3FT Hon
Entry Requirements: ***GCE:*** 220-260. ***SQAH:*** ABB-BBBC. ***IB:*** 24.

L1NF BA Economics/Business Entrepreneurship
Duration: 3FT Hon
Entry Requirements: ***GCE:*** 220-260. ***SQAH:*** ABB-BBBC. ***IB:*** 24.

G5N4 BSc Business Computing Systems/Accounting
Duration: 3FT Hon
Entry Requirements: ***GCE:*** 220-260. ***SQAH:*** ABB-BBBC. ***IB:*** 24.

NN14 FdA Business (Finance)
Duration: 2FT Fdg
Entry Requirements: ***GCE:*** 60-100. ***SQAH:*** BC-CC. ***IB:*** 24.

41NN HND Business (Finance)
Duration: 2FT HND
Entry Requirements: ***GCE:*** 60-100. ***SQAH:*** BC-CC. ***IB:*** 24.

N77 NORTHUMBRIA UNIVERSITY
TRINITY BUILDING
NORTHUMBERLAND ROAD
NEWCASTLE UPON TYNE NE1 8ST
t: 0191 243 7420 f: 0191 227 4561
e: er.admissions@northumbria.ac.uk
// www.northumbria.ac.uk

N1L1 BA Business with Economics
Duration: 3FT Hon
Entry Requirements: ***GCE:*** 280. ***SQAH:*** BBCCC. ***SQAAH:*** BCC. ***IB:*** 25. ***BTEC ND:*** DMM. ***OCR NED:*** M2

N1N3 BA Business with Finance
Duration: 3FT Hon
Entry Requirements: ***GCE:*** 280. ***SQAH:*** BBCCC. ***SQAAH:*** BCC. ***IB:*** 25. ***BTEC ND:*** DMM. ***OCR NED:*** M2

N91 NOTTINGHAM TRENT UNIVERSITY
DRYDEN CENTRE
BURTON STREET
NOTTINGHAM NG1 4BU
t: +44 (0) 115 848 4200 f: +44 (0) 115 848 8869
e: ask.ntu@ntu.ac.uk
// www.ntu.ac.uk/

NN24 BA Business Management and Accounting & Finance
Duration: 4SW Hon
Entry Requirements: ***GCE:*** 260. ***IB:*** 24. ***BTEC ND:*** MMM.

NNF3 BA Business Management and Accounting & Finance
Duration: 3FT Hon
Entry Requirements: ***GCE:*** 260. ***IB:*** 24. ***BTEC ND:*** MMM.

NL21 BA Business Management and Economics
Duration: 3FT Hon
Entry Requirements: ***GCE:*** 260. ***IB:*** 24. ***BTEC ND:*** MMM.

NL2C BA Business Management and Economics
Duration: 4SW Hon
Entry Requirements: ***GCE:*** 260. ***IB:*** 24. ***BTEC ND:*** MMM.

O66 OXFORD BROOKES UNIVERSITY
ADMISSIONS OFFICE
HEADINGTON CAMPUS
GIPSY LANE
OXFORD OX3 0BP
t: 01865 483040 f: 01865 483983
e: admissions@brookes.ac.uk
// www.brookes.ac.uk

LN13 BSc Economics, Finance and International Business
Duration: 3FT/4SW Hon
Entry Requirements: ***GCE:*** BCC.

P60 UNIVERSITY OF PLYMOUTH
DRAKE CIRCUS
PLYMOUTH PL4 8AA
t: 01752 588037 f: 01752 588050
e: admissions@plymouth.ac.uk
// www.plymouth.ac.uk

L1P1 BSc Business Economics with Information Management
Duration: 3FT/4SW Hon
Entry Requirements: ***GCE:*** 240. ***IB:*** 26. ***BTEC NC:*** DD. ***BTEC ND:*** MMM.

L1N5 BSc Business Economics with Marketing
Duration: 3FT/4SW Hon
Entry Requirements: ***GCE:*** 240. ***IB:*** 26. ***BTEC NC:*** DD. ***BTEC ND:*** MMM.

P80 UNIVERSITY OF PORTSMOUTH
ACADEMIC REGISTRY
UNIVERSITY HOUSE
WINSTON CHURCHILL AVENUE
PORTSMOUTH PO1 2UP
t: 023 9284 8484 f: 023 9284 3082
e: admissions@port.ac.uk
// www.port.ac.uk

NN41 BA Accounting and Business
Duration: 3FT/4SW Hon
Entry Requirements: ***GCE:*** 280. ***IB:*** 25. ***BTEC ND:*** DMM.

L1M2 BA Business Economics with Business Law
Duration: 3FT/4SW Hon
Entry Requirements: ***GCE:*** 260-300. ***IB:*** 24. ***BTEC ND:*** DMM.

NN31 BA Finance and Business
Duration: 3FT/4SW Hon
Entry Requirements: ***GCE:*** 260. ***IB:*** 24. ***BTEC ND:*** DMM.

N3Q3 BA Finance with Business English
Duration: 1FT/2FT Hon
Entry Requirements: Contact the institution for details.

Q50 QUEEN MARY, UNIVERSITY OF LONDON

MILE END ROAD
LONDON E1 4NS
t: 020 7882 5555 f: 020 7882 5500
e: admissions@qmul.ac.uk
// www.qmul.ac.uk

GN13 BSc Mathematics, Business Management and Finance

Duration: 3FT Hon

Entry Requirements: ***GCE:*** 320. ***IB:*** 34.

R12 THE UNIVERSITY OF READING

THE UNIVERSITY OF READING
PO BOX 217
READING RG6 6AH
t: 0118 378 8619 f: 0118 378 8924
e: student.recruitment@reading.ac.uk
// www.reading.ac.uk

DL61 BSc Food Marketing and Business Economics with Industrial Training

Duration: 4FT Hon

Entry Requirements: ***GCE:*** 300. ***BTEC ND:*** DDM. ***OCR NED:*** D2

R20 RICHMOND, THE AMERICAN INTERNATIONAL UNIVERSITY IN LONDON

QUEENS ROAD
RICHMOND
SURREY TW10 6JP
t: 020 8332 9000 f: 020 8332 1596
e: enroll@richmond.ac.uk
// www.richmond.ac.uk

NN13 BA Business Administration: Finance

Duration: 3FT/4FT Hon

Entry Requirements: ***GCE:*** 260. ***IB:*** 33.

S03 THE UNIVERSITY OF SALFORD

SALFORD M5 4WT
t: 0161 295 4545 f: 0161 295 3126
e: ugadmissions-exrel@salford.ac.uk
// www.salford.ac.uk

N1N3 BSc Business Studies with Financial Management

Duration: 3FT Hon

Entry Requirements: ***GCE:*** 240-260. ***IB:*** 28. ***BTEC NC:*** DD. ***BTEC ND:*** MMM. ***OCR ND:*** D ***OCR NED:*** M3

N1L1 BSc Business with Economics

Duration: 3FT Hon

Entry Requirements: Contact the institution for details.

N1LC BSc Business with Economics (with Professional Experience)

Duration: 4SW Hon

Entry Requirements: Contact the institution for details.

N1LD BSc Business with Economics (with Studies in Canada)

Duration: 3FT Hon

Entry Requirements: Contact thc institution for details.

NN23 FdSc Business Management (Finance)

Duration: 2FT Fdg

Entry Requirements: ***GCE:*** 100-120. ***IB:*** 24. ***BTEC NC:*** MP. ***BTEC ND:*** PPP. ***OCR ND:*** P2 ***OCR NED:*** P3

S18 THE UNIVERSITY OF SHEFFIELD

9 NORTHUMBERLAND ROAD
SHEFFIELD S10 2TT
t: 0114 222 1299 f: 0114 222 8032
e: ask@sheffield.ac.uk
// www.sheffield.ac.uk

NL21 BA Business Management and Economics

Duration: 3FT Hon

Entry Requirements: ***GCE:*** ABB. ***SQAH:*** AAAB. ***SQAAH:*** ABB. ***IB:*** 33. ***BTEC ND:*** DDM.

S21 SHEFFIELD HALLAM UNIVERSITY

CITY CAMPUS
HOWARD STREET
SHEFFIELD S1 1WB
t: 0114 225 5555 f: 0114 225 2167
e: admissions@shu.ac.uk
// www.shu.ac.uk

NN14 BA Business and Accounting

Duration: 3FT/4SW Hon

Entry Requirements: ***GCE:*** 240.

NN13 BA Business and Finance (2 year conversion)

Duration: 2FT Hon

Entry Requirements: Contact the institution for details.

NN1H BA Business and Financial Management

Duration: 3FT/4SW Hon

Entry Requirements: ***GCE:*** 240.

S30 SOUTHAMPTON SOLENT UNIVERSITY

EAST PARK TERRACE
SOUTHAMPTON
HAMPSHIRE SO14 0RT
t: +44 (0) 23 8031 9039 f: + 44 (0)23 8022 2259
e: admissions@solent.ac.uk or ask@solent.ac.uk
// www.solent.ac.uk/

N4N1 BA Accountancy (with Business Foundation)

Duration: 4FT Hon

Entry Requirements: ***GCE:*** 80. ***BTEC NC:*** PP. ***BTEC ND:*** PPP.

N1N3 BA Business Management with Finance
Duration: 3FT Hon
Entry Requirements: ***GCE:*** 220. ***SQAH:*** CC. ***SQAAH:*** C. ***BTEC NC:*** PP. ***BTEC ND:*** PPP.

N1NH BA Business Management with Finance (with foundation)
Duration: 4FT Hon
Entry Requirements: ***GCE:*** 80. ***BTEC NC:*** PP. ***BTEC ND:*** PPP.

NN13 BA Business and Finance (top-up)
Duration: 1FT Hon
Entry Requirements: HND required.

N3N2 BA Finance with Business Management
Duration: 3FT Hon
Entry Requirements: ***GCE:*** 200.

N3NF BA Finance with Business Management (with foundation)
Duration: 4FT Hon
Entry Requirements: ***GCE:*** 80.

S41 SOUTH CHESHIRE COLLEGE
DANE BANK AVENUE
CREWE CW2 8AB
t: 01270 654654 f: 01270 651515
e: admissions@s-cheshire.ac.uk
// www.s-cheshire.ac.uk

NN14 FdSc Business and Accountancy Management
Duration: 2FT/3SW Fdg
Entry Requirements: Interview required.

S72 STAFFORDSHIRE UNIVERSITY
COLLEGE ROAD
STOKE ON TRENT ST4 2DE
t: 01782 292753 f: 01782 292740
e: admissions@staffs.ac.uk
// www.staffs.ac.uk

NN41 BA Accounting and Business
Duration: 3FT Hon
Entry Requirements: ***GCE:*** BCC-BB. ***IB:*** 24. Interview required.

S75 THE UNIVERSITY OF STIRLING
STIRLING FK9 4LA
t: 01786 467044 f: 01786 466800
e: admissions@stir.ac.uk
// www.stir.ac.uk

LN11 BA Business Studies and Economics
Duration: 4FT Hon
Entry Requirements: ***GCE:*** CCC. ***SQAH:*** BBCC. ***SQAAH:*** AAA-CCC. ***IB:*** 30. ***BTEC ND:*** MMM.

NN13 BA Business Studies and Finance
Duration: 4FT Hon
Entry Requirements: ***GCE:*** BCC. ***SQAH:*** BBBB. ***SQAAH:*** AAA-CCC. ***IB:*** 30.

MN24 BAcc Accountancy and Business Law
Duration: 4FT Hon
Entry Requirements: ***GCE:*** CCC. ***SQAH:*** BBBB. ***SQAAH:*** AAA-CCC. ***IB:*** 30. ***BTEC ND:*** DMM.

NNF4 BAcc Accountancy and Business Studies
Duration: 4FT Hon
Entry Requirements: ***GCE:*** BCC. ***SQAH:*** BBBB. ***SQAAH:*** AAA-CCC. ***IB:*** 30.

S76 STOCKPORT COLLEGE
WELLINGTON ROAD SOUTH
STOCKPORT SK1 3UQ
t: 0161 958 3143 f: 0161 958 3663
e: susan.kelly@stockport.ac.uk
// www.stockport.ac.uk

NN13 FdA Business and Finance
Duration: 2FT Fdg
Entry Requirements: Interview required.

S78 THE UNIVERSITY OF STRATHCLYDE
GLASGOW G1 1XQ
t: 0141 552 4400 f: 0141 552 0775
// www.strath.ac.uk

NN41 BA Accounting and Business Enterprise
Duration: 4FT Hon
Entry Requirements: ***GCE:*** AAB. ***SQAH:*** AAAA-AAABB. ***IB:*** 36.

NM42 BA Accounting and Business Law
Duration: 4FT Hon
Entry Requirements: ***GCE:*** AAB. ***SQAH:*** AAAA-AAABB. ***IB:*** 36.

NG42 BA Accounting and Business Technology
Duration: 4FT Hon
Entry Requirements: ***GCE:*** AAB. ***SQAH:*** AAAA-AAABB. ***IB:*** 36.

NL11 BA Business Enterprise and Economics
Duration: 4FT Hon
Entry Requirements: ***GCE:*** ABB. ***SQAH:*** AABB-ABBBC. ***IB:*** 34.

NN13 BA Business Enterprise and Finance
Duration: 4FT Hon
Entry Requirements: ***GCE:*** ABB. ***SQAH:*** AABB-ABBBC. ***IB:*** 34.

GL21 BA Business Technology and Economics
Duration: 4FT Hon
Entry Requirements: ***GCE:*** ABB. ***SQAH:*** AABB-ABBBC. ***IB:*** 34.

GN23 BA Business Technology and Finance
Duration: 4FT Hon
Entry Requirements: ***GCE:*** ABB. ***SQAH:*** AABB-ABBBC. ***IB:*** 34.

LM12 BA Economics and Business Law
Duration: 4FT Hon
Entry Requirements: ***GCE:*** ABB. ***SQAH:*** AABB-ABBBC. ***IB:*** 34.

NM32 BA Finance and Business Law
Duration: 4FT Hon
Entry Requirements: ***GCE:*** ABB. ***SQAH:*** AABB-ABBBC. ***IB:*** 34.

NN14 BA International Business and Accounting
Duration: 4FT Hon
Entry Requirements: ***GCE:*** BBB. ***SQAH:*** AAAA-AAABB.

S82 UNIVERSITY CAMPUS SUFFOLK
WATERFRONT BUILDING
NEPTUNE QUAY
IPSWICH
SUFFOLK IP4 1QJ
t: 01473 338348 f: 01473 339900
e: info@ucs.ac.uk
// www.ucs.ac.uk

N2N3 BA Business Management with Finance
Duration: 3FT Hon
Entry Requirements: ***GCE:*** 240. ***IB:*** 24.

S84 UNIVERSITY OF SUNDERLAND
STUDENT HELPLINE
THE STUDENT GATEWAY
CHESTER ROAD
SUNDERLAND SR1 3SD
t: 0191 515 3000 f: 0191 515 3805
e: student-helpline@sunderland.ac.uk
// www.sunderland.ac.uk

NN1H BA Business and Financial Management
Duration: 3FT Hon
Entry Requirements: ***BTEC NC:*** DD. ***BTEC ND:*** MMM. ***OCR ND:*** D ***OCR NED:*** M3

S85 UNIVERSITY OF SURREY
STAG HILL
GUILDFORD
SURREY GU2 7XH
t: +44(0)1483 689305 f: +44(0)1483 689388
e: admissions@surrey.ac.uk
// www.surrey.ac.uk

LN11 BSc Business Economics (3 or 4 years)
Duration: 3FT/4SW Hon
Entry Requirements: ***GCE:*** ABB. ***SQAH:*** BBBBB. ***SQAAH:*** BBB. ***IB:*** 30.

S90 UNIVERSITY OF SUSSEX
UNDERGRADUATE ADMISSIONS
SUSSEX HOUSE
UNIVERSITY OF SUSSEX
BRIGHTON BN1 9RH
t: 01273 678416 f: 01273 678545
e: ug.applicants@sussex.ac.uk
// www.sussex.ac.uk

NN31 BSc Finance and Business
Duration: 3FT Hon
Entry Requirements: ***GCE:*** ABB-BBB. ***SQAH:*** AABBB-ABBBB.

S93 SWANSEA UNIVERSITY
SINGLETON PARK
SWANSEA SA2 8PP
t: 01792 295111 f: 01792 295110
e: admissions@swansea.ac.uk
// www.swansea.ac.uk

N1NK BA Business Management (Accounting)
Duration: 3FT Hon
Entry Requirements: ***GCE:*** ABB-BBB. ***BTEC ND:*** DDM.

N1N4 BSc Business Management (Accounting)
Duration: 3FT Hon
Entry Requirements: ***GCE:*** ABB-BBB. ***BTEC ND:*** DDM.

N1N3 BSc Business Management (Finance)
Duration: 3FT Hon
Entry Requirements: ***GCE:*** ABB-BBB. ***BTEC ND:*** DDM.

NL21 BSc Business Management and Economics
Duration: 3FT Hon
Entry Requirements: ***GCE:*** ABB. ***IB:*** 33. ***BTEC ND:*** DDM.

T40 THAMES VALLEY UNIVERSITY
ST MARY'S ROAD
EALING
LONDON W5 5RF
t: 0800 036 8888 f: 020 8566 1353
e: learning.advice@tvu.ac.uk
// www.tvu.ac.uk

N1NH BA Business Studies with Credit Management
Duration: 3FT Hon
Entry Requirements: ***GCE:*** 200. ***IB:*** 28.

N1N3 BA Business Studies with Finance
Duration: 3FT Hon
Entry Requirements: ***GCE:*** 200.

U20 UNIVERSITY OF ULSTER

COLERAINE
CO. LONDONDERRY
NORTHERN IRELAND BT52 1SA
t: 028 7032 4221 f: 028 7032 4908
e: online@ulster.ac.uk
// www.ulster.ac.uk

N1N4 BSc Business Studies with Accounting

Duration: 3FT Hon

Entry Requirements: ***GCE:*** 240. ***IB:*** 24. ***BTEC NC:*** MM. ***BTEC ND:*** MMM.

N1NK BSc Business with Accounting

Duration: 4SW Hon

Entry Requirements: ***GCE:*** 240. ***IB:*** 24. ***BTEC NC:*** MM. ***BTEC ND:*** MMM.

U80 UNIVERSITY COLLEGE LONDON (UNIVERSITY OF LONDON)

GOWER STREET
LONDON WC1E 6BT
t: 020 7679 3000 f: 020 7679 3001
// www.ucl.ac.uk

L1RR BA Economics & Business with East European Studies (with a Year Abroad) (4 years)

Duration: 4FT Hon

Entry Requirements: ***GCE:*** AABe-ABBe. ***SQAAH:*** AAB-ABB. Interview required.

L1R7 BA Economics and Business with East European Studies

Duration: 3FT Hon

Entry Requirements: ***GCE:*** AABe-ABBe. ***SQAAH:*** AAB-ABB. Interview required.

H1N3 BEng Engineering with Business Finance

Duration: 3FT Hon

Entry Requirements: ***GCE:*** AAAe-AABe. ***SQAAH:*** AAA-AAB. ***BTEC ND:*** DDD. Interview required.

H1NH MEng Engineering with Business Finance

Duration: 4FT Hon

Entry Requirements: ***GCE:*** A*AAe-AAAe. ***SQAAH:*** AAA. Interview required.

W50 UNIVERSITY OF WESTMINSTER

101 NEW CAVENDISH STREET
LONDON W1W 6XH
t: 020 7915 5511 f: 020 7911 5788
e: course-enquiries@westminster.ac.uk
// www.westminster.ac.uk

NL21 BA Business Management (Business Economics)

Duration: 3FT/4SW Hon

Entry Requirements: ***GCE:*** BCC. ***SQAH:*** BBBBB. ***SQAAH:*** BBB. ***IB:*** 28.

NN24 BA Business Management (Professional Accounting)

Duration: 3FT/4SW Hon

Entry Requirements: ***GCE:*** BCC. ***SQAH:*** BBBBB. ***SQAAH:*** BBB. ***IB:*** 28.

W75 UNIVERSITY OF WOLVERHAMPTON

ADMISSIONS UNIT
MX207, CAMP STREET
WOLVERHAMPTON
WEST MIDLANDS WV1 1AD
t: 01902 321000 f: 01902 321896
e: admissions@wlv.ac.uk
// www.wlv.ac.uk

NN14 BA Business and Accounting

Duration: 3FT Hon

Entry Requirements: ***GCE:*** 220. ***IB:*** 28. ***BTEC NC:*** DD. ***BTEC ND:*** MMM.

NN13 BA Business and Finance

Duration: 3FT Hon

Entry Requirements: Contact the institution for details.

W80 UNIVERSITY OF WORCESTER

HENWICK GROVE
WORCESTER WR2 6AJ
t: 01905 855111 f: 01905 857542
e: admissions@worc.ac.uk
// www.worcester.ac.uk

NLC1 BA Business, Accountancy & Economics

Duration: 3FT/4SW Hon

Entry Requirements: ***GCE:*** 280. ***IB:*** 25. ***BTEC NC:*** DD. ***BTEC ND:*** MMM. ***OCR ND:*** D ***OCR NED:*** M3

LN15 BA Business, Economics & Advertising

Duration: 3FT/4SW Hon

Entry Requirements: ***GCE:*** 280. ***IB:*** 25. ***BTEC NC:*** DD. ***BTEC ND:*** MMM. ***OCR ND:*** D ***OCR NED:*** M3

LN16 BA Business, Economics & Human Resource Management
Duration: 3FT/4SW Hon
Entry Requirements: ***GCE:*** 280. ***IB:*** 25. ***BTEC NC:*** DD. ***BTEC ND:*** MMM. ***OCR ND:*** D ***OCR NED:*** M3

LP12 BA Business, Economics & Public Relations
Duration: 3FT/4SW Hon
Entry Requirements: ***GCE:*** 280. ***IB:*** 25. ***BTEC NC:*** DD. ***BTEC ND:*** MMM. ***OCR ND:*** D ***OCR NED:*** M3

NN24 BA Business, Management & Accountancy
Duration: 3FT/4SW Hon
Entry Requirements: ***GCE:*** 280. ***IB:*** 25. ***BTEC NC:*** DD. ***BTEC ND:*** MMM. ***OCR ND:*** D ***OCR NED:*** M3

NL21 BA Business, Management & Economics
Duration: 3FT/4SW Hon
Entry Requirements: ***GCE:*** 280. ***IB:*** 25. ***BTEC NC:*** DD. ***BTEC ND:*** MMM. ***OCR ND:*** D ***OCR NED:*** M3

NL51 BA Business, Marketing & Economics
Duration: 3FT/4SW Hon
Entry Requirements: ***GCE:*** 280. ***IB:*** 25. ***BTEC NC:*** DD. ***BTEC ND:*** MMM. ***OCR ND:*** D ***OCR NED:*** M3

W81 WORCESTER COLLEGE OF TECHNOLOGY
DEANSWAY
WORCESTER WR1 2JF
t: 01905 725555 f: 01905 28906
// www.wortech.ac.uk

N1N4 FdA Business with Accounting
Duration: 2FT Hon
Entry Requirements: ***GCE:*** 80. Interview required.

Y50 THE UNIVERSITY OF YORK
ADMISSIONS AND UK/EU STUDENT RECRUITMENT
UNIVERSITY OF YORK
HESLINGTON
YORK YO10 5DD
t: 01904 433533 f: 01904 433538
e: admissions@york.ac.uk
// www.york.ac.uk

NN4F BSc Accounting, Business Finance & Management with a Year in Industry
Duration: 4SW Hon
Entry Requirements: ***GCE:*** AAB. ***SQAH:*** AAAAB. ***SQAAH:*** AB. ***IB:*** 34. ***BTEC ND:*** DDD.

NN42 BSc Accounting, Business Finance and Management
Duration: 3FT Hon
Entry Requirements: ***GCE:*** AAB. ***SQAH:*** AAAAB. ***SQAAH:*** AB. ***IB:*** 34. ***BTEC ND:*** DDD.

Y75 YORK ST JOHN UNIVERSITY
LORD MAYOR'S WALK
YORK YO31 7EX
t: 01904 876598 f: 01904 876940/876921
e: admissions@yorksj.ac.uk
// w3.yorksj.ac.uk

NN23 BA Business Management: Finance
Duration: 3FT Hon
Entry Requirements: ***Foundation:*** Pass. ***GCE:*** 200-240. ***IB:*** 24.

COMPUTING AND COMPUTER SCIENCE COMBINATIONS

A20 THE UNIVERSITY OF ABERDEEN
UNIVERSITY OFFICE
KING'S COLLEGE
ABERDEEN AB24 3FX
t: +44 (0) 1224 273504 f: +44 (0) 1224 272034
e: sras@abdn.ac.uk
// www.abdn.ac.uk/sras

N4G4 MA Accountancy with Computing
Duration: 4FT Hon
Entry Requirements: Contact the institution for details.

L1G4 MA Economics with Computing
Duration: 4FT Hon
Entry Requirements: Contact the institution for details.

N3G4 MA Finance with Computing
Duration: 4FT Hon
Entry Requirements: Contact the institution for details.

A40 ABERYSTWYTH UNIVERSITY
WELCOME CENTRE, ABERYSTWYTH UNIVERSITY
PENGLAIS CAMPUS
ABERYSTWYTH
CEREDIGION SY23 3FB
t: 01970 622021 f: 01970 627410
e: ug-admissions@aber.ac.uk
// www.aber.ac.uk

G4N4 BSc Computer Science with Accounting & Finance
Duration: 3FT Hon
Entry Requirements: ***GCE:*** 280. ***IB:*** 24.

N4G4 BScEcon Accounting & Finance with Computer Science
Duration: 3FT Hon
Entry Requirements: ***GCE:*** 280. ***IB:*** 27.

B84 BRUNEL UNIVERSITY
UXBRIDGE
MIDDLESEX UB8 3PH
t: 01895 265265 f: 01895 269790
e: admissions@brunel.ac.uk
// www.brunel.ac.uk

GN43 BSc Financial Computing
Duration: 3FT Hon
Entry Requirements: ***GCE:*** 260-300. ***IB:*** 31. ***BTEC ND:*** DDM.

GNK3 BSc Financial Computing (4 year Thick SW)
Duration: 4SW Hon
Entry Requirements: ***GCE:*** 260-300. ***IB:*** 31. ***BTEC ND:*** DDM.

B90 THE UNIVERSITY OF BUCKINGHAM
YEOMANRY HOUSE
HUNTER STREET
BUCKINGHAM MK18 1EG
t: 01280 820313 f: 01280 822245
e: info@buckingham.ac.uk
// www.buckingham.ac.uk

G4N4 BSc Computing with Accounting & Finance
Duration: 2FT Hon
Entry Requirements: ***GCE:*** 240. ***IB:*** 26. ***BTEC NC:*** DD. ***BTEC ND:*** MMM.

G4L1 BSc Computing with Economics
Duration: 2FT Hon
Entry Requirements: ***GCE:*** 240. ***IB:*** 26. ***BTEC NC:*** DD. ***BTEC ND:*** MMM.

L1G5 BScEcon Economics with Information Systems
Duration: 2FT Hon
Entry Requirements: ***GCE:*** 240. ***IB:*** 26. ***BTEC NC:*** DD. ***BTEC ND:*** MMM.

C30 UNIVERSITY OF CENTRAL LANCASHIRE
PRESTON
LANCS PR1 2HE
t: 01772 201201 f: 01772 894954
e: uadmissions@uclan.ac.uk
// www.uclan.ac.uk

NG45 BSc Accounting Information Systems
Duration: 3FT Hon
Entry Requirements: ***GCE:*** 240-280. ***SQAH:*** AABB-BBBB. ***IB:*** 28. ***BTEC NC:*** DD. ***OCR ND:*** D

C55 UNIVERSITY OF CHESTER
PARKGATE ROAD
CHESTER CH1 4BJ
t: 01244 511000 f: 01244 511300
e: enquiries@chester.ac.uk
// www.chester.ac.uk

LG14 BSc Economics and Computer Science
Duration: 3FT Hon
Entry Requirements: ***GCE:*** 240. ***SQAH:*** BBBB. ***IB:*** 24. ***BTEC NC:*** DM. ***BTEC ND:*** MMM.

L1G4 BSc Economics with Computer Science
Duration: 3FT Hon
Entry Requirements: ***GCE:*** 240. ***SQAH:*** BBBB. ***IB:*** 24. ***BTEC NC:*** DM. ***BTEC ND:*** MMM.

D26 DE MONTFORT UNIVERSITY
THE GATEWAY
LEICESTER LE1 9BH
t: 0116 255 1551 f: 0116 250 6204
e: enquiries@dmu.ac.uk
// www.dmu.ac.uk

NG44 BA/BSc Accounting and Computing
Duration: 3FT/4SW Hon
Entry Requirements: ***GCE:*** 240. ***IB:*** 24. ***OCR ND:*** D ***OCR NED:*** M3

D65 UNIVERSITY OF DUNDEE
DUNDEE DD1 4HN
t: 01382 383838 f: 01382 388150
e: ContactUs@dundee.ac.uk
// www.dundee.ac.uk/admissions/undergraduate/

GN44 BSc Accountancy and Applied Computing
Duration: 4FT Hon
Entry Requirements: ***GCE:*** BCC. ***SQAH:*** BBBB. ***IB:*** 30. ***BTEC ND:*** DMM.

GL41 BSc Applied Computing and Economics
Duration: 4FT Hon
Entry Requirements: ***GCE:*** BCC. ***SQAH:*** BBBB. ***IB:*** 30. ***BTEC ND:*** DMM.

GLK1 BSc Applied Computing and Financial Economics
Duration: 4FT Hon
Entry Requirements: ***GCE:*** BCC. ***SQAH:*** BBBB. ***IB:*** 30. ***BTEC ND:*** DMM.

E28 UNIVERSITY OF EAST LONDON

DOCKLANDS CAMPUS
UNIVERSITY WAY
LONDON E16 2RD
t: 020 8223 3333 f: 020 8223 2978
e: study@uel.ac.uk
// www.uel.ac.uk

GN54 BA/BSc Information Technology/Accounting

Duration: 3FT Hon
Entry Requirements: ***GCE:*** 200. ***IB:*** 24. ***BTEC NC:*** DM. ***BTEC ND:*** MMP.

G4N4 BSc Computer Networks with Accounting

Duration: 4SW Hon
Entry Requirements: ***GCE:*** 200. ***IB:*** 24. ***BTEC NC:*** DM. ***BTEC ND:*** MMP. ***OCR ND:*** M1 ***OCR NED:*** P1

G5N4 BSc Information Technology with Accounting

Duration: 3FT Hon
Entry Requirements: ***GCE:*** 200. ***IB:*** 24. ***BTEC NC:*** DM. ***BTEC ND:*** MMP. ***OCR ND:*** M1 ***OCR NED:*** P1

G6N4 BSc Software Engineering with Accounting

Duration: 3FT Hon
Entry Requirements: ***GCE:*** 200. ***IB:*** 24. ***BTEC NC:*** DM. ***BTEC ND:*** MMP. ***OCR ND:*** M1 ***OCR NED:*** P1

G28 UNIVERSITY OF GLASGOW

THE UNIVERSITY OF GLASGOW
THE FRASER BUILDING
65 HILLHEAD STREET
GLASGOW G12 8QF
t: 0141 330 6062 f: 0141 330 2961
e: ugenquiries@gla.ac.uk (UK/EU undergrad enquiries only)
// www.glasgow.ac.uk

GL41 BSc Computing Science/Economics

Duration: 4FT Hon
Entry Requirements: ***GCE:*** ABB. ***SQAH:*** ABBB. ***IB:*** 32.

GLK1 MA Computing Science/Economics

Duration: 4FT Hon
Entry Requirements: ***GCE:*** AAB. ***SQAH:*** AAAB-AABB. ***IB:*** 34.

GLL1 MA Computing/Economics

Duration: 4FT Hon
Entry Requirements: ***GCE:*** AAB. ***SQAH:*** AAAB-AABB. ***IB:*** 34.

H36 UNIVERSITY OF HERTFORDSHIRE

UNIVERSITY ADMISSIONS SERVICE
COLLEGE LANE
HATFIELD
HERTS AL10 9AB
t: 01707 284800 f: 01707 284870
// www.herts.ac.uk

NG45 BA Accounting/Information Systems

Duration: 3FT/4SW Hon
Entry Requirements: ***GCE:*** 260.

LG15 BA Economics/Information Systems

Duration: 3FT/4SW Hon
Entry Requirements: ***GCE:*** 240.

G5N3 BA Information Systems with Finance

Duration: 3FT/4SW Hon
Entry Requirements: ***GCE:*** 260.

H60 THE UNIVERSITY OF HUDDERSFIELD

QUEENSGATE
HUDDERSFIELD HD1 3DH
t: 01484 473969 f: 01484 472765
e: admissionsandrecords@hud.ac.uk
// www.hud.ac.uk

N4G5 BA Accountancy with Information Systems

Duration: 3FT/4SW Hon
Entry Requirements: ***GCE:*** 300. ***SQAH:*** BBCC. ***IB:*** 28.

K12 KEELE UNIVERSITY

STAFFS ST5 5BG
t: 01782 734005 f: 01782 632343
e: undergraduate@keele.ac.uk
// www.keele.ac.uk

GN43 BSc Computer Science and Finance

Duration: 3FT Hon
Entry Requirements: ***GCE:*** 300.

GN4H BSc Creative Computing and Finance

Duration: 3FT Hon
Entry Requirements: ***GCE:*** 300.

NG34 BSc Finance and Information Systems

Duration: 3FT Hon
Entry Requirements: ***GCE:*** 300.

K24 THE UNIVERSITY OF KENT

INFORMATION, RECRUITMENT & ADMISSIONS REGISTRY
UNIVERSITY OF KENT
CANTERBURY, KENT CT2 7NZ
t: 01227 827272 f: 01227 827077
e: information@kent.ac.uk
// www.kent.ac.uk

N4G4 BA Accounting & Finance with Computing

Duration: 3FT Hon
Entry Requirements: ***GCE:*** 300. ***IB:*** 33. ***BTEC NC:*** DD. ***BTEC ND:*** DMM. ***OCR ND:*** D

GN44 BA Computing and Accounting & Finance

Duration: 3FT Hon
Entry Requirements: ***GCE:*** 300. ***IB:*** 33. ***BTEC NC:*** DD. ***BTEC ND:*** DMM. ***OCR ND:*** D

L1G4 BSc Economics with Computing

Duration: 3FT Hon
Entry Requirements: ***GCE:*** 320. ***IB:*** 34. ***BTEC NC:*** DD. ***BTEC ND:*** DDM. ***OCR ND:*** D ***OCR NED:*** D2

L14 LANCASTER UNIVERSITY

THE UNIVERSITY
LANCASTER
LANCASHIRE LA1 4YW
t: 01524 592029 f: 01524 846243
e: ugadmissions@lancaster.ac.uk
// www.lancs.ac.uk

NG44 BSc Accounting, Finance and Computer Science

Duration: 3FT Hon
Entry Requirements: ***GCE:*** ABB. ***SQAH:*** BBBBB. ***SQAAH:*** ABB. ***IB:*** 32. ***BTEC ND:*** DDM.

L68 LONDON METROPOLITAN UNIVERSITY

166-220 HOLLOWAY ROAD
LONDON N7 8DB
t: 020 7133 4200
e: admissions@londonmet.ac.uk
// www.londonmet.ac.uk

N491 BA Accounting Information Systems

Duration: 3FT Hon
Entry Requirements: ***GCE:*** 240. ***IB:*** 28.

NG45 BA/BSc Accounting Information Systems and Computer Forensics

Duration: 3FT Hon
Entry Requirements: ***GCE:*** 240. ***IB:*** 28.

NG4K BA/BSc Accounting Information Systems and Computer Networking

Duration: 3FT Hon
Entry Requirements: ***GCE:*** 240. ***IB:*** 28.

NG4L BA/BSc Accounting Information Systems and Computing

Duration: 3FT Hon
Entry Requirements: ***GCE:*** 240. ***IB:*** 28.

NJ4X BA/BSc Accounting Information Systems and Logistics & Supply Chain Management

Duration: 3FT Hon
Entry Requirements: ***GCE:*** 240. ***IB:*** 28.

NG4C BA/BSc Accounting Information Systems and Mathematics

Duration: 3FT Hon
Entry Requirements: ***GCE:*** 240. ***IB:*** 28.

NG43 BA/BSc Accounting Information Systems and Statistics

Duration: 3FT Hon
Entry Requirements: ***GCE:*** 240. ***IB:*** 28.

NG44 BA/BSc Accounting and Computing

Duration: 3FT Hon
Entry Requirements: ***GCE:*** 240. ***IB:*** 28.

M20 THE UNIVERSITY OF MANCHESTER

OXFORD ROAD
MANCHESTER M13 9PL
t: 0161 275 2077 f: 0161 275 2106
e: ug-admissions@manchester.ac.uk
// www.manchester.ac.uk

NG45 BA Accounting, Management and Information Systems

Duration: 3FT Hon
Entry Requirements: ***GCE:*** AAB. ***SQAAH:*** AAB. ***IB:*** 35. ***BTEC ND:*** DDM.

M40 THE MANCHESTER METROPOLITAN UNIVERSITY

ADMISSIONS OFFICE
ALL SAINTS (GMS)
ALL SAINTS
MANCHESTER M15 6BH
t: 0161 247 2000
// www.mmu.ac.uk

GLL1 BSc Computer Music Technology/Economics

Duration: 3FT Hon
Entry Requirements: ***GCE:*** 220. ***IB:*** 26.

GL41 BSc Computing/Economics
Duration: 3FT Hon
Entry Requirements: ***GCE:*** 220. ***IB:*** 26.

N38 UNIVERSITY OF NORTHAMPTON
PARK CAMPUS
BOUGHTON GREEN ROAD
NORTHAMPTON NN2 7AL
t: 0800 358 2232 f: 01604 722083
e: admissions@northampton.ac.uk
// www.northampton.ac.uk

N4G4 BA Accounting/Computing
Duration: 3FT Hon
Entry Requirements: ***GCE:*** 220-260. ***SQAH:*** ABB-BBBC. ***IB:*** 24.

L1G4 BA Economics/Computing
Duration: 3FT Hon
Entry Requirements: ***GCE:*** 220-260. ***SQAH:*** ABB-BBBC. ***IB:*** 24.

G4N4 BSc Computing/Accounting
Duration: 3FT Hon
Entry Requirements: ***GCE:*** 220-260. ***SQAH:*** ABB-BBBC. ***IB:*** 24.

G4L1 BSc Computing/Economics
Duration: 3FT Hon
Entry Requirements: ***GCE:*** 220-260. ***SQAH:*** ABB-BBBC. ***IB:*** 24.

S36 UNIVERSITY OF ST ANDREWS
ST KATHARINE'S WEST
16 THE SCORES
ST ANDREWS
FIFE KY16 9AX
t: 01334 462150 f: 01334 463330
e: admissions@st-andrews.ac.uk
// www.st-and.ac.uk

GL41 BSc Computer Science-Economics
Duration: 4FT Hon
Entry Requirements: ***GCE:*** AAA. ***SQAH:*** AAAA. ***IB:*** 38.

LG14 BSc Economics-Internet Computer Science
Duration: 4FT Hon
Entry Requirements: ***GCE:*** AAA. ***SQAH:*** AAAA. ***IB:*** 38.

S72 STAFFORDSHIRE UNIVERSITY
COLLEGE ROAD
STOKE ON TRENT ST4 2DE
t: 01782 292753 f: 01782 292740
e: admissions@staffs.ac.uk
// www.staffs.ac.uk

NG45 BA Accounting Information Systems
Duration: 3FT/4SW Hon
Entry Requirements: ***GCE:*** BCC-BB. ***IB:*** 24. Interview required.

S73 STAFFORDSHIRE UNIVERSITY REGIONAL FEDERATION
COLLEGE ROAD
STOKE ON TRENT ST4 2DE
t: 01782 292753 f: 01782 292740
e: admissions@staffs.ac.uk
// www.surf.ac.uk

NG45 BSc Information Systems Accounting
Duration: 5FT Hon
Entry Requirements: Contact the institution for details.

S75 THE UNIVERSITY OF STIRLING
STIRLING FK9 4LA
t: 01786 467044 f: 01786 466800
e: admissions@stir.ac.uk
// www.stir.ac.uk

NG34 BA Finance and Computing Science
Duration: 4FT Hon
Entry Requirements: ***GCE:*** CCC. ***SQAH:*** BBBB. ***SQAAH:*** AAA-CCC. ***BTEC ND:*** DMM.

GN44 BAcc Accountancy and Computing Science
Duration: 4FT Hon
Entry Requirements: ***GCE:*** CCC. ***SQAH:*** BBBB. ***SQAAH:*** AAA-CCC. ***IB:*** 30. ***BTEC ND:*** DMM.

GL41 BSc Computing Science and Economics
Duration: 4FT Hon
Entry Requirements: ***GCE:*** CCC. ***SQAH:*** BBCC. ***SQAAH:*** AAA-CCC. ***IB:*** 30. ***BTEC ND:*** MMM.

S93 SWANSEA UNIVERSITY
SINGLETON PARK
SWANSEA SA2 8PP
t: 01792 295111 f: 01792 295110
e: admissions@swansea.ac.uk
// www.swansea.ac.uk

G4L1 BSc Computing with Finance
Duration: 3FT Hon
Entry Requirements: ***GCE:*** ABB. ***IB:*** 33. ***BTEC ND:*** DDM.

U20 UNIVERSITY OF ULSTER
COLERAINE
CO. LONDONDERRY
NORTHERN IRELAND BT52 1SA
t: 028 7032 4221 f: 028 7032 4908
e: online@ulster.ac.uk
// www.ulster.ac.uk

G4N4 BSc Computing with Accounting
Duration: 4SW Hon
Entry Requirements: ***GCE:*** 260. ***IB:*** 24. ***BTEC ND:*** DMM.

G4NK BSc Computing with Accounting

Duration: 4SW Hon

Entry Requirements: ***GCE:*** 260. ***IB:*** 24. ***BTEC ND:*** DMM.

G4L1 BSc Computing with Economic Studies

Duration: 4SW Hon

Entry Requirements: ***GCE:*** 260. ***IB:*** 24. ***BTEC ND:*** DMM.

GEOGRAPHY AND GEOLOGY COMBINATIONS

A20 THE UNIVERSITY OF ABERDEEN

UNIVERSITY OFFICE
KING'S COLLEGE
ABERDEEN AB24 3FX
t: +44 (0) 1224 273504 f: +44 (0) 1224 272034
e: sras@abdn.ac.uk
// www.abdn.ac.uk/sras

NL47 MA Accountancy and Geography

Duration: 4FT Hon

Entry Requirements: ***GCE:*** BBB. ***SQAH:*** BBBB. ***IB:*** 30. ***BTEC ND:*** MMM.

LL17 MA Economics and Geography

Duration: 4FT Hon

Entry Requirements: ***GCE:*** BBB. ***SQAH:*** BBBB. ***IB:*** 30. ***BTEC ND:*** MMM.

LN73 MA Finance and Geography

Duration: 4FT Hon

Entry Requirements: ***GCE:*** BBB. ***SQAH:*** BBBB. ***IB:*** 30. ***BTEC ND:*** MMM.

A40 ABERYSTWYTH UNIVERSITY

WELCOME CENTRE, ABERYSTWYTH UNIVERSITY
PENGLAIS CAMPUS
ABERYSTWYTH
CEREDIGION SY23 3FB
t: 01970 622021 f: 01970 627410
e: ug-admissions@aber.ac.uk
// www.aber.ac.uk

L7L1 BA Human Geography with Economics

Duration: 3FT Hon

Entry Requirements: ***GCE:*** 300-320. ***IB:*** 28.

L1L7 BScEcon Economics with Human Geography

Duration: 3FT Hon

Entry Requirements: ***GCE:*** 280. ***IB:*** 27.

B32 THE UNIVERSITY OF BIRMINGHAM

EDGBASTON
BIRMINGHAM B15 2TT
t: 0121 415 8900 f: 0121 414 7159
e: admissions@bham.ac.uk
// www.bham.ac.uk

LL71 BSc Geography and Economics

Duration: 3FT Hon

Entry Requirements: ***GCE:*** AAB. ***SQAH:*** AAABB. ***SQAAH:*** AAB-ABB.

C55 UNIVERSITY OF CHESTER

PARKGATE ROAD
CHESTER CH1 4BJ
t: 01244 511000 f: 01244 511300
e: enquiries@chester.ac.uk
// www.chester.ac.uk

LF18 BSc Economics and Geography

Duration: 3FT Hon

Entry Requirements: ***GCE:*** 240. ***SQAH:*** BBBB. ***IB:*** 24. ***BTEC NC:*** DM. ***BTEC ND:*** MMM.

L1F8 BSc Economics with Geography

Duration: 3FT Hon

Entry Requirements: ***GCE:*** 240. ***SQAH:*** BBBB. ***IB:*** 24. ***BTEC NC:*** DM. ***BTEC ND:*** MMM.

F8L1 BSc Geography with Economics

Duration: 3FT Hon

Entry Requirements: ***GCE:*** 240. ***SQAH:*** BBBB. ***IB:*** 24. ***BTEC NC:*** DM. ***BTEC ND:*** MMM.

D39 UNIVERSITY OF DERBY

KEDLESTON ROAD
DERBY DE22 1GB
t: 08701 202330 f: 01332 597724
e: askadmissions@derby.ac.uk
// www.derby.ac.uk

FN84 BSc Accounting and Geography

Duration: 3FT Hon

Entry Requirements: ***Foundation:*** Merit. ***GCE:*** 180-240. ***IB:*** 26. ***BTEC NC:*** DM. ***BTEC ND:*** MMP.

FN64 BSc Accounting and Geology

Duration: 3FT Hon

Entry Requirements: ***Foundation:*** Merit. ***GCE:*** 180-240. ***IB:*** 26. ***BTEC NC:*** DM. ***BTEC ND:*** MMP.

E56 THE UNIVERSITY OF EDINBURGH

STUDENT RECRUITMENT & ADMISSIONS
57 GEORGE SQUARE
EDINBURGH EH8 9JU
t: 0131 650 4360 f: 0131 651 1236
e: sra.enquiries@ed.ac.uk
// www.ed.ac.uk/studying/undergraduate/

LL71 MA Geography and Economics
Duration: 4FT Hon
Entry Requirements: ***GCE:*** AAA-ABB. ***SQAH:*** AAAA-ABBB.

G28 UNIVERSITY OF GLASGOW

THE UNIVERSITY OF GLASGOW
THE FRASER BUILDING
65 HILLHEAD STREET
GLASGOW G12 8QF
t: 0141 330 6062 f: 0141 330 2961
e: ugenquiries@gla.ac.uk (UK/EU undergrad enquiries only)
// www.glasgow.ac.uk

LL17 MA Economics/Geography
Duration: 4FT Hon
Entry Requirements: ***GCE:*** AAB. ***SQAH:*** AAAB-AABB. ***IB:*** 34.

H36 UNIVERSITY OF HERTFORDSHIRE

UNIVERSITY ADMISSIONS SERVICE
COLLEGE LANE
HATFIELD
HERTS AL10 9AB
t: 01707 284800 f: 01707 284870
// www.herts.ac.uk

L1L7 BSc Economics/Human Geography
Duration: 3FT/4SW Hon
Entry Requirements: ***GCE:*** 220.

L7L1 BSc Human Geography/Economics
Duration: 3FT/4SW Hon
Entry Requirements: ***GCE:*** 220.

K12 KEELE UNIVERSITY

STAFFS ST5 5BG
t: 01782 734005 f: 01782 632343
e: undergraduate@keele.ac.uk
// www.keele.ac.uk

NL47 BA Accounting and Geography
Duration: 3FT Hon
Entry Requirements: ***GCE:*** 300-320.

NL4R BA Accounting and Human Geography
Duration: 3FT Hon
Entry Requirements: ***GCE:*** 300-320.

LLC7 BA Economics and Geography
Duration: 3FT Hon
Entry Requirements: ***GCE:*** 300.

LLD7 BA Economics and Human Geography
Duration: 3FT Hon
Entry Requirements: ***GCE:*** 300.

NF46 BSc Accounting and Geology
Duration: 3FT Hon
Entry Requirements: ***GCE:*** 300.

NF48 BSc Accounting and Physical Geography
Duration: 3FT Hon
Entry Requirements: ***GCE:*** 300.

FL61 BSc Economics and Geology
Duration: 3FT Hon
Entry Requirements: ***GCE:*** 300.

FL81 BSc Economics and Physical Geography
Duration: 3FT Hon
Entry Requirements: ***GCE:*** 300.

FN63 BSc Finance and Geology
Duration: 3FT Hon
Entry Requirements: ***GCE:*** 300.

K84 KINGSTON UNIVERSITY

STUDENT INFORMATION & ADVICE CENTRE
COOPER HOUSE
40-46 SURBITON ROAD
KINGSTON UPON THAMES KT1 2HX
t: 0844 8552177 f: 020 8547 7080
e: aps@kingston.ac.uk
// www.kingston.ac.uk

L1L7 BA Economics (Applied) with Human Geography
Duration: 3FT Hon
Entry Requirements: ***GCE:*** 260-360. ***IB:*** 24.

FL81 BA/BSc Geography and Applied Economics
Duration: 3FT Hon
Entry Requirements: ***GCE:*** 200-280.

LL71 BA/BSc Human Geography with Economics
Duration: 3FT Hon
Entry Requirements: ***GCE:*** 200-280. ***IB:*** 30.

FL61 BSc Geology and Applied Economics
Duration: 3FT Hon
Entry Requirements: ***GCE:*** 200-280.

L14 LANCASTER UNIVERSITY

THE UNIVERSITY
LANCASTER
LANCASHIRE LA1 4YW
t: 01524 592029 f: 01524 846243
e: ugadmissions@lancaster.ac.uk
// www.lancs.ac.uk

LL71 BA Economics and Geography

Duration: 3FT Hon
Entry Requirements: ***GCE:*** ABB. ***SQAH:*** BBBBB. ***SQAAH:*** ABB. ***IB:*** 32. ***BTEC ND:*** DDM.

L23 UNIVERSITY OF LEEDS

THE UNIVERSITY OF LEEDS
LEEDS LS2 9JT
t: 0113 343 3999
e: admissions@adm.leeds.ac.uk
// www.leeds.ac.uk

LL17 BA Economics and Geography

Duration: 3FT Hon
Entry Requirements: ***GCE:*** ABB. ***SQAAH:*** ABB. ***IB:*** 33.

L72 LONDON SCHOOL OF ECONOMICS AND POLITICAL SCIENCE (UNIVERSITY OF LONDON)

HOUGHTON STREET
LONDON WC2A 2AE
t: 020 7955 7125/7769 f: 020 7955 6001
e: ug-admissions@lse.ac.uk
// www.lse.ac.uk

L7L1 BSc Geography with Economics

Duration: 3FT Hon
Entry Requirements: ***GCE:*** AAB. ***SQAH:*** AAAAA-AAAAB. ***SQAAH:*** AAB. ***IB:*** 37.

L79 LOUGHBOROUGH UNIVERSITY

LOUGHBOROUGH
LEICESTERSHIRE LE11 3TU
t: 01509 223522 f: 01509 223905
e: admissions@lboro.ac.uk
// www.lboro.ac.uk

L1F8 BSc Economics with Geography

Duration: 3FT Hon
Entry Requirements: ***GCE:*** AAB. ***SQAH:*** AABBB. ***SQAAH:*** AB. ***IB:*** 34. ***BTEC ND:*** DDM.

LL17 BSc Geography with Economics

Duration: 3FT Hon
Entry Requirements: ***GCE:*** 300-320. ***IB:*** 32.

M40 THE MANCHESTER METROPOLITAN UNIVERSITY

ADMISSIONS OFFICE
ALL SAINTS (GMS)
ALL SAINTS
MANCHESTER M15 6BH
t: 0161 247 2000
// www.mmu.ac.uk

LLC7 BA/BSc Economics/Geography

Duration: 3FT Hon
Entry Requirements: ***GCE:*** 260. ***IB:*** 28.

N38 UNIVERSITY OF NORTHAMPTON

PARK CAMPUS
BOUGHTON GREEN ROAD
NORTHAMPTON NN2 7AL
t: 0800 358 2232 f: 01604 722083
e: admissions@northampton.ac.uk
// www.northampton.ac.uk

N4F8 BA Accounting/Physical Geography

Duration: 3FT Hon
Entry Requirements: ***GCE:*** 220-260. ***SQAH:*** ABB-BBBC. ***IB:*** 24.

L1L7 BA Economics/Human Geography

Duration: 3FT Hon
Entry Requirements: ***GCE:*** 220-260. ***SQAH:*** ABB-BBBC. ***IB:*** 24.

L7L1 BA Human Geography/Economics

Duration: 3FT Hon
Entry Requirements: ***GCE:*** 220-260. ***SQAH:*** ABB-BBBC. ***IB:*** 24.

F8N4 BSc Physical Geography/Accounting

Duration: 3FT Hon
Entry Requirements: ***GCE:*** 220-260. ***SQAH:*** ABB-BBBC. ***IB:*** 24.

P60 UNIVERSITY OF PLYMOUTH

DRAKE CIRCUS
PLYMOUTH PL4 8AA
t: 01752 588037 f: 01752 588050
e: admissions@plymouth.ac.uk
// www.plymouth.ac.uk

L1FW BSc Economics with Geography

Duration: 3FT/4SW Hon
Entry Requirements: ***GCE:*** 240. ***IB:*** 26.

Q50 QUEEN MARY, UNIVERSITY OF LONDON

MILE END ROAD
LONDON E1 4NS
t: 020 7882 5555 f: 020 7882 5500
e: admissions@qmul.ac.uk
// www.qmul.ac.uk

LL71 BScEcon Geography and Economics

Duration: 3FT Hon

Entry Requirements: ***GCE:*** AAB. ***SQAAH:*** AAB. ***IB:*** 34.

R12 THE UNIVERSITY OF READING

THE UNIVERSITY OF READING
PO BOX 217
READING RG6 6AH
t: 0118 378 8619 f: 0118 378 8924
e: student.recruitment@reading.ac.uk
// www.reading.ac.uk

LL17 BSc Geography and Economics (Regional Science)

Duration: 3FT Hon

Entry Requirements: ***GCE:*** 320.

S09 SCHOOL OF ORIENTAL AND AFRICAN STUDIES (UNIVERSITY OF LONDON)

THORNHAUGH STREET
RUSSELL SQUARE
LONDON WC1H 0XG
t: 020 7074 5106 f: 020 7898 4039
e: undergradadmissions@soas.ac.uk
// www.soas.ac.uk

LL17 BA Geography and Economics

Duration: 3FT Hon

Entry Requirements: Contact the institution for details.

S36 UNIVERSITY OF ST ANDREWS

ST KATHARINE'S WEST
16 THE SCORES
ST ANDREWS
FIFE KY16 9AX
t: 01334 462150 f: 01334 463330
e: admissions@st-andrews.ac.uk
// www.st-and.ac.uk

LL17 MA Economics-Geography

Duration: 4FT Hon

Entry Requirements: ***GCE:*** AAA. ***SQAH:*** AAAA. ***IB:*** 38.

S78 THE UNIVERSITY OF STRATHCLYDE

GLASGOW G1 1XQ
t: 0141 552 4400 f: 0141 552 0775
// www.strath.ac.uk

LL17 BA Economics and Geography

Duration: 4FT Hon

Entry Requirements: ***GCE:*** ABB. ***SQAH:*** ABBB-BBBBC. ***IB:*** 34.

S84 UNIVERSITY OF SUNDERLAND

STUDENT HELPLINE
THE STUDENT GATEWAY
CHESTER ROAD
SUNDERLAND SR1 3SD
t: 0191 515 3000 f: 0191 515 3805
e: student-helpline@sunderland.ac.uk
// www.sunderland.ac.uk

NL37 BA Financial Management and Geography

Duration: 3FT Hon

Entry Requirements: ***GCE:*** 220-360. ***BTEC NC:*** DM. ***BTEC ND:*** MMM. ***OCR ND:*** D ***OCR NED:*** M3

N3L7 BA Financial Management with Geography

Duration: 3FT Hon

Entry Requirements: ***GCE:*** 220-360. ***BTEC NC:*** DM. ***BTEC ND:*** MMM. ***OCR ND:*** D ***OCR NED:*** M3

L7N3 BA Geography with Financial Management

Duration: 3FT Hon

Entry Requirements: ***GCE:*** 220-360. ***BTEC NC:*** DM. ***BTEC ND:*** MMM. ***OCR ND:*** D ***OCR NED:*** M3

S93 SWANSEA UNIVERSITY

SINGLETON PARK
SWANSEA SA2 8PP
t: 01792 295111 f: 01792 295110
e: admissions@swansea.ac.uk
// www.swansea.ac.uk

LL17 BA Geography and Economics

Duration: 3FT Hon

Entry Requirements: ***GCE:*** ABB. ***IB:*** 33. ***BTEC ND:*** DDM.

LL71 BSc Economics and Geography

Duration: 3FT Hon

Entry Requirements: ***GCE:*** ABB. ***IB:*** 33. ***BTEC ND:*** DDM.

U80 UNIVERSITY COLLEGE LONDON (UNIVERSITY OF LONDON)
GOWER STREET
LONDON WC1E 6BT
t: 020 7679 3000 f: 020 7679 3001
// www.ucl.ac.uk

LL17 BScEcon Economics and Geography
Duration: 3FT Hon
Entry Requirements: ***GCE:*** AAAe-AABe. ***SQAAH:*** AAA-AAB. Interview required.

LANGUAGE COMBINATIONS

A20 THE UNIVERSITY OF ABERDEEN
UNIVERSITY OFFICE
KING'S COLLEGE
ABERDEEN AB24 3FX
t: +44 (0) 1224 273504 f: +44 (0) 1224 272034
e: sras@abdn.ac.uk
// www.abdn.ac.uk/sras

NR41 MA Accountancy and French
Duration: 5FT Hon
Entry Requirements: ***GCE:*** BBB. ***SQAH:*** BBBB. ***IB:*** 30. ***BTEC ND:*** MMM.

NR42 MA Accountancy and German
Duration: 5FT Hon
Entry Requirements: ***GCE:*** BBB. ***SQAH:*** BBBB. ***IB:*** 30. ***BTEC ND:*** MMM.

NR44 MA Accountancy and Hispanic Studies
Duration: 5FT Hon
Entry Requirements: ***GCE:*** BBB. ***SQAH:*** BBBB. ***IB:*** 30. ***BTEC ND:*** MMM.

N4R1 MA Accountancy with French
Duration: 4FT Hon
Entry Requirements: ***GCE:*** BBB. ***SQAH:*** BBBB. ***IB:*** 30. ***BTEC ND:*** MMM.

N4R2 MA Accountancy with German
Duration: 4FT Hon
Entry Requirements: ***GCE:*** BBB. ***SQAH:*** BBBB. ***IB:*** 30. ***BTEC ND:*** MMM.

LQ13 MA Economics and English
Duration: 4FT Hon
Entry Requirements: ***GCE:*** BBB. ***SQAH:*** BBBB. ***IB:*** 30. ***BTEC ND:*** MMM.

LR11 MA Economics and French
Duration: 5FT Hon
Entry Requirements: ***GCE:*** BBB. ***SQAH:*** BBBB. ***IB:*** 30. ***BTEC ND:*** MMM.

RL11 MA Economics and French (4 years)
Duration: 4FT Hon
Entry Requirements: ***GCE:*** BBB. ***SQAH:*** BBBB. ***IB:*** 30. ***BTEC ND:*** MMM.

QL51 MA Economics and Gaelic Studies
Duration: 4FT Hon
Entry Requirements: ***GCE:*** BBB. ***SQAH:*** BBBB. ***IB:*** 30. ***BTEC ND:*** MMM.

LR12 MA Economics and German
Duration: 5FT Hon
Entry Requirements: ***GCE:*** BBB. ***SQAH:*** BBBB. ***IB:*** 30. ***BTEC ND:*** MMM.

RL21 MA Economics and German (4 years)
Duration: 4FT Hon
Entry Requirements: ***GCE:*** BBB. ***SQAH:*** BBBB. ***IB:*** 30. ***BTEC ND:*** MMM.

LR14 MA Economics and Hispanic Studies
Duration: 5FT Hon
Entry Requirements: ***GCE:*** BBB. ***SQAH:*** BBBB. ***IB:*** 30. ***BTEC ND:*** MMM.

RL41 MA Economics and Hispanic Studies (4 years)
Duration: 4FT Hon
Entry Requirements: ***GCE:*** BBB. ***SQAH:*** BBBB. ***IB:*** 30. ***BTEC ND:*** MMM.

LQ12 MA Economics and Literature in a World Context
Duration: 4FT Hon
Entry Requirements: ***GCE:*** BBB. ***SQAH:*** BBBB. ***IB:*** 30. ***BTEC ND:*** MMM.

NQ33 MA English and Finance
Duration: 4FT Hon
Entry Requirements: ***GCE:*** BBB. ***SQAH:*** BBBB. ***IB:*** 30. ***BTEC ND:*** MMM.

NR31 MA Finance and French
Duration: 5FT Hon
Entry Requirements: ***GCE:*** BBB. ***SQAH:*** BBBB. ***IB:*** 30. ***BTEC ND:*** MMM.

RN13 MA Finance and French (4 years)
Duration: 4FT Hon
Entry Requirements: ***GCE:*** BBB. ***SQAH:*** BBBB. ***IB:*** 30. ***BTEC ND:*** MMM.

NR32 MA Finance and German
Duration: 5FT Hon
Entry Requirements: ***GCE:*** BBB. ***SQAH:*** BBBB. ***IB:*** 30. ***BTEC ND:*** MMM.

RN23 MA Finance and German (4 years)
Duration: 4FT Hon
Entry Requirements: ***GCE:*** BBB. ***SQAH:*** BBBB. ***IB:*** 30. ***BTEC ND:*** MMM.

RN43 MA Finance and Hispanic Studies
Duration: 5FT Hon
Entry Requirements: ***GCE:*** BBB. ***SQAH:*** BBBB. ***IB:*** 30. ***BTEC ND:*** MMM.

RNK3 MA Finance and Hispanic Studies (4 years)
Duration: 4FT Hon
Entry Requirements: ***GCE:*** BBB. ***SQAH:*** BBBB. ***IB:*** 30. ***BTEC ND:*** MMM.

NQ32 MA Finance and Literature in a World Context
Duration: 4FT Hon
Entry Requirements: ***GCE:*** BBB. ***SQAH:*** BBBB. ***IB:*** 30. ***BTEC ND:*** MMM.

A40 ABERYSTWYTH UNIVERSITY
WELCOME CENTRE, ABERYSTWYTH UNIVERSITY
PENGLAIS CAMPUS
ABERYSTWYTH
CEREDIGION SY23 3FB
t: 01970 622021 f: 01970 627410
e: ug-admissions@aber.ac.uk
// www.aber.ac.uk

R1L1 BA French with Economics (4 years)
Duration: 4FT Hon
Entry Requirements: ***GCE:*** 260. ***IB:*** 28.

R4L1 BA Spanish with Economics (4 years)
Duration: 4FT Hon
Entry Requirements: ***GCE:*** 260. ***IB:*** 28.

N4Q5 BScEcon Accounting & Finance with Cymraeg
Duration: 3FT Hon
Entry Requirements: ***GCE:*** 280. ***IB:*** 27.

N4R1 BScEcon Accounting & Finance with French (4 years)
Duration: 4FT Hon
Entry Requirements: ***GCE:*** 280. ***IB:*** 27.

N4R2 BScEcon Accounting & Finance with German (4 years)
Duration: 4FT Hon
Entry Requirements: ***GCE:*** 280. ***IB:*** 27.

N4R4 BScEcon Accounting & Finance with Spanish (4 years)
Duration: 4FT Hon
Entry Requirements: ***GCE:*** 280. ***IB:*** 27.

NR41 BScEcon Accounting & Finance/French
Duration: 4FT Hon
Entry Requirements: ***GCE:*** 280. ***IB:*** 28.

NR44 BScEcon Accounting & Finance/Spanish
Duration: 4FT Hon
Entry Requirements: ***GCE:*** 280. ***IB:*** 28.

L1R1 BScEcon Economics with French (4 years)
Duration: 4FT Hon
Entry Requirements: ***GCE:*** 280. ***IB:*** 27.

L1R2 BScEcon Economics with German (4 years)
Duration: 4FT Hon
Entry Requirements: ***GCE:*** 280. ***IB:*** 27.

L1R4 BScEcon Economics with Spanish (4 years)
Duration: 4FT Hon
Entry Requirements: ***GCE:*** 280. ***IB:*** 27.

LR11 BScEcon Economics/French
Duration: 4FT Hon
Entry Requirements: ***GCE:*** 280. ***IB:*** 27.

B06 BANGOR UNIVERSITY
BANGOR
GWYNEDD LL57 2DG
t: 01248 382016/2017 f: 01248 370451
e: admissions@bangor.ac.uk
// www.bangor.ac.uk

NR43 BA Accounting/Italian (4 years)
Duration: 4FT Hon
Entry Requirements: ***GCE:*** 240-260. ***IB:*** 28.

NR44 BA Accounting/Spanish (4 years)
Duration: 4FT Hon
Entry Requirements: ***GCE:*** 240-260. ***IB:*** 28.

LR13 BA Economics/Italian (4 years)
Duration: 4FT Hon
Entry Requirements: ***GCE:*** 260-300. ***IB:*** 28.

LR14 BA Economics/Spanish (4 years)
Duration: 4FT Hon
Entry Requirements: ***GCE:*** 260-300. ***IB:*** 28.

NR41 BA French/Accounting (4 years)
Duration: 4FT Hon
Entry Requirements: ***GCE:*** 240-260. ***IB:*** 28.

LR11 BA French/Economics (4 years)
Duration: 4FT Hon
Entry Requirements: ***GCE:*** 240-260. ***IB:*** 28.

NR42 BA German/Accounting (4 years)
Duration: 4FT Hon
Entry Requirements: ***GCE:*** 240-260. ***IB:*** 28.

LR12 BA German/Economics (4 years)
Duration: 4FT Hon
Entry Requirements: ***GCE:*** 240-260. ***IB:*** 28.

B32 THE UNIVERSITY OF BIRMINGHAM
EDGBASTON
BIRMINGHAM B15 2TT
t: 0121 415 8900 f: 0121 414 7159
e: admissions@bham.ac.uk
// www.bham.ac.uk

RL71 BA Russian Studies and Economics (4 years)
Duration: 4FT Hon
Entry Requirements: ***GCE:*** ABB-BBB. ***SQAH:*** AABBB-ABBBB. ***SQAAH:*** AB.

L1R9 BSc Economics with Central & East European Studies
Duration: 3FT Hon
Entry Requirements: ***GCE:*** AAB. ***SQAH:*** AAABB. ***SQAAH:*** AAB-ABB.

L1R1 BSc Economics with French (4 years)
Duration: 4FT Hon
Entry Requirements: ***GCE:*** AAB. ***SQAH:*** AAABB. ***SQAAH:*** AAB-ABB.

L1R2 BSc Economics with German (4 years)
Duration: 4FT Hon
Entry Requirements: ***GCE:*** AAB. ***SQAH:*** AAABB. ***SQAAH:*** AAB-ABB.

L1R3 BSc Economics with Italian (4 years)
Duration: 4FT Hon
Entry Requirements: ***GCE:*** AAB. ***SQAH:*** AAABB. ***SQAAH:*** AAB-ABB.

L1T2 BSc Economics with Japanese (4 years)
Duration: 4FT Hon
Entry Requirements: ***GCE:*** AAB. ***SQAH:*** AAABB. ***SQAAH:*** AAB-ABB.

L1R5 BSc Economics with Portuguese (4 years)
Duration: 4FT Hon
Entry Requirements: ***GCE:*** AAB. ***SQAH:*** AAABB. ***SQAAH:*** AAB-ABB.

L1R7 BSc Economics with Russian Studies
Duration: 3FT Hon
Entry Requirements: ***GCE:*** AAB. ***SQAH:*** AAABB. ***SQAAH:*** AAB-ABB.

L1R4 BSc Economics with Spanish (4 years)
Duration: 4FT Hon
Entry Requirements: ***GCE:*** AAB. ***SQAH:*** AAABB. ***SQAAH:*** AAB-ABB.

B90 THE UNIVERSITY OF BUCKINGHAM
YEOMANRY HOUSE
HUNTER STREET
BUCKINGHAM MK18 1EG
t: 01280 820313 f: 01280 822245
e: info@buckingham.ac.uk
// www.buckingham.ac.uk

L1QH BSc Economics with English Language Studies
Duration: 2FT Hon
Entry Requirements: ***GCE:*** 240. ***IB:*** 26. ***BTEC NC:*** DD. ***BTEC ND:*** MMM.

L1Q3 BSc Economics with English as a Foreign Language
Duration: 2FT Hon
Entry Requirements: ***GCE:*** 240. ***IB:*** 26. ***BTEC NC:*** DD. ***BTEC ND:*** MMM.

L1R1 BSc Economics with French
Duration: 2FT Hon
Entry Requirements: ***GCE:*** 240. ***IB:*** 26. ***BTEC NC:*** DD. ***BTEC ND:*** MMM.

L1R4 BSc Economics with Spanish
Duration: 2FT Hon
Entry Requirements: ***GCE:*** 240. ***IB:*** 26. ***BTEC NC:*** DD. ***BTEC ND:*** MMM.

C15 CARDIFF UNIVERSITY
PO BOX 927
30-36 NEWPORT ROAD
CARDIFF CF24 0DE
t: 029 2087 9999 f: 029 2087 6138
e: admissions@cardiff.ac.uk
// www.cardiff.ac.uk

RL11 BA Economics/French (4 years)
Duration: 4FT Hon
Entry Requirements: ***GCE:*** AAB. ***SQAH:*** AAABB. ***SQAAH:*** ABB. ***IB:*** 35. ***BTEC ND:*** DDD. ***OCR NED:*** D2

RL21 BA Economics/German (4 years)
Duration: 4FT Hon
Entry Requirements: ***GCE:*** AAB-BBB. ***SQAH:*** AAABB-AABBB. ***SQAAH:*** AAB-BBB. ***IB:*** 33.

RL31 BA Economics/Italian (4 years)
Duration: 4FT Hon
Entry Requirements: ***GCE:*** AAB-BBB. ***SQAH:*** AAABB-AABBB. ***SQAAH:*** AAB-BBB. ***IB:*** 33. ***BTEC ND:*** DDD. ***OCR NED:*** D2

LR14 BA Economics/Spanish (4 years)
Duration: 4FT Hon
Entry Requirements: ***GCE:*** AAB-ABB. ***SQAH:*** AAABB-AABBB. ***SQAAH:*** AAB-ABB. ***IB:*** 33. ***OCR NED:*** D2

C55 UNIVERSITY OF CHESTER

PARKGATE ROAD
CHESTER CH1 4BJ
t: 01244 511000 f: 01244 511300
e: enquiries@chester.ac.uk
// www.chester.ac.uk

LR11 BA Economics and French

Duration: 3FT Hon

Entry Requirements: ***GCE:*** 240. ***SQAH:*** BBBB. ***IB:*** 24. ***BTEC NC:*** DM. ***BTEC ND:*** MMM.

LR12 BA Economics and German

Duration: 3FT Hon

Entry Requirements: ***GCE:*** 240. ***SQAH:*** BBBB. ***IB:*** 24. ***BTEC NC:*** DM. ***BTEC ND:*** MMM.

LR14 BA Economics and Spanish

Duration: 3FT Hon

Entry Requirements: ***Foundation:*** Pass. ***GCE:*** 240. ***SQAH:*** BBBB. ***IB:*** 24. ***BTEC NC:*** DM. ***BTEC ND:*** MMM.

R2L1 BA German with Economics

Duration: 3FT Hon

Entry Requirements: ***GCE:*** 240. ***SQAH:*** BBBB. ***IB:*** 24. ***BTEC NC:*** DM. ***BTEC ND:*** MMM.

R4L1 BA Spanish with Economics

Duration: 3FT Hon

Entry Requirements: ***Foundation:*** Pass. ***GCE:*** 240. ***SQAH:*** BBBB. ***IB:*** 24. ***BTEC NC:*** DM. ***BTEC ND:*** MMM.

L1R1 BSc Economics with French

Duration: 3FT Hon

Entry Requirements: ***GCE:*** 240. ***SQAH:*** BBBB. ***IB:*** 24. ***BTEC NC:*** DM. ***BTEC ND:*** MMM.

L1R2 BSc Economics with German

Duration: 3FT Hon

Entry Requirements: ***GCE:*** 240. ***SQAH:*** BBBB. ***IB:*** 24. ***BTEC NC:*** DM. ***BTEC ND:*** MMM.

L1R4 BSc Economics with Spanish

Duration: 3FT Hon

Entry Requirements: ***Foundation:*** Pass. ***GCE:*** 240. ***SQAH:*** BBBB. ***IB:*** 24. ***BTEC NC:*** DM. ***BTEC ND:*** MMM.

C58 UNIVERSITY OF CHICHESTER

BISHOP OTTER CAMPUS
COLLEGE LANE
CHICHESTER
WEST SUSSEX PO19 6PE
t: 01243 816002 f: 01243 816161
e: admissions@chi.ac.uk
// www.chiuni.ac.uk

N4Q3 BA Accounting & Finance with International English Studies

Duration: 3FT Hon

Entry Requirements: ***GCE:*** CCC. ***SQAAH:*** CCC. ***IB:*** 28. ***BTEC ND:*** MMM.

NQ43 BA Accounting and International English Studies

Duration: 3FT Hon

Entry Requirements: ***GCE:*** CCC. ***SQAAH:*** CCC. ***IB:*** 28. ***BTEC ND:*** MMM.

D39 UNIVERSITY OF DERBY

KEDLESTON ROAD
DERBY DE22 1GB
t: 08701 202330 f: 01332 597724
e: askadmissions@derby.ac.uk
// www.derby.ac.uk

NT47 BA Accounting and American Studies

Duration: 3FT Hon

Entry Requirements: ***Foundation:*** Merit. ***GCE:*** 180-240. ***IB:*** 26. ***BTEC NC:*** DM. ***BTEC ND:*** MMP.

NQ43 BA Accounting and English

Duration: 3FT Hon

Entry Requirements: ***Foundation:*** Merit. ***GCE:*** 180-240. ***IB:*** 26. ***BTEC NC:*** DM. ***BTEC ND:*** MMP.

D65 UNIVERSITY OF DUNDEE

DUNDEE DD1 4HN
t: 01382 383838 f: 01382 388150
e: ContactUs@dundee.ac.uk
// www.dundee.ac.uk/admissions/undergraduate/

LR18 MA Economics and European Studies

Duration: 4FT Hon

Entry Requirements: ***GCE:*** BCC. ***SQAH:*** BBBB. ***IB:*** 30. ***BTEC ND:*** DMM.

L1R1 MA Economics with French

Duration: 4FT Hon

Entry Requirements: ***GCE:*** BCC. ***SQAH:*** BBBB. ***IB:*** 30. ***BTEC ND:*** DMM.

L1R2 MA Economics with German

Duration: 4FT Hon

Entry Requirements: ***GCE:*** BCC. ***SQAH:*** BBBB. ***IB:*** 30. ***BTEC ND:*** DMM.

L1R4 MA Economics with Spanish
Duration: 4FT Hon
Entry Requirements: ***GCE:*** BCC. ***SQAH:*** BBBB. ***IB:*** 30. ***BTEC ND:*** DMM.

L1RC MA Financial Economics with French
Duration: 4FT Hon
Entry Requirements: ***GCE:*** BCC. ***SQAH:*** BBBB. ***IB:*** 30. ***BTEC ND:*** DMM.

L1RF MA Financial Economics with German
Duration: 4FT Hon
Entry Requirements: ***GCE:*** BCC. ***SQAH:*** BBBB. ***IB:*** 30. ***BTEC ND:*** DMM.

L1RK MA Financial Economics with Spanish
Duration: 4FT Hon
Entry Requirements: ***GCE:*** BCC. ***SQAH:*** BBBB. ***IB:*** 30. ***BTEC ND:*** DMM.

D86 DURHAM UNIVERSITY
DURHAM UNIVERSITY
UNIVERSITY OFFICE
DURHAM DH1 3HP
t: 0191 334 2000 f: 0191 334 6055
e: admissions@durham.ac.uk
// www.durham.ac.uk

L1R1 BA Economics with French
Duration: 4FT Hon
Entry Requirements: ***GCE:*** AAA. ***SQAAH:*** AAA. ***IB:*** 37.

E56 THE UNIVERSITY OF EDINBURGH
STUDENT RECRUITMENT & ADMISSIONS
57 GEORGE SQUARE
EDINBURGH EH8 9JU
t: 0131 650 4360 f: 0131 651 1236
e: sra.enquiries@ed.ac.uk
// www.ed.ac.uk/studying/undergraduate/

TL61 MA Arabic and Economics
Duration: 4FT Hon
Entry Requirements: ***GCE:*** AAA-BBB. ***SQAH:*** AABB-BBBB. ***IB:*** 34.

LT11 MA Economics and Chinese
Duration: 4FT Hon
Entry Requirements: ***GCE:*** AAA-BBB. ***SQAH:*** AABB-BBBB. ***IB:*** 34.

E70 THE UNIVERSITY OF ESSEX
WIVENHOE PARK
COLCHESTER
ESSEX CO4 3SQ
t: 01206 873666 f: 01206 873423
e: admit@essex.ac.uk
// www.essex.ac.uk

L1R1 BA Economics with French
Duration: 3FT Hon
Entry Requirements: ***GCE:*** 320. ***SQAH:*** AAAB. ***IB:*** 34. ***BTEC NC:*** DD. ***BTEC ND:*** DDM.

L1RC BA Economics with French (International Exchange)
Duration: 4FT Hon
Entry Requirements: ***GCE:*** 320. ***SQAH:*** AAAB. ***IB:*** 34. ***BTEC NC:*** DD. ***BTEC ND:*** DDM.

L1R2 BA Economics with German
Duration: 3FT Hon
Entry Requirements: ***GCE:*** 320. ***SQAH:*** AAAB. ***IB:*** 34. ***BTEC NC:*** DD. ***BTEC ND:*** DDM.

L1RF BA Economics with German (International Exchange)
Duration: 4FT Hon
Entry Requirements: ***GCE:*** 320. ***SQAH:*** AAAB. ***IB:*** 34. ***BTEC NC:*** DD. ***BTEC ND:*** DDM.

L1R3 BA Economics with Italian
Duration: 3FT Hon
Entry Requirements: ***GCE:*** 320. ***SQAH:*** AAAB. ***IB:*** 34. ***BTEC NC:*** DD. ***BTEC ND:*** DDM.

L1RH BA Economics with Italian (International Exchange)
Duration: 4FT Hon
Entry Requirements: ***GCE:*** 320. ***SQAH:*** AAAB. ***IB:*** 34. ***BTEC NC:*** DD. ***BTEC ND:*** DDM.

L1R5 BA Economics with Portuguese
Duration: 4FT Hon
Entry Requirements: ***GCE:*** 320. ***SQAH:*** AAAB. ***IB:*** 34. ***BTEC NC:*** DD. ***BTEC ND:*** DDM.

L1RM BA Economics with Portuguese (International Exchange)
Duration: 4FT Hon
Entry Requirements: ***GCE:*** 320. ***SQAH:*** AAAB. ***IB:*** 34. ***BTEC NC:*** DD. ***BTEC ND:*** DDM.

L1R4 BA Economics with Spanish
Duration: 3FT Hon
Entry Requirements: ***GCE:*** 320. ***SQAH:*** AAAB. ***IB:*** 34. ***BTEC NC:*** DD. ***BTEC ND:*** DDM.

L1RK BA Economics with Spanish (International Exchange)
Duration: 4FT Hon
Entry Requirements: ***GCE:*** 320. ***SQAH:*** AAAB. ***IB:*** 34. ***BTEC NC:*** DD. ***BTEC ND:*** DDM.

G14 UNIVERSITY OF GLAMORGAN, CARDIFF AND PONTYPRIDD
ENQUIRIES AND ADMISSIONS UNIT
PONTYPRIDD CF37 1DL
t: 0800 716925 f: 01443 654050
e: enquiries@glam.ac.uk
// www.glam.ac.uk

N4Q5 BA Accounting with Professional Welsh
Duration: 3FT Hon
Entry Requirements: ***GCE:*** 220-260. ***BTEC NC:*** DD. ***BTEC ND:*** MMM. Interview required.

G28 UNIVERSITY OF GLASGOW
THE UNIVERSITY OF GLASGOW
THE FRASER BUILDING
65 HILLHEAD STREET
GLASGOW G12 8QF
t: 0141 330 6062 f: 0141 330 2961
e: ugenquiries@gla.ac.uk (UK/EU undergrad enquiries only)
// www.glasgow.ac.uk

N4T9 BAcc Accountancy with Languages
Duration: 4FT Hon
Entry Requirements: ***GCE:*** AAB. ***SQAH:*** AAABB. ***IB:*** 34.

RL81 MA Central & East European Studies/Economics
Duration: 4FT Hon
Entry Requirements: ***GCE:*** AAB. ***SQAH:*** AAAB-AABB. ***IB:*** 34.

LQC2 MA Comparative Literature/Economics
Duration: 4FT Hon
Entry Requirements: ***GCE:*** AAB. ***SQAH:*** AAAB-AABB. ***IB:*** 34.

RL7C MA Czech/Economics
Duration: 5FT Hon
Entry Requirements: ***GCE:*** AAB. ***SQAH:*** AAAB-AABB. ***IB:*** 34.

L1RT MA Economics with Czech Language
Duration: 5FT Hon
Entry Requirements: ***GCE:*** AAB. ***SQAH:*** AAAB-AABB. ***IB:*** 34.

L1R1 MA Economics with French Language
Duration: 5FT Hon
Entry Requirements: ***GCE:*** AAB. ***SQAH:*** AAAB-AABB. ***IB:*** 34.

L1RR MA Economics with Polish Language
Duration: 5FT Hon
Entry Requirements: ***GCE:*** AAB. ***SQAH:*** AAAB-AABB. ***IB:*** 34.

L1R7 MA Economics with Russian Language
Duration: 5FT Hon
Entry Requirements: ***GCE:*** AAB. ***SQAH:*** AAAB-AABB. ***IB:*** 34.

L1RK MA Economics with Spanish
Duration: 5FT Hon
Entry Requirements: ***GCE:*** AAB. ***SQAH:*** AAAB-AABB. ***IB:*** 34.

LQ1H MA Economics/English Language
Duration: 4FT Hon
Entry Requirements: ***GCE:*** AAB. ***SQAH:*** AAAB-AABB. ***IB:*** 34.

LQD3 MA Economics/English Literature
Duration: 4FT Hon
Entry Requirements: ***GCE:*** AAB. ***SQAH:*** AAAB-AABB. ***IB:*** 34.

LR11 MA Economics/French
Duration: 5FT Hon
Entry Requirements: ***GCE:*** AAB. ***SQAH:*** AAAB-AABB. ***IB:*** 34.

LQ17 MA Economics/Greek
Duration: 4FT Hon
Entry Requirements: ***GCE:*** AAB. ***SQAH:*** AAAB-AABB. ***IB:*** 34.

LQ16 MA Economics/Latin
Duration: 4FT Hon
Entry Requirements: ***GCE:*** AAB. ***SQAH:*** AAAB-AABB. ***IB:*** 34.

LRC7 MA Economics/Polish
Duration: 5FT Hon
Entry Requirements: ***GCE:*** AAB. ***SQAH:*** AAAB-AABB. ***IB:*** 34.

LR17 MA Economics/Russian
Duration: 5FT Hon
Entry Requirements: ***GCE:*** AAB. ***SQAH:*** AAAB-AABB. ***IB:*** 34.

LQ12 MA Economics/Scottish Literature
Duration: 4FT Hon
Entry Requirements: ***GCE:*** AAB. ***SQAH:*** AAAB-AABB. ***IB:*** 34.

RL41 MA Spanish/Economics
Duration: 5FT Hon
Entry Requirements: ***GCE:*** AAB. ***SQAH:*** AAAB-AABB. ***IB:*** 34.

H36 UNIVERSITY OF HERTFORDSHIRE
UNIVERSITY ADMISSIONS SERVICE
COLLEGE LANE
HATFIELD
HERTS AL10 9AB
t: 01707 284800 f: 01707 284870
// www.herts.ac.uk

NR41 BA Accounting with French
Duration: 3FT/4SW Hon
Entry Requirements: ***GCE:*** 240.

NR42 BA Accounting with German
Duration: 3FT/4SW Hon
Entry Requirements: ***GCE:*** 240.

NR43 BA Accounting with Italian
Duration: 3FT/4SW Hon
Entry Requirements: ***GCE:*** 260.

N4T1 BA Accounting with Mandarin Chinese
Duration: 3FT/4SW Hon
Entry Requirements: ***GCE:*** 260.

NR44 BA Accounting with Spanish
Duration: 3FT/4SW Hon
Entry Requirements: ***GCE:*** 260.

NR48 BA Accounting/European Studies
Duration: 3FT/4SW Hon
Entry Requirements: ***GCE:*** 260.

LR11 BA Economics with French
Duration: 3FT/4SW Hon
Entry Requirements: ***GCE:*** 240.

LR12 BA Economics with German
Duration: 3FT/4SW Hon
Entry Requirements: ***GCE:*** 240.

LR13 BA Economics with Italian
Duration: 3FT/4SW Hon
Entry Requirements: ***GCE:*** 240.

L1T1 BA Economics with Mandarin Chinese
Duration: 3FT/4SW Hon
Entry Requirements: ***GCE:*** 260.

LR14 BA Economics with Spanish
Duration: 3FT/4SW Hon
Entry Requirements: ***GCE:*** 200-240.

LR18 BA Economics/European Studies
Duration: 3FT/4SW Hon
Entry Requirements: ***GCE:*** 260.

R8N3 BA European Studies with Finance
Duration: 3FT/4SW Hon
Entry Requirements: ***GCE:*** 260.

L1Q1 BSc Economics/English Language & Communication
Duration: 3FT/4SW Hon
Entry Requirements: ***GCE:*** 220.

Q1L1 BSc English Language & Communication/Economics
Duration: 3FT/4SW Hon
Entry Requirements: ***GCE:*** 220.

K12 KEELE UNIVERSITY
STAFFS ST5 5BG
t: 01782 734005 f: 01782 632343
e: undergraduate@keele.ac.uk
// www.keele.ac.uk

NQ43 BA Accounting and English
Duration: 3FT Hon
Entry Requirements: ***GCE:*** 300-320.

NT37 BA American Studies and Finance
Duration: 3FT Hon
Entry Requirements: ***GCE:*** 300-320.

LQ13 BA Economics and English
Duration: 3FT Hon
Entry Requirements: ***GCE:*** 300-320.

NQ33 BA English and Finance
Duration: 3FT Hon
Entry Requirements: ***GCE:*** 300-320.

K24 THE UNIVERSITY OF KENT
INFORMATION, RECRUITMENT & ADMISSIONS REGISTRY
UNIVERSITY OF KENT
CANTERBURY, KENT CT2 7NZ
t: 01227 827272 f: 01227 827077
e: information@kent.ac.uk
// www.kent.ac.uk

L1R4 BSc Economics with a Language (Spanish)
Duration: 3FT Hon
Entry Requirements: ***GCE:*** 320. ***IB:*** 34. ***BTEC NC:*** DD. ***BTEC ND:*** DDM. ***OCR ND:*** D ***OCR NED:*** D2

K84 KINGSTON UNIVERSITY
STUDENT INFORMATION & ADVICE CENTRE
COOPER HOUSE
40-46 SURBITON ROAD
KINGSTON UPON THAMES KT1 2HX
t: 0844 8552177 f: 020 8547 7080
e: aps@kingston.ac.uk
// www.kingston.ac.uk

L1Q3 BA Economics (Applied) with English Language & Communication
Duration: 3FT Hon
Entry Requirements: ***GCE:*** 260-360. ***IB:*** 24.

L1R1 BA Economics (Applied) with French
Duration: 3FT Hon
Entry Requirements: ***GCE:*** 260-360. ***IB:*** 24.

L1R4 BA Economics (Applied) with Spanish
Duration: 3FT Hon
Entry Requirements: ***GCE:*** 260-360. ***IB:*** 24.

Q3L1 BA English Language & Communication with Economics (Applied)
Duration: 3FT Hon
Entry Requirements: ***GCE:*** 240-360.

L23 UNIVERSITY OF LEEDS
THE UNIVERSITY OF LEEDS
LEEDS LS2 9JT
t: 0113 343 3999
e: admissions@adm.leeds.ac.uk
// www.leeds.ac.uk

LT13 BA Asia Pacific Studies and Economics
Duration: 3FT Hon
Entry Requirements: ***GCE:*** ABB. ***SQAAH:*** ABB.

LT11 BA Chinese and Economics
Duration: 4FT Hon
Entry Requirements: ***GCE:*** ABB. ***SQAAH:*** ABB.

RL11 BA Economics and French
Duration: 4FT Hon
Entry Requirements: ***GCE:*** AAB. ***SQAAH:*** ABB.

RL21 BA Economics and German
Duration: 4FT Hon
Entry Requirements: ***GCE:*** ABB. ***SQAAH:*** ABB.

LR13 BA Economics and Italian A
Duration: 4FT Hon
Entry Requirements: ***GCE:*** ABB. ***SQAAH:*** ABB.

LRC3 BA Economics and Italian B
Duration: 4FT Hon
Entry Requirements: ***GCE:*** ABB. ***SQAAH:*** ABB.

TL21 BA Economics and Japanese
Duration: 4FT Hon
Entry Requirements: ***GCE:*** AAB. ***SQAAH:*** AAB.

RL71 BA Economics and Russian A
Duration: 4FT Hon
Entry Requirements: ***GCE:*** ABB. ***SQAAH:*** ABB.

RLR1 BA Economics and Russian B
Duration: 4FT Hon
Entry Requirements: ***GCE:*** ABB. ***SQAAH:*** ABB.

RLT1 BA Economics and Russian Civilisation
Duration: 3FT Hon
Entry Requirements: ***GCE:*** ABB. ***SQAAH:*** ABB.

LT1H BA Economics and South East Asian Studies
Duration: 4FT Hon
Entry Requirements: ***GCE:*** ABB. ***SQAAH:*** ABB.

RL41 BA Economics and Spanish
Duration: 4FT Hon
Entry Requirements: ***GCE:*** ABB. ***SQAAH:*** ABB.

LT1J BA Economics and Thai & South East Asian Studies
Duration: 4FT Hon
Entry Requirements: ***GCE:*** ABB. ***SQAAH:*** ABB.

L75 LONDON SOUTH BANK UNIVERSITY
103 BOROUGH ROAD
LONDON SE1 0AA
t: 020 7815 7815 f: 020 7815 8273
e: enquiry@lsbu.ac.uk
// www.lsbu.ac.uk

N4Q3 BA Accounting with English Language Studies
Duration: 3FT Hon
Entry Requirements: ***GCE:*** 160. ***IB:*** 24. ***BTEC NC:*** MM. ***BTEC ND:*** MPP.

QN34 BA English Language Studies and Accounting
Duration: 3FT Hon
Entry Requirements: ***GCE:*** 160. ***IB:*** 24. ***BTEC NC:*** MM. ***BTEC ND:*** MPP.

M40 THE MANCHESTER METROPOLITAN UNIVERSITY
ADMISSIONS OFFICE
ALL SAINTS (GMS)
ALL SAINTS
MANCHESTER M15 6BH
t: 0161 247 2000
// www.mmu.ac.uk

NQ33 BA Financial Management/English
Duration: 3FT Hon
Entry Requirements: ***GCE:*** 260. ***BTEC ND:*** MMM.

LR19 BA/BSc Economics/European Studies
Duration: 3FT Hon
Entry Requirements: ***GCE:*** 220. ***IB:*** 26.

LR1Y BA/BSc Economics/Language(s)
Duration: 3FT/4FT Hon
Entry Requirements: ***GCE:*** 240. ***IB:*** 27.

LQ1C BA/BSc Economics/Linguistics
Duration: 3FT Hon
Entry Requirements: ***GCE:*** 240. ***IB:*** 27.

N38 UNIVERSITY OF NORTHAMPTON

PARK CAMPUS
BOUGHTON GREEN ROAD
NORTHAMPTON NN2 7AL
t: 0800 358 2232 f: 01604 722083
e: admissions@northampton.ac.uk
// www.northampton.ac.uk

N4Q3 BA Accounting/English

Duration: 3FT Hon
Entry Requirements: ***GCE:*** 220-260. ***SQAH:*** ABB-BBBC. ***IB:*** 24.

N4R2 BA Accounting/German

Duration: 3FT Hon
Entry Requirements: ***GCE:*** 220-260. ***SQAH:*** ABB-BBBC. ***IB:*** 24.

L1Q3 BA Economics/English

Duration: 3FT Hon
Entry Requirements: ***GCE:*** 220-260. ***SQAH:*** ABB-BBBC. ***IB:*** 24.

L1R1 BA Economics/French

Duration: 3FT Hon
Entry Requirements: ***GCE:*** 220-260. ***SQAH:*** ABB-BBBC. ***IB:*** 24.

Q3N4 BA English/Accounting

Duration: 3FT Hon
Entry Requirements: ***GCE:*** 220-260. ***SQAH:*** ABB-BBBC. ***IB:*** 24.

Q3L1 BA English/Economics

Duration: 3FT Hon
Entry Requirements: ***GCE:*** 220-260. ***SQAH:*** ABB-BBBC. ***IB:*** 24.

R1L1 BA French/Economics

Duration: 3FT Hon
Entry Requirements: ***GCE:*** 220-260. ***SQAH:*** ABB-BBBC. ***IB:*** 24.

R2N4 BA German/Accounting

Duration: 3FT Hon
Entry Requirements: ***GCE:*** 220-260. ***SQAH:*** ABB-BBBC. ***IB:*** 24.

N84 THE UNIVERSITY OF NOTTINGHAM

THE ADMISSIONS OFFICE
THE UNIVERSITY OF NOTTINGHAM
UNIVERSITY PARK
NOTTINGHAM NG7 2RD
t: 0115 951 5151 f: 0115 951 4668
// www.nottingham.ac.uk

L1T1 BA Economics with Chinese Studies

Duration: 3FT Hon
Entry Requirements: ***GCE:*** AAA-AABB. ***SQAAH:*** AAA. ***IB:*** 38.

L1R1 BA Economics with French

Duration: 4FT Hon
Entry Requirements: ***GCE:*** AAA-AABB. ***SQAAH:*** AAA. ***IB:*** 38.

L1R2 BA Economics with German

Duration: 4FT Hon
Entry Requirements: ***GCE:*** AAA-AABB. ***SQAAH:*** AAA. ***IB:*** 38.

L1R4 BA Economics with Hispanic Studies

Duration: 4FT Hon
Entry Requirements: ***GCE:*** AAA-AABB. ***SQAAH:*** AAA. ***IB:*** 38.

L1R7 BA Economics with Russian

Duration: 4FT Hon
Entry Requirements: ***GCE:*** AAA-AABB. ***SQAAH:*** AAA. ***IB:*** 38.

P60 UNIVERSITY OF PLYMOUTH

DRAKE CIRCUS
PLYMOUTH PL4 8AA
t: 01752 588037 f: 01752 588050
e: admissions@plymouth.ac.uk
// www.plymouth.ac.uk

N4R1 BA Accounting with French

Duration: 3FT/4SW Hon
Entry Requirements: ***GCE:*** 240. ***IB:*** 26.

N4R9 BA Accounting with Modern Languages

Duration: 3FT/4SW Hon
Entry Requirements: ***GCE:*** 240. ***IB:*** 26. ***BTEC NC:*** DD. ***BTEC ND:*** MMM.

N4R4 BA Accounting with Spanish

Duration: 3FT/4SW Hon
Entry Requirements: ***GCE:*** 240. ***IB:*** 26.

P80 UNIVERSITY OF PORTSMOUTH

ACADEMIC REGISTRY
UNIVERSITY HOUSE
WINSTON CHURCHILL AVENUE
PORTSMOUTH PO1 2UP
t: 023 9284 8484 f: 023 9284 3082
e: admissions@port.ac.uk
// www.port.ac.uk

LQ13 BA International Trade and English

Duration: 3FT Hon
Entry Requirements: Contact the institution for details.

Q75 QUEEN'S UNIVERSITY BELFAST

UNIVERSITY ROAD
BELFAST BT7 1NN
t: 028 9097 3838 f: 028 9097 2828
e: admissions@qub.ac.uk
// www.qub.ac.uk

QL51 BA Irish & Celtic/Linguistics

Duration: 3FT Hon
Entry Requirements: ***GCE:*** BBB-BBCb.

N4R1 BSc Accounting with French (4 years)

Duration: 4FT Hon
Entry Requirements: ***GCE:*** AAB-ABBa. ***SQAH:*** AAAA-AAABB. ***SQAAH:*** AAB. ***IB:*** 34.

N4R4 BSc Accounting with Spanish (4 years)
Duration: 4FT Hon
Entry Requirements: ***GCE:*** AAB-ABBa. ***SQAH:*** AAAA-AAABB. ***SQAAH:*** AAB. ***IB:*** 34.

L1R1 BSc Economics with French
Duration: 3FT Hon
Entry Requirements: ***GCE:*** BBB-BBCb. ***SQAH:*** BBBBB. ***SQAAH:*** BBB. ***IB:*** 32.

L1R4 BSc Economics with Spanish
Duration: 3FT Hon
Entry Requirements: ***GCE:*** BBB-BBCb. ***SQAH:*** BBBBB. ***SQAAH:*** BBB. ***IB:*** 32.

R12 THE UNIVERSITY OF READING
THE UNIVERSITY OF READING
PO BOX 217
READING RG6 6AH
t: 0118 378 8619 f: 0118 378 8924
e: student.recruitment@reading.ac.uk
// www.reading.ac.uk

LR11 BA French and Economics
Duration: 4FT Hon
Entry Requirements: ***GCE:*** 300-320. ***OCR ND:*** M1 ***OCR NED:*** D2

LR12 BA German and Economics
Duration: 4FT Hon
Entry Requirements: ***GCE:*** 300-320.

LR13 BA Italian and Economics
Duration: 4FT Hon
Entry Requirements: ***GCE:*** 300-320.

R72 ROYAL HOLLOWAY, UNIVERSITY OF LONDON
ROYAL HOLLOWAY, UNIVERSITY OF LONDON
EGHAM
SURREY TW20 0EX
t: 01784 434455 f: 01784 473662
e: Admissions@rhul.ac.uk
// www.rhul.ac.uk

L1R1 BA Economics with French
Duration: 3FT Hon
Entry Requirements: ***GCE:*** AAA-ABB. ***SQAH:*** AAAAA-AABBB. ***SQAAH:*** AAA-ABB. ***IB:*** 32. ***BTEC NC:*** DM. ***BTEC ND:*** DDM.

L1R2 BA Economics with German
Duration: 3FT Hon
Entry Requirements: ***GCE:*** AAA-ABB. ***SQAH:*** AAAAA-AABBB. ***SQAAH:*** AAA-ABB. ***IB:*** 32. ***BTEC NC:*** DM. ***BTEC ND:*** DDM.

L1R3 BA Economics with Italian
Duration: 3FT Hon
Entry Requirements: ***GCE:*** AAA-ABB. ***SQAH:*** AAAAA-AABBB. ***SQAAH:*** AAA-ABB. ***IB:*** 32. ***BTEC NC:*** DM. ***BTEC ND:*** DDM.

L1R4 BA Economics with Spanish
Duration: 3FT Hon
Entry Requirements: ***GCE:*** AAA-ABB. ***SQAH:*** AAAAA-AABBB. ***SQAAH:*** AAA-ABB. ***IB:*** 32. ***BTEC NC:*** DM. ***BTEC ND:*** DDM.

S09 SCHOOL OF ORIENTAL AND AFRICAN STUDIES (UNIVERSITY OF LONDON)
THORNHAUGH STREET
RUSSELL SQUARE
LONDON WC1H 0XG
t: 020 7074 5106 f: 020 7898 4039
e: undergradadmissions@soas.ac.uk
// www.soas.ac.uk

TL41 BA Bengali and Economics
Duration: 4FT Hon
Entry Requirements: ***GCE:*** AAA. ***SQAH:*** AABBB-BBBBB. ***SQAAH:*** ABB-BBB. ***IB:*** 36.

TL51 BA Economics and African Studies
Duration: 3FT Hon
Entry Requirements: Contact the institution for details.

LT16 BA Economics and Arabic
Duration: 4FT Hon
Entry Requirements: Contact the institution for details.

LT1H BA Economics and Burmese
Duration: 3FT Hon
Entry Requirements: Contact the institution for details.

LT11 BA Economics and Chinese
Duration: 4FT Hon
Entry Requirements: Contact the institution for details.

LQ13 BA Economics and Linguistics
Duration: 3FT Hon
Entry Requirements: Contact the institution for details.

TLJC BA Economics and South-East Asian Studies
Duration: 3FT Hon
Entry Requirements: ***GCE:*** AAA. ***SQAH:*** AABBB-BBBBB. ***SQAAH:*** ABB-BBB. ***IB:*** 36. ***BTEC ND:*** DDM.

LT19 BA Georgian and Economics
Duration: 3FT Hon
Entry Requirements: Contact the institution for details.

LTC5 BA Hausa and Economics
Duration: 4FT Hon
Entry Requirements: Contact the institution for details.

LQ14 BA Hebrew and Economics
Duration: 4FT Hon
Entry Requirements: Contact the institution for details.

LTC3 BA Hindi and Economics
Duration: 4FT Hon
Entry Requirements: Contact the institution for details.

LTCH BA Indonesian and Economics
Duration: 3FT Hon
Entry Requirements: Contact the institution for details.

TL21 BA Japanese Studies and Economics
Duration: 3FT Hon
Entry Requirements: ***GCE:*** AAA.

LT12 BA Japanese and Economics
Duration: 4FT Hon
Entry Requirements: Contact the institution for details.

LTCL BA Korean and Economics
Duration: 4FT Hon
Entry Requirements: Contact the institution for details.

TL61 BA Middle Eastern Studies and Economics
Duration: 3FT Hon
Entry Requirements: ***GCE:*** AAA. ***SQAH:*** AABBB-BBBBB. ***SQAAH:*** ABB-BBB. ***IB:*** 36. ***BTEC ND:*** DDM.

LTD3 BA Nepali and Economics
Duration: 4FT Hon
Entry Requirements: Contact the institution for details.

LTD6 BA Persian and Economics
Duration: 3FT Hon
Entry Requirements: Contact the institution for details.

LQ19 BA Sanskrit and Economics
Duration: 3FT Hon
Entry Requirements: ***GCE:*** AAA. ***SQAH:*** AABBB-BBBBB. ***SQAAH:*** ABB-BBB. ***IB:*** 36. ***BTEC ND:*** DDM.

TLH1 BA South Asian Studies and Economics
Duration: 3FT Hon
Entry Requirements: Contact the institution for details.

LTD5 BA Swahili and Economics
Duration: 4FT Hon
Entry Requirements: Contact the institution for details.

TL31 BA Thai and Economics
Duration: 3FT Hon
Entry Requirements: Contact the institution for details.

LTC6 BA Turkish and Economics
Duration: 4FT Hon
Entry Requirements: Contact the institution for details.

TL3D BA Vietnamese and Economics
Duration: 3FT Hon
Entry Requirements: Contact the institution for details.

S18 THE UNIVERSITY OF SHEFFIELD
9 NORTHUMBERLAND ROAD
SHEFFIELD S10 2TT
t: 0114 222 1299 f: 0114 222 8032
e: ask@sheffield.ac.uk
// www.sheffield.ac.uk

RL11 BA French and Economics
Duration: 4FT Hon
Entry Requirements: ***GCE:*** BBB. ***SQAH:*** AABB. ***SQAAH:*** BBB. ***IB:*** 32. ***BTEC ND:*** DDM.

RL21 BA German and Economics
Duration: 4FT Hon
Entry Requirements: ***GCE:*** BBB. ***SQAH:*** AABB. ***SQAAH:*** BBB. ***IB:*** 32. ***BTEC ND:*** DDM.

RL41 BA Hispanic Studies and Economics
Duration: 4FT Hon
Entry Requirements: ***GCE:*** BBB. ***SQAH:*** AABB. ***SQAAH:*** BBB. ***IB:*** 32. ***BTEC ND:*** DDM.

RL71 BA Russian and Economics
Duration: 4FT Hon
Entry Requirements: ***GCE:*** BBB. ***SQAH:*** AABB. ***SQAAH:*** BBB. ***IB:*** 32. ***BTEC ND:*** DDM.

S30 SOUTHAMPTON SOLENT UNIVERSITY
EAST PARK TERRACE
SOUTHAMPTON
HAMPSHIRE SO14 0RT
t: +44 (0) 23 8031 9039 f: + 44 (0)23 8022 2259
e: admissions@solent.ac.uk or ask@solent.ac.uk
// www.solent.ac.uk/

N4QH BA Accountancy (International only) Language Fdn Year
Duration: 4FT Hon
Entry Requirements: Contact the institution for details.

N4Q3 BA Accountancy with Language Fdn Year
Duration: 4FT Hon
Entry Requirements: Contact the institution for details.

S36 UNIVERSITY OF ST ANDREWS
ST KATHARINE'S WEST
16 THE SCORES
ST ANDREWS
FIFE KY16 9AX
t: 01334 462150 f: 01334 463330
e: admissions@st-andrews.ac.uk
// www.st-and.ac.uk

LT16 MA Arabic-Economics
Duration: 4FT Hon
Entry Requirements: ***GCE:*** AAA. ***SQAH:*** AAAA. ***IB:*** 38.

L1R2 MA Economics with German
Duration: 4FT Hon
Entry Requirements: ***GCE:*** AAA. ***SQAH:*** AAAA. ***IB:*** 38.

L1RF MA Economics with German (with Integrated year Abroad)
Duration: 5FT Hon
Entry Requirements: ***GCE:*** AAA. ***SQAH:*** AAAA. ***IB:*** 38.

L1RT MA Economics with Russian
Duration: 4FT Hon
Entry Requirements: ***GCE:*** AAA. ***SQAH:*** AAAA. ***IB:*** 38.

L1RR MA Economics with Russian (with Integrated Year Abroad)
Duration: 5FT Hon
Entry Requirements: ***GCE:*** AAA. ***SQAH:*** AAAA. ***IB:*** 38.

L1RK MA Economics with Spanish
Duration: 4FT Hon
Entry Requirements: ***GCE:*** AAA. ***SQAH:*** AAAA. ***IB:*** 38.

L1RL MA Economics with Spanish (with Integrated Year Abroad)
Duration: 5FT Hon
Entry Requirements: ***GCE:*** AAA. ***SQAH:*** AAAA. ***IB:*** 38.

LQ13 MA Economics-English
Duration: 4FT Hon
Entry Requirements: ***GCE:*** AAA. ***SQAH:*** AAAA. ***IB:*** 38.

LR12 MA Economics-German
Duration: 4FT Hon
Entry Requirements: ***GCE:*** AAA. ***SQAH:*** AAAA. ***IB:*** 38.

LRC2 MA Economics-German with Year Abroad
Duration: 5FT Hon
Entry Requirements: ***GCE:*** AAA. ***SQAH:*** AAAA. ***IB:*** 38.

LR13 MA Economics-Italian
Duration: 4FT Hon
Entry Requirements: ***GCE:*** AAA. ***SQAH:*** AAAA. ***IB:*** 38.

LRC3 MA Economics-Italian with Year Abroad
Duration: 5FT Hon
Entry Requirements: ***GCE:*** AAA. ***SQAH:*** AAAA. ***IB:*** 38.

TL61 MA Economics-Middle East Studies
Duration: 4FT Hon
Entry Requirements: ***GCE:*** AAA. ***SQAH:*** AAAA. ***IB:*** 38.

LR17 MA Economics-Russian
Duration: 4FT Hon
Entry Requirements: ***GCE:*** AAA. ***SQAH:*** AAAA. ***IB:*** 38.

LRC7 MA Economics-Russian with Year Abroad
Duration: 5FT Hon
Entry Requirements: ***GCE:*** AAA. ***SQAH:*** AAAA. ***IB:*** 38.

LR14 MA Economics-Spanish
Duration: 4FT Hon
Entry Requirements: ***GCE:*** AAA. ***SQAH:*** AAAA. ***IB:*** 38.

LRC4 MA Economics-Spanish with Year Abroad
Duration: 5FT Hon
Entry Requirements: ***GCE:*** AAA. ***SQAH:*** AAAA. ***IB:*** 38.

S75 THE UNIVERSITY OF STIRLING
STIRLING FK9 4LA
t: 01786 467044 f: 01786 466800
e: admissions@stir.ac.uk
// www.stir.ac.uk

LR11 BA Economics and French
Duration: 4FT Hon
Entry Requirements: ***GCE:*** CCC. ***SQAH:*** BBBC. ***SQAAH:*** AAA-CCC. ***IB:*** 28. ***BTEC ND:*** DMM.

LR14 BA Economics and Spanish
Duration: 4FT Hon
Entry Requirements: ***GCE:*** CCC. ***SQAH:*** BBBC. ***SQAAH:*** AAA-CCC. ***IB:*** 28. ***BTEC ND:*** DMM.

N3R1 BA Finance and French
Duration: 4FT Hon
Entry Requirements: ***GCE:*** CCC. ***SQAH:*** BBBC. ***SQAAH:*** AAA-CCC. ***IB:*** 28. ***BTEC ND:*** DMM.

N3R4 BA Finance and Spanish
Duration: 4FT Hon
Entry Requirements: ***GCE:*** CCC. ***SQAH:*** BBBC. ***SQAAH:*** AAA-CCC. ***IB:*** 28. ***BTEC ND:*** DMM.

NR41 BAcc Accountancy and French
Duration: 4FT Hon
Entry Requirements: ***GCE:*** CCC. ***SQAH:*** BBBB. ***SQAAH:*** AAA-CCC. ***IB:*** 30. ***BTEC ND:*** DMM.

NR44 BAcc Accountancy and Spanish
Duration: 4FT Hon
Entry Requirements: ***GCE:*** CCC. ***SQAH:*** BBBB. ***SQAAH:*** AAA-CCC. ***IB:*** 30. ***BTEC ND:*** DMM.

S78 THE UNIVERSITY OF STRATHCLYDE
GLASGOW G1 1XQ
t: 0141 552 4400 f: 0141 552 0775
// www.strath.ac.uk

NR41 BA Accounting and French
Duration: 5FT Hon
Entry Requirements: ***GCE:*** AAB. ***SQAH:*** AAAA-AAABB. ***IB:*** 36.

NR43 BA Accounting and Italian
Duration: 5FT Hon
Entry Requirements: ***GCE:*** AAB. ***SQAH:*** AAAA-AAABB. ***IB:*** 36.

LR11 BA Economics and French
Duration: 5FT Hon
Entry Requirements: ***GCE:*** ABB. ***SQAH:*** ABBB-BBBBC. ***IB:*** 34.

LR13 BA Economics and Italian
Duration: 5FT Hon
Entry Requirements: ***GCE:*** ABB. ***SQAH:*** ABBB-BBBBC. ***IB:*** 34.

LR14 BA Economics and Spanish
Duration: 5FT Hon
Entry Requirements: ***GCE:*** ABB. ***SQAH:*** ABBB-BBBBC. ***IB:*** 34.

S84 UNIVERSITY OF SUNDERLAND
STUDENT HELPLINE
THE STUDENT GATEWAY
CHESTER ROAD
SUNDERLAND SR1 3SD
t: 0191 515 3000 f: 0191 515 3805
e: student-helpline@sunderland.ac.uk
// www.sunderland.ac.uk

T7N3 BA American Studies with Financial Management
Duration: 3FT Hon
Entry Requirements: ***GCE:*** 220-360. ***BTEC NC:*** DM. ***BTEC ND:*** MMM. ***OCR ND:*** D ***OCR NED:*** M3

Q1N3 BA English Language/Linguistics with Financial Management
Duration: 3FT Hon
Entry Requirements: ***GCE:*** 220-360. ***BTEC NC:*** DM. ***BTEC ND:*** MMM. ***OCR ND:*** D ***OCR NED:*** M3

Q3N3 BA English with Financial Management
Duration: 3FT Hon
Entry Requirements: ***GCE:*** 220-360. ***BTEC NC:*** DM. ***BTEC ND:*** MMM. ***OCR ND:*** D ***OCR NED:*** M3

NT37 BA Financial Management and American Studies
Duration: 3FT Hon
Entry Requirements: ***GCE:*** 220-360. ***BTEC NC:*** DM. ***BTEC ND:*** MMM. ***OCR ND:*** D ***OCR NED:*** M3

NQ33 BA Financial Management and English
Duration: 3FT Hon
Entry Requirements: ***GCE:*** 220-360. ***BTEC NC:*** DM. ***BTEC ND:*** MMM. ***OCR ND:*** D ***OCR NED:*** M3

NQ31 BA Financial Management and English Language/Linguistics
Duration: 3FT Hon
Entry Requirements: ***GCE:*** 220-360. ***BTEC NC:*** DM. ***BTEC ND:*** MMM. ***OCR ND:*** D ***OCR NED:*** M3

NR31 BA Financial Management and MFL French
Duration: 3FT Hon
Entry Requirements: ***GCE:*** 220-360. ***BTEC NC:*** DM. ***BTEC ND:*** MMM. ***OCR ND:*** D ***OCR NED:*** M3

NR32 BA Financial Management and MFL German
Duration: 3FT Hon
Entry Requirements: ***GCE:*** 220-360. ***BTEC NC:*** DM. ***BTEC ND:*** MMM. ***OCR ND:*** D ***OCR NED:*** M3

NR34 BA Financial Management and MFL Spanish
Duration: 3FT Hon
Entry Requirements: ***GCE:*** 220-360. ***BTEC NC:*** DM. ***BTEC ND:*** MMM. ***OCR ND:*** D ***OCR NED:*** M3

NQ3H BA Financial Management and Modern Foreign Language (English)
Duration: 3FT Hon
Entry Requirements: ***GCE:*** 220-360. ***BTEC NC:*** DM. ***BTEC ND:*** MMM. ***OCR ND:*** D ***OCR NED:*** M3

N3T7 BA Financial Management with American Studies
Duration: 3FT Hon
Entry Requirements: ***GCE:*** 220-360. ***BTEC NC:*** DM. ***BTEC ND:*** MMM. ***OCR ND:*** D ***OCR NED:*** M3

N3Q3 BA Financial Management with English
Duration: 3FT Hon
Entry Requirements: ***GCE:*** 220-360. ***BTEC NC:*** DM. ***BTEC ND:*** MMM. ***OCR ND:*** D ***OCR NED:*** M3

N3Q1 BA Financial Management with English Language/Linguistics
Duration: 3FT Hon
Entry Requirements: ***GCE:*** 220-360. ***BTEC NC:*** DM. ***BTEC ND:*** MMM. ***OCR ND:*** D ***OCR NED:*** M3

N3R1 BA Financial Management with MFL French
Duration: 3FT Hon
Entry Requirements: ***GCE:*** 220-360. ***BTEC NC:*** DM. ***BTEC ND:*** MMM. ***OCR ND:*** D ***OCR NED:*** M3

N3R2 BA Financial Management with MFL German
Duration: 3FT Hon
Entry Requirements: ***GCE:*** 220-360. ***BTEC NC:*** DM. ***BTEC ND:*** MMM. ***OCR ND:*** D ***OCR NED:*** M3

N3R4 BA Financial Management with MFL Spanish
Duration: 3FT Hon
Entry Requirements: ***GCE:*** 220-360. ***BTEC NC:*** DM. ***BTEC ND:*** MMM. ***OCR ND:*** D ***OCR NED:*** M3

N3QH BA Financial Management with Modern Foreign Language (English)
Duration: 3FT Hon
Entry Requirements: ***GCE:*** 220-360. ***BTEC NC:*** DM. ***BTEC ND:*** MMM. ***OCR ND:*** D ***OCR NED:*** M3

QN33 BA Modern Foreign Language (English) and Financial Management
Duration: 3FT Hon
Entry Requirements: ***GCE:*** 220-360. ***IB:*** 31. ***BTEC NC:*** DM. ***BTEC ND:*** MMM. ***OCR ND:*** D ***OCR NED:*** M3

S93 SWANSEA UNIVERSITY
SINGLETON PARK
SWANSEA SA2 8PP
t: 01792 295111 f: 01792 295110
e: admissions@swansea.ac.uk
// www.swansea.ac.uk

LR11 BA French and Economics (4 years)
Duration: 4FT Hon
Entry Requirements: ***GCE:*** ABB. ***IB:*** 33. ***BTEC ND:*** DDM.

LR12 BA German and Economics (4 years)
Duration: 4FT Hon
Entry Requirements: ***GCE:*** ABB. ***IB:*** 33. ***BTEC ND:*** DDM.

LR13 BA Italian and Economics (4 years)
Duration: 4FT Hon
Entry Requirements: ***GCE:*** ABB. ***IB:*** 33. ***BTEC ND:*** DDM.

LR14 BA Spanish and Economics (4 years)
Duration: 4FT Hon
Entry Requirements: ***GCE:*** ABB. ***IB:*** 33. ***BTEC ND:*** DDM.

LQ15 BA Welsh and Economics (3 or 4 years)
Duration: 3FT Hon
Entry Requirements: ***GCE:*** ABB. ***IB:*** 33. ***BTEC ND:*** DDM.

U20 UNIVERSITY OF ULSTER
COLERAINE
CO. LONDONDERRY
NORTHERN IRELAND BT52 1SA
t: 028 7032 4221 f: 028 7032 4908
e: online@ulster.ac.uk
// www.ulster.ac.uk

R1N4 BA French with Accounting
Duration: 4SW Hon
Entry Requirements: ***GCE:*** 240. ***IB:*** 24. ***BTEC NC:*** MM. ***BTEC ND:*** MMM.

R2N4 BA German with Accounting
Duration: 4SW Hon
Entry Requirements: ***GCE:*** 240. ***IB:*** 24. ***BTEC NC:*** MM. ***BTEC ND:*** MMM.

Q5N4 BA Irish with Accounting
Duration: 4SW Hon
Entry Requirements: ***GCE:*** 240. ***IB:*** 24. ***BTEC NC:*** MM. ***BTEC ND:*** MMM.

R4N4 BA Spanish with Accounting
Duration: 4SW Hon
Entry Requirements: ***GCE:*** 240. ***IB:*** 24. ***BTEC NC:*** MM. ***BTEC ND:*** MMM.

U80 UNIVERSITY COLLEGE LONDON (UNIVERSITY OF LONDON)
GOWER STREET
LONDON WC1E 6BT
t: 020 7679 3000 f: 020 7679 3001
// www.ucl.ac.uk

GLR0 BSc Statistics, Economics and a Language
Duration: 3FT Hon
Entry Requirements: ***GCE:*** A*AAe-AAAe. ***SQAAH:*** AAA. Interview required.

LAW COMBINATIONS

A20 THE UNIVERSITY OF ABERDEEN
UNIVERSITY OFFICE
KING'S COLLEGE
ABERDEEN AB24 3FX
t: +44 (0) 1224 273504 f: +44 (0) 1224 272034
e: sras@abdn.ac.uk
// www.abdn.ac.uk/sras

M1N4 LLB Law with options in Accountancy
Duration: 3FT/4FT Ord/Hon
Entry Requirements: ***GCE:*** BBB. ***SQAH:*** ABBBB-AABB. ***SQAAH:*** BBB. ***IB:*** 34.

M1L1 LLB Law with options in Economics
Duration: 3FT/4FT Ord/Hon
Entry Requirements: ***GCE:*** BBB. ***SQAH:*** ABBBB-AABB. ***SQAAH:*** BBB. ***IB:*** 34.

NM49 MA Accountancy and Legal Studies
Duration: 4FT Hon
Entry Requirements: ***GCE:*** BBB. ***SQAH:*** BBBB. ***IB:*** 30. ***BTEC ND:*** MMM.

LM19 MA Economics and Legal Studies
Duration: 4FT Hon
Entry Requirements: ***GCE:*** BBB. ***SQAH:*** BBBB. ***IB:*** 30. ***BTEC ND:*** MMM.

NM31 MA Finance and Legal Studies

Duration: 4FT Hon

Entry Requirements: ***GCE:*** BBB. ***SQAH:*** BBBB. ***IB:*** 30. ***BTEC ND:*** MMM.

A40 ABERYSTWYTH UNIVERSITY

WELCOME CENTRE, ABERYSTWYTH UNIVERSITY
PENGLAIS CAMPUS
ABERYSTWYTH
CEREDIGION SY23 3FB
t: 01970 622021 f: 01970 627410
e: ug-admissions@aber.ac.uk
// www.aber.ac.uk

M1N4 BA Law with Accounting & Finance

Duration: 3FT Hon

Entry Requirements: ***GCE:*** 300. ***IB:*** 28.

M1L1 BA Law with Economics

Duration: 3FT Hon

Entry Requirements: ***GCE:*** 300. ***IB:*** 28.

N4M1 BScEcon Accounting & Finance with Law

Duration: 3FT Hon

Entry Requirements: ***GCE:*** 280. ***IB:*** 27.

L1M1 BScEcon Economics with Law

Duration: 3FT Hon

Entry Requirements: ***GCE:*** 280. ***IB:*** 27.

B06 BANGOR UNIVERSITY

BANGOR
GWYNEDD LL57 2DG
t: 01248 382016/2017 f: 01248 370451
e: admissions@bangor.ac.uk
// www.bangor.ac.uk

M1N4 LLB Law with Accounting & Finance

Duration: 3FT Hon

Entry Requirements: ***GCE:*** 280. ***IB:*** 28.

B40 BLACKBURN COLLEGE

FEILDEN STREET
BLACKBURN BB2 1LH
t: 01254 292594 f: 01254 679647
e: he-admissions@blackburn.ac.uk
// www.blackburn.ac.uk

NM31 FdA Financial Services and Law

Duration: 2FT Fdg

Entry Requirements: ***GCE:*** 80.

B44 THE UNIVERSITY OF BOLTON

DEANE ROAD
BOLTON BL3 5AB
t: 01204 900600 f: 01204 399074
e: enquiries@bolton.ac.uk
// www.bolton.ac.uk

NM41 BA Accountancy and Law

Duration: 3FT Hon

Entry Requirements: ***GCE:*** 260. ***IB:*** 24. ***BTEC ND:*** DMM.

M1N4 LLB LLB Law with Accountancy

Duration: 3FT Hon

Entry Requirements: ***GCE:*** 260. ***IB:*** 24. ***BTEC ND:*** DMM.

B50 BOURNEMOUTH UNIVERSITY

TALBOT CAMPUS
FERN BARROW
POOLE
DORSET BH12 5BB
t: 01202 524111
// www.bournemouth.ac.uk

NM41 BA Accounting and Law

Duration: 3FT Hon

Entry Requirements: ***GCE:*** 320. ***IB:*** 32. ***BTEC ND:*** DDM.

NM3C BA Finance and Law (Top-up)

Duration: 1FT Hon

Entry Requirements: HND required.

NM31 FdA Finance and Law

Duration: 2FT Fdg

Entry Requirements: ***GCE:*** 80.

B60 BRADFORD COLLEGE: AN ASSOCIATE COLLEGE OF LEEDS METROPOLITAN UNIVERSITY

GREAT HORTON ROAD
BRADFORD
WEST YORKSHIRE BD7 1AY
t: 01274 433333 f: 01274 433241
e: admissions@bradfordcollege.ac.uk
// www.bradfordcollege.ac.uk

NM41 BA Accountancy and Law

Duration: 3FT Hon

Entry Requirements: ***GCE:*** 240. ***BTEC NC:*** MM. ***BTEC ND:*** MPP.

B90 THE UNIVERSITY OF BUCKINGHAM

YEOMANRY HOUSE
HUNTER STREET
BUCKINGHAM MK18 1EG
t: 01280 820313 f: 01280 822245
e: info@buckingham.ac.uk
// www.buckingham.ac.uk

M1L1 LLB Law with Economics

Duration: 2FT Hon

Entry Requirements: ***GCE:*** 300. ***IB:*** 28. ***BTEC NC:*** DD. ***BTEC ND:*** DMM. ***OCR NED:*** M2 Interview required.

C30 UNIVERSITY OF CENTRAL LANCASHIRE

PRESTON
LANCS PR1 2HE
t: 01772 201201 f: 01772 894954
e: uadmissions@uclan.ac.uk
// www.uclan.ac.uk

MN14 BA Accounting and Law

Duration: 3FT Hon

Entry Requirements: ***GCE:*** 260-300. ***IB:*** 28. ***BTEC NC:*** DM. ***BTEC ND:*** DMM. ***OCR ND:*** D ***OCR NED:*** M2

C55 UNIVERSITY OF CHESTER

PARKGATE ROAD
CHESTER CH1 4BJ
t: 01244 511000 f: 01244 511300
e: enquiries@chester.ac.uk
// www.chester.ac.uk

LM11 BA Economics and Law

Duration: 3FT Hon

Entry Requirements: ***GCE:*** 240. ***SQAH:*** BBBB. ***IB:*** 24. ***BTEC NC:*** DM. ***BTEC ND:*** MMM.

M1L1 BA Law with Economics

Duration: 3FT Hon

Entry Requirements: ***GCE:*** 240. ***SQAH:*** BBBB. ***IB:*** 24. ***BTEC NC:*** DM. ***BTEC ND:*** MMM.

L1M1 BSc Economics with Law

Duration: 3FT Hon

Entry Requirements: ***GCE:*** 240. ***SQAH:*** BBBB. ***IB:*** 24. ***BTEC NC:*** DM. ***BTEC ND:*** MMM.

D26 DE MONTFORT UNIVERSITY

THE GATEWAY
LEICESTER LE1 9BH
t: 0116 255 1551 f: 0116 250 6204
e: enquiries@dmu.ac.uk
// www.dmu.ac.uk

MN14 BA Accounting and Law

Duration: 3FT/4SW Hon

Entry Requirements: ***GCE:*** 240. ***IB:*** 24. ***BTEC NC:*** DD. ***BTEC ND:*** MMM. ***OCR ND:*** D ***OCR NED:*** M3 Interview required.

D39 UNIVERSITY OF DERBY

KEDLESTON ROAD
DERBY DE22 1GB
t: 08701 202330 f: 01332 597724
e: askadmissions@derby.ac.uk
// www.derby.ac.uk

NM49 BA Accounting and Criminology

Duration: 3FT Hon

Entry Requirements: ***Foundation:*** Merit. ***GCE:*** 180-240. ***IB:*** 26. ***BTEC NC:*** DM. ***BTEC ND:*** MMP.

MN1K BA Accounting and Law

Duration: 3FT Hon

Entry Requirements: ***Foundation:*** Merit. ***GCE:*** 180-240. ***IB:*** 26. ***BTEC NC:*** DM. ***BTEC ND:*** MMP.

E28 UNIVERSITY OF EAST LONDON

DOCKLANDS CAMPUS
UNIVERSITY WAY
LONDON E16 2RD
t: 020 8223 3333 f: 020 8223 2978
e: study@uel.ac.uk
// www.uel.ac.uk

N4M1 BA Accounting/Law

Duration: 3FT Hon

Entry Requirements: ***GCE:*** 240. ***IB:*** 28. ***BTEC NC:*** DD. ***BTEC ND:*** MMM.

M1NK BA Law with Accounting

Duration: 3FT Hon

Entry Requirements: ***GCE:*** 240. ***IB:*** 28. ***BTEC NC:*** DD. ***BTEC ND:*** MMM.

N4MC BSc Accounting with Law

Duration: 3FT Hon

Entry Requirements: ***GCE:*** 200. ***IB:*** 28.

E56 THE UNIVERSITY OF EDINBURGH

STUDENT RECRUITMENT & ADMISSIONS
57 GEORGE SQUARE
EDINBURGH EH8 9JU
t: 0131 650 4360 f: 0131 651 1236
e: sra.enquiries@ed.ac.uk
// www.ed.ac.uk/studying/undergraduate/

MN14 LLB Law and Accountancy

Duration: 4FT Hon
Entry Requirements: ***GCE:*** AAA-BBB. ***SQAH:*** AAAB-BBBB. ***IB:*** 34.

ML11 LLB Law and Economics

Duration: 4FT Hon
Entry Requirements: ***GCE:*** AAA-BBB. ***SQAH:*** AAAB-BBBB. ***IB:*** 34.

LM11 MA Economics and Law

Duration: 4FT Hon
Entry Requirements: ***GCE:*** AAA-BBB. ***SQAH:*** AABB-BBBB. ***IB:*** 34.

E59 EDINBURGH NAPIER UNIVERSITY

CRAIGLOCKHART CAMPUS
EDINBURGH EH14 1DJ
t: +44 (0)8452 60 60 40 f: 0131 455 6464
e: info@napier.ac.uk
// www.napier.ac.uk

N4M1 BA Accounting with Law

Duration: 3FT/4FT Ord/Hon
Entry Requirements: ***GCE:*** 230.

G14 UNIVERSITY OF GLAMORGAN, CARDIFF AND PONTYPRIDD

ENQUIRIES AND ADMISSIONS UNIT
PONTYPRIDD CF37 1DL
t: 0800 716925 f: 01443 654050
e: enquiries@glam.ac.uk
// www.glam.ac.uk

MN14 BA Accounting and Law

Duration: 3FT Hon
Entry Requirements: ***GCE:*** 220-260. ***BTEC NC:*** DD. ***BTEC ND:*** MMM. Interview required.

M1N4 LLB Law with Accounting

Duration: 3FT Hon
Entry Requirements: ***GCE:*** 300-340. ***IB:*** 30. ***BTEC NC:*** DD. ***BTEC ND:*** DMM. Interview required.

G28 UNIVERSITY OF GLASGOW

THE UNIVERSITY OF GLASGOW
THE FRASER BUILDING
65 HILLHEAD STREET
GLASGOW G12 8QF
t: 0141 330 6062 f: 0141 330 2961
e: ugenquiries@gla.ac.uk (UK/EU undergrad enquiries only)
// www.glasgow.ac.uk

ML11 LLB Law/Economics

Duration: 4FT Hon
Entry Requirements: ***GCE:*** AAB. ***SQAH:*** AAAAB. ***IB:*** 34.
Admissions Test required.

G70 UNIVERSITY OF GREENWICH

GREENWICH CAMPUS
OLD ROYAL NAVAL COLLEGE
PARK ROW
LONDON SE10 9LS
t: 0800 005 006 f: 020 8331 8145
e: courseinfo@gre.ac.uk
// www.gre.ac.uk

L1M1 BA Economics with Law

Duration: 3FT Hon
Entry Requirements: ***GCE:*** 180. ***IB:*** 24.

ML11 BA Law and Economics

Duration: 3FT Hon
Entry Requirements: ***GCE:*** 180. ***IB:*** 24.

H36 UNIVERSITY OF HERTFORDSHIRE

UNIVERSITY ADMISSIONS SERVICE
COLLEGE LANE
HATFIELD
HERTS AL10 9AB
t: 01707 284800 f: 01707 284870
// www.herts.ac.uk

L1M1 BSc Economics/Law

Duration: 3FT/4SW Hon
Entry Requirements: ***GCE:*** 260.

M1L1 BSc Law/Economics

Duration: 3FT/4SW Hon
Entry Requirements: ***GCE:*** 260.

H60 THE UNIVERSITY OF HUDDERSFIELD

QUEENSGATE
HUDDERSFIELD HD1 3DH
t: 01484 473969 f: 01484 472765
e: admissionsandrecords@hud.ac.uk
// www.hud.ac.uk

MN14 BA Law and Accountancy

Duration: 3FT/4SW Hon
Entry Requirements: ***GCE:*** 300. ***SQAH:*** BBCC. ***IB:*** 28.

N4M1 BA(Hons) Accountancy with Law

Duration: 3FT/4SW Hon
Entry Requirements: ***GCE:*** 300. ***SQAH:*** BBCC. ***IB:*** 28.

K12 KEELE UNIVERSITY

STAFFS ST5 5BG
t: 01782 734005 f: 01782 632343
e: undergraduate@keele.ac.uk
// www.keele.ac.uk

NM49 BA Accounting and Criminology

Duration: 3FT Hon
Entry Requirements: ***GCE:*** 320.

NM41 BA Accounting and Law

Duration: 3FT Hon
Entry Requirements: ***GCE:*** 320-340.

LM19 BA Criminology and Economics

Duration: 3FT Hon
Entry Requirements: ***GCE:*** 280-340.

MNX3 BA Criminology and Finance

Duration: 3FT Hon
Entry Requirements: ***GCE:*** 320.

LM11 BA Economics and Law

Duration: 3FT Hon
Entry Requirements: ***GCE:*** 300-320.

K24 THE UNIVERSITY OF KENT

INFORMATION, RECRUITMENT & ADMISSIONS
REGISTRY
UNIVERSITY OF KENT
CANTERBURY, KENT CT2 7NZ
t: 01227 827272 f: 01227 827077
e: information@kent.ac.uk
// www.kent.ac.uk

NM41 BA Law and Accounting & Finance (4 years)

Duration: 4FT Hon
Entry Requirements: ***GCE:*** AAB. ***SQAH:*** AAAAB. ***IB:*** 35. ***BTEC NC:*** DD. ***BTEC ND:*** DDM. ***OCR ND:*** D ***OCR NED:*** M1

ML11 BA Law and Economics

Duration: 3FT Hon
Entry Requirements: ***GCE:*** AAB. ***SQAH:*** AAAAB. ***IB:*** 35. ***BTEC NC:*** DD. ***BTEC ND:*** DDM. ***OCR ND:*** D

K84 KINGSTON UNIVERSITY

STUDENT INFORMATION & ADVICE CENTRE
COOPER HOUSE
40-46 SURBITON ROAD
KINGSTON UPON THAMES KT1 2HX
t: 0844 8552177 f: 020 8547 7080
e: aps@kingston.ac.uk
// www.kingston.ac.uk

M9L1 BA Criminology with Economics (Applied)

Duration: 3FT Hon
Entry Requirements: ***GCE:*** 220-320. ***SQAH:*** BBCCC. ***SQAAH:*** BBC.

L1M9 BA Economics (Applied) with Criminology

Duration: 3FT Hon
Entry Requirements: ***GCE:*** 260-360. ***IB:*** 24.

L1LF BA Economics (Applied) with Human Rights

Duration: 3FT Hon
Entry Requirements: ***GCE:*** 220-360. ***IB:*** 24.

L1M1 BA Economics (Applied) with Law

Duration: 3FT Hon
Entry Requirements: ***GCE:*** 280-360. ***IB:*** 25.

L2LC BA Human Rights with Applied Economics

Duration: 3FT Hon
Entry Requirements: ***GCE:*** 220-360.

ML11 BA Law and Economics (Applied)

Duration: 3FT Hon
Entry Requirements: ***GCE:*** 280-360. ***IB:*** 25.

L23 UNIVERSITY OF LEEDS

THE UNIVERSITY OF LEEDS
LEEDS LS2 9JT
t: 0113 343 3999
e: admissions@adm.leeds.ac.uk
// www.leeds.ac.uk

MN14 BA Accounting and Law

Duration: 4FT Hon
Entry Requirements: ***GCE:*** AAB. ***SQAAH:*** AAB. ***IB:*** 36. Admissions Test required.

L34 UNIVERSITY OF LEICESTER
UNIVERSITY ROAD
LEICESTER LE1 7RH
t: 0116 252 5281 f: 0116 252 2447
e: admissions@le.ac.uk
// www.le.ac.uk

LM11 BA Economics and Law
Duration: 3FT Hon
Entry Requirements: ***GCE:*** ABB. ***SQAH:*** AABBB. ***SQAAH:*** ABB. ***IB:*** 32. ***BTEC ND:*** DDM.

L39 UNIVERSITY OF LINCOLN
ADMISSIONS
BRAYFORD POOL
LINCOLN LN6 7TS
t: 01522 886097 f: 01522 886146
e: admissions@lincoln.ac.uk
// www.lincoln.ac.uk

NM31 LLB Law and Finance
Duration: 3FT Hon
Entry Requirements: ***GCE:*** 280.

L68 LONDON METROPOLITAN UNIVERSITY
166-220 HOLLOWAY ROAD
LONDON N7 8DB
t: 020 7133 4200
e: admissions@londonmet.ac.uk
// www.londonmet.ac.uk

MN14 BA Accounting and Law
Duration: 3FT Hon
Entry Requirements: ***GCE:*** 240. ***IB:*** 28.

LM1C BA Economics and Law
Duration: 3FT Hon
Entry Requirements: ***GCE:*** 240. ***IB:*** 28.

LM1D BA/BSc Economics and International Law & International Politics
Duration: 3FT Hon
Entry Requirements: ***GCE:*** 240. ***IB:*** 28.

LMC1 BA/BSc International Economics and International Law & International Politics
Duration: 3FT Hon
Entry Requirements: ***GCE:*** 240. ***IB:*** 28.

L75 LONDON SOUTH BANK UNIVERSITY
103 BOROUGH ROAD
LONDON SE1 0AA
t: 020 7815 7815 f: 020 7815 8273
e: enquiry@lsbu.ac.uk
// www.lsbu.ac.uk

N4M1 BA Accounting with Law
Duration: 3FT Hon
Entry Requirements: ***GCE:*** 240. ***IB:*** 24.

M1N4 LLB Law with Accounting
Duration: 3FT Hon
Entry Requirements: ***GCE:*** 240. ***IB:*** 24.

M20 THE UNIVERSITY OF MANCHESTER
OXFORD ROAD
MANCHESTER M13 9PL
t: 0161 275 2077 f: 0161 275 2106
e: ug-admissions@manchester.ac.uk
// www.manchester.ac.uk

LM19 BAEcon Economics and Criminology
Duration: 3FT Hon
Entry Requirements: ***GCE:*** ABB. ***SQAH:*** AABBB. ***SQAAH:*** ABB. ***IB:*** 34. ***BTEC ND:*** DDM. Interview required.

M40 THE MANCHESTER METROPOLITAN UNIVERSITY
ADMISSIONS OFFICE
ALL SAINTS (GMS)
ALL SAINTS
MANCHESTER M15 6BH
t: 0161 247 2000
// www.mmu.ac.uk

NM32 BA Financial Management/Legal Studies
Duration: 3FT Hon
Entry Requirements: ***GCE:*** 260. ***BTEC ND:*** MMM.

ML91 BSc Criminology/Economics
Duration: 3FT Hon
Entry Requirements: ***GCE:*** 240. ***IB:*** 27.

N37 UNIVERSITY OF WALES, NEWPORT
CAERLEON CAMPUS
LODGE ROAD
CAERLEON
NEWPORT NP18 3QT
t: 01633 432030 f: 01633 432850
e: admissions@newport.ac.uk
// www.newport.ac.uk

MN14 BSc Accounting and Law
Duration: 3FT Hon
Entry Requirements: ***GCE:*** 240. ***IB:*** 24.

LM11 BSc Economics and Law
Duration: 3FT Hon
Entry Requirements: ***GCE:*** 240. ***IB:*** 24.

N38 UNIVERSITY OF NORTHAMPTON
PARK CAMPUS
BOUGHTON GREEN ROAD
NORTHAMPTON NN2 7AL
t: 0800 358 2232 f: 01604 722083
e: admissions@northampton.ac.uk
// www.northampton.ac.uk

N4M1 BA Accounting/Law
Duration: 3FT Hon
Entry Requirements: ***GCE:*** 220-260. ***SQAH:*** ABB-BBBC. ***IB:*** 24.

M9L1 BA Criminology/Economics
Duration: 3FT Hon
Entry Requirements: ***GCE:*** 220-260. ***SQAH:*** ABB-BBBC. ***IB:*** 24.

L1M9 BA Economics/Criminology
Duration: 3FT Hon
Entry Requirements: ***GCE:*** 220-260. ***SQAH:*** ABB-BBBC. ***IB:*** 24.

L1M1 BA Economics/Law
Duration: 3FT Hon
Entry Requirements: ***GCE:*** 220-260. ***SQAH:*** ABB-BBBC. ***IB:*** 24.

M1N4 BA Law/Accounting
Duration: 3FT Hon
Entry Requirements: ***GCE:*** 220-260. ***SQAH:*** ABB-BBBC. ***IB:*** 24.

M1L1 BA Law/Economics
Duration: 3FT Hon
Entry Requirements: ***GCE:*** 220-260. ***SQAH:*** ABB-BBBC. ***IB:*** 24.

P60 UNIVERSITY OF PLYMOUTH
DRAKE CIRCUS
PLYMOUTH PL4 8AA
t: 01752 588037 f: 01752 588050
e: admissions@plymouth.ac.uk
// www.plymouth.ac.uk

L1MG BSc Economics with Law
Duration: 3FT/4SW Hon
Entry Requirements: ***GCE:*** 240. ***IB:*** 26.

S03 THE UNIVERSITY OF SALFORD
SALFORD M5 4WT
t: 0161 295 4545 f: 0161 295 3126
e: ugadmissions-exrel@salford.ac.uk
// www.salford.ac.uk

M1N3 LLB Law with Finance
Duration: 3FT Hon
Entry Requirements: ***GCE:*** 300. ***IB:*** 29. ***BTEC ND:*** DMM. ***OCR NED:*** M2 Interview required.

S09 SCHOOL OF ORIENTAL AND AFRICAN STUDIES (UNIVERSITY OF LONDON)
THORNHAUGH STREET
RUSSELL SQUARE
LONDON WC1H 0XG
t: 020 7074 5106 f: 020 7898 4039
e: undergradadmissions@soas.ac.uk
// www.soas.ac.uk

LM11 BA Law and Economics
Duration: 3FT Hon
Entry Requirements: Contact the institution for details.

S72 STAFFORDSHIRE UNIVERSITY
COLLEGE ROAD
STOKE ON TRENT ST4 2DE
t: 01782 292753 f: 01782 292740
e: admissions@staffs.ac.uk
// www.staffs.ac.uk

NM42 BA Accounting and Legal Studies
Duration: 3FT Hon
Entry Requirements: ***GCE:*** BCC-BB. ***IB:*** 24.

L1M2 BA Economics with Legal Studies
Duration: 3FT Hon
Entry Requirements: ***GCE:*** BCC-BB. ***IB:*** 24. ***BTEC NC:*** DM. ***BTEC ND:*** MMM.

LM11 BA/BSc LLB with Economics
Duration: 3FT Hon
Entry Requirements: ***GCE:*** ABB-BB. ***SQAAH:*** ABB-BB. ***IB:*** 26. ***BTEC NC:*** DM. ***BTEC ND:*** DDM. ***OCR ND:*** D

M1N4 LLB LLB with Accounting
Duration: 3FT Hon
Entry Requirements: ***GCE:*** ABB-BB. ***SQAAH:*** ABB-BB. ***IB:*** 26. ***BTEC NC:*** DM. ***BTEC ND:*** DDM. ***OCR ND:*** D

S75 THE UNIVERSITY OF STIRLING
STIRLING FK9 4LA
t: 01786 467044 f: 01786 466800
e: admissions@stir.ac.uk
// www.stir.ac.uk

ML11 BA Economics and Law
Duration: 4FT Hon
Entry Requirements: ***GCE:*** CCC. ***SQAH:*** BBBB. ***SQAAH:*** AAA-CCC. ***IB:*** 30. ***BTEC ND:*** DMM.

MN13 BA Finance and Law
Duration: 4FT Hon
Entry Requirements: ***GCE:*** CCC. ***SQAH:*** BBBB. ***SQAAH:*** AAA-CCC. ***IB:*** 30. ***BTEC ND:*** DMM.

S78 THE UNIVERSITY OF STRATHCLYDE

GLASGOW G1 1XQ
t: 0141 552 4400 f: 0141 552 0775
// www.strath.ac.uk

LM11 BA Economics and Law

Duration: 4FT Hon
Entry Requirements: ***GCE:*** ABB. ***SQAH:*** ABBB-BBBBC. ***IB:*** 34.

S84 UNIVERSITY OF SUNDERLAND

STUDENT HELPLINE
THE STUDENT GATEWAY
CHESTER ROAD
SUNDERLAND SR1 3SD
t: 0191 515 3000 f: 0191 515 3805
e: student-helpline@sunderland.ac.uk
// www.sunderland.ac.uk

M9N3 BA Criminology with Financial Management

Duration: 3FT Hon
Entry Requirements: ***GCE:*** 220-360. ***BTEC NC:*** DM. ***BTEC ND:*** MMM. ***OCR ND:*** D ***OCR NED:*** M3

NM39 BA Financial Management and Criminology

Duration: 3FT Hon
Entry Requirements: ***GCE:*** 220-360. ***BTEC NC:*** DM. ***BTEC ND:*** MMM. ***OCR ND:*** D ***OCR NED:*** M3

NM31 BA Financial Management and Law

Duration: 3FT Hon
Entry Requirements: ***GCE:*** 220-360. ***BTEC NC:*** DM. ***BTEC ND:*** MMM. ***OCR ND:*** D ***OCR NED:*** M3

N3M9 BA Financial Management with Criminology

Duration: 3FT Hon
Entry Requirements: ***GCE:*** 220-360. ***BTEC NC:*** DM. ***BTEC ND:*** MMM. ***OCR ND:*** D ***OCR NED:*** M3

N3M1 BA Financial Management with Law

Duration: 3FT Hon
Entry Requirements: ***GCE:*** 220-360. ***BTEC NC:*** DM. ***BTEC ND:*** MMM. ***OCR ND:*** D ***OCR NED:*** M3

M1N3 BA Law with Financial Management

Duration: 3FT Hon
Entry Requirements: ***GCE:*** 220-360. ***BTEC NC:*** DM. ***BTEC ND:*** MMM. ***OCR ND:*** D ***OCR NED:*** M3

S90 UNIVERSITY OF SUSSEX

UNDERGRADUATE ADMISSIONS
SUSSEX HOUSE
UNIVERSITY OF SUSSEX
BRIGHTON BN1 9RH
t: 01273 678416 f: 01273 678545
e: ug.applicants@sussex.ac.uk
// www.sussex.ac.uk

M1L1 LLB Law with Politics

Duration: 3FT Hon
Entry Requirements: ***GCE:*** AAB. ***SQAH:*** AAABB. ***IB:*** 36. ***BTEC ND:*** DDD. ***OCR NED:*** D1

S93 SWANSEA UNIVERSITY

SINGLETON PARK
SWANSEA SA2 8PP
t: 01792 295111 f: 01792 295110
e: admissions@swansea.ac.uk
// www.swansea.ac.uk

ML11 LLB Law and Economics

Duration: 3FT Hon
Entry Requirements: ***GCE:*** AAB. ***IB:*** 34.

U20 UNIVERSITY OF ULSTER

COLERAINE
CO. LONDONDERRY
NORTHERN IRELAND BT52 1SA
t: 028 7032 4221 f: 028 7032 4908
e: online@ulster.ac.uk
// www.ulster.ac.uk

NM41 BSc Accounting and Law

Duration: 4FT/5SW Hon
Entry Requirements: ***GCE:*** AAA. ***SQAH:*** AAAAA. ***SQAAH:*** AAA. ***IB:*** 39. ***BTEC NC:*** DD. ***BTEC ND:*** DDD.

M1N4 LLB Law with Accounting

Duration: 3FT Hon
Entry Requirements: ***GCE:*** ABB. ***SQAH:*** AAABC. ***SQAAH:*** ABB. ***IB:*** 26. ***BTEC ND:*** DDM.

W50 UNIVERSITY OF WESTMINSTER

101 NEW CAVENDISH STREET
LONDON W1W 6XH
t: 020 7915 5511 f: 020 7911 5788
e: course-enquiries@westminster.ac.uk
// www.westminster.ac.uk

LM19 BA Development and Criminology

Duration: 3FT Hon
Entry Requirements: Contact the institution for details.

W75 UNIVERSITY OF WOLVERHAMPTON
ADMISSIONS UNIT
MX207, CAMP STREET
WOLVERHAMPTON
WEST MIDLANDS WV1 1AD
t: 01902 321000 f: 01902 321896
e: admissions@wlv.ac.uk
// www.wlv.ac.uk

MN1L BA Accounting and Law
Duration: 3FT Hon
Entry Requirements: ***GCE:*** 160-220. ***IB:*** 28.

NM31 BA Finance and Law
Duration: 3FT Hon
Entry Requirements: Contact the institution for details.

W76 UNIVERSITY OF WINCHESTER
WINCHESTER
HANTS SO22 4NR
t: 01962 827234 f: 01962 827288
e: course.enquiries@winchester.ac.uk
// www.winchester.ac.uk

NM41 BA Accounting and Law
Duration: 3FT Hon
Entry Requirements: ***Foundation:*** Distinction. ***GCE:*** 260-300. ***IB:*** 25. ***BTEC NC:*** DD. ***BTEC ND:*** DMM. ***OCR ND:*** D ***OCR NED:*** M2

MANAGEMENT COMBINATIONS

A20 THE UNIVERSITY OF ABERDEEN
UNIVERSITY OFFICE
KING'S COLLEGE
ABERDEEN AB24 3FX
t: +44 (0) 1224 273504 f: +44 (0) 1224 272034
e: sras@abdn.ac.uk
// www.abdn.ac.uk/sras

NN24 MA Accountancy and Management Studies
Duration: 4FT Hon
Entry Requirements: ***GCE:*** BBB. ***SQAH:*** BBBB. ***IB:*** 30. ***BTEC ND:*** MMM.

LNC2 MA Economics and Management Studies
Duration: 4FT Hon
Entry Requirements: ***GCE:*** BBB. ***SQAH:*** BBBB. ***IB:*** 30. ***BTEC ND:*** MMM.

NN32 MA Finance and Management Studies
Duration: 4FT Hon
Entry Requirements: ***GCE:*** BBB. ***SQAH:*** BBBB. ***IB:*** 30. ***BTEC ND:*** MMM.

A30 UNIVERSITY OF ABERTAY DUNDEE
BELL STREET
DUNDEE DD1 1HG
t: 01382 308080 f: 01382 308081
e: sro@abertay.ac.uk
// www.abertay.ac.uk

LN12 BA European Economy and Management
Duration: 4FT Hon
Entry Requirements: ***GCE:*** DDD. ***SQAH:*** BBC. ***IB:*** 24. ***BTEC NC:*** DM. ***BTEC ND:*** MMP.

A40 ABERYSTWYTH UNIVERSITY
WELCOME CENTRE, ABERYSTWYTH UNIVERSITY
PENGLAIS CAMPUS
ABERYSTWYTH
CEREDIGION SY23 3FB
t: 01970 622021 f: 01970 627410
e: ug-admissions@aber.ac.uk
// www.aber.ac.uk

N4P1 BScEcon Accounting & Finance with Information Management
Duration: 3FT Hon
Entry Requirements: ***GCE:*** 280. ***IB:*** 27.

N4N2 BScEcon Accounting & Finance with Management
Duration: 3FT Hon
Entry Requirements: ***GCE:*** 280. ***IB:*** 27.

L1N2 BScEcon Economics with Management
Duration: 3FT Hon
Entry Requirements: ***GCE:*** 280. ***IB:*** 27.

P1N4 BScEcon Information Management with Accounting & Finance
Duration: 3FT Hon
Entry Requirements: ***GCE:*** 180. ***IB:*** 24.

P1L1 BScEcon Information Management with Economics
Duration: 3FT Hon
Entry Requirements: ***GCE:*** 180. ***IB:*** 24.

A80 ASTON UNIVERSITY, BIRMINGHAM
ASTON TRIANGLE
BIRMINGHAM B4 7ET
t: 0121 204 4444 f: 0121 204 3696
e: admissions@aston.ac.uk
// www.aston.ac.uk

LN12 BSc Economics and Management
Duration: 4SW Hon
Entry Requirements: ***GCE:*** 320-340. ***SQAH:*** AAAAB-AAABB. ***SQAAH:*** AAB-ABB. ***IB:*** 34. ***BTEC ND:*** DDM. ***OCR NED:*** D2

B06 BANGOR UNIVERSITY

BANGOR
GWYNEDD LL57 2DG
t: 01248 382016/2017 f: 01248 370451
e: admissions@bangor.ac.uk
// www.bangor.ac.uk

N2N4 BA Management with Accounting

Duration: 3FT Hon

Entry Requirements: ***GCE:*** 260-300. ***IB:*** 28.

N2NK BSc Management with Accounting

Duration: 3FT Hon

Entry Requirements: ***GCE:*** 260-300. ***IB:*** 28.

B25 BIRMINGHAM CITY UNIVERSITY

CITY NORTH CAMPUS
PERRY BARR
BIRMINGHAM B42 2SU
t: 0121 331 5595 f: 0121 331 7994
e: choices@bcu.ac.uk
// www.bcu.ac.uk/courses/choices/contact-choices

NN42 BA Accountancy and Management

Duration: 3FT/4SW Hon

Entry Requirements: ***GCE:*** 260. ***IB:*** 30. ***BTEC NC:*** DD. ***BTEC ND:*** DMM. ***OCR ND:*** D ***OCR NED:*** M3 Interview required. Portfolio required.

LK12 BSc Construction Management and Economics

Duration: 3FT Hon

Entry Requirements: ***GCE:*** 220. ***IB:*** 28. ***BTEC NC:*** DD. ***BTEC ND:*** DMM.

B77 BRISTOL, CITY OF BRISTOL COLLEGE

ASHLEY DOWN CENTRE
PO BOX 2887
BRISTOL BS2 2BB
t: 0117 312 5211 f: 0117 312 5050
e: admissions@cityofbristol.ac.uk
// www.cityofbristol.ac.uk

N4NF Cert HE Accounting with Management

Duration: 1FT Cer

Entry Requirements: Contact the institution for details.

B78 UNIVERSITY OF BRISTOL

UNDERGRADUATE ADMISSIONS OFFICE
SENATE HOUSE
TYNDALL AVENUE
BRISTOL BS8 1TH
t: 0117 928 9000 f: 0117 925 1424
e: ug-admissions@bristol.ac.uk
// www.bristol.ac.uk

NN42 BSc Accounting and Management

Duration: 3FT Hon

Entry Requirements: ***GCE:*** A*AA-ABB. ***SQAAH:*** AAA-AAB. ***BTEC ND:*** DDD.

LN12 BSc Economics and Management

Duration: 3FT Hon

Entry Requirements: ***GCE:*** A*AA-ABB. ***SQAAH:*** AAA-AAB. ***BTEC ND:*** DDD.

B84 BRUNEL UNIVERSITY

UXBRIDGE
MIDDLESEX UB8 3PH
t: 01895 265265 f: 01895 269790
e: admissions@brunel.ac.uk
// www.brunel.ac.uk

LNC2 BSc Economics and Management

Duration: 3FT Hon

Entry Requirements: ***GCE:*** 280-320. ***IB:*** 32. ***BTEC NC:*** DM. ***BTEC ND:*** DDM.

LND2 BSc Economics and Management (4 year Thick SW)

Duration: 4SW Hon

Entry Requirements: ***GCE:*** 280-320. ***IB:*** 32. ***BTEC NC:*** DM. ***BTEC ND:*** DDM.

C15 CARDIFF UNIVERSITY

PO BOX 927
30-36 NEWPORT ROAD
CARDIFF CF24 0DE
t: 029 2087 9999 f: 029 2087 6138
e: admissions@cardiff.ac.uk
// www.cardiff.ac.uk

NN24 BScEcon Accounting and Management

Duration: 3FT Hon

Entry Requirements: ***GCE:*** AAB. ***SQAH:*** AAABB. ***SQAAH:*** AAB. ***IB:*** 35. ***BTEC ND:*** DDD. ***OCR NED:*** D2

LN12 BScEcon Economics and Management Studies

Duration: 3FT Hon

Entry Requirements: ***GCE:*** AAB. ***SQAH:*** AAABB. ***SQAAH:*** AAB. ***IB:*** 35. ***BTEC ND:*** DDD. ***OCR NED:*** D2

C30 UNIVERSITY OF CENTRAL LANCASHIRE

PRESTON
LANCS PR1 2HE
t: 01772 201201 f: 01772 894954
e: uadmissions@uclan.ac.uk
// www.uclan.ac.uk

NN24 BA Accounting and Management

Duration: 3FT Hon
Entry Requirements: ***GCE:*** 240-280. ***SQAH:*** AABB-BBBB. ***IB:*** 28. ***BTEC NC:*** DD. ***OCR ND:*** D

C55 UNIVERSITY OF CHESTER

PARKGATE ROAD
CHESTER CH1 4BJ
t: 01244 511000 f: 01244 511300
e: enquiries@chester.ac.uk
// www.chester.ac.uk

LN12 BA Economics and Management

Duration: 3FT Hon
Entry Requirements: ***GCE:*** 240. ***SQAH:*** BBBB. ***IB:*** 24. ***BTEC NC:*** DM. ***BTEC ND:*** MMM.

N2L1 BA Management with Economics

Duration: 3FT Hon
Entry Requirements: ***GCE:*** 240. ***SQAH:*** BBBB. ***IB:*** 24. ***BTEC NC:*** DM. ***BTEC ND:*** MMM.

LF17 BSc Economics and Natural Hazard Management

Duration: 3FT Hon
Entry Requirements: ***GCE:*** 240. ***SQAH:*** BBBB. ***IB:*** 24. ***BTEC NC:*** DM. ***BTEC ND:*** MMM.

L1N2 BSc Economics with Management

Duration: 3FT Hon
Entry Requirements: ***GCE:*** 240. ***SQAH:*** BBBB. ***IB:*** 24. ***BTEC NC:*** DM. ***BTEC ND:*** MMM.

L1F7 BSc Economics with Natural Hazard Management

Duration: 3FT Hon
Entry Requirements: ***GCE:*** 240. ***SQAH:*** BBBB. ***IB:*** 24. ***BTEC NC:*** DM. ***BTEC ND:*** MMM.

F7L1 BSc Natural Hazard Management with Economics

Duration: 3FT Hon
Entry Requirements: ***GCE:*** 240. ***SQAH:*** BBBB. ***IB:*** 24. ***BTEC NC:*** DM. ***BTEC ND:*** MMM.

C58 UNIVERSITY OF CHICHESTER

BISHOP OTTER CAMPUS
COLLEGE LANE
CHICHESTER
WEST SUSSEX PO19 6PE
t: 01243 816002 f: 01243 816161
e: admissions@chi.ac.uk
// www.chiuni.ac.uk

NN84 BA Event Management and Accounting & Finance

Duration: 3FT Hon
Entry Requirements: ***GCE:*** CCC. ***SQAAH:*** CCC. ***IB:*** 28. ***BTEC ND:*** MMM.

NN83 BA Event Management and Finance

Duration: 3FT Hon
Entry Requirements: ***GCE:*** CCC. ***SQAAH:*** CCC. ***IB:*** 28. ***BTEC ND:*** MMM.

NN8J BA Event Management and Finance - Placement

Duration: 4SW Hon
Entry Requirements: ***GCE:*** CCC. ***SQAAH:*** CCC. ***IB:*** 28. ***BTEC ND:*** MMM.

NN8H BA Tourism Management and Finance

Duration: 3FT Hon
Entry Requirements: ***GCE:*** CCC. ***SQAAH:*** CCC. ***IB:*** 28. ***BTEC ND:*** MMM.

D39 UNIVERSITY OF DERBY

KEDLESTON ROAD
DERBY DE22 1GB
t: 08701 202330 f: 01332 597724
e: askadmissions@derby.ac.uk
// www.derby.ac.uk

NN42 BA Accounting and Enterprise Management

Duration: 3FT Hon
Entry Requirements: ***Foundation:*** Merit. ***GCE:*** 180-240. ***IB:*** 26. ***BTEC NC:*** DM. ***BTEC ND:*** MMP.

NN46 BA Accounting and Human Resource Management

Duration: 3FT Hon
Entry Requirements: ***Foundation:*** Merit. ***GCE:*** 180-240. ***IB:*** 26. ***BTEC NC:*** DM. ***BTEC ND:*** MMP.

E14 UNIVERSITY OF EAST ANGLIA
NORWICH NR4 7TJ
t: 01603 591515 f: 01603 458596
e: admissions@uea.ac.uk
// www.uea.ac.uk

N4N2 BSc Accounting with Management
Duration: 3FT Hon
Entry Requirements: ***GCE:*** BBB. ***SQAH:*** ABBBB. ***SQAAH:*** BBB. ***IB:*** 31. ***BTEC NC:*** DD. ***BTEC ND:*** DDM. ***OCR ND:*** M1 ***OCR NED:*** M1

E28 UNIVERSITY OF EAST LONDON
DOCKLANDS CAMPUS
UNIVERSITY WAY
LONDON E16 2RD
t: 020 8223 3333 f: 020 8223 2978
e: study@uel.ac.uk
// www.uel.ac.uk

N2N4 BSc Health Services Management with Accounting
Duration: 3FT Hon
Entry Requirements: ***GCE:*** 200. ***IB:*** 24. ***BTEC NC:*** DM. ***BTEC ND:*** MMP. ***OCR ND:*** M1 ***OCR NED:*** P1

E56 THE UNIVERSITY OF EDINBURGH
STUDENT RECRUITMENT & ADMISSIONS
57 GEORGE SQUARE
EDINBURGH EH8 9JU
t: 0131 650 4360 f: 0131 651 1236
e: sra.enquiries@ed.ac.uk
// www.ed.ac.uk/studying/undergraduate/

L1N2 MA Economics with Management Science
Duration: 4FT Hon
Entry Requirements: ***GCE:*** AAA-BBB. ***SQAH:*** AABB-BBBB. ***IB:*** 34.

E59 EDINBURGH NAPIER UNIVERSITY
CRAIGLOCKHART CAMPUS
EDINBURGH EH14 1DJ
t: +44 (0)8452 60 60 40 f: 0131 455 6464
e: info@napier.ac.uk
// www.napier.ac.uk

N4N6 BA Accounting with Human Resource Management
Duration: 3FT/4FT Ord/Hon
Entry Requirements: ***GCE:*** 230.

N4N5 BA Accounting with Marketing Management
Duration: 3FT/4FT Ord/Hon
Entry Requirements: ***GCE:*** 230.

L1N2 BA Economics with Management
Duration: 3FT/4FT Ord/Hon
Entry Requirements: ***GCE:*** 230.

E70 THE UNIVERSITY OF ESSEX
WIVENHOE PARK
COLCHESTER
ESSEX CO4 3SQ
t: 01206 873666 f: 01206 873423
e: admit@essex.ac.uk
// www.essex.ac.uk

NN24 BA Accounting & Management
Duration: 3FT Hon
Entry Requirements: ***GCE:*** 320. ***SQAH:*** AAAB. ***IB:*** 34. ***BTEC NC:*** DD. ***BTEC ND:*** DDM. ***OCR ND:*** D

NN42 BA Accounting and Management (four year)
Duration: 4FT Hon
Entry Requirements: ***GCE:*** 180. ***SQAH:*** CCCD. ***IB:*** 24. ***BTEC NC:*** DM. ***BTEC ND:*** MMP.

NGL0 BSc Management, Mathematics and Economics
Duration: 3FT Hon
Entry Requirements: ***GCE:*** 300. ***SQAH:*** AABB. ***IB:*** 32. ***BTEC NC:*** DM. ***BTEC ND:*** DDM.

NGL1 BSc Management, Mathematics and Economics (4 years including foundation year)
Duration: 4FT Hon
Entry Requirements: ***GCE:*** 180. ***SQAH:*** CCCD. ***IB:*** 24. ***BTEC NC:*** DM. ***BTEC ND:*** MMP.

LGN0 BSc Management, Mathematics and Economics with a year in the USA
Duration: 4FT Hon
Entry Requirements: ***GCE:*** 300. ***SQAH:*** AABB. ***IB:*** 32. ***BTEC NC:*** DM. ***BTEC ND:*** DDM.

H36 UNIVERSITY OF HERTFORDSHIRE
UNIVERSITY ADMISSIONS SERVICE
COLLEGE LANE
HATFIELD
HERTS AL10 9AB
t: 01707 284800 f: 01707 284870
// www.herts.ac.uk

NN4V BA Accounting/Event Management
Duration: 3FT/4SW Hon
Entry Requirements: ***GCE:*** 260.

LN1V BA Economics/Event Management
Duration: 3FT/4SW Hon
Entry Requirements: ***GCE:*** 260.

N8N3 BA Event Management with Finance
Duration: 3FT/4SW Hon
Entry Requirements: ***GCE:*** 260.

H72 THE UNIVERSITY OF HULL

THE UNIVERSITY OF HULL
COTTINGHAM ROAD
HULL HU6 7RX
t: 01482 466100 f: 01482 442290
e: admissions@hull.ac.uk
// www.hull.ac.uk

NN24 BA Management and Accounting
Duration: 3FT Hon
Entry Requirements: ***GCE:*** 280. ***IB:*** 28.

NN2K BA Management and Accounting (International) (4 years)
Duration: 4FT Hon
Entry Requirements: ***GCE:*** 280. ***IB:*** 28.

NN2L BA Management and Accounting (with Professional Experience) (4 years)
Duration: 4FT Hon
Entry Requirements: ***GCE:*** 280. ***IB:*** 28.

NL21 BA Management and Economics
Duration: 3FT Hon
Entry Requirements: ***GCE:*** 280. ***IB:*** 28.

NL2C BA Management and Economics (International) (4 years)
Duration: 4FT Hon
Entry Requirements: ***GCE:*** 280. ***IB:*** 28.

NL2D BA Management and Economics (with Professional Experience) (4 years)
Duration: 4FT Hon
Entry Requirements: ***GCE:*** 280. ***IB:*** 28.

NN23 BA Management and Financial Management
Duration: 3FT Hon
Entry Requirements: ***GCE:*** 280. ***IB:*** 28.

NN2H BA Management and Financial Management (International) (4 years)
Duration: 4FT Hon
Entry Requirements: ***GCE:*** 280. ***IB:*** 28.

NN2J BA Management and Financial Management (with Professional Experience) (4 years)
Duration: 4FT Hon
Entry Requirements: ***GCE:*** 280. ***IB:*** 28.

NN53 BA Marketing and Financial Management
Duration: 3FT Hon
Entry Requirements: ***GCE:*** 280. ***IB:*** 28.

NNM3 BA Marketing and Financial Management (International) (4 years)
Duration: 4FT Hon
Entry Requirements: ***GCE:*** 280. ***IB:*** 28.

NNN3 BA Marketing and Financial Management (with Professional Experience) (4 years)
Duration: 4FT Hon
Entry Requirements: ***GCE:*** 280. ***IB:*** 28.

NN32 BSc Financial Management and Logistics
Duration: 3FT Hon
Entry Requirements: ***GCE:*** 280. ***IB:*** 28.

NN3F BSc Financial Management and Logistics (International) (4 years)
Duration: 4FT Hon
Entry Requirements: ***GCE:*** 280. ***IB:*** 28.

NNH2 BSc Financial Management and Logistics (with Professional Experience) (4 years)
Duration: 4FT Hon
Entry Requirements: ***GCE:*** 280. ***IB:*** 28.

K12 KEELE UNIVERSITY

STAFFS ST5 5BG
t: 01782 734005 f: 01782 632343
e: undergraduate@keele.ac.uk
// www.keele.ac.uk

NN46 BA Accounting and Human Resource Management
Duration: 3FT Hon
Entry Requirements: ***GCE:*** 320-340.

LN16 BA Economics and Human Resource Management
Duration: 3FT Hon
Entry Requirements: ***GCE:*** 280-340.

NN36 BA Finance and Human Resource Management
Duration: 3FT Hon
Entry Requirements: ***GCE:*** 280-340.

K24 THE UNIVERSITY OF KENT

INFORMATION, RECRUITMENT & ADMISSIONS REGISTRY
UNIVERSITY OF KENT
CANTERBURY, KENT CT2 7NZ
t: 01227 827272 f: 01227 827077
e: information@kent.ac.uk
// www.kent.ac.uk

NN24 BA Accounting & Finance and Management Science

Duration: 3FT Hon
Entry Requirements: ***GCE:*** 300. ***IB:*** 33. ***BTEC NC:*** DD. ***BTEC ND:*** DMM. ***OCR ND:*** D

NN46 BA Employment Relations and Human Resource Management (Accounting)

Duration: 3FT Hon
Entry Requirements: ***GCE:*** 300. ***IB:*** 33. ***BTEC NC:*** DD. ***BTEC ND:*** DDM. ***OCR ND:*** D ***OCR NED:*** M1

LN16 BA Employment Relations and Human Resource Management (Economics)

Duration: 3FT Hon
Entry Requirements: ***GCE:*** 300. ***IB:*** 33. ***BTEC NC:*** DD. ***BTEC ND:*** DDM. ***OCR ND:*** D ***OCR NED:*** M1

L14 LANCASTER UNIVERSITY

THE UNIVERSITY
LANCASTER
LANCASHIRE LA1 4YW
t: 01524 592029 f: 01524 846243
e: ugadmissions@lancaster.ac.uk
// www.lancs.ac.uk

NN24 BSc Accounting and Management Studies

Duration: 3FT Hon
Entry Requirements: ***GCE:*** AAB. ***SQAH:*** ABBBB. ***SQAAH:*** AAB. ***IB:*** 34. ***BTEC ND:*** DDM.

NN23 BSc Finance and Management Studies

Duration: 3FT Hon
Entry Requirements: ***GCE:*** AAB. ***SQAH:*** ABBBB. ***SQAAH:*** AAB. ***IB:*** 34.

L23 UNIVERSITY OF LEEDS

THE UNIVERSITY OF LEEDS
LEEDS LS2 9JT
t: 0113 343 3999
e: admissions@adm.leeds.ac.uk
// www.leeds.ac.uk

NN42 BA Accounting & Management

Duration: 3FT Hon
Entry Requirements: ***GCE:*** AAB. ***SQAH:*** AAAAB. ***SQAAH:*** AAB. ***IB:*** 35.

LN12 BA Economics and Management

Duration: 3FT Hon
Entry Requirements: ***GCE:*** AAB. ***SQAH:*** AAAAB. ***SQAAH:*** AAB. ***IB:*** 34.

L34 UNIVERSITY OF LEICESTER

UNIVERSITY ROAD
LEICESTER LE1 7RH
t: 0116 252 5281 f: 0116 252 2447
e: admissions@le.ac.uk
// www.le.ac.uk

NL21 BA Management Studies and Economics

Duration: 3FT Hon
Entry Requirements: ***GCE:*** ABB. ***SQAH:*** AABBB. ***SQAAH:*** ABB. ***IB:*** 30. ***BTEC ND:*** DDM.

L39 UNIVERSITY OF LINCOLN

ADMISSIONS
BRAYFORD POOL
LINCOLN LN6 7TS
t: 01522 886097 f: 01522 886146
e: admissions@lincoln.ac.uk
// www.lincoln.ac.uk

NN42 BA Management and Accountancy

Duration: 3FT Hon
Entry Requirements: ***GCE:*** 260.

NN32 BA Management and Finance

Duration: 3FT Hon
Entry Requirements: ***GCE:*** 260.

L68 LONDON METROPOLITAN UNIVERSITY

166-220 HOLLOWAY ROAD
LONDON N7 8DB
t: 020 7133 4200
e: admissions@londonmet.ac.uk
// www.londonmet.ac.uk

NJ49 BA/BSc Accounting and Logistics & Supply Chain Management

Duration: 3FT Hon
Entry Requirements: ***GCE:*** 240. ***IB:*** 28.

NP43 BA/BSc Accounting and Music & Media Management
Duration: 3FT Hon
Entry Requirements: ***GCE:*** 240. ***IB:*** 28.

NL21 BA/BSc Community Sector Management and Economics
Duration: 3FT Hon
Entry Requirements: ***GCE:*** 280. ***IB:*** 28. Interview required.

L79 LOUGHBOROUGH UNIVERSITY
LOUGHBOROUGH
LEICESTERSHIRE LE11 3TU
t: 01509 223522 f: 01509 223905
e: admissions@lboro.ac.uk
// www.lboro.ac.uk

G1N4 BSc Mathematics and Accounting and Financial Management
Duration: 3FT Hon
Entry Requirements: ***GCE:*** AAB. ***SQAH:*** AAABBB. ***SQAAH:*** AB. ***IB:*** 34. ***BTEC ND:*** DDM.

G1NK BSc Mathematics and Accounting and Financial Management (4 year SW)
Duration: 4SW Hon
Entry Requirements: ***GCE:*** AAB. ***SQAH:*** AAABBB. ***SQAAH:*** AB. ***IB:*** 34. ***BTEC ND:*** DDM.

M20 THE UNIVERSITY OF MANCHESTER
OXFORD ROAD
MANCHESTER M13 9PL
t: 0161 275 2077 f: 0161 275 2106
e: ug-admissions@manchester.ac.uk
// www.manchester.ac.uk

NN24 BSc Management (Accounting and Finance)
Duration: 3FT Hon
Entry Requirements: ***GCE:*** AAB. ***SQAAH:*** AAB. ***IB:*** 35. ***BTEC ND:*** DDM.

M40 THE MANCHESTER METROPOLITAN UNIVERSITY
ADMISSIONS OFFICE
ALL SAINTS (GMS)
ALL SAINTS
MANCHESTER M15 6BH
t: 0161 247 2000
// www.mmu.ac.uk

LN53 BA Abuse Studies/Financial Management
Duration: 3FT Hon
Entry Requirements: ***GCE:*** 260. ***BTEC ND:*** MMM.

NX33 BA Childhood & Youth Studies/Financial Management
Duration: 3FT Hon
Entry Requirements: Contact the institution for details.

XN13 BA Coaching Studies/Financial Management
Duration: 3FT Hon
Entry Requirements: ***GCE:*** 260.

WN33 BA Creative Music Production/Financial Management
Duration: 3FT Hon
Entry Requirements: ***GCE:*** 260.

WN43 BA Drama/Financial Management
Duration: 3FT Hon
Entry Requirements: ***GCE:*** 260.

NW38 BA Financial Management/Creative Writing
Duration: 3FT Hon
Entry Requirements: ***GCE:*** 260. ***BTEC ND:*** DMM.

NL3H BA Financial Management/Crime Studies
Duration: 3FT Hon
Entry Requirements: ***GCE:*** 260. ***BTEC ND:*** MMM.

NN35 BA Financial Management/Marketing
Duration: 3FT Hon
Entry Requirements: ***GCE:*** 260. ***BTEC ND:*** MMM.

NW33 BA Financial Management/Music
Duration: 3FT Hon
Entry Requirements: ***GCE:*** 260. ***BTEC ND:*** DMM.

NLJ3 BA Financial Management/Sociology
Duration: 3FT Hon
Entry Requirements: ***GCE:*** 260. ***BTEC ND:*** MMM.

NV35 BA Philosophy/Financial Management
Duration: 3FT Hon
Entry Requirements: ***GCE:*** 260.

LN1P BA/BSc Economics/Human Resource Management
Duration: 3FT Hon
Entry Requirements: ***GCE:*** 240. ***IB:*** 27.

LNCF BA/BSc Economics/Project Management
Duration: 3FT Hon
Entry Requirements: ***GCE:*** 240. ***IB:*** 27.

LN1F BA/BSc Economics/Public Management Studies
Duration: 3FT Hon
Entry Requirements: ***GCE:*** 220. ***IB:*** 26.

LN93 BA/BSc Justice and the Environment/Financial Management
Duration: 3FT Hon
Entry Requirements: ***GCE:*** 260.

LP1D BSc Economics/Information Management
Duration: 3FT Hon
Entry Requirements: ***GCE:*** 220. ***IB:*** 26.

LNC2 BSc Economics/Management Systems
Duration: 3FT Hon
Entry Requirements: ***GCE:*** 240. ***IB:*** 27.

NN36 BSc Financial Management/Human Resource Management
Duration: 3FT Hon
Entry Requirements: ***GCE:*** 260. ***BTEC ND:*** MMM.

NC36 BSc Financial Management/Sport
Duration: 3FT Hon
Entry Requirements: ***GCE:*** 260. ***BTEC ND:*** MMM.

N38 UNIVERSITY OF NORTHAMPTON
PARK CAMPUS
BOUGHTON GREEN ROAD
NORTHAMPTON NN2 7AL
t: 0800 358 2232 f: 01604 722083
e: admissions@northampton.ac.uk
// www.northampton.ac.uk

N4NG BA Accounting with Applied Management
Duration: 3FT Hon
Entry Requirements: ***GCE:*** 220-260. ***SQAH:*** ABB-BBBC. ***IB:*** 24.

N4NV BA Accounting/Events Management
Duration: 3FT Hon
Entry Requirements: ***GCE:*** 220-260. ***SQAH:*** ABB-BBBC. ***IB:*** 24.

N4DK BA Accounting/Heritage Management
Duration: 3FT Hon
Entry Requirements: ***GCE:*** 220-260. ***SQAH:*** ABB-BBBC. ***IB:*** 24.

N4NW BA Accounting/Leisure & Lifestyle Management
Duration: 3FT Hon
Entry Requirements: ***GCE:*** 220-260. ***SQAH:*** ABB-BBBC. ***IB:*** 24.

N4N2 BA Accounting/Management
Duration: 3FT Hon
Entry Requirements: ***GCE:*** 220-260. ***SQAH:*** ABB-BBBC. ***IB:*** 24.

N4FV BA Accounting/Wastes Management
Duration: 3FT Hon
Entry Requirements: ***GCE:*** 220-260. ***SQAH:*** ABB-BBBC. ***IB:*** 24.

L1NA BA Economics with Applied Management
Duration: 3FT Hon
Entry Requirements: ***GCE:*** 220-260. ***SQAH:*** ABB-BBBC. ***IB:*** 24.

L1NV BA Economics/Events Management
Duration: 3FT Hon
Entry Requirements: ***GCE:*** 220-260. ***SQAH:*** ABB-BBBC. ***IB:*** 24.

L1N6 BA Economics/Human Resource Management
Duration: 3FT Hon
Entry Requirements: ***GCE:*** 220-260. ***SQAH:*** ABB-BBBC. ***IB:*** 24.

L1N2 BA Economics/Management
Duration: 3FT Hon
Entry Requirements: ***GCE:*** 220-260. ***SQAH:*** ABB-BBBC. ***IB:*** 24.

N8NK BA Events Management/Accounting
Duration: 3FT Hon
Entry Requirements: ***GCE:*** 220-260. ***SQAH:*** ABB-BBBC. ***IB:*** 24.

N8LC BA Events Management/Economics
Duration: 3FT Hon
Entry Requirements: ***GCE:*** 220-260. ***SQAH:*** ABB-BBBC. ***IB:*** 24.

D4N4 BA Heritage Management/Accounting
Duration: 3FT Hon
Entry Requirements: ***GCE:*** 220-260. ***SQAH:*** ABB-BBBC. ***IB:*** 24.

N6L1 BA Human Resource Management/Economics
Duration: 3FT Hon
Entry Requirements: ***GCE:*** 220-260. ***SQAH:*** ABB-BBBC. ***IB:*** 24.

NN84 BA Leisure & Lifestyle Management/Accounting
Duration: 3FT Hon
Entry Requirements: ***GCE:*** 220-260. ***SQAH:*** ABB-BBBC. ***IB:*** 24.

N2N4 BA Management/Accounting
Duration: 3FT Hon
Entry Requirements: ***GCE:*** 220-260. ***SQAH:*** ABB-BBBC. ***IB:*** 24.

N2L1 BA Management/Economics
Duration: 3FT Hon
Entry Requirements: ***GCE:*** 220-260. ***SQAH:*** ABB-BBBC. ***IB:*** 24.

F8NK BSc Wastes Management/Accounting
Duration: 3FT Hon
Entry Requirements: ***GCE:*** 220-260. ***SQAH:*** ABB-BBBC. ***IB:*** 24.

N77 NORTHUMBRIA UNIVERSITY

TRINITY BUILDING
NORTHUMBERLAND ROAD
NEWCASTLE UPON TYNE NE1 8ST
t: 0191 243 7420 f: 0191 227 4561
e: er.admissions@northumbria.ac.uk
// www.northumbria.ac.uk

N390 BA Finance and Investment Management

Duration: 3FT Hon

Entry Requirements: ***GCE:*** 300. ***SQAH:*** BBBBC. ***SQAAH:*** BBC. ***IB:*** 26. ***BTEC ND:*** DDM. ***OCR NED:*** D2

O33 OXFORD UNIVERSITY

UNDERGRADUATE ADMISSIONS OFFICE
UNIVERSITY OF OXFORD
WELLINGTON SQUARE
OXFORD OX1 2JD
t: 01865 288000 f: 01865 270212
e: undergraduate.admissions@admin.ox.ac.uk
// www.admissions.ox.ac.uk

LN12 BA Economics and Management

Duration: 3FT Hon

Entry Requirements: ***GCE:*** AAA. ***SQAH:*** AAAAA-AAAAB. ***SQAAH:*** AAB. Interview required. Admissions Test required.

Q50 QUEEN MARY, UNIVERSITY OF LONDON

MILE END ROAD
LONDON E1 4NS
t: 020 7882 5555 f: 020 7882 5500
e: admissions@qmul.ac.uk
// www.qmul.ac.uk

LN12 BSc Economics, Finance and Management

Duration: 3FT Hon

Entry Requirements: ***GCE:*** AAB. ***SQAAH:*** AAB. ***IB:*** 36.

Q75 QUEEN'S UNIVERSITY BELFAST

UNIVERSITY ROAD
BELFAST BT7 1NN
t: 028 9097 3838 f: 028 9097 2828
e: admissions@qub.ac.uk
// www.qub.ac.uk

N323 BSc Actuarial Science and Risk Management

Duration: 4SW Hon

Entry Requirements: ***GCE:*** AAAa. ***SQAAH:*** AAA.

LNC2 BSc Economics and Management

Duration: 3FT Hon

Entry Requirements: ***GCE:*** BBB-BBCb. ***SQAH:*** BBBBB. ***SQAAH:*** BBB. ***IB:*** 32.

R12 THE UNIVERSITY OF READING

THE UNIVERSITY OF READING
PO BOX 217
READING RG6 6AH
t: 0118 378 8619 f: 0118 378 8924
e: student.recruitment@reading.ac.uk
// www.reading.ac.uk

NN24 BA Accounting and Management

Duration: 3FT Hon

Entry Requirements: ***GCE:*** AAB. ***SQAH:*** AAAAB. ***SQAAH:*** AAB.

R36 THE ROBERT GORDON UNIVERSITY

ROBERT GORDON UNIVERSITY
SCHOOLHILL
ABERDEEN
SCOTLAND AB10 1FR
t: 01224 26 27 28 f: 01224 262147
e: admissions@rgu.ac.uk
// www.rgu.ac.uk

N2L1 BA Management with Economics

Duration: 4FT Hon

Entry Requirements: ***GCE:*** CCC. ***SQAH:*** BBCC. ***IB:*** 26. ***BTEC ND:*** MMM.

N2N3 BA Management with Finance

Duration: 4FT Hon

Entry Requirements: ***GCE:*** CCC. ***SQAH:*** BBCC. ***IB:*** 26. ***BTEC ND:*** MMM.

R72 ROYAL HOLLOWAY, UNIVERSITY OF LONDON

ROYAL HOLLOWAY, UNIVERSITY OF LONDON
EGHAM
SURREY TW20 0EX
t: 01784 434455 f: 01784 473662
e: Admissions@rhul.ac.uk
// www.rhul.ac.uk

LN12 BSc Economics and Management

Duration: 3FT Hon

Entry Requirements: ***GCE:*** AAA-ABB. ***SQAH:*** AAAAA-AABBB. ***SQAAH:*** AAA-ABB. ***IB:*** 32. ***BTEC NC:*** DM. ***BTEC ND:*** DDM.

N2N4 BSc Management with Accounting

Duration: 3FT Hon

Entry Requirements: ***GCE:*** AAB. ***SQAH:*** AAABB. ***SQAAH:*** ABB. ***IB:*** 35.

S03 THE UNIVERSITY OF SALFORD

SALFORD M5 4WT
t: 0161 295 4545 f: 0161 295 3126
e: ugadmissions-exrel@salford.ac.uk
// www.salford.ac.uk

K4N3 BSc Property Management and Investment

Duration: 3FT Hon
Entry Requirements: ***GCE:*** 280. ***BTEC NC:*** DD. ***BTEC ND:*** DMM.

S18 THE UNIVERSITY OF SHEFFIELD

9 NORTHUMBERLAND ROAD
SHEFFIELD S10 2TT
t: 0114 222 1299 f: 0114 222 8032
e: ask@sheffield.ac.uk
// www.sheffield.ac.uk

NP41 BA Accounting & Financial Management and Information Management

Duration: 3FT Hon
Entry Requirements: ***GCE:*** BBB. ***SQAH:*** AABB. ***SQAAH:*** BB. ***IB:*** 32. ***BTEC ND:*** DDM.

NG41 BA Accounting & Financial Management and Mathematics

Duration: 3FT Hon
Entry Requirements: ***GCE:*** ABB. ***SQAH:*** AAAB. ***SQAAH:*** ABB. ***IB:*** 33. ***BTEC ND:*** DDM.

S27 UNIVERSITY OF SOUTHAMPTON

HIGHFIELD
SOUTHAMPTON SO17 1BJ
t: 023 8059 4732 f: 023 8059 3037
e: admissions@soton.ac.uk
// www.southampton.ac.uk

NN24 BSc Management Sciences and Accounting

Duration: 3FT Hon
Entry Requirements: ***GCE:*** AAB. ***SQAH:*** AAABB. ***SQAAH:*** AB. ***IB:*** 34. ***BTEC NC:*** DD. ***BTEC ND:*** DDD.

S36 UNIVERSITY OF ST ANDREWS

ST KATHARINE'S WEST
16 THE SCORES
ST ANDREWS
FIFE KY16 9AX
t: 01334 462150 f: 01334 463330
e: admissions@st-andrews.ac.uk
// www.st-and.ac.uk

LNC2 BSc Economics-Management

Duration: 4FT Hon
Entry Requirements: ***GCE:*** AAA. ***SQAH:*** AAAA. ***IB:*** 38.

LN12 BSc Economics-Management Science

Duration: 4FT Hon
Entry Requirements: ***GCE:*** AAA. ***SQAH:*** AAAA. ***IB:*** 38.

NL21 MA Economics-Management

Duration: 4FT Hon
Entry Requirements: ***GCE:*** AAA. ***SQAH:*** AAAA. ***IB:*** 38.

S75 THE UNIVERSITY OF STIRLING

STIRLING FK9 4LA
t: 01786 467044 f: 01786 466800
e: admissions@stir.ac.uk
// www.stir.ac.uk

NNH6 BA Finance and Human Resource Management

Duration: 4FT Hon
Entry Requirements: ***GCE:*** BCC. ***SQAH:*** BBBB. ***SQAAH:*** AAA-CCC. ***IB:*** 30.

NN32 BA Finance and Management Science

Duration: 4FT Hon
Entry Requirements: ***GCE:*** BCC. ***SQAH:*** BBBB. ***SQAAH:*** AAA-CCC. ***IB:*** 30.

NL61 BA Human Resource Management and Economics

Duration: 4FT Hon
Entry Requirements: ***GCE:*** CCC. ***SQAH:*** BBBB. ***SQAAH:*** AAA-CCC. ***IB:*** 30. ***BTEC ND:*** DMM.

NN24 BAcc Accountancy and Management Science

Duration: 4FT Hon
Entry Requirements: ***GCE:*** BCC. ***SQAH:*** BBBB. ***SQAAH:*** AAA-CCC. ***IB:*** 30.

LN12 BSc Economics and Management Science

Duration: 4FT Hon
Entry Requirements: ***GCE:*** CCC. ***SQAH:*** BBBB. ***SQAAH:*** AAA-CCC. ***IB:*** 30. ***BTEC ND:*** MMM.

S78 THE UNIVERSITY OF STRATHCLYDE

GLASGOW G1 1XQ
t: 0141 552 4400 f: 0141 552 0775
// www.strath.ac.uk

NN46 BA Accounting and Human Resource Management

Duration: 4FT Hon
Entry Requirements: ***GCE:*** AAB. ***SQAH:*** AAAA-AAABB. ***IB:*** 36.

NN42 BA Accounting and Management

Duration: 4FT Hon
Entry Requirements: ***GCE:*** AAB. ***SQAH:*** AAAA-AAABB. ***IB:*** 36.

GN24 BA Accounting and Management Science

Duration: 4FT Hon
Entry Requirements: ***GCE:*** AAB. ***SQAH:*** AAAA-AAABB. ***IB:*** 36.

LN16 BA Economics and Human Resource Management
Duration: 4FT Hon
Entry Requirements: ***GCE:*** ABB. ***SQAH:*** AABB-ABBBC. ***IB:*** 34.

LN12 BA Economics and Management
Duration: 4FT Hon
Entry Requirements: ***GCE:*** ABB. ***SQAH:*** AABB-ABBBC. ***IB:*** 34.

LG12 BA Economics and Management Science
Duration: 4FT Hon
Entry Requirements: ***GCE:*** ABB. ***SQAH:*** AABB-ABBBC. ***IB:*** 34.

NN36 BA Finance and Human Resource Management
Duration: 4FT Hon
Entry Requirements: ***GCE:*** ABB. ***SQAH:*** AABB-ABBBC. ***IB:*** 34.

NN32 BA Finance and Management
Duration: 4FT Hon
Entry Requirements: ***GCE:*** ABB. ***SQAH:*** AABB-ABBBC. ***IB:*** 34.

NG32 BA Finance and Management Science
Duration: 4FT Hon
Entry Requirements: ***GCE:*** ABB. ***SQAH:*** AABB-ABBBC. ***IB:*** 34.

H3N3 MEng Mechanical Engineering with Financial Management (d)
Duration: 5FT Hon
Entry Requirements: ***GCE:*** AAA. ***SQAH:*** AAAAB-AAAABB. ***SQAAH:*** AAA. ***IB:*** 36. Interview required.

S84 UNIVERSITY OF SUNDERLAND
STUDENT HELPLINE
THE STUDENT GATEWAY
CHESTER ROAD
SUNDERLAND SR1 3SD
t: 0191 515 3000 f: 0191 515 3805
e: student-helpline@sunderland.ac.uk
// www.sunderland.ac.uk

XNH3 BA Childhood Studies and Financial Management
Duration: 3FT Hon
Entry Requirements: Contact the institution for details.

X3N3 BA Childhood Studies with Financial Management
Duration: 3FT Hon
Entry Requirements: Contact the institution for details.

B9N3 BA Community Health with Financial Management
Duration: 3FT Hon
Entry Requirements: ***GCE:*** 220-360. ***BTEC NC:*** DM. ***BTEC ND:*** MMM. ***OCR ND:*** D ***OCR NED:*** M3

W5N3 BA Dance with Financial Management
Duration: 3FT Hon
Entry Requirements: ***GCE:*** 220-360. ***BTEC NC:*** DM. ***BTEC ND:*** MMM. ***OCR ND:*** D ***OCR NED:*** M3

W4N3 BA Drama with Financial Management
Duration: 3FT Hon
Entry Requirements: ***GCE:*** 220-360. ***BTEC NC:*** DM. ***BTEC ND:*** MMM. ***OCR ND:*** D ***OCR NED:*** M3

NB39 BA Financial Management and Community Health
Duration: 3FT Hon
Entry Requirements: ***GCE:*** 220-360. ***BTEC NC:*** DM. ***BTEC ND:*** MMM. ***OCR ND:*** D ***OCR NED:*** M3

NW35 BA Financial Management and Dance
Duration: 3FT Hon
Entry Requirements: ***GCE:*** 220-360. ***BTEC NC:*** DM. ***BTEC ND:*** MMM. ***OCR ND:*** D ***OCR NED:*** M3

NW34 BA Financial Management and Drama
Duration: 3FT Hon
Entry Requirements: ***GCE:*** 220-360. ***BTEC NC:*** DM. ***BTEC ND:*** MMM. ***OCR ND:*** D ***OCR NED:*** M3

NX33 BA Financial Management and Education
Duration: 3FT Hon
Entry Requirements: ***GCE:*** 220-360. ***BTEC NC:*** DM. ***BTEC ND:*** MMM. ***OCR ND:*** D ***OCR NED:*** M3

NV31 BA Financial Management and History
Duration: 3FT Hon
Entry Requirements: ***GCE:*** 220-360. ***BTEC NC:*** DM. ***BTEC ND:*** MMM. ***OCR ND:*** D ***OCR NED:*** M3

NP35 BA Financial Management and Journalism
Duration: 3FT Hon
Entry Requirements: ***GCE:*** 220-360. ***BTEC NC:*** DM. ***BTEC ND:*** MMM. ***OCR ND:*** D ***OCR NED:*** M3

NP33 BA Financial Management and Media Studies
Duration: 3FT Hon
Entry Requirements: ***GCE:*** 220-360. ***BTEC NC:*** DM. ***BTEC ND:*** MMM. ***OCR ND:*** D ***OCR NED:*** M3

NW33 BA Financial Management and Music
Duration: 3FT Hon
Entry Requirements: ***GCE:*** 220-360. ***BTEC NC:*** DM. ***BTEC ND:*** MMM. ***OCR ND:*** D ***OCR NED:*** M3

NW36 BA Financial Management and Photography
Duration: 3FT Hon
Entry Requirements: ***GCE:*** 220-360. ***BTEC NC:*** DM. ***BTEC ND:*** MMM. ***OCR ND:*** D ***OCR NED:*** M3

NL32 BA Financial Management and Politics
Duration: 3FT Hon

Entry Requirements: ***GCE:*** 220-360. ***BTEC NC:*** DM. ***BTEC ND:*** MMM. ***OCR ND:*** D ***OCR NED:*** M3

NC38 BA Financial Management and Psychology
Duration: 3FT Hon

Entry Requirements: ***GCE:*** 220-360. ***BTEC NC:*** DM. ***BTEC ND:*** MMM. ***OCR ND:*** D ***OCR NED:*** M3

NP32 BA Financial Management and Public Relations
Duration: 3FT Hon

Entry Requirements: ***GCE:*** 220-360. ***BTEC NC:*** DM. ***BTEC ND:*** MMM. ***OCR ND:*** D ***OCR NED:*** M3

NL33 BA Financial Management and Sociology
Duration: 3FT Hon

Entry Requirements: ***GCE:*** 220-360. ***BTEC NC:*** DM. ***BTEC ND:*** MMM. ***OCR ND:*** D ***OCR NED:*** M3

NC36 BA Financial Management and Sport
Duration: 3FT Hon

Entry Requirements: ***GCE:*** 220-360. ***BTEC NC:*** DM. ***BTEC ND:*** MMM. ***OCR ND:*** D ***OCR NED:*** M3

NX31 BA Financial Management and TESOL
Duration: 3FT Hon

Entry Requirements: ***GCE:*** 220-360. ***BTEC NC:*** DM. ***BTEC ND:*** MMM. ***OCR ND:*** D ***OCR NED:*** M3

NN38 BA Financial Management and Tourism
Duration: 3FT Hon

Entry Requirements: ***GCE:*** 220-360. ***BTEC NC:*** DM. ***BTEC ND:*** MMM. ***OCR ND:*** D ***OCR NED:*** M3

N3XH BA Financial Management with Childhood Studies
Duration: 3FT Hon

Entry Requirements: Contact the institution for details.

N3B9 BA Financial Management with Community Health
Duration: 3FT Hon

Entry Requirements: ***GCE:*** 220-360. ***BTEC NC:*** DM. ***BTEC ND:*** MMM. ***OCR ND:*** D ***OCR NED:*** M3

N3W5 BA Financial Management with Dance
Duration: 3FT Hon

Entry Requirements: ***GCE:*** 220-360. ***BTEC NC:*** DM. ***BTEC ND:*** MMM. ***OCR ND:*** D ***OCR NED:*** M3

N3W4 BA Financial Management with Drama
Duration: 3FT Hon

Entry Requirements: ***GCE:*** 220-360. ***BTEC NC:*** DM. ***BTEC ND:*** MMM. ***OCR ND:*** D ***OCR NED:*** M3

N3X3 BA Financial Management with Education
Duration: 3FT Hon

Entry Requirements: ***GCE:*** 220-360. ***BTEC NC:*** DM. ***BTEC ND:*** MMM. ***OCR ND:*** D ***OCR NED:*** M3

N3L5 BA Financial Management with Health & Social Care
Duration: 3FT Hon

Entry Requirements: Contact the institution for details.

N3V1 BA Financial Management with History
Duration: 3FT Hon

Entry Requirements: ***GCE:*** 220-360. ***BTEC NC:*** DM. ***BTEC ND:*** MMM. ***OCR ND:*** D ***OCR NED:*** M3

N3P5 BA Financial Management with Journalism
Duration: 3FT Hon

Entry Requirements: ***GCE:*** 220-360. ***BTEC NC:*** DM. ***BTEC ND:*** MMM. ***OCR ND:*** D ***OCR NED:*** M3

N3P3 BA Financial Management with Media Studies
Duration: 3FT Hon

Entry Requirements: ***GCE:*** 220-360. ***BTEC NC:*** DM. ***BTEC ND:*** MMM. ***OCR ND:*** D ***OCR NED:*** M3

N3W3 BA Financial Management with Music
Duration: 3FT Hon

Entry Requirements: ***GCE:*** 220-360. ***BTEC NC:*** DM. ***BTEC ND:*** MMM. ***OCR ND:*** D ***OCR NED:*** M3

N3W6 BA Financial Management with Photography
Duration: 3FT Hon

Entry Requirements: ***GCE:*** 220-360. ***BTEC NC:*** DM. ***BTEC ND:*** MMM. ***OCR ND:*** D ***OCR NED:*** M3

N3L2 BA Financial Management with Politics
Duration: 3FT Hon

Entry Requirements: ***GCE:*** 220-360. ***BTEC NC:*** DM. ***BTEC ND:*** MMM. ***OCR ND:*** D ***OCR NED:*** M3

N3C8 BA Financial Management with Psychology
Duration: 3FT Hon

Entry Requirements: ***GCE:*** 220-360. ***BTEC NC:*** DM. ***BTEC ND:*** MMM. ***OCR ND:*** D ***OCR NED:*** M3

N3P2 BA Financial Management with Public Relations
Duration: 3FT Hon

Entry Requirements: ***GCE:*** 220-360. ***BTEC NC:*** DM. ***BTEC ND:*** MMM. ***OCR ND:*** D ***OCR NED:*** M3

N3L3 BA Financial Management with Sociology
Duration: 3FT Hon
Entry Requirements: ***GCE:*** 220-360. ***BTEC NC:*** DM. ***BTEC ND:*** MMM. ***OCR ND:*** D ***OCR NED:*** M3

N3C6 BA Financial Management with Sport
Duration: 3FT Hon
Entry Requirements: ***GCE:*** 220-360. ***BTEC NC:*** DM. ***BTEC ND:*** MMM. ***OCR ND:*** D ***OCR NED:*** M3

N3X1 BA Financial Management with TESOL
Duration: 3FT Hon
Entry Requirements: ***GCE:*** 220-360. ***BTEC NC:*** DM. ***BTEC ND:*** MMM. ***OCR ND:*** D ***OCR NED:*** M3

N3N8 BA Financial Management with Tourism
Duration: 3FT Hon
Entry Requirements: ***GCE:*** 220-360. ***BTEC NC:*** DM. ***BTEC ND:*** MMM. ***OCR ND:*** D ***OCR NED:*** M3

LN53 BA Health & Social Care and Financial Management
Duration: 3FT Hon
Entry Requirements: Contact the institution for details.

L5N3 BA Health & Social Care with Financial Management
Duration: 3FT Hon
Entry Requirements: Contact the institution for details.

V1N3 BA History with Financial Management
Duration: 3FT Hon
Entry Requirements: ***GCE:*** 220-360. ***BTEC NC:*** DM. ***BTEC ND:*** MMM. ***OCR ND:*** D ***OCR NED:*** M3

P5N3 BA Journalism with Financial Management
Duration: 3FT Hon
Entry Requirements: ***GCE:*** 220-360. ***BTEC NC:*** DM. ***BTEC ND:*** MMM. ***OCR ND:*** D ***OCR NED:*** M3

P3N3 BA Media with Financial Management
Duration: 3FT Hon
Entry Requirements: ***GCE:*** 220-360. ***BTEC NC:*** DM. ***BTEC ND:*** MMM. ***OCR ND:*** D ***OCR NED:*** M3

W3N3 BA Music with Financial Management
Duration: 3FT Hon
Entry Requirements: ***GCE:*** 220-360. ***IB:*** 31. ***BTEC NC:*** DM. ***BTEC ND:*** MMM. ***OCR ND:*** D ***OCR NED:*** M3

L2N3 BA Politics with Financial Management
Duration: 3FT Hon
Entry Requirements: ***GCE:*** 220-360. ***BTEC NC:*** DM. ***BTEC ND:*** MMM. ***OCR ND:*** D ***OCR NED:*** M3

P2N3 BA Public Relations with Financial Management
Duration: 3FT Hon
Entry Requirements: ***GCE:*** 220-360. ***BTEC NC:*** DM. ***BTEC ND:*** MMM. ***OCR ND:*** D ***OCR NED:*** M3

L3N3 BA Sociology with Financial Management
Duration: 3FT Hon
Entry Requirements: ***GCE:*** 220-360. ***BTEC NC:*** DM. ***BTEC ND:*** MMM. ***OCR ND:*** D ***OCR NED:*** M3

C6N3 BA Sport with Financial Management
Duration: 3FT Hon
Entry Requirements: ***GCE:*** 220-360. ***BTEC NC:*** DM. ***BTEC ND:*** MMM. ***OCR ND:*** D ***OCR NED:*** M3

X1N3 BA Teaching English to Speakers of another Language with Financial Management
Duration: 3FT Hon
Entry Requirements: ***GCE:*** 220-360. ***BTEC NC:*** DM. ***BTEC ND:*** MMM. ***OCR ND:*** D ***OCR NED:*** M3

N8N3 BA Tourism with Financial Management
Duration: 3FT Hon
Entry Requirements: ***GCE:*** 220-360. ***BTEC NC:*** DM. ***BTEC ND:*** MMM. ***OCR ND:*** D ***OCR NED:*** M3

C8N3 BSc Psychology with Financial Management
Duration: 3FT Hon
Entry Requirements: ***GCE:*** 220-360. ***BTEC NC:*** DM. ***BTEC ND:*** MMM. ***OCR ND:*** D ***OCR NED:*** M3

S90 UNIVERSITY OF SUSSEX
UNDERGRADUATE ADMISSIONS
SUSSEX HOUSE
UNIVERSITY OF SUSSEX
BRIGHTON BN1 9RH
t: 01273 678416 f: 01273 678545
e: ug.applicants@sussex.ac.uk
// www.sussex.ac.uk

LN12 BSc Economics and Management Studies
Duration: 3FT Hon
Entry Requirements: ***GCE:*** ABB-BBB. ***SQAH:*** AABBB-ABBBB.

S93 SWANSEA UNIVERSITY

SINGLETON PARK
SWANSEA SA2 8PP
t: 01792 295111 f: 01792 295110
e: admissions@swansea.ac.uk
// www.swansea.ac.uk

N2N4 BSc Management Science (Accounting)

Duration: 3FT Hon

Entry Requirements: ***GCE:*** ABB-BBB. ***BTEC ND:*** DDM.

N2N3 BSc Management Science (Finance)

Duration: 3FT Hon

Entry Requirements: ***GCE:*** ABB-BBB. ***BTEC ND:*** DDM.

U20 UNIVERSITY OF ULSTER

COLERAINE
CO. LONDONDERRY
NORTHERN IRELAND BT52 1SA
t: 028 7032 4221 f: 028 7032 4908
e: online@ulster.ac.uk
// www.ulster.ac.uk

NN46 BSc Accounting and Human Resource Management

Duration: 4SW Hon

Entry Requirements: ***GCE:*** 240. ***IB:*** 24. ***BTEC NC:*** MM. ***BTEC ND:*** MMM.

W36 WEST CHESHIRE COLLEGE

EATON ROAD
HANDBRIDGE
CHESTER
CHESHIRE CH4 7ER
t: 01244 670600 f: 01244 670687
e: info@west-cheshire.ac.uk
// www.west-cheshire.ac.uk

N4N2 FdA Accounting with Management

Duration: 2FT Fdg

Entry Requirements: Contact the institution for details.

W50 UNIVERSITY OF WESTMINSTER

101 NEW CAVENDISH STREET
LONDON W1W 6XH
t: 020 7915 5511 f: 020 7911 5788
e: course-enquiries@westminster.ac.uk
// www.westminster.ac.uk

N3N2 BA Finance with Management

Duration: 3FT/4SW Hon

Entry Requirements: ***GCE:*** BBC. ***SQAH:*** BBBBB. ***SQAAH:*** BBB. ***IB:*** 28.

N4N2 BSc Accounting with Management

Duration: 3FT/4SW Hon

Entry Requirements: ***GCE:*** BBB. ***SQAH:*** BBBBB. ***SQAAH:*** BBB. ***IB:*** 28. ***BTEC ND:*** DMM.

W76 UNIVERSITY OF WINCHESTER

WINCHESTER
HANTS SO22 4NR
t: 01962 827234 f: 01962 827288
e: course.enquiries@winchester.ac.uk
// www.winchester.ac.uk

NN42 BA Accounting and Management

Duration: 3FT Hon

Entry Requirements: ***Foundation:*** Distinction. ***GCE:*** 260-300. ***IB:*** 25. ***BTEC NC:*** DD. ***BTEC ND:*** DMM. ***OCR ND:*** D ***OCR NED:*** M2

Y50 THE UNIVERSITY OF YORK

ADMISSIONS AND UK/EU STUDENT RECRUITMENT
UNIVERSITY OF YORK
HESLINGTON
YORK YO10 5DD
t: 01904 433533 f: 01904 433538
e: admissions@york.ac.uk
// www.york.ac.uk

CL91 BSc Environment, Economics & Environmental Management

Duration: 3FT Hon

Entry Requirements: ***GCE:*** ABB-BBB. ***SQAH:*** AAABB. ***IB:*** 32. ***BTEC ND:*** DDM.

MARKETING COMBINATIONS

A40 ABERYSTWYTH UNIVERSITY

WELCOME CENTRE, ABERYSTWYTH UNIVERSITY
PENGLAIS CAMPUS
ABERYSTWYTH
CEREDIGION SY23 3FB
t: 01970 622021 f: 01970 627410
e: ug-admissions@aber.ac.uk
// www.aber.ac.uk

N4N5 BScEcon Accounting & Finance with Marketing

Duration: 3FT Hon

Entry Requirements: ***GCE:*** 280. ***IB:*** 27.

LN15 BScEcon Economics/Marketing

Duration: 3FT Hon

Entry Requirements: ***GCE:*** 280. ***IB:*** 27.

N5N4 BScEcon Marketing with Accounting & Finance

Duration: 3FT Hon

Entry Requirements: ***GCE:*** 260. ***IB:*** 27.

N5L1 BScEcon Marketing with Economics

Duration: 3FT Hon

Entry Requirements: ***GCE:*** 260. ***IB:*** 27.

B25 BIRMINGHAM CITY UNIVERSITY

CITY NORTH CAMPUS
PERRY BARR
BIRMINGHAM B42 2SU
t: 0121 331 5595 f: 0121 331 7994
e: choices@bcu.ac.uk
// www.bcu.ac.uk/courses/choices/contact-choices

NLM1 BA Advertising and Economics

Duration: 3FT/4SW Hon

Entry Requirements: ***GCE:*** 260. ***IB:*** 30. ***BTEC NC:*** DD. ***BTEC ND:*** DMM. ***OCR ND:*** D ***OCR NED:*** M3 Interview required. Portfolio required.

NL51 BA Marketing and Economics

Duration: 3FT/4SW Hon

Entry Requirements: ***GCE:*** 260. ***IB:*** 30. ***BTEC NC:*** DD. ***BTEC ND:*** DMM. ***OCR ND:*** D ***OCR NED:*** M3 Interview required. Portfolio required.

B56 THE UNIVERSITY OF BRADFORD

RICHMOND ROAD
BRADFORD
WEST YORKSHIRE BD7 1DP
t: 0800 073 1225 f: 01274 235585
e: course-enquiries@bradford.ac.uk
// www.bradford.ac.uk

L1N5 BSc Economics with Marketing

Duration: 3FT Hon

Entry Requirements: ***GCE:*** 240-260. ***IB:*** 28.

C10 CANTERBURY CHRIST CHURCH UNIVERSITY

NORTH HOLMES ROAD
CANTERBURY
KENT CT1 1QU
t: 01227 782900 f: 01227 782888
e: admissions@canterbury.ac.uk
// www.canterbury.ac.uk

N5N4 BSc Marketing with Accounting

Duration: 3FT Hon

Entry Requirements: ***GCE:*** 240. ***IB:*** 24.

C30 UNIVERSITY OF CENTRAL LANCASHIRE

PRESTON
LANCS PR1 2HE
t: 01772 201201 f: 01772 894954
e: uadmissions@uclan.ac.uk
// www.uclan.ac.uk

NN54 BA Accounting and Marketing

Duration: 3FT Hon

Entry Requirements: ***GCE:*** 240-280. ***SQAH:*** AABB-BBBB. ***IB:*** 28. ***BTEC NC:*** DD. ***OCR ND:*** D

C58 UNIVERSITY OF CHICHESTER

BISHOP OTTER CAMPUS
COLLEGE LANE
CHICHESTER
WEST SUSSEX PO19 6PE
t: 01243 816002 f: 01243 816161
e: admissions@chi.ac.uk
// www.chiuni.ac.uk

NN53 BA Marketing and Finance

Duration: 3FT Hon

Entry Requirements: ***GCE:*** CCC. ***SQAAH:*** CCC. ***IB:*** 28. ***BTEC ND:*** MMM.

D26 DE MONTFORT UNIVERSITY

THE GATEWAY
LEICESTER LE1 9BH
t: 0116 255 1551 f: 0116 250 6204
e: enquiries@dmu.ac.uk
// www.dmu.ac.uk

NN45 BA Accounting and Marketing

Duration: 3FT Hon

Entry Requirements: ***GCE:*** 240. ***IB:*** 24. ***BTEC NC:*** DD. ***BTEC ND:*** MMM. ***OCR ND:*** D ***OCR NED:*** M3 Interview required.

D39 UNIVERSITY OF DERBY

KEDLESTON ROAD
DERBY DE22 1GB
t: 08701 202330 f: 01332 597724
e: askadmissions@derby.ac.uk
// www.derby.ac.uk

NN45 BA Accounting and Marketing

Duration: 3FT Hon

Entry Requirements: ***Foundation:*** Merit. ***GCE:*** 180-240. ***IB:*** 26. ***BTEC NC:*** DM. ***BTEC ND:*** MMP.

E70 THE UNIVERSITY OF ESSEX

WIVENHOE PARK
COLCHESTER
ESSEX CO4 3SQ
t: 01206 873666 f: 01206 873423
e: admit@essex.ac.uk
// www.essex.ac.uk

NN53 BSc Marketing and Finance

Duration: 3FT Hon
Entry Requirements: ***GCE:*** 320. ***SQAH:*** AAAB. ***IB:*** 34. ***BTEC NC:*** DD. ***BTEC ND:*** DDM.

H24 HERIOT-WATT UNIVERSITY, EDINBURGH

EDINBURGH CAMPUS
EDINBURGH EH14 4AS
t: 0131 449 5111 f: 0131 451 3630
e: ugadmissions@hw.ac.uk
// www.hw.ac.uk

LN15 MA Economics and Marketing

Duration: 4FT Hon
Entry Requirements: ***GCE:*** ABC-BBB. ***SQAH:*** AAAB-BBBBC. ***SQAAH:*** BB. ***IB:*** 29.

H36 UNIVERSITY OF HERTFORDSHIRE

UNIVERSITY ADMISSIONS SERVICE
COLLEGE LANE
HATFIELD
HERTS AL10 9AB
t: 01707 284800 f: 01707 284870
// www.herts.ac.uk

NN45 BA Accounting/Marketing

Duration: 3FT/4SW Hon
Entry Requirements: ***GCE:*** 260.

LN1M BA Economics/Marketing

Duration: 3FT/4SW Hon
Entry Requirements: ***GCE:*** 260.

N5N3 BA Marketing with Finance

Duration: 3FT/4SW Hon
Entry Requirements: ***GCE:*** 260.

H72 THE UNIVERSITY OF HULL

THE UNIVERSITY OF HULL
COTTINGHAM ROAD
HULL HU6 7RX
t: 01482 466100 f: 01482 442290
e: admissions@hull.ac.uk
// www.hull.ac.uk

NN54 BA Marketing and Accounting

Duration: 3FT Hon
Entry Requirements: ***GCE:*** 280. ***IB:*** 28.

NN5K BA Marketing and Accounting (International) (4 years)

Duration: 4FT Hon
Entry Requirements: ***GCE:*** 280. ***IB:*** 28.

NNM4 BA Marketing and Accounting (with Professional Experience) (4 years)

Duration: 4FT Hon
Entry Requirements: ***GCE:*** 280. ***IB:*** 28.

NL5C BA Marketing and Economics

Duration: 3FT Hon
Entry Requirements: ***GCE:*** 280. ***IB:*** 28.

NLN1 BA Marketing and Economics (International) (4 years)

Duration: 4FT Hon
Entry Requirements: ***GCE:*** 280. ***IB:*** 28.

NLMC BA Marketing and Economics (with Professional Experience) (4 years)

Duration: 4FT Hon
Entry Requirements: ***GCE:*** 280. ***IB:*** 28.

K12 KEELE UNIVERSITY

STAFFS ST5 5BG
t: 01782 734005 f: 01782 632343
e: undergraduate@keele.ac.uk
// www.keele.ac.uk

NN45 BA Accounting and Marketing

Duration: 3FT Hon
Entry Requirements: ***GCE:*** 320-340.

LN15 BA Economics and Marketing

Duration: 3FT Hon
Entry Requirements: ***GCE:*** 280-340.

NN35 BA Finance and Marketing

Duration: 3FT Hon
Entry Requirements: ***GCE:*** 280-340.

L39 UNIVERSITY OF LINCOLN

ADMISSIONS
BRAYFORD POOL
LINCOLN LN6 7TS
t: 01522 886097 f: 01522 886146
e: admissions@lincoln.ac.uk
// www.lincoln.ac.uk

NN45 BA/BSc Accountancy and Marketing

Duration: 3FT Hon
Entry Requirements: ***GCE:*** 260.

L68 LONDON METROPOLITAN UNIVERSITY
166-220 HOLLOWAY ROAD
LONDON N7 8DB
t: 020 7133 4200
e: admissions@londonmet.ac.uk
// www.londonmet.ac.uk

NN35 BA Financial Services and Marketing
Duration: 3FT Hon
Entry Requirements: ***GCE:*** 240. ***IB:*** 28.

L75 LONDON SOUTH BANK UNIVERSITY
103 BOROUGH ROAD
LONDON SE1 0AA
t: 020 7815 7815 f: 020 7815 8273
e: enquiry@lsbu.ac.uk
// www.lsbu.ac.uk

N4N5 BA Accounting with Marketing
Duration: 3FT Hon
Entry Requirements: ***GCE:*** 160. ***IB:*** 24. ***BTEC NC:*** MM. ***BTEC ND:*** MPP.

N5N4 BA Digital Marketing with Accounting
Duration: 3FT Hon
Entry Requirements: ***GCE:*** 160. ***IB:*** 24. ***BTEC NC:*** MM. ***BTEC ND:*** MPP.

NN45 BA Marketing and Accounting
Duration: 3FT Hon
Entry Requirements: ***GCE:*** 160. ***IB:*** 24. ***BTEC NC:*** MM. ***BTEC ND:*** MPP.

N5NK BA Marketing with Accounting
Duration: 3FT Hon
Entry Requirements: ***GCE:*** 160. ***IB:*** 24. ***BTEC NC:*** MM. ***BTEC ND:*** MPP.

NN54 BA/BSc Digital Marketing and Accounting
Duration: 3FT Hon
Entry Requirements: ***GCE:*** 160. ***IB:*** 24. ***BTEC NC:*** MM. ***BTEC ND:*** MPP.

N38 UNIVERSITY OF NORTHAMPTON
PARK CAMPUS
BOUGHTON GREEN ROAD
NORTHAMPTON NN2 7AL
t: 0800 358 2232 f: 01604 722083
e: admissions@northampton.ac.uk
// www.northampton.ac.uk

N4NM BA Accounting/Advertising
Duration: 3FT Hon
Entry Requirements: ***GCE:*** 220-260. ***SQAH:*** ABB-BBBC. ***IB:*** 24.

N4N5 BA Accounting/Marketing
Duration: 3FT Hon
Entry Requirements: ***GCE:*** 220-260. ***SQAH:*** ABB-BBBC. ***IB:*** 24.

N5NK BA Advertising/Accounting
Duration: 3FT Hon
Entry Requirements: ***GCE:*** 220-260. ***SQAH:*** ABB-BBBC. ***IB:*** 24.

N5LC BA Advertising/Economics
Duration: 3FT Hon
Entry Requirements: ***GCE:*** 220-260. ***SQAH:*** ABB-BBBC. ***IB:*** 24.

L1NM BA Economics/Advertising
Duration: 3FT Hon
Entry Requirements: ***GCE:*** 220-260. ***SQAH:*** ABB-BBBC. ***IB:*** 24.

L1N5 BA Economics/Marketing
Duration: 3FT Hon
Entry Requirements: ***GCE:*** 220-260. ***SQAH:*** ABB-BBBC. ***IB:*** 24.

N5N4 BA Marketing/Accounting
Duration: 3FT Hon
Entry Requirements: ***GCE:*** 220-260. ***SQAH:*** ABB-BBBC. ***IB:*** 24.

N5L1 BA Marketing/Economics
Duration: 3FT Hon
Entry Requirements: ***GCE:*** 220-260. ***SQAH:*** ABB-BBBC. ***IB:*** 24.

S75 THE UNIVERSITY OF STIRLING
STIRLING FK9 4LA
t: 01786 467044 f: 01786 466800
e: admissions@stir.ac.uk
// www.stir.ac.uk

NL51 BA Economics and Marketing
Duration: 4FT Hon
Entry Requirements: ***GCE:*** CCC. ***SQAH:*** BBBB. ***SQAAH:*** AAA-CCC. ***IB:*** 30. ***BTEC ND:*** MMM.

NN35 BA Finance and Marketing
Duration: 4FT Hon
Entry Requirements: ***GCE:*** BCC. ***SQAH:*** BBBB. ***SQAAH:*** AAA-CCC. ***IB:*** 30.

NN45 BAcc Accountancy and Marketing
Duration: 4FT Hon
Entry Requirements: ***GCE:*** BCC. ***SQAH:*** BBBB. ***SQAAH:*** AAA-CCC. ***IB:*** 30.

S78 THE UNIVERSITY OF STRATHCLYDE
GLASGOW G1 1XQ
t: 0141 552 4400 f: 0141 552 0775
// www.strath.ac.uk

NN45 BA Accounting and Marketing
Duration: 4FT Hon
Entry Requirements: ***GCE:*** AAB. ***SQAH:*** AAAA-AAABB. ***IB:*** 36.

LN15 BA Economics and Marketing
Duration: 4FT Deg
Entry Requirements: ***GCE:*** ABB. ***SQAH:*** AABB-ABBBC. ***IB:*** 34.

NN35 BA Finance and Marketing
Duration: 4FT Hon
Entry Requirements: ***GCE:*** ABB. ***SQAH:*** AABB-ABBBC. ***IB:*** 34.

U20 UNIVERSITY OF ULSTER
COLERAINE
CO. LONDONDERRY
NORTHERN IRELAND BT52 1SA
t: 028 7032 4221 f: 028 7032 4908
e: online@ulster.ac.uk
// www.ulster.ac.uk

NN4M BSc Accounting and Advertising
Duration: 4SW Hon
Entry Requirements: ***GCE:*** 240. ***IB:*** 24. ***BTEC NC:*** MM. ***BTEC ND:*** MMM.

NN45 BSc Accounting and Marketing
Duration: 4SW Hon
Entry Requirements: ***GCE:*** 240. ***IB:*** 24. ***BTEC NC:*** MM. ***BTEC ND:*** MMM.

N5N4 BSc Advertising with Accounting
Duration: 4FT Hon
Entry Requirements: ***GCE:*** 240. ***IB:*** 24. ***BTEC NC:*** MM. ***BTEC ND:*** MMM.

L1N5 BSc Economics with Marketing
Duration: 4SW Hon
Entry Requirements: ***GCE:*** 240. ***IB:*** 24. ***BTEC NC:*** MM. ***BTEC ND:*** MMM.

MATHEMATICS AND STATISTICS COMBINATIONS

A20 THE UNIVERSITY OF ABERDEEN
UNIVERSITY OFFICE
KING'S COLLEGE
ABERDEEN AB24 3FX
t: +44 (0) 1224 273504 f: +44 (0) 1224 272034
e: sras@abdn.ac.uk
// www.abdn.ac.uk/sras

LG11 MA Economics and Mathematics
Duration: 4FT Hon
Entry Requirements: ***GCE:*** BBB. ***SQAH:*** BBBB. ***IB:*** 30. ***BTEC ND:*** MMM.

A40 ABERYSTWYTH UNIVERSITY
WELCOME CENTRE, ABERYSTWYTH UNIVERSITY
PENGLAIS CAMPUS
ABERYSTWYTH
CEREDIGION SY23 3FB
t: 01970 622021 f: 01970 627410
e: ug-admissions@aber.ac.uk
// www.aber.ac.uk

G1N3 BSc Financial Mathematics
Duration: 3FT Hon
Entry Requirements: ***GCE:*** 300. ***IB:*** 27.

G1N4 BSc Mathematics with Accounting & Finance
Duration: 3FT Hon
Entry Requirements: ***GCE:*** 300. ***IB:*** 27.

G1L1 BSc Mathematics with Economics
Duration: 3FT Hon
Entry Requirements: ***GCE:*** 300. ***IB:*** 27.

N4G1 BScEcon Accounting & Finance with Mathematics
Duration: 3FT Hon
Entry Requirements: ***GCE:*** 280. ***IB:*** 27.

N4G3 BScEcon Accounting & Finance with Statistics
Duration: 3FT Hon
Entry Requirements: ***GCE:*** 280. ***IB:*** 27.

L1G1 BScEcon Economics with Mathematics
Duration: 3FT Hon
Entry Requirements: ***GCE:*** 280. ***IB:*** 27.

A80 ASTON UNIVERSITY, BIRMINGHAM
ASTON TRIANGLE
BIRMINGHAM B4 7ET
t: 0121 204 4444 f: 0121 204 3696
e: admissions@aston.ac.uk
// www.aston.ac.uk

G1L1 BSc Mathematics with Economics
Duration: 3FT/4SW Hon
Entry Requirements: ***GCE:*** 320-340. ***SQAH:*** ABBBB. ***SQAAH:*** ABB. ***IB:*** 33. ***BTEC ND:*** DDM.

B32 THE UNIVERSITY OF BIRMINGHAM

EDGBASTON
BIRMINGHAM B15 2TT
t: 0121 415 8900 f: 0121 414 7159
e: admissions@bham.ac.uk
// www.bham.ac.uk

LG13 BSc Mathematical Economics and Statistics

Duration: 3FT Hon

Entry Requirements: ***GCE:*** AAB. ***SQAH:*** AAABB. ***SQAAH:*** AAB-ABB.

B44 THE UNIVERSITY OF BOLTON

DEANE ROAD
BOLTON BL3 5AB
t: 01204 900600 f: 01204 399074
e: enquiries@bolton.ac.uk
// www.bolton.ac.uk

GN14 BA/BSc Accountancy and Mathematics

Duration: 3FT Hon

Entry Requirements: ***GCE:*** 260. ***IB:*** 24. ***BTEC ND:*** DMM.

B72 UNIVERSITY OF BRIGHTON

MITHRAS HOUSE
LEWES ROAD
BRIGHTON BN2 4AT
t: 01273 644644 f: 01273 642607
e: admissions@brighton.ac.uk
// www.brighton.ac.uk

G1N3 BSc Mathematics with Finance

Duration: 3FT/4SW Hon

Entry Requirements: ***GCE:*** BBC. ***IB:*** 28.

B78 UNIVERSITY OF BRISTOL

UNDERGRADUATE ADMISSIONS OFFICE
SENATE HOUSE
TYNDALL AVENUE
BRISTOL BS8 1TH
t: 0117 928 9000 f: 0117 925 1424
e: ug-admissions@bristol.ac.uk
// www.bristol.ac.uk

LG11 BSc Economics and Mathematics

Duration: 3FT Hon

Entry Requirements: ***GCE:*** A*AA-AAB. ***SQAH:*** AAAAA-AAAAB. ***SQAAH:*** AA-AB. ***BTEC ND:*** DDD.

B84 BRUNEL UNIVERSITY

UXBRIDGE
MIDDLESEX UB8 3PH
t: 01895 265265 f: 01895 269790
e: admissions@brunel.ac.uk
// www.brunel.ac.uk

GN13 BSc Financial Mathematics

Duration: 3FT Hon

Entry Requirements: ***GCE:*** 280-320. ***IB:*** 32. ***BTEC ND:*** DDM.

GND3 BSc Financial Mathematics (4 year Thick SW)

Duration: 4SW Hon

Entry Requirements: ***GCE:*** 280-320. ***IB:*** 32. ***BTEC ND:*** DDM.

GN1H MMath Financial Mathematics (4 years)

Duration: 4FT Hon

Entry Requirements: ***GCE:*** 320-360. ***IB:*** 33.

GN1J MMath Financial Mathematics (5 year Thick SW)

Duration: 5FT Hon

Entry Requirements: ***GCE:*** 320-360. ***IB:*** 33.

C55 UNIVERSITY OF CHESTER

PARKGATE ROAD
CHESTER CH1 4BJ
t: 01244 511000 f: 01244 511300
e: enquiries@chester.ac.uk
// www.chester.ac.uk

LG11 BSc Economics and Mathematics

Duration: 3FT Hon

Entry Requirements: ***GCE:*** 240. ***SQAH:*** BBBB. ***IB:*** 24. ***BTEC NC:*** MM. ***BTEC ND:*** MPP.

L1G1 BSc Economics with Mathematics

Duration: 3FT Hon

Entry Requirements: ***GCE:*** 240. ***SQAH:*** BBBB. ***IB:*** 24. ***BTEC NC:*** MM. ***BTEC ND:*** MPP.

G1L1 BSc Mathematics with Economics

Duration: 3FT Hon

Entry Requirements: ***GCE:*** 240. ***SQAH:*** BBBB. ***IB:*** 24. ***BTEC NC:*** MM. ***BTEC ND:*** MPP.

C60 CITY UNIVERSITY
NORTHAMPTON SQUARE
LONDON EC1V 0HB
t: 020 7040 5060 f: 020 7040 8995
e: ugadmissions@city.ac.uk
// www.city.ac.uk

G1L1 BSc Mathematical Science with Finance & Economics (3 years or 4 year SW)
Duration: 3FT Hon
Entry Requirements: ***GCE:*** 280-300. ***IB:*** 28.

GN13 BSc Mathematics and Finance (3 years or 4 year SW)
Duration: 3FT Hon
Entry Requirements: ***GCE:*** BBB. ***IB:*** 28.

GN1H BSc Mathematics and Finance (Foundation)
Duration: 4FT Hon
Entry Requirements: ***GCE:*** DD. ***IB:*** 24.

D39 UNIVERSITY OF DERBY
KEDLESTON ROAD
DERBY DE22 1GB
t: 08701 202330 f: 01332 597724
e: askadmissions@derby.ac.uk
// www.derby.ac.uk

GN14 BSc Accounting and Mathematics
Duration: 3FT Hon
Entry Requirements: ***Foundation:*** Merit. ***GCE:*** 180-240. ***IB:*** 26. ***BTEC NC:*** DM. ***BTEC ND:*** MMP.

D65 UNIVERSITY OF DUNDEE
DUNDEE DD1 4HN
t: 01382 383838 f: 01382 388150
e: ContactUs@dundee.ac.uk
// www.dundee.ac.uk/admissions/undergraduate/

GN14 BSc Accountancy and Mathematics
Duration: 4FT Hon
Entry Requirements: ***GCE:*** CCC. ***SQAH:*** BBBB. ***IB:*** 30. ***BTEC ND:*** DMM.

GL11 BSc Mathematics and Economics
Duration: 4FT Hon
Entry Requirements: ***GCE:*** CCC. ***SQAH:*** BBBB. ***IB:*** 30. ***BTEC ND:*** DMM.

GLD1 BSc Mathematics and Financial Economics
Duration: 4FT Hon
Entry Requirements: ***GCE:*** CCC. ***SQAH:*** BBBB. ***IB:*** 30. ***BTEC ND:*** DMM.

E14 UNIVERSITY OF EAST ANGLIA
NORWICH NR4 7TJ
t: 01603 591515 f: 01603 458596
e: admissions@uea.ac.uk
// www.uea.ac.uk

G1L1 BSc Mathematics with Economics
Duration: 3FT Hon
Entry Requirements: ***GCE:*** ABB-ABC. ***SQAH:*** ABBB. ***SQAAH:*** ABB. ***IB:*** 32.

E28 UNIVERSITY OF EAST LONDON
DOCKLANDS CAMPUS
UNIVERSITY WAY
LONDON E16 2RD
t: 020 8223 3333 f: 020 8223 2978
e: study@uel.ac.uk
// www.uel.ac.uk

N4G1 BA Accounting with Mathematics
Duration: 3FT Hon
Entry Requirements: Contact the institution for details.

E56 THE UNIVERSITY OF EDINBURGH
STUDENT RECRUITMENT & ADMISSIONS
57 GEORGE SQUARE
EDINBURGH EH8 9JU
t: 0131 650 4360 f: 0131 651 1236
e: sra.enquiries@ed.ac.uk
// www.ed.ac.uk/studying/undergraduate/

LG11 MA Economics and Mathematics
Duration: 4FT Hon
Entry Requirements: ***GCE:*** AAA-ABC. ***SQAH:*** AABB-ABBC. ***IB:*** 34.

LG13 MA Economics and Statistics
Duration: 4FT Hon
Entry Requirements: ***GCE:*** AAA-ABC. ***SQAH:*** AABB-ABBC. ***IB:*** 34.

E70 THE UNIVERSITY OF ESSEX
WIVENHOE PARK
COLCHESTER
ESSEX CO4 3SQ
t: 01206 873666 f: 01206 873423
e: admit@essex.ac.uk
// www.essex.ac.uk

GN14 BSc Accounting and Mathematics
Duration: 3FT Hon
Entry Requirements: ***GCE:*** 300. ***SQAH:*** AABB. ***IB:*** 32. ***BTEC NC:*** DM. ***BTEC ND:*** DDM.

GN1K BSc Accounting and Mathematics with a year in the USA
Duration: 4FT Hon
Entry Requirements: ***GCE:*** 300. ***SQAH:*** AABB. ***IB:*** 32. ***BTEC NC:*** DM. ***BTEC ND:*** DDM.

LG11 BSc Economics and Mathematics
Duration: 3FT Hon
Entry Requirements: ***GCE:*** 300. ***SQAH:*** AABB. ***IB:*** 32. ***BTEC NC:*** DM. ***BTEC ND:*** DDM.

LG1C BSc Economics and Mathematics with a year in the USA
Duration: 4FT Hon
Entry Requirements: ***GCE:*** 300. ***SQAH:*** AABB. ***IB:*** 32. ***BTEC NC:*** DM. ***BTEC ND:*** DDM.

L1G1 BSc Economics with Mathematics
Duration: 3FT Hon
Entry Requirements: ***GCE:*** 320. ***SQAH:*** AAAB. ***IB:*** 34. ***BTEC NC:*** DD. ***BTEC ND:*** DDM.

GN13 BSc Finance and Mathematics
Duration: 3FT Hon
Entry Requirements: ***GCE:*** 300. ***SQAH:*** AABB. ***IB:*** 32. ***BTEC NC:*** DM. ***BTEC ND:*** DDM.

GN1H BSc Finance and Mathematics with a year in the USA
Duration: 4FT Hon
Entry Requirements: ***GCE:*** 300. ***SQAH:*** AABB. ***IB:*** 32. ***BTEC NC:*** DM. ***BTEC ND:*** DDM.

G1L1 BSc Mathematics with Economics
Duration: 3FT Hon
Entry Requirements: ***GCE:*** 300. ***SQAH:*** AABB. ***IB:*** 32. ***BTEC NC:*** DM. ***BTEC ND:*** DDM.

G1LC BSc Mathematics with Economics with a year in the USA
Duration: 4FT Hon
Entry Requirements: ***GCE:*** 300. ***SQAH:*** AABB. ***IB:*** 32. ***BTEC NC:*** DM. ***BTEC ND:*** DDM.

E84 UNIVERSITY OF EXETER
LAVER BUILDING
NORTH PARK ROAD
EXETER
DEVON EX4 4QE
t: 01392 263855 f: 01392 263857/262479
e: admissions@exeter.ac.uk
// www.exeter.ac.uk/admissions

G1N4 BSc Mathematics with Accounting
Duration: 3FT Hon
Entry Requirements: ***GCE:*** AAA-ABB. ***SQAH:*** AAAAB-AABBB. ***SQAAH:*** AAB-BBB. ***BTEC ND:*** DDD.

G1L1 BSc Mathematics with Economics
Duration: 3FT Hon
Entry Requirements: ***GCE:*** AAA-ABB. ***SQAH:*** AAAAB-AABBB. ***SQAAH:*** AAB-BBB. ***BTEC ND:*** DDD.

G1N3 BSc Mathematics with Finance
Duration: 3FT Hon
Entry Requirements: ***GCE:*** AAA-ABB. ***SQAH:*** AAAAB-AABBB. ***SQAAH:*** AAB-BBB. ***BTEC ND:*** DDD.

G14 UNIVERSITY OF GLAMORGAN, CARDIFF AND PONTYPRIDD
ENQUIRIES AND ADMISSIONS UNIT
PONTYPRIDD CF37 1DL
t: 0800 716925 f: 01443 654050
e: enquiries@glam.ac.uk
// www.glam.ac.uk

G1N3 BSc Financial Mathematics
Duration: 3FT/4SW Hon
Entry Requirements: ***GCE:*** 300-340. Interview required.

GN1K BSc Mathematics and Accounting
Duration: 3FT Hon
Entry Requirements: ***GCE:*** 240-280. ***BTEC NC:*** MP. ***BTEC ND:*** PPP. Interview required.

G1NK BSc Mathematics with Accounting
Duration: 3FT Hon
Entry Requirements: ***GCE:*** 240-280. ***BTEC NC:*** MP. ***BTEC ND:*** MPP. Interview required.

G28 UNIVERSITY OF GLASGOW
THE UNIVERSITY OF GLASGOW
THE FRASER BUILDING
65 HILLHEAD STREET
GLASGOW G12 8QF
t: 0141 330 6062 f: 0141 330 2961
e: ugenquiries@gla.ac.uk (UK/EU undergrad enquiries only)
// www.glasgow.ac.uk

NG41 BSc Accounting and Applied Mathematics
Duration: 4FT Hon
Entry Requirements: ***GCE:*** AAB. ***SQAH:*** AAABB. ***IB:*** 32.

NG4C BSc Accounting and Mathematics
Duration: 4FT Hon
Entry Requirements: ***GCE:*** AAB. ***SQAH:*** AAABB. ***IB:*** 34.

NG4D BSc Accounting and Pure Mathematics
Duration: 4FT Hon
Entry Requirements: ***GCE:*** AAB. ***SQAH:*** AAABB. ***IB:*** 34.

GN34 BSc Accounting and Statistics
Duration: 4FT Hon
Entry Requirements: ***GCE:*** AAB. ***SQAH:*** AAABB. ***IB:*** 34.

LG1C BSc Applied Mathematics and Economics
Duration: 3FT/4FT Deg/Hon
Entry Requirements: ***GCE:*** ABB. ***SQAH:*** ABBB. ***IB:*** 32.

GN13 BSc Finance and Applied Mathematics
Duration: 4FT Hon
Entry Requirements: ***GCE:*** AAB. ***SQAH:*** AAABB. ***IB:*** 34.

NG3C BSc Finance and Mathematics
Duration: 4FT Hon
Entry Requirements: ***GCE:*** AAB. ***SQAH:*** AAABB. ***IB:*** 34.

NG31 BSc Finance and Pure Mathematics
Duration: 4FT Hon
Entry Requirements: ***GCE:*** AAB. ***SQAH:*** AAABB. ***IB:*** 34.

GN33 BSc Finance and Statistics
Duration: 4FT Hon
Entry Requirements: ***GCE:*** AAB. ***SQAH:*** AAABB. ***IB:*** 34.

LG1D BSc Mathematics/Economics
Duration: 4FT Hon
Entry Requirements: ***GCE:*** ABB. ***SQAH:*** ABBB. ***IB:*** 32.

GL31 BSc Statistics and Economics
Duration: 4FT Hon
Entry Requirements: ***GCE:*** ABB. ***SQAH:*** ABBB. ***IB:*** 32.

GL11 MA Economics/Mathematics
Duration: 4FT Hon
Entry Requirements: ***GCE:*** AAB. ***SQAH:*** AAAB-AABB. ***IB:*** 34.

GLC1 MA Economics/Mathematics
Duration: 4FT Hon
Entry Requirements: ***GCE:*** AAB. ***SQAH:*** AAAB-AABB. ***IB:*** 34.

G70 UNIVERSITY OF GREENWICH
GREENWICH CAMPUS
OLD ROYAL NAVAL COLLEGE
PARK ROW
LONDON SE10 9LS
t: 0800 005 006 f: 020 8331 8145
e: courseinfo@gre.ac.uk
// www.gre.ac.uk

GL11 BSc Economics and Mathematics
Duration: 3FT Hon
Entry Requirements: ***GCE:*** 180. ***IB:*** 24.

LG13 BSc Economics and Statistics
Duration: 3FT Hon
Entry Requirements: ***GCE:*** 180. ***IB:*** 24.

G1L1 BSc Mathematics with Economics
Duration: 3FT Hon
Entry Requirements: ***GCE:*** 160. ***IB:*** 24.

H24 HERIOT-WATT UNIVERSITY, EDINBURGH
EDINBURGH CAMPUS
EDINBURGH EH14 4AS
t: 0131 449 5111 f: 0131 451 3630
e: ugadmissions@hw.ac.uk
// www.hw.ac.uk

G1N3 BSc Mathematics with Finance
Duration: 3FT/4FT Hon
Entry Requirements: ***GCE:*** BBB. ***SQAH:*** BBBCC. ***SQAAH:*** BBB. ***IB:*** 26.

H36 UNIVERSITY OF HERTFORDSHIRE
UNIVERSITY ADMISSIONS SERVICE
COLLEGE LANE
HATFIELD
HERTS AL10 9AB
t: 01707 284800 f: 01707 284870
// www.herts.ac.uk

L1G9 BSc Economics/Financial Mathematics
Duration: 3FT/4SW Hon
Entry Requirements: ***GCE:*** 220.

L1G1 BSc Economics/Mathematics
Duration: 3FT/4SW Hon
Entry Requirements: ***GCE:*** 220.

GN13 BSc Financial Mathematics
Duration: 3FT/4SW Hon
Entry Requirements: ***GCE:*** 180.

G9L1 BSc Financial Mathematics/Economics
Duration: 3FT/4SW Hon
Entry Requirements: ***GCE:*** 220.

G1L1 BSc Mathematics/Economics
Duration: 3FT/4SW Hon
Entry Requirements: ***GCE:*** 220.

K12 KEELE UNIVERSITY
STAFFS ST5 5BG
t: 01782 734005 f: 01782 632343
e: undergraduate@keele.ac.uk
// www.keele.ac.uk

NG41 BSc Accounting and Mathematics
Duration: 3FT Hon
Entry Requirements: ***GCE:*** 300.

GL11 BSc Economics and Mathematics
Duration: 3FT Hon
Entry Requirements: ***GCE:*** 300.

GN13 BSc Finance and Mathematics
Duration: 3FT Hon
Entry Requirements: ***GCE:*** 300.

K24 THE UNIVERSITY OF KENT

INFORMATION, RECRUITMENT & ADMISSIONS
REGISTRY
UNIVERSITY OF KENT
CANTERBURY, KENT CT2 7NZ
t: 01227 827272 f: 01227 827077
e: information@kent.ac.uk
// www.kent.ac.uk

GN14 BA Mathematics and Accounting & Finance (3 or 4 years)

Duration: 3FT/4SW Hon
Entry Requirements: ***GCE:*** 300. ***IB:*** 33. ***BTEC NC:*** MM. ***BTEC ND:*** MMP. ***OCR ND:*** M2 ***OCR NED:*** M3

GN13 BSc Financial Mathematics

Duration: 3FT/4SW Hon
Entry Requirements: ***GCE:*** 300. ***IB:*** 33. ***BTEC NC:*** MM. ***BTEC ND:*** MMP. ***OCR ND:*** M2 ***OCR NED:*** M3

K84 KINGSTON UNIVERSITY

STUDENT INFORMATION & ADVICE CENTRE
COOPER HOUSE
40-46 SURBITON ROAD
KINGSTON UPON THAMES KT1 2HX
t: 0844 8552177 f: 020 8547 7080
e: aps@kingston.ac.uk
// www.kingston.ac.uk

G9L1 BSc Financial Mathematics with Applied Economics

Duration: 3FT Hon
Entry Requirements: ***GCE:*** 260.

G9LC BSc Financial Mathematics with Applied Economics

Duration: 4SW Hon
Entry Requirements: ***GCE:*** 260.

G9LD BSc Financial Mathematics with Applied Economics

Duration: 4FT Hon
Entry Requirements: ***GCE:*** 40.

GL1C BSc Mathematics & Applied Economics (including year 0)

Duration: 5SW Hon
Entry Requirements: ***GCE:*** 40.

GLC1 BSc Mathematics & Applied Economics (including year 0)

Duration: 4FT Hon
Entry Requirements: ***GCE:*** 40.

GL11 BSc Mathematics and Applied Economics

Duration: 3FT Hon
Entry Requirements: ***GCE:*** 260.

GLH1 BSc Medical Statistics & Applied Economics (including year 0)

Duration: 4FT Hon
Entry Requirements: ***GCE:*** 40.

GLHC BSc Medical Statistics & Applied Economics (including year 0)

Duration: 5SW Hon
Entry Requirements: ***GCE:*** 40.

GL3C BSc Medical Statistics and Applied Economics

Duration: 3FT Hon
Entry Requirements: ***GCE:*** 260.

GL3D BSc Medical Statistics and Applied Economics

Duration: 4SW Hon
Entry Requirements: ***GCE:*** 260.

GL31 BSc Statistics and Applied Economics

Duration: 3FT Hon
Entry Requirements: ***GCE:*** 260.

LG13 BSc Statistics and Applied Economics

Duration: 4SW Hon
Entry Requirements: ***GCE:*** 260.

GLJ1 BSc Statistics and Applied Economics (including year 0)

Duration: 4FT Hon
Entry Requirements: ***GCE:*** 40.

GLJC BSc Statistics and Applied Economics (including year 0)

Duration: 5SW Hon
Entry Requirements: ***GCE:*** 40.

L14 LANCASTER UNIVERSITY

THE UNIVERSITY
LANCASTER
LANCASHIRE LA1 4YW
t: 01524 592029 f: 01524 846243
e: ugadmissions@lancaster.ac.uk
// www.lancs.ac.uk

GL11 BA Economics and Mathematics

Duration: 3FT Hon
Entry Requirements: ***GCE:*** ABB. ***SQAH:*** BBBBB. ***SQAAH:*** ABB. ***IB:*** 32. ***BTEC ND:*** DDM.

NG41 BSc Accounting, Finance and Mathematics

Duration: 3FT Hon
Entry Requirements: ***GCE:*** ABB. ***SQAH:*** BBBBB. ***SQAAH:*** ABB. ***IB:*** 32. ***BTEC ND:*** DDM.

GN13 BSc Financial Mathematics
Duration: 3FT Hon
Entry Requirements: ***GCE:*** ABB. ***SQAH:*** BBBBB. ***SQAAH:*** ABB. ***IB:*** 32. ***BTEC ND:*** DDM.

L23 UNIVERSITY OF LEEDS
THE UNIVERSITY OF LEEDS
LEEDS LS2 9JT
t: 0113 343 3999
e: admissions@adm.leeds.ac.uk
// www.leeds.ac.uk

NG31 BSc Actuarial Mathematics
Duration: 3FT/4FT Hon
Entry Requirements: ***GCE:*** AAB. ***SQAAH:*** AAB. ***IB:*** 34.

GL11 BSc Economics and Mathematics
Duration: 3FT Hon
Entry Requirements: ***GCE:*** AAB. ***SQAAH:*** AAB.

G1N3 BSc Mathematics with Finance
Duration: 3FT Hon
Entry Requirements: ***GCE:*** AAB. ***SQAAH:*** AAB. ***IB:*** 34.

L34 UNIVERSITY OF LEICESTER
UNIVERSITY ROAD
LEICESTER LE1 7RH
t: 0116 252 5281 f: 0116 252 2447
e: admissions@le.ac.uk
// www.le.ac.uk

GN13 BSc Financial Mathematics
Duration: 3FT Hon
Entry Requirements: ***GCE:*** AAB. ***SQAH:*** AAAAB-AAABB. ***SQAAH:*** AAB. ***BTEC ND:*** DDD.

G1L1 BSc Mathematics with Economics
Duration: 3FT Hon
Entry Requirements: ***GCE:*** AAB. ***SQAH:*** AAAAB-AAABB. ***SQAAH:*** AAB. ***BTEC ND:*** DDD.

L41 THE UNIVERSITY OF LIVERPOOL
THE FOUNDATION BUILDING
BROWNLOW HILL
LIVERPOOL L69 7ZX
t: 0151 794 2000 f: 0151 708 6502
e: ugrecruitment@liv.ac.uk
// www.liv.ac.uk

GL11 BA Economics and Mathematics
Duration: 3FT Hon
Entry Requirements: ***GCE:*** ABB. ***SQAAH:*** ABB. ***IB:*** 33. ***BTEC ND:*** DDD.

G1N3 BSc Mathematics with Finance
Duration: 3FT Hon
Entry Requirements: ***GCE:*** ABB. ***SQAAH:*** ABB. ***IB:*** 33. ***BTEC ND:*** DDD.

L68 LONDON METROPOLITAN UNIVERSITY
166-220 HOLLOWAY ROAD
LONDON N7 8DB
t: 020 7133 4200
e: admissions@londonmet.ac.uk
// www.londonmet.ac.uk

NG41 BA/BSc Accounting and Mathematics
Duration: 3FT Hon
Entry Requirements: ***GCE:*** 240. ***IB:*** 28.

NG31 BSc Financial Mathematics
Duration: 3FT Hon
Entry Requirements: ***GCE:*** 200. ***IB:*** 28.

L72 LONDON SCHOOL OF ECONOMICS AND POLITICAL SCIENCE (UNIVERSITY OF LONDON)
HOUGHTON STREET
LONDON WC2A 2AE
t: 020 7955 7125/7769 f: 020 7955 6001
e: ug-admissions@lse.ac.uk
// www.lse.ac.uk

GL11 BSc Mathematics and Economics
Duration: 3FT Hon
Entry Requirements: ***GCE:*** A*AA. ***SQAH:*** AAAAA. ***SQAAH:*** AAA. ***IB:*** 38.

G1L1 BSc Mathematics with Economics
Duration: 3FT Hon
Entry Requirements: ***GCE:*** A*AA. ***SQAH:*** AAAAA. ***SQAAH:*** AAA. ***IB:*** 38.

G3N3 BSc Statistics with Finance
Duration: 3FT Hon
Entry Requirements: ***GCE:*** AAA. ***SQAH:*** AAAAA. ***SQAAH:*** AAA. ***IB:*** 38.

L79 LOUGHBOROUGH UNIVERSITY
LOUGHBOROUGH
LEICESTERSHIRE LE11 3TU
t: 01509 223522 f: 01509 223905
e: admissions@lboro.ac.uk
// www.lboro.ac.uk

GN13 BSc Financial Mathematics
Duration: 3FT Hon
Entry Requirements: ***GCE:*** AAB. ***SQAH:*** AAABBB. ***SQAAH:*** AB. ***IB:*** 34. ***BTEC ND:*** DDM.

GNC3 BSc Financial Mathematics (4 year SW)
Duration: 4SW Hon
Entry Requirements: ***GCE:*** AAB. ***SQAH:*** AAABBB. ***SQAAH:*** AB. ***IB:*** 34. ***BTEC ND:*** DDM.

G1L1 BSc Mathematics with Economics

Duration: 3FT Hon

Entry Requirements: ***GCE:*** AAB. ***SQAH:*** AAABBB. ***SQAAH:*** AB. ***IB:*** 34. ***BTEC ND:*** DDM.

G1LC BSc Mathematics with Economics (4 year SW)

Duration: 4SW Hon

Entry Requirements: ***GCE:*** AAB. ***SQAH:*** AAABBB. ***SQAAH:*** AB. ***IB:*** 34. ***BTEC ND:*** DDM.

M20 THE UNIVERSITY OF MANCHESTER

OXFORD ROAD
MANCHESTER M13 9PL
t: 0161 275 2077 f: 0161 275 2106
e: ug-admissions@manchester.ac.uk
// www.manchester.ac.uk

NG31 BSc Actuarial Science and Mathematics

Duration: 3FT Hon

Entry Requirements: ***GCE:*** A*AB-AAA. ***SQAH:*** AAAAB. ***SQAAH:*** AAB. ***IB:*** 36. ***BTEC ND:*** MMP. Interview required.

G1N3 BSc Mathematics with Finance

Duration: 3FT Hon

Entry Requirements: ***GCE:*** A*AB-AAA. ***SQAH:*** AAAAB. ***SQAAH:*** AAB. ***IB:*** 36. ***BTEC ND:*** MMP. Interview required.

G1NH BSc Mathematics with Financial Mathematics

Duration: 3FT Hon

Entry Requirements: ***GCE:*** A*AB-AAA. ***SQAH:*** AAAAB. ***SQAAH:*** AAB. ***IB:*** 36. ***BTEC ND:*** MMP. Interview required.

G1NJ MMath Mathematics with Financial Mathematics

Duration: 4FT Hon

Entry Requirements: ***GCE:*** A*AB-AAA. ***SQAH:*** AAAAB. ***SQAAH:*** AAB. ***IB:*** 36. ***BTEC ND:*** MMP. Interview required.

M40 THE MANCHESTER METROPOLITAN UNIVERSITY

ADMISSIONS OFFICE
ALL SAINTS (GMS)
ALL SAINTS
MANCHESTER M15 6BH
t: 0161 247 2000
// www.mmu.ac.uk

GL11 BSc Economics/Mathematics

Duration: 3FT Hon

Entry Requirements: ***GCE:*** 220. ***IB:*** 26.

M80 MIDDLESEX UNIVERSITY

MIDDLESEX UNIVERSITY
THE BURROUGHS
LONDON NW4 4BT
t: 020 8411 5555 f: 020 8411 5649
e: enquiries@mdx.ac.uk
// www.mdx.ac.uk

NG43 BSc Accounting and Statistics

Duration: 3FT Hon

Entry Requirements: ***GCE:*** 200-300. ***IB:*** 28.

N21 NEWCASTLE UNIVERSITY

KING'S GATE
NEWCASTLE UPON TYNE NE1 7RU
t: 0191 208 3333 f: 0191 222 6143
e: enquiries@ncl.ac.uk
// www.ncl.ac.uk

NG41 BSc Accounting and Mathematics

Duration: 3FT Hon

Entry Requirements: ***GCE:*** ABB. ***SQAH:*** AABBB. ***IB:*** 32.

NG43 BSc Accounting and Statistics

Duration: 3FT Hon

Entry Requirements: ***GCE:*** ABB. ***SQAH:*** AABBB. ***IB:*** 32.

GL11 BSc Economics and Mathematics

Duration: 3FT Hon

Entry Requirements: ***GCE:*** ABB. ***SQAH:*** AABBB. ***IB:*** 32.

GL31 BSc Economics and Statistics

Duration: 3FT Hon

Entry Requirements: ***GCE:*** ABB. ***SQAH:*** AABBB. ***IB:*** 32.

GN13 BSc Financial Mathematics

Duration: 3FT Hon

Entry Requirements: ***GCE:*** AAB. ***SQAH:*** AAABB.

N84 THE UNIVERSITY OF NOTTINGHAM

THE ADMISSIONS OFFICE
THE UNIVERSITY OF NOTTINGHAM
UNIVERSITY PARK
NOTTINGHAM NG7 2RD
t: 0115 951 5151 f: 0115 951 4668
// www.nottingham.ac.uk

GL11 BSc Mathematics and Economics

Duration: 3FT Hon

Entry Requirements: ***GCE:*** AAA. ***SQAAH:*** AAA. ***IB:*** 38.

N91 NOTTINGHAM TRENT UNIVERSITY

DRYDEN CENTRE
BURTON STREET
NOTTINGHAM NG1 4BU
t: +44 (0) 115 848 4200 f: +44 (0) 115 848 8869
e: ask.ntu@ntu.ac.uk
// www.ntu.ac.uk/

GN13 BSc Financial Mathematics

Duration: 3FT/4SW Hon

Entry Requirements: ***GCE:*** 260. ***IB:*** 24. ***BTEC ND:*** DMM.

P60 UNIVERSITY OF PLYMOUTH

DRAKE CIRCUS
PLYMOUTH PL4 8AA
t: 01752 588037 f: 01752 588050
e: admissions@plymouth.ac.uk
// www.plymouth.ac.uk

G1N3 BSc Mathematics with Finance

Duration: 3FT Hon

Entry Requirements: ***GCE:*** 300. ***IB:*** 29.

Q50 QUEEN MARY, UNIVERSITY OF LONDON

MILE END ROAD
LONDON E1 4NS
t: 020 7882 5555 f: 020 7882 5500
e: admissions@qmul.ac.uk
// www.qmul.ac.uk

G1N4 BSc Mathematics with Finance & Accounting

Duration: 3FT Hon

Entry Requirements: ***GCE:*** 320. ***IB:*** 34.

GL11 BSc Mathematics, Statistics and Financial Economics

Duration: 3FT Hon

Entry Requirements: ***GCE:*** AAB. ***IB:*** 36.

LG11 BScEcon Economics, Statistics and Mathematics

Duration: 3FT Hon

Entry Requirements: ***GCE:*** AAB. ***SQAAH:*** AAB. ***IB:*** 36.

R12 THE UNIVERSITY OF READING

THE UNIVERSITY OF READING
PO BOX 217
READING RG6 6AH
t: 0118 378 8619 f: 0118 378 8924
e: student.recruitment@reading.ac.uk
// www.reading.ac.uk

GL11 BSc Mathematics and Economics

Duration: 3FT Hon

Entry Requirements: ***GCE:*** 320-340.

R72 ROYAL HOLLOWAY, UNIVERSITY OF LONDON

ROYAL HOLLOWAY, UNIVERSITY OF LONDON
EGHAM
SURREY TW20 0EX
t: 01784 434455 f: 01784 473662
e: Admissions@rhul.ac.uk
// www.rhul.ac.uk

LG11 BSc Economics and Mathematics

Duration: 3FT Hon

Entry Requirements: ***GCE:*** AAA-ABB. ***SQAH:*** AAAAA-AABBB. ***SQAAH:*** AAA-ABB. ***IB:*** 34. ***BTEC NC:*** DM. ***BTEC ND:*** DDM.

NG31 BSc Finance and Mathematics

Duration: 3FT Hon

Entry Requirements: ***GCE:*** AAA-ABB. ***SQAH:*** AAAAA-AABBB. ***SQAAH:*** AAA-ABB. ***IB:*** 34. ***BTEC NC:*** DM. ***BTEC ND:*** DDM.

S18 THE UNIVERSITY OF SHEFFIELD

9 NORTHUMBERLAND ROAD
SHEFFIELD S10 2TT
t: 0114 222 1299 f: 0114 222 8032
e: ask@sheffield.ac.uk
// www.sheffield.ac.uk

LG11 BSc Economics and Mathematics

Duration: 3FT Hon

Entry Requirements: ***GCE:*** AAB. ***SQAH:*** AAAA. ***SQAAH:*** AAB. ***IB:*** 35. ***BTEC NC:*** DM.

GN13 BSc Financial Mathematics

Duration: 3FT Hon

Entry Requirements: ***GCE:*** AAB. ***SQAH:*** AAAA. ***SQAAH:*** AAB. ***IB:*** 35. ***BTEC ND:*** DDD.

S27 UNIVERSITY OF SOUTHAMPTON

HIGHFIELD
SOUTHAMPTON SO17 1BJ
t: 023 8059 4732 f: 023 8059 3037
e: admissions@soton.ac.uk
// www.southampton.ac.uk

G1N3 BSc Mathematics with Actuarial Science

Duration: 3FT Hon

Entry Requirements: ***GCE:*** AAA-AAB. ***SQAH:*** AABBB. ***SQAAH:*** BBB. ***IB:*** 36.

G1L1 BSc Mathematics with Economics

Duration: 3FT Hon

Entry Requirements: ***GCE:*** AAA-AAB. ***SQAH:*** AABBB. ***SQAAH:*** BBB. ***IB:*** 36.

G1NH BSc Mathematics with Finance

Duration: 3FT Hon

Entry Requirements: ***GCE:*** AAA-AAB. ***SQAH:*** AABBB. ***SQAAH:*** BBB. ***IB:*** 36.

S36 UNIVERSITY OF ST ANDREWS

ST KATHARINE'S WEST
16 THE SCORES
ST ANDREWS
FIFE KY16 9AX
t: 01334 462150 f: 01334 463330
e: admissions@st-andrews.ac.uk
// www.st-and.ac.uk

GLC1 BSc Economics-Mathematics (Science)

Duration: 4FT Hon
Entry Requirements: ***GCE:*** AAA. ***SQAH:*** AAAA. ***IB:*** 38.

GL31 BSc Economics-Statistics

Duration: 4FT Hon
Entry Requirements: ***GCE:*** AAA. ***SQAH:*** AAAA. ***IB:*** 38.

GL11 MA Economics-Mathematics

Duration: 4FT Hon
Entry Requirements: ***GCE:*** AAA. ***SQAH:*** AAAA. ***IB:*** 38.

GLH1 MA Economics-Statistics

Duration: 4FT Hon
Entry Requirements: ***GCE:*** AAA. ***SQAH:*** AAAA. ***IB:*** 38.

S75 THE UNIVERSITY OF STIRLING

STIRLING FK9 4LA
t: 01786 467044 f: 01786 466800
e: admissions@stir.ac.uk
// www.stir.ac.uk

GL11 BA Economics and Mathematics

Duration: 4FT Hon
Entry Requirements: ***GCE:*** CCD. ***SQAH:*** AAAAA-BBCC. ***SQAAH:*** AAA-CCC. ***IB:*** 26. ***BTEC ND:*** MMM.

GN13 BA Finance and Mathematics

Duration: 4FT Hon
Entry Requirements: ***GCE:*** CCD. ***SQAH:*** BBCC. ***SQAAH:*** AAA-CCC. ***IB:*** 26. ***BTEC ND:*** MMM.

GN14 BAcc Accountancy and Mathematics

Duration: 4FT Hon
Entry Requirements: ***GCE:*** CCC. ***SQAH:*** BBBB. ***SQAAH:*** AAA-CCC. ***IB:*** 30. ***BTEC ND:*** MMM.

S78 THE UNIVERSITY OF STRATHCLYDE

GLASGOW G1 1XQ
t: 0141 552 4400 f: 0141 552 0775
// www.strath.ac.uk

NG41 BA Accounting and Mathematics & Statistics

Duration: 4FT Hon
Entry Requirements: ***GCE:*** AAB. ***SQAH:*** AAAA-AAABB. ***IB:*** 36.

LG11 BA Economics, Mathematics and Statistics

Duration: 4FT Hon
Entry Requirements: ***GCE:*** ABB. ***SQAH:*** AABB-ABBBC. ***IB:*** 34.

NG33 BA Finance, Mathematics and Statistics

Duration: 4FT Hon
Entry Requirements: ***GCE:*** ABB. ***SQAH:*** AABB-ABBBC. ***IB:*** 34.

GN34 BSc Mathematics, Statistics and Accounting

Duration: 4FT Hon
Entry Requirements: ***GCE:*** AAB. ***SQAH:*** AAAA. ***IB:*** 36.

G1L1 BSc Mathematics, Statistics and Economics

Duration: 4FT Hon
Entry Requirements: ***GCE:*** ABC. ***SQAH:*** ABBB-ABBBC. ***IB:*** 32.

GN33 BSc Mathematics, Statistics and Finance

Duration: 4FT Hon
Entry Requirements: ***GCE:*** ABC. ***SQAH:*** ABBB-ABBBC. ***IB:*** 32.

S90 UNIVERSITY OF SUSSEX

UNDERGRADUATE ADMISSIONS
SUSSEX HOUSE
UNIVERSITY OF SUSSEX
BRIGHTON BN1 9RH
t: 01273 678416 f: 01273 678545
e: ug.applicants@sussex.ac.uk
// www.sussex.ac.uk

G1L1 BSc Mathematics with Economics

Duration: 3FT Hon
Entry Requirements: ***GCE:*** AAA-AAB. ***SQAH:*** AAAAA-AAABB. ***IB:*** 36.

G1LC MMath Mathematics with Economics (4 years)

Duration: 4FT Hon
Entry Requirements: ***GCE:*** AAA. ***SQAH:*** AAAAA. ***IB:*** 36.

S93 SWANSEA UNIVERSITY

SINGLETON PARK
SWANSEA SA2 8PP
t: 01792 295111 f: 01792 295110
e: admissions@swansea.ac.uk
// www.swansea.ac.uk

GL11 BSc Economics and Mathematics

Duration: 3FT Hon
Entry Requirements: ***GCE:*** ABB. ***IB:*** 33. ***BTEC ND:*** DDM.

U80 UNIVERSITY COLLEGE LONDON (UNIVERSITY OF LONDON)

GOWER STREET
LONDON WC1E 6BT
t: 020 7679 3000 f: 020 7679 3001
// www.ucl.ac.uk

G1L1 BSc Mathematics with Economics

Duration: 3FT Hon

Entry Requirements: ***GCE:*** A*AAe. ***SQAAH:*** AAA. ***IB:*** 39. Interview required.

GLN0 BSc Statistics, Economics and Finance

Duration: 3FT Hon

Entry Requirements: ***GCE:*** A*AAe-AAAe. ***SQAAH:*** AAA. Interview required.

LG13 BScEcon Economics and Statistics

Duration: 3FT Hon

Entry Requirements: ***GCE:*** A*AAe-AAAe. ***SQAAH:*** AAA. Interview required.

G1LC MSci Mathematics with Economics

Duration: 4FT Hon

Entry Requirements: ***GCE:*** A*AAe. ***SQAAH:*** AAA. ***IB:*** 39. Interview required.

W20 THE UNIVERSITY OF WARWICK

COVENTRY CV4 8UW
t: 024 7652 3723 f: 024 7652 4649
e: ugadmissions@warwick.ac.uk
// www.warwick.ac.uk

GL11 BSc Mathematics and Economics

Duration: 3FT Hon

Entry Requirements: ***GCE:*** A*AAa-AAB. ***SQAH:*** AAABB. ***SQAAH:*** AA.

GLN0 BSc Mathematics, Operational Research, Statistics, Economics

Duration: 3FT Hon

Entry Requirements: ***GCE:*** A*AA-AABa. ***SQAAH:*** AA. ***IB:*** 39. Interview required.

G0L0 BSc.MMORSE Mathematics, Operational Research, Statistics and Economics option - Econometrics and Mathematical Economics

Duration: 4FT Hon

Entry Requirements: ***GCE:*** A*AA-AABa. ***SQAAH:*** AA. ***IB:*** 39. Interview required.

G0L0 BSc.MMORSE Mathematics, Operational Research, Statistics and Economics

Duration: 4FT Hon

Entry Requirements: ***GCE:*** A*AA-AABa. ***SQAAH:*** AA. ***IB:*** 39. Interview required.

G0L0 BSc.MMORSE Mathematics, Operational Research, Statistics and Economics option - Actuarial and Financial Mathematics

Duration: 4FT Hon

Entry Requirements: ***GCE:*** A*AA-AABa. ***SQAAH:*** AA. ***IB:*** 39. Interview required.

G0L0 BSc.MMORSE Mathematics, Operational Research, Statistics and Economics option - Operational Research and Statistics

Duration: 4FT Hon

Entry Requirements: ***GCE:*** A*AA-AABa. ***SQAAH:*** AA. ***IB:*** 39. Interview required.

G0L0 BSc.MMORSE Mathematics, Operational Research, Statistics and Economics option - Statistics with Mathematics

Duration: 4FT Hon

Entry Requirements: ***GCE:*** A*AA-AABa. ***SQAAH:*** AA. ***IB:*** 39. Interview required.

Y50 THE UNIVERSITY OF YORK

ADMISSIONS AND UK/EU STUDENT RECRUITMENT
UNIVERSITY OF YORK
HESLINGTON
YORK YO10 5DD
t: 01904 433533 f: 01904 433538
e: admissions@york.ac.uk
// www.york.ac.uk

LG11 BA/BSc Economics/Mathematics (Equal)

Duration: 3FT Hon

Entry Requirements: ***GCE:*** AAB. ***SQAH:*** AAAAB. ***SQAAH:*** AB. ***IB:*** 34. ***BTEC ND:*** DDD.

GL11 BSc Mathematics / Finance (Equal)

Duration: 3FT Hon

Entry Requirements: ***GCE:*** AAB. ***SQAH:*** AAAAB. ***SQAAH:*** AB. ***IB:*** 34. ***BTEC ND:*** DDM.

POLITICS COMBINATIONS

A20 THE UNIVERSITY OF ABERDEEN
UNIVERSITY OFFICE
KING'S COLLEGE
ABERDEEN AB24 3FX
t: +44 (0) 1224 273504 f: +44 (0) 1224 272034
e: sras@abdn.ac.uk
// www.abdn.ac.uk/sras

LL12 MA Economics and Politics
Duration: 4FT Hon
Entry Requirements: ***GCE:*** BBB. ***SQAH:*** BBBB. ***IB:*** 30. ***BTEC ND:*** MMM.

NL32 MA Finance and Politics
Duration: 4FT Hon
Entry Requirements: ***GCE:*** BBB. ***SQAH:*** BBBB. ***IB:*** 30. ***BTEC ND:*** MMM.

A40 ABERYSTWYTH UNIVERSITY
WELCOME CENTRE, ABERYSTWYTH UNIVERSITY
PENGLAIS CAMPUS
ABERYSTWYTH
CEREDIGION SY23 3FB
t: 01970 622021 f: 01970 627410
e: ug-admissions@aber.ac.uk
// www.aber.ac.uk

L1LF BScEcon Economics with International Politics
Duration: 3FT Hon
Entry Requirements: ***GCE:*** 280. ***IB:*** 27.

L1L2 BScEcon Economics with Politics
Duration: 3FT Hon
Entry Requirements: ***GCE:*** 280. ***IB:*** 27.

L2L1 BScEcon International Politics with Economics
Duration: 3FT Hon
Entry Requirements: ***GCE:*** 280. ***IB:*** 28.

B16 UNIVERSITY OF BATH
CLAVERTON DOWN
BATH BA2 7AY
t: 01225 383019 f: 01225 386366
e: admissions@bath.ac.uk
// www.bath.ac.uk

LL12 BSc Economics and Politics
Duration: 3FT Hon
Entry Requirements: ***GCE:*** AAA-AAB. ***SQAAH:*** AAB. ***IB:*** 38. ***BTEC NC:*** DD. ***BTEC ND:*** DDD.

LLC2 BSc Economics and Politics (4 year sandwich)
Duration: 4SW Hon
Entry Requirements: ***GCE:*** AAA-AAB. ***SQAAH:*** AAB. ***IB:*** 38. ***BTEC NC:*** DD. ***BTEC ND:*** DDD.

L2L1 BSc Politics with Economics
Duration: 3FT Hon
Entry Requirements: ***GCE:*** AAA-AAB. ***SQAAH:*** AAB. ***IB:*** 38.

L2LC BSc Politics with Economics (4 year sandwich)
Duration: 4SW Hon
Entry Requirements: ***GCE:*** AAA-AAB. ***SQAAH:*** AAB. ***IB:*** 38.

B32 THE UNIVERSITY OF BIRMINGHAM
EDGBASTON
BIRMINGHAM B15 2TT
t: 0121 415 8900 f: 0121 414 7159
e: admissions@bham.ac.uk
// www.bham.ac.uk

LL2C BSc European Politics, Society and Economics
Duration: 3FT Hon
Entry Requirements: ***GCE:*** ABB. ***SQAH:*** AABBB. ***SQAAH:*** AB.

B78 UNIVERSITY OF BRISTOL
UNDERGRADUATE ADMISSIONS OFFICE
SENATE HOUSE
TYNDALL AVENUE
BRISTOL BS8 1TH
t: 0117 928 9000 f: 0117 925 1424
e: ug-admissions@bristol.ac.uk
// www.bristol.ac.uk

LL12 BSc Economics and Politics
Duration: 3FT Hon
Entry Requirements: ***GCE:*** A*AA-AAB. ***SQAH:*** AAAAA-AAAAB. ***SQAAH:*** AAA-ABB. ***BTEC ND:*** DDD.

B84 BRUNEL UNIVERSITY
UXBRIDGE
MIDDLESEX UB8 3PH
t: 01895 265265 f: 01895 269790
e: admissions@brunel.ac.uk
// www.brunel.ac.uk

LLC2 BSc Politics and Economics
Duration: 3FT Hon
Entry Requirements: ***GCE:*** 280-320. ***IB:*** 32. ***BTEC NC:*** DM. ***BTEC ND:*** DDM.

LL12 BSc Politics and Economics (4 year Thick SW)
Duration: 4SW Hon
Entry Requirements: ***GCE:*** 280-320. ***IB:*** 32. ***BTEC NC:*** DM. ***DTEC ND.*** DDM.

B90 THE UNIVERSITY OF BUCKINGHAM

YEOMANRY HOUSE
HUNTER STREET
BUCKINGHAM MK18 1EG
t: 01280 820313 f: 01280 822245
e: info@buckingham.ac.uk
// www.buckingham.ac.uk

L1L2 BSc Economics with Politics

Duration: 2FT Hon

Entry Requirements: ***GCE:*** 240. ***IB:*** 26. ***BTEC NC:*** DD. ***BTEC ND:*** MMM.

C15 CARDIFF UNIVERSITY

PO BOX 927
30-36 NEWPORT ROAD
CARDIFF CF24 0DE
t: 029 2087 9999 f: 029 2087 6138
e: admissions@cardiff.ac.uk
// www.cardiff.ac.uk

LL12 BScEcon Politics and Economics

Duration: 3FT Hon

Entry Requirements: ***GCE:*** AAB. ***SQAH:*** AAABB. ***SQAAH:*** AAB. ***IB:*** 35. ***BTEC ND:*** DDD. ***OCR NED:*** D2

C55 UNIVERSITY OF CHESTER

PARKGATE ROAD
CHESTER CH1 4BJ
t: 01244 511000 f: 01244 511300
e: enquiries@chester.ac.uk
// www.chester.ac.uk

LL21 BA Politics and Economics

Duration: 3FT Hon

Entry Requirements: ***GCE:*** 240. ***SQAH:*** BBBB. ***IB:*** 24. ***BTEC NC:*** DM. ***BTEC ND:*** MMM.

L2P9 BA Politics with Communication Studies

Duration: 3FT Hon

Entry Requirements: ***GCE:*** 240. ***SQAH:*** BBBB. ***IB:*** 24. ***BTEC NC:*** DM. ***BTEC ND:*** MMM.

L2L1 BA Politics with Economics

Duration: 3FT Hon

Entry Requirements: ***GCE:*** 240. ***SQAH:*** BBBB. ***IB:*** 24. ***BTEC NC:*** DM. ***BTEC ND:*** MMM.

L1L2 BSc Economics with Politics

Duration: 3FT Hon

Entry Requirements: ***GCE:*** 240. ***SQAH:*** BBBB. ***IB:*** 24. ***BTEC NC:*** DM. ***BTEC ND:*** MMM.

D65 UNIVERSITY OF DUNDEE

DUNDEE DD1 4HN
t: 01382 383838 f: 01382 388150
e: ContactUs@dundee.ac.uk
// www.dundee.ac.uk/admissions/undergraduate/

LL12 MA Economics and Politics

Duration: 4FT Hon

Entry Requirements: ***GCE:*** BCC. ***SQAH:*** BBBB. ***IB:*** 30. ***BTEC ND:*** DMM.

D86 DURHAM UNIVERSITY

DURHAM UNIVERSITY
UNIVERSITY OFFICE
DURHAM DH1 3HP
t: 0191 334 2000 f: 0191 334 6055
e: admissions@durham.ac.uk
// www.durham.ac.uk

LL12 BA Economics and Politics

Duration: 3FT Hon

Entry Requirements: ***GCE:*** AAA. ***SQAH:*** AAAAA. ***SQAAH:*** AAA. ***IB:*** 37.

E14 UNIVERSITY OF EAST ANGLIA

NORWICH NR4 7TJ
t: 01603 591515 f: 01603 458596
e: admissions@uea.ac.uk
// www.uea.ac.uk

LL12 BA Politics and Economics

Duration: 3FT Hon

Entry Requirements: ***GCE:*** ABB-BBB. ***SQAH:*** AAAB. ***SQAAH:*** ABB. ***IB:*** 32. ***BTEC NC:*** DD. ***BTEC ND:*** DDM. ***OCR ND:*** M1 ***OCR NED:*** D2

E56 THE UNIVERSITY OF EDINBURGH

STUDENT RECRUITMENT & ADMISSIONS
57 GEORGE SQUARE
EDINBURGH EH8 9JU
t: 0131 650 4360 f: 0131 651 1236
e: sra.enquiries@ed.ac.uk
// www.ed.ac.uk/studying/undergraduate/

LL12 MA Economics and Politics

Duration: 4FT Hon

Entry Requirements: ***GCE:*** AAA-BBB. ***SQAH:*** AABB-BBBB. ***IB:*** 34.

E70 THE UNIVERSITY OF ESSEX

WIVENHOE PARK
COLCHESTER
ESSEX CO4 3SQ
t: 01206 873666 f: 01206 873423
e: admit@essex.ac.uk
// www.essex.ac.uk

LL12 BA Economics and Politics

Duration: 3FT Hon

Entry Requirements: ***GCE:*** 320. ***SQAH:*** AAAB. ***IB:*** 34. ***BTEC ND:*** DDM.

LL1F BA Economics and Politics (International Exchange)

Duration: 4FT Hon

Entry Requirements: ***GCE:*** 320. ***SQAH:*** AAAB. ***IB:*** 34. ***BTEC ND:*** DDM.

L0VA BA Philosophy, Politics and Economics (International Exchange)

Duration: 4SW Hon

Entry Requirements: ***GCE:*** 320. ***SQAH:*** AAAB. ***IB:*** 34. ***BTEC ND:*** DDM.

E84 UNIVERSITY OF EXETER

LAVER BUILDING
NORTH PARK ROAD
EXETER
DEVON EX4 4QE
t: 01392 263855 f: 01392 263857/262479
e: admissions@exeter.ac.uk
// www.exeter.ac.uk/admissions

LL12 BA Economics and Politics

Duration: 3FT Hon

Entry Requirements: ***GCE:*** AAA-AAB. ***SQAH:*** AAAAB-AAABB. ***SQAAH:*** AAB-ABB. ***BTEC ND:*** DDD.

LL1F BA Economics and Politics with European Study (4 years)

Duration: 4FT Hon

Entry Requirements: ***GCE:*** AAA-AAB. ***SQAH:*** AAAAB-AAABB. ***SQAAH:*** AAB-ABB. ***BTEC ND:*** DDD.

LL1G BA Economics and Politics with Industrial Experience (4 years)

Duration: 4FT Hon

Entry Requirements: ***GCE:*** AAA-AAB. ***SQAH:*** AAAAB-AAABB. ***SQAAH:*** AAB-ABB. ***BTEC ND:*** DDD.

LLCF BA Economics and Politics with International Study (4 years)

Duration: 4FT Hon

Entry Requirements: ***GCE:*** AAA-AAB. ***SQAH:*** AAAAB-AAABB. ***SQAAH:*** AAB-ABB. ***BTEC ND:*** DDD.

G28 UNIVERSITY OF GLASGOW

THE UNIVERSITY OF GLASGOW
THE FRASER BUILDING
65 HILLHEAD STREET
GLASGOW G12 8QF
t: 0141 330 6062 f: 0141 330 2961
e: ugenquiries@gla.ac.uk (UK/EU undergrad enquiries only)
// www.glasgow.ac.uk

LL12 MA Economics/Politics

Duration: 4FT Hon

Entry Requirements: ***GCE:*** AAB. ***SQAH:*** AAAB-AABB. ***IB:*** 34.

G56 GOLDSMITHS, UNIVERSITY OF LONDON

LEWISHAM WAY
NEW CROSS
LONDON SE14 6NW
t: 020 7919 7766 f: 020 7919 7509
e: admissions@gold.ac.uk
// www.goldsmiths.ac.uk

LL12 BA Economics, Politics and Public Policy

Duration: 3FT Hon

Entry Requirements: ***GCE:*** ABB. ***SQAH:*** AABBB. ***SQAAH:*** ABB. ***BTEC NC:*** DD. ***BTEC ND:*** DDM.

L2L1 BA Politics with Economics

Duration: 3FT Hon

Entry Requirements: ***GCE:*** ABB. ***SQAH:*** BBBBB. ***SQAAH:*** BBB. ***IB:*** 32. ***BTEC NC:*** DD. ***BTEC ND:*** DDM.

G70 UNIVERSITY OF GREENWICH

GREENWICH CAMPUS
OLD ROYAL NAVAL COLLEGE
PARK ROW
LONDON SE10 9LS
t: 0800 005 006 f: 020 8331 8145
e: courseinfo@gre.ac.uk
// www.gre.ac.uk

LL21 BA Politics and Economics

Duration: 3FT Hon

Entry Requirements: ***GCE:*** 180. ***IB:*** 24.

K12 KEELE UNIVERSITY

STAFFS ST5 5BG
t: 01782 734005 f: 01782 632343
e: undergraduate@keele.ac.uk
// www.keele.ac.uk

NL4F BA Accounting and Politics

Duration: 3FT Hon

Entry Requirements: ***GCE:*** 320-340.

LL12 BA Economics and Politics
Duration: 3FT Hon
Entry Requirements: ***GCE:*** 320.

LN23 BA Finance and Politics
Duration: 3FT Hon
Entry Requirements: ***GCE:*** 320.

K24 THE UNIVERSITY OF KENT
INFORMATION, RECRUITMENT & ADMISSIONS REGISTRY
UNIVERSITY OF KENT
CANTERBURY, KENT CT2 7NZ
t: 01227 827272 f: 01227 827077
e: information@kent.ac.uk
// www.kent.ac.uk

LN24 BA Accounting & Finance and Politics
Duration: 3FT Hon
Entry Requirements: ***GCE:*** 300. ***IB:*** 33. ***BTEC NC:*** DD. ***BTEC ND:*** DMM. ***OCR ND:*** D

LL12 BA Economics and Politics
Duration: 3FT Hon
Entry Requirements: ***GCE:*** 320. ***IB:*** 34. ***BTEC NC:*** DD. ***BTEC ND:*** DDM. ***OCR ND:*** D ***OCR NED:*** D2

K84 KINGSTON UNIVERSITY
STUDENT INFORMATION & ADVICE CENTRE
COOPER HOUSE
40-46 SURBITON ROAD
KINGSTON UPON THAMES KT1 2HX
t: 0844 8552177 f: 020 8547 7080
e: aps@kingston.ac.uk
// www.kingston.ac.uk

L1L2 BA Economics (Applied) with Politics
Duration: 3FT Hon
Entry Requirements: ***GCE:*** 260-360. ***IB:*** 24.

L2L1 BA Politics with Economics (Applied)
Duration: 3FT Hon
Entry Requirements: ***GCE:*** 260-360.

L14 LANCASTER UNIVERSITY
THE UNIVERSITY
LANCASTER
LANCASHIRE LA1 4YW
t: 01524 592029 f: 01524 846243
e: ugadmissions@lancaster.ac.uk
// www.lancs.ac.uk

LL21 BA Economics and Politics
Duration: 3FT Hon
Entry Requirements: ***GCE:*** ABB. ***SQAH:*** BBBBB. ***SQAAH:*** ABB. ***IB:*** 32. ***BTEC ND:*** DDM.

L23 UNIVERSITY OF LEEDS
THE UNIVERSITY OF LEEDS
LEEDS LS2 9JT
t: 0113 343 3999
e: admissions@adm.leeds.ac.uk
// www.leeds.ac.uk

LL12 BA Economics and Politics
Duration: 3FT Hon
Entry Requirements: ***GCE:*** ABB. ***SQAAH:*** ABB. ***IB:*** 34.

L34 UNIVERSITY OF LEICESTER
UNIVERSITY ROAD
LEICESTER LE1 7RH
t: 0116 252 5281 f: 0116 252 2447
e: admissions@le.ac.uk
// www.le.ac.uk

LL12 BA Politics and Economics
Duration: 3FT Hon
Entry Requirements: ***GCE:*** AAB. ***SQAH:*** AAAAB. ***SQAAH:*** AAB. ***IB:*** 32. ***BTEC ND:*** DDD.

L68 LONDON METROPOLITAN UNIVERSITY
166-220 HOLLOWAY ROAD
LONDON N7 8DB
t: 020 7133 4200
e: admissions@londonmet.ac.uk
// www.londonmet.ac.uk

LLCG BA International Economics and Politics
Duration: 3FT Hon
Entry Requirements: ***GCE:*** 240. ***IB:*** 28.

L79 LOUGHBOROUGH UNIVERSITY
LOUGHBOROUGH
LEICESTERSHIRE LE11 3TU
t: 01509 223522 f: 01509 223905
e: admissions@lboro.ac.uk
// www.lboro.ac.uk

L1L2 BSc Economics with Politics
Duration: 3FT Hon
Entry Requirements: ***GCE:*** AAB. ***SQAH:*** AABBB. ***SQAAH:*** AB. ***IB:*** 34. ***BTEC ND:*** DDM.

M20 THE UNIVERSITY OF MANCHESTER
OXFORD ROAD
MANCHESTER M13 9PL
t: 0161 275 2077 f: 0161 275 2106
e: ug-admissions@manchester.ac.uk
// www.manchester.ac.uk

LL12 BA Economics and Politics
Duration: 3FT Hon
Entry Requirements: ***GCE:*** ABB. ***SQAH:*** AABBB. ***SQAAH:*** ABB. ***IB:*** 34. ***BTEC ND:*** DDM. Interview required.

M40 THE MANCHESTER METROPOLITAN UNIVERSITY

ADMISSIONS OFFICE
ALL SAINTS (GMS)
ALL SAINTS
MANCHESTER M15 6BH
t: 0161 247 2000
// www.mmu.ac.uk

LL1F BA/BSc Economics/International Politics
Duration: 3FT Hon
Entry Requirements: ***GCE:*** 220. ***IB:*** 26.

LL1G BA/BSc Economics/Politics
Duration: 3FT Hon
Entry Requirements: ***GCE:*** 220. ***IB:*** 26.

N21 NEWCASTLE UNIVERSITY

KING'S GATE
NEWCASTLE UPON TYNE NE1 7RU
t: 0191 208 3333 f: 0191 222 6143
e: enquiries@ncl.ac.uk
// www.ncl.ac.uk

LL21 BA Politics and Economics
Duration: 3FT Hon
Entry Requirements: ***GCE:*** AAA-BBB. ***SQAH:*** AAAAA-BBBBB. ***IB:*** 35.

N38 UNIVERSITY OF NORTHAMPTON

PARK CAMPUS
BOUGHTON GREEN ROAD
NORTHAMPTON NN2 7AL
t: 0800 358 2232 f: 01604 722083
e: admissions@northampton.ac.uk
// www.northampton.ac.uk

N4L2 BA Accounting/Politics
Duration: 3FT Hon
Entry Requirements: ***GCE:*** 220-260. ***SQAH:*** ABB-BBBC. ***IB:*** 24.

L2N4 BA Politics/Accounting
Duration: 3FT Hon
Entry Requirements: ***GCE:*** 220-260. ***SQAH:*** ABB-BBBC. ***IB:*** 24.

N84 THE UNIVERSITY OF NOTTINGHAM

THE ADMISSIONS OFFICE
THE UNIVERSITY OF NOTTINGHAM
UNIVERSITY PARK
NOTTINGHAM NG7 2RD
t: 0115 951 5151 f: 0115 951 4668
// www.nottingham.ac.uk

LL21 BA Politics and Economics
Duration: 3FT Hon
Entry Requirements: Contact the institution for details.

O66 OXFORD BROOKES UNIVERSITY

ADMISSIONS OFFICE
HEADINGTON CAMPUS
GIPSY LANE
OXFORD OX3 0BP
t: 01865 483040 f: 01865 483983
e: admissions@brookes.ac.uk
// www.brookes.ac.uk

LL12 BA/BSc Economics/Politics
Duration: 3FT Hon
Entry Requirements: ***GCE:*** BBC.

P60 UNIVERSITY OF PLYMOUTH

DRAKE CIRCUS
PLYMOUTH PL4 8AA
t: 01752 588037 f: 01752 588050
e: admissions@plymouth.ac.uk
// www.plymouth.ac.uk

L1LB BSc Economics with Politics
Duration: 3FT/4SW Hon
Entry Requirements: ***GCE:*** 240. ***IB:*** 26.

L2L1 BSc Politics with Economics
Duration: 3FT Hon
Entry Requirements: Contact the institution for details.

Q50 QUEEN MARY, UNIVERSITY OF LONDON

MILE END ROAD
LONDON E1 4NS
t: 020 7882 5555 f: 020 7882 5500
e: admissions@qmul.ac.uk
// www.qmul.ac.uk

LL12 BScEcon Economics and Politics
Duration: 3FT Hon
Entry Requirements: ***GCE:*** AAB. ***SQAAH:*** AAB. ***IB:*** 36.

R12 THE UNIVERSITY OF READING

THE UNIVERSITY OF READING
PO BOX 217
READING RG6 6AH
t: 0118 378 8619 f: 0118 378 8924
e: student.recruitment@reading.ac.uk
// www.reading.ac.uk

LL12 BA Politics and Economics
Duration: 3FT Hon
Entry Requirements: ***GCE:*** 300-320.

R72 ROYAL HOLLOWAY, UNIVERSITY OF LONDON

ROYAL HOLLOWAY, UNIVERSITY OF LONDON
EGHAM
SURREY TW20 0EX
t: 01784 434455 f: 01784 473662
e: Admissions@rhul.ac.uk
// www.rhul.ac.uk

LL12 BSc Economics, Politics & International Relations

Duration: 3FT Hon

Entry Requirements: ***GCE:*** AAA-ABB. ***SQAH:*** AAAAA-AABBB. ***SQAAH:*** AAA-ABB. ***IB:*** 32. ***BTEC NC:*** DM. ***BTEC ND:*** DDM.

S09 SCHOOL OF ORIENTAL AND AFRICAN STUDIES (UNIVERSITY OF LONDON)

THORNHAUGH STREET
RUSSELL SQUARE
LONDON WC1H 0XG
t: 020 7074 5106 f: 020 7898 4039
e: undergradadmissions@soas.ac.uk
// www.soas.ac.uk

LL12 BA Politics and Economics

Duration: 3FT Hon

Entry Requirements: Contact the institution for details.

S18 THE UNIVERSITY OF SHEFFIELD

9 NORTHUMBERLAND ROAD
SHEFFIELD S10 2TT
t: 0114 222 1299 f: 0114 222 8032
e: ask@sheffield.ac.uk
// www.sheffield.ac.uk

LL12 BA Economics and Politics

Duration: 3FT Hon

Entry Requirements: ***GCE:*** AAB. ***SQAH:*** AAAA. ***SQAAH:*** AAB. ***IB:*** 35. ***BTEC ND:*** DDD.

S27 UNIVERSITY OF SOUTHAMPTON

HIGHFIELD
SOUTHAMPTON SO17 1BJ
t: 023 8059 4732 f: 023 8059 3037
e: admissions@soton.ac.uk
// www.southampton.ac.uk

LL12 BSc Politics and Economics

Duration: 3FT Hon

Entry Requirements: ***GCE:*** AAB. ***SQAH:*** AAABB. ***SQAAH:*** AB. ***IB:*** 34. ***BTEC NC:*** DD. ***BTEC ND:*** DDD.

S75 THE UNIVERSITY OF STIRLING

STIRLING FK9 4LA
t: 01786 467044 f: 01786 466800
e: admissions@stir.ac.uk
// www.stir.ac.uk

LL12 BA Economics and Politics

Duration: 4FT Hon

Entry Requirements: ***GCE:*** CCC. ***SQAH:*** BBBB. ***SQAAH:*** AAA-CCC. ***IB:*** 30. ***BTEC ND:*** MMM.

S78 THE UNIVERSITY OF STRATHCLYDE

GLASGOW G1 1XQ
t: 0141 552 4400 f: 0141 552 0775
// www.strath.ac.uk

LL12 BA Economics and Politics

Duration: 4FT Hon

Entry Requirements: ***GCE:*** ABB. ***SQAH:*** ABBB-BBBBC. ***IB:*** 34.

S90 UNIVERSITY OF SUSSEX

UNDERGRADUATE ADMISSIONS
SUSSEX HOUSE
UNIVERSITY OF SUSSEX
BRIGHTON BN1 9RH
t: 01273 678416 f: 01273 678545
e: ug.applicants@sussex.ac.uk
// www.sussex.ac.uk

LL12 BA Economics and Politics

Duration: 3FT Hon

Entry Requirements: ***GCE:*** ABB-BBB. ***SQAH:*** AABBB-ABBBB.

S93 SWANSEA UNIVERSITY

SINGLETON PARK
SWANSEA SA2 8PP
t: 01792 295111 f: 01792 295110
e: admissions@swansea.ac.uk
// www.swansea.ac.uk

LL12 BA Economics and Politics

Duration: 3FT Hon

Entry Requirements: ***GCE:*** ABB. ***IB:*** 33. ***BTEC ND:*** DDM.

U20 UNIVERSITY OF ULSTER

COLERAINE
CO. LONDONDERRY
NORTHERN IRELAND BT52 1SA
t: 028 7032 4221 f: 028 7032 4908
e: online@ulster.ac.uk
// www.ulster.ac.uk

L2LD BA International Politics with Economic Studies

Duration: 3FT Hon

Entry Requirements: ***GCE:*** 240. ***IB:*** 24. ***BTEC NC:*** MM. ***BTEC ND:*** MMM.

L1LF BSc Economics with Politics

Duration: 3FT Hon

Entry Requirements: ***GCE:*** 240. ***IB:*** 24. ***BTEC NC:*** MM. ***BTEC ND:*** MMM.

W20 THE UNIVERSITY OF WARWICK

COVENTRY CV4 8UW
t: 024 7652 3723 f: 024 7652 4649
e: ugadmissions@warwick.ac.uk
// www.warwick.ac.uk

LLD2 BA Economics, Politics and International Studies

Duration: 3FT Hon

Entry Requirements: ***GCE:*** A*AAb - AAAb. ***SQAAH:*** AA. ***IB:*** 38.

Y50 THE UNIVERSITY OF YORK

ADMISSIONS AND UK/EU STUDENT RECRUITMENT
UNIVERSITY OF YORK
HESLINGTON
YORK YO10 5DD
t: 01904 433533 f: 01904 433538
e: admissions@york.ac.uk
// www.york.ac.uk

LL12 BA Economics/Politics (Equal)

Duration: 3FT Hon

Entry Requirements: ***GCE:*** AAB. ***SQAH:*** AAAAB. ***SQAAH:*** AB. ***IB:*** 34. ***BTEC ND:*** DDD.

SCIENCE COMBINATIONS

A20 THE UNIVERSITY OF ABERDEEN

UNIVERSITY OFFICE
KING'S COLLEGE
ABERDEEN AB24 3FX
t: +44 (0) 1224 273504 f: +44 (0) 1224 272034
e: sras@abdn.ac.uk
// www.abdn.ac.uk/sras

F1N4 BSc Chemistry with Accountancy

Duration: 4FT Hon

Entry Requirements: ***GCE:*** BBB. ***SQAH:*** BBBB. ***IB:*** 30. ***BTEC ND:*** DDD.

D39 UNIVERSITY OF DERBY

KEDLESTON ROAD
DERBY DE22 1GB
t: 08701 202330 f: 01332 597724
e: askadmissions@derby.ac.uk
// www.derby.ac.uk

NC41 BA/BSc Accounting and Biology

Duration: 3FT Hon

Entry Requirements: ***Foundation:*** Merit. ***GCE:*** 180-240. ***IB:*** 26. ***BTEC NC:*** DM. ***BTEC ND:*** MMP.

H36 UNIVERSITY OF HERTFORDSHIRE

UNIVERSITY ADMISSIONS SERVICE
COLLEGE LANE
HATFIELD
HERTS AL10 9AB
t: 01707 284800 f: 01707 284870
// www.herts.ac.uk

L1B1 BSc Economics/Human Biology

Duration: 3FT/4SW Hon

Entry Requirements: ***GCE:*** 220.

B1L1 BSc Human Biology/Economics

Duration: 3FT/4SW Hon

Entry Requirements: ***GCE:*** 220.

K12 KEELE UNIVERSITY

STAFFS ST5 5BG
t: 01782 734005 f: 01782 632343
e: undergraduate@keele.ac.uk
// www.keele.ac.uk

NF45 BSc Accounting and Astrophysics

Duration: 3FT Hon

Entry Requirements: ***GCE:*** 300-320.

NC47 BSc Accounting and Biochemistry

Duration: 3FT Hon

Entry Requirements: ***GCE:*** 300-320.

NC41 BSc Accounting and Biology

Duration: 3FT Hon

Entry Requirements: ***GCE:*** 300-320.

NF44 BSc Accounting and Forensic Science

Duration: 3FT Hon

Entry Requirements: ***GCE:*** 300-320.

NB41 BSc Accounting and Neuroscience

Duration: 3FT Hon

Entry Requirements: ***GCE:*** 280-300.

NF43 BSc Accounting and Physics

Duration: 3FT Hon

Entry Requirements: ***GCE:*** 300-320.

FNX3 BSc Applied Environmental Science and Finance
Duration: 3FT Hon
Entry Requirements: ***GCE:*** 300.

FL51 BSc Astrophysics and Economics
Duration: 3FT Hon
Entry Requirements: ***GCE:*** 300-320.

CL71 BSc Biochemistry and Economics
Duration: 3FT Hon
Entry Requirements: ***GCE:*** 300.

CN73 BSc Biochemistry and Finance
Duration: 3FT Hon
Entry Requirements: ***GCE:*** 300.

CL11 BSc Biology and Economics
Duration: 3FT Hon
Entry Requirements: ***GCE:*** 300.

CN13 BSc Biology and Finance
Duration: 3FT Hon
Entry Requirements: ***GCE:*** 300.

FNC3 BSc Chemistry and Finance
Duration: 3FT Hon
Entry Requirements: ***GCE:*** 300.

FL41 BSc Economics and Forensic Science
Duration: 3FT Hon
Entry Requirements: ***GCE:*** 300.

LC1C BSc Economics and Human Biology
Duration: 3FT Hon
Entry Requirements: ***GCE:*** 280-300. ***BTEC NC:*** DD. ***BTEC ND:*** DMM.

BL11 BSc Economics and Neuroscience
Duration: 3FT Hon
Entry Requirements: ***GCE:*** 280-300.

FL31 BSc Economics and Physics
Duration: 3FT Hon
Entry Requirements: ***GCE:*** 300-320.

NC3C BSc Finance and Human Biology
Duration: 3FT Hon
Entry Requirements: ***GCE:*** 280-300. ***BTEC NC:*** DD. ***BTEC ND:*** DMM.

FN13 BSc Finance and Medicinal Chemistry
Duration: 3FT Hon
Entry Requirements: ***GCE:*** 300.

BN13 BSc Finance and Neuroscience
Duration: 3FT Hon
Entry Requirements: ***GCE:*** 280-300.

M40 THE MANCHESTER METROPOLITAN UNIVERSITY
ADMISSIONS OFFICE
ALL SAINTS (GMS)
ALL SAINTS
MANCHESTER M15 6BH
t: 0161 247 2000
// www.mmu.ac.uk

CLC1 BSc Biology/Economics
Duration: 3FT Hon
Entry Requirements: ***GCE:*** 220. ***IB:*** 26.

FL11 BSc Chemistry/Economics
Duration: 3FT Hon
Entry Requirements: ***GCE:*** 220. ***IB:*** 26.

N38 UNIVERSITY OF NORTHAMPTON
PARK CAMPUS
BOUGHTON GREEN ROAD
NORTHAMPTON NN2 7AL
t: 0800 358 2232 f: 01604 722083
e: admissions@northampton.ac.uk
// www.northampton.ac.uk

N4C1 BA Accounting/Biological Conservation
Duration: 3FT Hon
Entry Requirements: ***GCE:*** 220-260. ***SQAH:*** ABB-BBBC. ***IB:*** 24.

L1C1 BA Economics/Biological Conservation
Duration: 3FT Hon
Entry Requirements: ***GCE:*** 220-260. ***SQAH:*** ABB-BBBC. ***IB:*** 24.

C1N4 BSc Biological Conservation/Accounting
Duration: 3FT Hon
Entry Requirements: ***GCE:*** 220-260. ***SQAH:*** ABB-BBBC. ***IB:*** 24.

C1L1 BSc Biological Conservation/Economics
Duration: 3FT Hon
Entry Requirements: ***GCE:*** 220-260. ***SQAH:*** ABB-BBBC. ***IB:*** 24.

Q50 QUEEN MARY, UNIVERSITY OF LONDON
MILE END ROAD
LONDON E1 4NS
t: 020 7882 5555 f: 020 7882 5500
e: admissions@qmul.ac.uk
// www.qmul.ac.uk

F3N3 BSc Physics with Finance
Duration: 3FT Hon
Entry Requirements: ***GCE:*** 300. ***IB:*** 30. ***BTEC NC:*** DD. ***BTEC ND:*** DMM.

S36 UNIVERSITY OF ST ANDREWS

ST KATHARINE'S WEST
16 THE SCORES
ST ANDREWS
FIFE KY16 9AX
t: 01334 462150 f: 01334 463330
e: admissions@st-andrews.ac.uk
// www.st-and.ac.uk

CL11 BSc Biology-Economics

Duration: 4FT Hon

Entry Requirements: ***GCE:*** AAA. ***SQAH:*** AAAA. ***IB:*** 38.

S75 THE UNIVERSITY OF STIRLING

STIRLING FK9 4LA
t: 01786 467044 f: 01786 466800
e: admissions@stir.ac.uk
// www.stir.ac.uk

FL91 BSc Economics and Environmental Science

Duration: 4FT Hon

Entry Requirements: ***GCE:*** CCC. ***SQAH:*** BBCC. ***SQAAH:*** AAA-CCC. ***IB:*** 26. ***BTEC ND:*** MMM.

S85 UNIVERSITY OF SURREY

STAG HILL
GUILDFORD
SURREY GU2 7XH
t: +44(0)1483 689305 f: +44(0)1483 689388
e: admissions@surrey.ac.uk
// www.surrey.ac.uk

F3N3 BSc Physics with Finance (3 or 4 years)

Duration: 3FT Hon

Entry Requirements: ***GCE:*** AAB. ***SQAH:*** BBBBB. ***IB:*** 28. Interview required.

F3NH MPhys Physics with Finance (4 years)

Duration: 4FT Hon

Entry Requirements: ***GCE:*** AAB. ***SQAH:*** ABBBB. ***IB:*** 32. Interview required.

SOCIOLOGY AND SOCIAL SCIENCE COMBINATIONS

A20 THE UNIVERSITY OF ABERDEEN

UNIVERSITY OFFICE
KING'S COLLEGE
ABERDEEN AB24 3FX
t: +44 (0) 1224 273504 f: +44 (0) 1224 272034
e: sras@abdn.ac.uk
// www.abdn.ac.uk/sras

LN64 MA Accountancy and Anthropology

Duration: 4FT Hon

Entry Requirements: ***GCE:*** BBB. ***SQAH:*** BBBB. ***IB:*** 30. ***BTEC ND:*** MMM.

NL43 MA Accountancy and Sociology

Duration: 4FT Hon

Entry Requirements: ***GCE:*** BBB. ***SQAH:*** BBBB. ***IB:*** 30. ***BTEC ND:*** MMM.

LL61 MA Anthropology and Economics

Duration: 4FT Hon

Entry Requirements: ***GCE:*** BBB. ***SQAH:*** BBBB. ***IB:*** 30. ***BTEC ND:*** MMM.

LN63 MA Anthropology and Finance

Duration: 4FT Hon

Entry Requirements: ***GCE:*** BBB. ***SQAH:*** BBBB. ***IB:*** 30. ***BTEC ND:*** MMM.

LL13 MA Economics and Sociology

Duration: 4FT Hon

Entry Requirements: ***GCE:*** BBB. ***SQAH:*** BBBB. ***IB:*** 30. ***BTEC ND:*** MMM.

NL33 MA Finance and Sociology

Duration: 4FT Hon

Entry Requirements: ***GCE:*** BBB. ***SQAH:*** BBBB. ***IB:*** 30. ***BTEC ND:*** MMM.

A40 ABERYSTWYTH UNIVERSITY

WELCOME CENTRE, ABERYSTWYTH UNIVERSITY
PENGLAIS CAMPUS
ABERYSTWYTH
CEREDIGION SY23 3FB
t: 01970 622021 f: 01970 627410
e: ug-admissions@aber.ac.uk
// www.aber.ac.uk

V3L1 BA Economic & Social History with Economics

Duration: 3FT Hon

Entry Requirements: ***GCE:*** 300. ***IB:*** 30.

L1V3 BScEcon Economics with Economic & Social History
Duration: 3FT Hon
Entry Requirements: ***GCE:*** 280. ***IB:*** 27.

B06 BANGOR UNIVERSITY
BANGOR
GWYNEDD LL57 2DG
t: 01248 382016/2017 f: 01248 370451
e: admissions@bangor.ac.uk
// www.bangor.ac.uk

LL14 BA Social Policy/Economics
Duration: 3FT Hon
Entry Requirements: ***GCE:*** 240-280. ***IB:*** 28.

LL13 BA Sociology/Economics
Duration: 3FT Hon
Entry Requirements: ***GCE:*** 240-280. ***IB:*** 28.

B56 THE UNIVERSITY OF BRADFORD
RICHMOND ROAD
BRADFORD
WEST YORKSHIRE BD7 1DP
t: 0800 073 1225 f: 01274 235585
e: course-enquiries@bradford.ac.uk
// www.bradford.ac.uk

L1L4 BSc Economics with Social Policy
Duration: 3FT Hon
Entry Requirements: ***GCE:*** 240-260. ***IB:*** 28.

L1LH BSc Economics with Sociology
Duration: 3FT Hon
Entry Requirements: ***GCE:*** 240-260. ***IB:*** 28.

C55 UNIVERSITY OF CHESTER
PARKGATE ROAD
CHESTER CH1 4BJ
t: 01244 511000 f: 01244 511300
e: enquiries@chester.ac.uk
// www.chester.ac.uk

LL13 BSc Economics and Sociology
Duration: 3FT Hon
Entry Requirements: ***GCE:*** 240. ***SQAH:*** BBBB. ***IB:*** 24. ***BTEC NC:*** DM. ***BTEC ND:*** MMM.

L1L3 BSc Economics with Sociology
Duration: 3FT Hon
Entry Requirements: ***GCE:*** 240. ***SQAH:*** BBBB. ***IB:*** 24. ***BTEC NC:*** DM. ***BTEC ND:*** MMM.

L3L1 BSc Sociology with Economics
Duration: 3FT Hon
Entry Requirements: ***GCE:*** 240. ***SQAH:*** BBBB. ***IB:*** 24. ***BTEC NC:*** DM. ***BTEC ND:*** MMM.

E28 UNIVERSITY OF EAST LONDON
DOCKLANDS CAMPUS
UNIVERSITY WAY
LONDON E16 2RD
t: 020 8223 3333 f: 020 8223 2978
e: study@uel.ac.uk
// www.uel.ac.uk

N4L6 BA Accounting with Anthropology
Duration: 3FT Hon
Entry Requirements: ***GCE:*** 200. ***IB:*** 24. ***BTEC NC:*** DM. ***BTEC ND:*** MMP. ***OCR ND:*** M1 ***OCR NED:*** P1

NL46 BA Accounting/Anthropology
Duration: 3FT Hon
Entry Requirements: ***GCE:*** 200. ***IB:*** 24. ***BTEC NC:*** DM. ***BTEC ND:*** MMP. ***OCR ND:*** M1 ***OCR NED:*** P1

NC48 BA Accounting/Psychosocial Studies
Duration: 3FT Hon
Entry Requirements: ***GCE:*** 200. ***IB:*** 24. ***BTEC NC:*** DM. ***BTEC ND:*** MMP. ***OCR ND:*** M1 ***OCR NED:*** P1

E56 THE UNIVERSITY OF EDINBURGH
STUDENT RECRUITMENT & ADMISSIONS
57 GEORGE SQUARE
EDINBURGH EH8 9JU
t: 0131 650 4360 f: 0131 651 1236
e: sra.enquiries@ed.ac.uk
// www.ed.ac.uk/studying/undergraduate/

LL13 MA Economics and Sociology
Duration: 4FT Hon
Entry Requirements: ***GCE:*** AAA-BBB. ***SQAH:*** AABB-BBBB. ***IB:*** 34.

LL41 MA Social Policy and Economics
Duration: 4FT Hon
Entry Requirements: ***GCE:*** BBB. ***SQAH:*** BBBB. ***IB:*** 34.

G28 UNIVERSITY OF GLASGOW
THE UNIVERSITY OF GLASGOW
THE FRASER BUILDING
65 HILLHEAD STREET
GLASGOW G12 8QF
t: 0141 330 6062 f: 0141 330 2961
e: ugenquiries@gla.ac.uk (UK/EU undergrad enquiries only)
// www.glasgow.ac.uk

LVC3 MA Economic & Social History/Economics
Duration: 4FT Hon
Entry Requirements: ***GCE:*** AAB. ***SQAH:*** AAAB-AABB. ***IB:*** 34.

LL61 MA Sociology & Anthropology/Economics
Duration: 4FT Hon
Entry Requirements: ***GCE:*** AAB. ***SQAH:*** AAAB-AABB. ***IB:*** 34.

K12 KEELE UNIVERSITY

STAFFS ST5 5BG
t: 01782 734005 f: 01782 632343
e: undergraduate@keele.ac.uk
// www.keele.ac.uk

N4L0 BA Accounting & Finance with Social Sciences Foundation Year

Duration: 4FT Hon
Entry Requirements: ***GCE:*** 160.

NL43 BA Accounting and Social Science Foundation Year

Duration: 4FT Hon
Entry Requirements: ***GCE:*** 160.

NL4H BA Accounting and Sociology

Duration: 3FT Hon
Entry Requirements: ***GCE:*** 320-340.

LL13 BA Economics and Sociology

Duration: 3FT Hon
Entry Requirements: ***GCE:*** 300-320.

LLC3 BA Economics with Social Science Foundation Year

Duration: 4FT Hon
Entry Requirements: ***GCE:*** 160.

LN33 BA Finance and Sociology

Duration: 3FT Hon
Entry Requirements: ***GCE:*** 320.

N3L3 BA Finance with Social Science Foundation Year

Duration: 4FT Hon
Entry Requirements: ***GCE:*** 160.

NL33 BSc Actuarial Science and Social Science Foundation Year

Duration: 4FT Hon
Entry Requirements: Contact the institution for details.

K24 THE UNIVERSITY OF KENT

INFORMATION, RECRUITMENT & ADMISSIONS REGISTRY
UNIVERSITY OF KENT
CANTERBURY, KENT CT2 7NZ
t: 01227 827272 f: 01227 827077
e: information@kent.ac.uk
// www.kent.ac.uk

NL43 BA Accounting & Finance and Sociology

Duration: 3FT Hon
Entry Requirements: ***GCE:*** 300. ***IB:*** 33. ***BTEC NC:*** DD. ***BTEC ND:*** DMM. ***OCR ND:*** D

LL16 BA Social Anthropology and Economics

Duration: 3FT Hon
Entry Requirements: ***GCE:*** 300. ***IB:*** 33. ***BTEC NC:*** DD. ***BTEC ND:*** DMM. ***OCR ND:*** D ***OCR NED:*** M2

LL13 BA Sociology and Economics

Duration: 3FT Hon
Entry Requirements: ***GCE:*** 300. ***IB:*** 33. ***BTEC NC:*** DD. ***BTEC ND:*** DMM. ***OCR ND:*** D ***OCR NED:*** M2

K84 KINGSTON UNIVERSITY

STUDENT INFORMATION & ADVICE CENTRE
COOPER HOUSE
40-46 SURBITON ROAD
KINGSTON UPON THAMES KT1 2HX
t: 0844 8552177 f: 020 8547 7080
e: aps@kingston.ac.uk
// www.kingston.ac.uk

L1L3 BA Economics (Applied) with Sociology

Duration: 3FT Hon
Entry Requirements: ***GCE:*** 220-360. ***IB:*** 24.

L3L1 BA Sociology with Economics (Applied)

Duration: 3FT Hon
Entry Requirements: ***GCE:*** 220-360.

L72 LONDON SCHOOL OF ECONOMICS AND POLITICAL SCIENCE (UNIVERSITY OF LONDON)

HOUGHTON STREET
LONDON WC2A 2AE
t: 020 7955 7125/7769 f: 020 7955 6001
e: ug-admissions@lse.ac.uk
// www.lse.ac.uk

LLK1 BSc Social Policy and Economics

Duration: 3FT Hon
Entry Requirements: ***GCE:*** ABB. ***SQAH:*** AAABB-AABBB. ***SQAAH:*** ABB. ***IB:*** 37.

L79 LOUGHBOROUGH UNIVERSITY

LOUGHBOROUGH
LEICESTERSHIRE LE11 3TU
t: 01509 223522 f: 01509 223905
e: admissions@lboro.ac.uk
// www.lboro.ac.uk

L1L4 BSc Economics with Social Policy

Duration: 3FT Hon
Entry Requirements: ***GCE:*** AAB. ***SQAH:*** AABBB. ***SQAAH:*** AB. ***IB:*** 34. ***BTEC ND:*** DDM.

L1L3 BSc Economics with Sociology

Duration: 3FT Hon
Entry Requirements: ***GCE:*** AAB. ***SQAH:*** AABBB. ***SQAAH:*** AB. ***IB:*** 34. ***BTEC ND:*** DDM.

M20 THE UNIVERSITY OF MANCHESTER

OXFORD ROAD
MANCHESTER M13 9PL
t: 0161 275 2077 f: 0161 275 2106
e: ug-admissions@manchester.ac.uk
// www.manchester.ac.uk

LVC3 BA Economics and Economic & Social History

Duration: 3FT Hon

Entry Requirements: ***GCE:*** ABB. ***SQAH:*** AABBB. ***SQAAH:*** ABB. ***IB:*** 34. ***BTEC ND:*** DDM. Interview required.

LL13 BA Economics and Sociology

Duration: 3FT Hon

Entry Requirements: ***GCE:*** ABB. ***SQAH:*** AABBB. ***SQAAH:*** ABB. ***IB:*** 34. ***BTEC ND:*** DDM.

M40 THE MANCHESTER METROPOLITAN UNIVERSITY

ADMISSIONS OFFICE
ALL SAINTS (GMS)
ALL SAINTS
MANCHESTER M15 6BH
t: 0161 247 2000
// www.mmu.ac.uk

LVD3 BA/BSc Economics/Social History

Duration: 3FT Hon

Entry Requirements: ***GCE:*** 220. ***IB:*** 26.

LLD3 BSc Economics/Sociology

Duration: 3FT Hon

Entry Requirements: ***GCE:*** 240. ***IB:*** 27.

N38 UNIVERSITY OF NORTHAMPTON

PARK CAMPUS
BOUGHTON GREEN ROAD
NORTHAMPTON NN2 7AL
t: 0800 358 2232 f: 01604 722083
e: admissions@northampton.ac.uk
// www.northampton.ac.uk

N4NA BA Accounting/Social Enterprise Development

Duration: 3FT Hon

Entry Requirements: ***GCE:*** 220-260. ***SQAH:*** ABB-BBBC. ***IB:*** 24.

N4L3 BA Accounting/Sociology

Duration: 3FT Hon

Entry Requirements: ***GCE:*** 220-260. ***SQAH:*** ABB-BBBC. ***IB:*** 24.

L1L5 BA Economics/Social Care

Duration: 3FT Hon

Entry Requirements: ***GCE:*** 220-260. ***SQAH:*** ABB-BBBC. ***IB:*** 24.

L1L3 BA Economics/Sociology

Duration: 3FT Hon

Entry Requirements: ***GCE:*** 220-260. ***SQAH:*** ABB-BBBC. ***IB:*** 24.

L5L1 BA Social Care/Economics

Duration: 3FT Hon

Entry Requirements: ***GCE:*** 220-260. ***SQAH:*** ABB-BBBC. ***IB:*** 24.

N2NL BA Social Enterprise Development/Accounting

Duration: 3FT Hon

Entry Requirements: ***GCE:*** 220-260. ***SQAH:*** ABB-BBBC. ***IB:*** 24.

L3N4 BA Sociology/Accounting

Duration: 3FT Hon

Entry Requirements: ***GCE:*** 220-260. ***SQAH:*** ABB-BBBC. ***IB:*** 24.

L3L1 BA Sociology/Economics

Duration: 3FT Hon

Entry Requirements: ***GCE:*** 220-260. ***SQAH:*** ABB-BBBC. ***IB:*** 24.

P60 UNIVERSITY OF PLYMOUTH

DRAKE CIRCUS
PLYMOUTH PL4 8AA
t: 01752 588037 f: 01752 588050
e: admissions@plymouth.ac.uk
// www.plymouth.ac.uk

L1L3 BSc Economics with Sociology

Duration: 3FT/4SW Hon

Entry Requirements: ***GCE:*** 240. ***IB:*** 26.

Q50 QUEEN MARY, UNIVERSITY OF LONDON

MILE END ROAD
LONDON E1 4NS
t: 020 7882 5555 f: 020 7882 5500
e: admissions@qmul.ac.uk
// www.qmul.ac.uk

LL31 BA Cities, Economies and Social Change

Duration: 3FT Hon

Entry Requirements: ***GCE:*** 300-340. ***IB:*** 32. ***BTEC NC:*** DD. ***BTEC ND:*** DDM.

S09 SCHOOL OF ORIENTAL AND AFRICAN STUDIES (UNIVERSITY OF LONDON)

THORNHAUGH STREET
RUSSELL SQUARE
LONDON WC1H 0XG
t: 020 7074 5106 f: 020 7898 4039
e: undergradadmissions@soas.ac.uk
// www.soas.ac.uk

LL16 BA Social Anthropology and Economics

Duration: 3FT Hon

Entry Requirements: Contact the institution for details.

S36 UNIVERSITY OF ST ANDREWS

ST KATHARINE'S WEST
16 THE SCORES
ST ANDREWS
FIFE KY16 9AX
t: 01334 462150 f: 01334 463330
e: admissions@st-andrews.ac.uk
// www.st-and.ac.uk

L1L6 MA Economics with Social Anthropology

Duration: 4FT Hon

Entry Requirements: ***GCE:*** AAA. ***SQAH:*** AAAA. ***IB:*** 38.

LL16 MA Economics-Social Anthropology

Duration: 4FT Hon

Entry Requirements: ***GCE:*** AAA. ***SQAH:*** AAAA. ***IB:*** 38.

S75 THE UNIVERSITY OF STIRLING

STIRLING FK9 4LA
t: 01786 467044 f: 01786 466800
e: admissions@stir.ac.uk
// www.stir.ac.uk

LL13 BA Economics and Sociology

Duration: 4FT Hon

Entry Requirements: ***GCE:*** CCC. ***SQAH:*** BBBB. ***SQAAH:*** AAA-CCC. ***IB:*** 30. ***BTEC ND:*** MMM.

S78 THE UNIVERSITY OF STRATHCLYDE

GLASGOW G1 1XQ
t: 0141 552 4400 f: 0141 552 0775
// www.strath.ac.uk

LL13 BA Economics and Sociology

Duration: 4FT Hon

Entry Requirements: ***GCE:*** ABB. ***SQAH:*** ABBB-BBBBC. ***IB:*** 34.

S93 SWANSEA UNIVERSITY

SINGLETON PARK
SWANSEA SA2 8PP
t: 01792 295111 f: 01792 295110
e: admissions@swansea.ac.uk
// www.swansea.ac.uk

LL41 BA Economics and Social Policy

Duration: 3FT Hon

Entry Requirements: ***GCE:*** ABB. ***IB:*** 33. ***BTEC ND:*** DDM.

W50 UNIVERSITY OF WESTMINSTER

101 NEW CAVENDISH STREET
LONDON W1W 6XH
t: 020 7915 5511 f: 020 7911 5788
e: course-enquiries@westminster.ac.uk
// www.westminster.ac.uk

LL13 BA Development and Sociology

Duration: 3FT Hon

Entry Requirements: Contact the institution for details.

Y50 THE UNIVERSITY OF YORK

ADMISSIONS AND UK/EU STUDENT RECRUITMENT
UNIVERSITY OF YORK
HESLINGTON
YORK YO10 5DD
t: 01904 433533 f: 01904 433538
e: admissions@york.ac.uk
// www.york.ac.uk

LL13 BA Economics/Sociology (Equal)

Duration: 3FT Hon

Entry Requirements: ***GCE:*** ABB. ***SQAH:*** AABBB. ***SQAAH:*** AB. ***IB:*** 32. ***BTEC ND:*** DDM.

ECONOMICS AND OTHER COMBINATIONS

A20 THE UNIVERSITY OF ABERDEEN

UNIVERSITY OFFICE
KING'S COLLEGE
ABERDEEN AB24 3FX
t: +44 (0) 1224 273504 f: +44 (0) 1224 272034
e: sras@abdn.ac.uk
// www.abdn.ac.uk/sras

NL21 MA Economics and Entrepreneurship

Duration: 4FT Hon

Entry Requirements: ***GCE:*** BBB. ***SQAH:*** BBBB. ***IB:*** 30. ***BTEC ND:*** MMM.

LV11 MA Economics and History

Duration: 4FT Hon

Entry Requirements: ***GCE:*** BBB. ***SQAH:*** BBBB. ***IB:*** 30. ***BTEC ND:*** MMM.

LLC2 MA Economics and International Relations

Duration: 4FT Hon

Entry Requirements: ***GCE:*** BBB. ***SQAH:*** BBBB. ***IB:*** 30. ***BTEC ND:*** MMM.

LV15 MA Economics and Philosophy

Duration: 4FT Hon

Entry Requirements: ***GCE:*** BBB. ***SQAH:*** BBBB. ***IB:*** 30. ***BTEC ND:*** MMM.

LK12 MA Economics and Property
Duration: 4FT Hon
Entry Requirements: ***GCE:*** BBB. ***SQAH:*** BBBB. ***IB:*** 30. ***BTEC ND:*** MMM.

LC18 MA Economics and Psychology
Duration: 4FT Hon
Entry Requirements: ***GCE:*** BBB. ***SQAH:*** BBBB. ***IB:*** 30. ***BTEC ND:*** MMM.

A40 ABERYSTWYTH UNIVERSITY
WELCOME CENTRE, ABERYSTWYTH UNIVERSITY
PENGLAIS CAMPUS
ABERYSTWYTH
CEREDIGION SY23 3FB
t: 01970 622021 f: 01970 627410
e: ug-admissions@aber.ac.uk
// www.aber.ac.uk

CL81 BScEcon Psychology/Economics
Duration: 3FT Hon
Entry Requirements: ***GCE:*** 260. ***IB:*** 27.

B06 BANGOR UNIVERSITY
BANGOR
GWYNEDD LL57 2DG
t: 01248 382016/2017 f: 01248 370451
e: admissions@bangor.ac.uk
// www.bangor.ac.uk

LLC3 BA Economics/Cymdeithaseg
Duration: 3FT Hon
Entry Requirements: ***GCE:*** 260-300. ***IB:*** 28.

LLC4 BA Economics/Polisi Cymdeithasol
Duration: 3FT Hon
Entry Requirements: ***GCE:*** 260-300. ***IB:*** 28.

LV11 BA History/Economics
Duration: 3FT Hon
Entry Requirements: ***GCE:*** 240-280. ***IB:*** 28.

B16 UNIVERSITY OF BATH
CLAVERTON DOWN
BATH BA2 7AY
t: 01225 383019 f: 01225 386366
e: admissions@bath.ac.uk
// www.bath.ac.uk

LL19 BSc Economics and International Development
Duration: 3FT Hon
Entry Requirements: ***GCE:*** AAA-AAB. ***SQAAH:*** AAB. ***IB:*** 38. ***BTEC NC:*** DD. ***BTEC ND:*** DDD.

LLC9 BSc Economics and International Development (4 year sandwich)
Duration: 4SW Hon
Entry Requirements: ***GCE:*** AAA-AAB. ***SQAAH:*** AAB. ***IB:*** 38. ***BTEC NC:*** DD. ***BTEC ND:*** DDD.

B32 THE UNIVERSITY OF BIRMINGHAM
EDGBASTON
BIRMINGHAM B15 2TT
t: 0121 415 8900 f: 0121 414 7159
e: admissions@bham.ac.uk
// www.bham.ac.uk

LL21 BA International Studies with Economics
Duration: 3FT Hon
Entry Requirements: ***GCE:*** AAB-ABB. ***SQAH:*** AAABB-AABBB. ***SQAAH:*** ABB-AA.

LL12 BSc Economics and Political Science
Duration: 3FT Hon
Entry Requirements: ***GCE:*** AAB. ***SQAH:*** AAABB. ***SQAAH:*** AAB-ABB.

KL41 BSc Urban & Regional Planning and Economics
Duration: 3FT Hon
Entry Requirements: ***GCE:*** ABB. ***SQAH:*** AABBB. ***SQAAH:*** AB.

B56 THE UNIVERSITY OF BRADFORD
RICHMOND ROAD
BRADFORD
WEST YORKSHIRE BD7 1DP
t: 0800 073 1225 f: 01274 235585
e: course-enquiries@bradford.ac.uk
// www.bradford.ac.uk

L1L9 BSc Economics with Development Studies
Duration: 3FT Hon
Entry Requirements: ***GCE:*** 240-260. ***IB:*** 28.

L1L2 BSc Economics with International Relations
Duration: 3FT Hon
Entry Requirements: ***GCE:*** 240-260. ***IB:*** 28.

L1C8 BSc Economics with Psychology
Duration: 3FT Hon
Entry Requirements: ***GCE:*** 240-260. ***IB:*** 28.

B78 UNIVERSITY OF BRISTOL

UNDERGRADUATE ADMISSIONS OFFICE
SENATE HOUSE
TYNDALL AVENUE
BRISTOL BS8 1TH
t: 0117 928 9000 f: 0117 925 1424
e: ug-admissions@bristol.ac.uk
// www.bristol.ac.uk

VL51 BSc Philosophy and Economics

Duration: 3FT Hon
Entry Requirements: ***GCE:*** A*AA-AAB. ***SQAH:*** AAAAA-AAAAB. ***SQAAH:*** AAA-ABB. ***BTEC ND:*** DDD.

B90 THE UNIVERSITY OF BUCKINGHAM

YEOMANRY HOUSE
HUNTER STREET
BUCKINGHAM MK18 1EG
t: 01280 820313 f: 01280 822245
e: info@buckingham.ac.uk
// www.buckingham.ac.uk

L1V1 BSc Economics with History

Duration: 2FT Hon
Entry Requirements: ***GCE:*** 240. ***IB:*** 26. ***BTEC NC:*** DD. ***BTEC ND:*** MMM.

C05 UNIVERSITY OF CAMBRIDGE

CAMBRIDGE ADMISSIONS OFFICE
FITZWILLIAM HOUSE
32 TRUMPINGTON STREET
CAMBRIDGE CB2 1QY
t: 01223 333 308 f: 01223 746 868
e: admissions@cam.ac.uk
// www.cam.ac.uk/admissions/undergraduate/

KL41 BA Land Economy

Duration: 3FT Hon
Entry Requirements: ***GCE:*** A*AA. ***SQAAH:*** AAA-AAB. Interview required.

C15 CARDIFF UNIVERSITY

PO BOX 927
30-36 NEWPORT ROAD
CARDIFF CF24 0DE
t: 029 2087 9999 f: 029 2087 6138
e: admissions@cardiff.ac.uk
// www.cardiff.ac.uk

VL11 BA Economics/History

Duration: 3FT Hon
Entry Requirements: ***GCE:*** AAB-ABB. ***SQAH:*** AAABB-AABBB. ***SQAAH:*** AAB-ABB. ***IB:*** 33. ***OCR NED:*** D2

VL51 BA Economics/Philosophy

Duration: 3FT Hon
Entry Requirements: ***GCE:*** AAB. ***SQAH:*** AAABB. ***SQAAH:*** AAB. ***IB:*** 35. ***BTEC ND:*** DDD. ***OCR NED:*** D2

C55 UNIVERSITY OF CHESTER

PARKGATE ROAD
CHESTER CH1 4BJ
t: 01244 511000 f: 01244 511300
e: enquiries@chester.ac.uk
// www.chester.ac.uk

LV11 BA Economics and History

Duration: 3FT Hon
Entry Requirements: ***GCE:*** 240. ***SQAH:*** BBBB. ***IB:*** 24. ***BTEC NC:*** DM. ***BTEC ND:*** MPP.

V1L1 BA History with Economics

Duration: 3FT Hon
Entry Requirements: ***GCE:*** 240. ***SQAH:*** BBBB. ***IB:*** 24. ***BTEC NC:*** DM. ***BTEC ND:*** MPP.

LL19 BSc Economics and International Development Studies

Duration: 3FT Hon
Entry Requirements: ***GCE:*** 240. ***SQAH:*** BBBB. ***IB:*** 24. ***BTEC NC:*** DM. ***BTEC ND:*** MMM.

LC18 BSc Economics and Psychology

Duration: 3FT Hon
Entry Requirements: ***GCE:*** 240. ***SQAH:*** BBBB. ***IB:*** 24. ***BTEC NC:*** DM. ***BTEC ND:*** MMM.

L1V1 BSc Economics with History

Duration: 3FT Hon
Entry Requirements: ***GCE:*** 240. ***SQAH:*** BBBB. ***IB:*** 24. ***BTEC NC:*** DM. ***BTEC ND:*** MPP.

L1L9 BSc Economics with International Development Studies

Duration: 3FT Hon
Entry Requirements: ***GCE:*** 240. ***SQAH:*** BBBB. ***IB:*** 24. ***BTEC NC:*** DM. ***BTEC ND:*** MMM.

L1C8 BSc Economics with Psychology

Duration: 3FT Hon
Entry Requirements: ***GCE:*** 240. ***SQAH:*** BBBB. ***IB:*** 24. ***BTEC NC:*** DM. ***BTEC ND:*** MMM.

L9L1 BSc International Development Studies with Economics

Duration: 3FT Hon
Entry Requirements: ***GCE:*** 240. ***SQAH:*** BBBB. ***IB:*** 24. ***BTEC NC:*** DM. ***BTEC ND:*** MMM.

C8L1 BSc Psychology with Economics

Duration: 3FT Hon
Entry Requirements: ***GCE:*** 240. ***SQAH:*** BBBB. ***IB:*** 24. ***BTEC NC:*** DM. ***BTEC ND:*** MMM.

C60 CITY UNIVERSITY

NORTHAMPTON SQUARE
LONDON EC1V 0HB
t: 020 7040 5060 f: 020 7040 8995
e: ugadmissions@city.ac.uk
// www.city.ac.uk

LP15 BA Journalism/Economics (3 years or 4 year SW)

Duration: 3FT Hon

Entry Requirements: ***GCE:*** ABB. ***IB:*** 32.

C85 COVENTRY UNIVERSITY

THE STUDENT CENTRE
COVENTRY UNIVERSITY
1 GULSON ROAD
COVENTRY CV1 2JH
t: 024 7615 2222 f: 024 7615 2223
e: studentenquiries@coventry.ac.uk
// www.coventry.ac.uk

LN11 BA International Economics and Trade

Duration: 3FT Hon

Entry Requirements: ***GCE:*** 260-320. ***IB:*** 30. Interview required.

D26 DE MONTFORT UNIVERSITY

THE GATEWAY
LEICESTER LE1 9BH
t: 0116 255 1551 f: 0116 250 6204
e: enquiries@dmu.ac.uk
// www.dmu.ac.uk

LL12 BA Economics and Government

Duration: 3FT/4SW Hon

Entry Requirements: ***GCE:*** 240. ***IB:*** 24. ***BTEC NC:*** DD. ***BTEC ND:*** MMM. ***OCR ND:*** D ***OCR NED:*** M3 Interview required.

D65 UNIVERSITY OF DUNDEE

DUNDEE DD1 4HN
t: 01382 383838 f: 01382 388150
e: ContactUs@dundee.ac.uk
// www.dundee.ac.uk/admissions/undergraduate/

LV11 MA Economics and History

Duration: 4FT Hon

Entry Requirements: ***GCE:*** BCC. ***SQAH:*** BBBB. ***IB:*** 30. ***BTEC ND:*** DMM.

LLD2 MA Economics and International Relations

Duration: 4FT Hon

Entry Requirements: ***GCE:*** BCC. ***SQAH:*** BBBB. ***IB:*** 30. ***BTEC ND:*** DMM.

LK14 MA Spatial Economics and Development

Duration: 4FT Hon

Entry Requirements: ***GCE:*** BCC. ***SQAH:*** BBBB. ***IB:*** 30. ***BTEC ND:*** DMM.

E14 UNIVERSITY OF EAST ANGLIA

NORWICH NR4 7TJ
t: 01603 591515 f: 01603 458596
e: admissions@uea.ac.uk
// www.uea.ac.uk

L2L1 BA International Development with Economics

Duration: 3FT Hon

Entry Requirements: ***GCE:*** ABB. ***SQAH:*** AAABB. ***SQAAH:*** ABB. ***IB:*** 32. ***BTEC NC:*** DD. ***BTEC ND:*** DDM. ***OCR ND:*** M1 ***OCR NED:*** D2

L2LC BA International Development with Economics with Overseas Experience

Duration: 3FT Hon

Entry Requirements: ***GCE:*** ABB. ***SQAH:*** AAABB. ***SQAAH:*** ABB. ***IB:*** 32. ***BTEC NC:*** DD. ***BTEC ND:*** DDM. ***OCR ND:*** M1 ***OCR NED:*** D2

LC18 BSc Economics and Economic Psychology

Duration: 3FT Hon

Entry Requirements: ***GCE:*** AAA-AAB. ***SQAH:*** AAAA. ***SQAAH:*** AAA-AAB. ***IB:*** 33. ***BTEC NC:*** DD. ***BTEC ND:*** DDD.

E56 THE UNIVERSITY OF EDINBURGH

STUDENT RECRUITMENT & ADMISSIONS
57 GEORGE SQUARE
EDINBURGH EH8 9JU
t: 0131 650 4360 f: 0131 651 1236
e: sra.enquiries@ed.ac.uk
// www.ed.ac.uk/studying/undergraduate/

LV13 MA Economics and Economic History

Duration: 4FT Hon

Entry Requirements: ***GCE:*** AAA-BBB. ***SQAH:*** AABB-BBBB. ***IB:*** 34.

L1F9 MA Economics with Environmental Studies

Duration: 4FT Hon

Entry Requirements: ***GCE:*** AAA-BBB. ***SQAH:*** AABB-BBBB. ***IB:*** 34.

VL51 MA Philosophy and Economics

Duration: 4FT Hon

Entry Requirements: ***GCE:*** AAA-BBB. ***SQAH:*** AABB-BBBB. ***IB:*** 34.

E70 THE UNIVERSITY OF ESSEX

WIVENHOE PARK
COLCHESTER
ESSEX CO4 3SQ
t: 01206 873666 f: 01206 873423
e: admit@essex.ac.uk
// www.essex.ac.uk

LV11 BA History and Economics

Duration: 3FT Hon

Entry Requirements: ***GCE:*** 300-320. ***SQAH:*** AAAB-AABB. ***IB:*** 34. ***BTEC NC:*** DM. ***BTEC ND:*** MMP.

E84 UNIVERSITY OF EXETER

LAVER BUILDING
NORTH PARK ROAD
EXETER
DEVON EX4 4QE
t: 01392 263855 f: 01392 263857/262479
e: admissions@exeter.ac.uk
// www.exeter.ac.uk/admissions

L190 BA Economics with Econometrics
Duration: 3FT Hon
Entry Requirements: ***GCE:*** AAA-AAB. ***SQAH:*** AAAAB-AAABB. ***SQAAH:*** AAB-ABB. ***BTEC ND:*** DDD.

L191 BA Economics with Econometrics with European Study (4 years)
Duration: 4FT Hon
Entry Requirements: ***GCE:*** AAA-AAB. ***SQAH:*** AAAAB-AAABB. ***SQAAH:*** AAB-ABB. ***BTEC ND:*** DDD.

L193 BA Economics with Econometrics with Industrial Experience (4 years)
Duration: 4FT Hon
Entry Requirements: ***GCE:*** AAA-AAB. ***SQAH:*** AAAAB-AAABB. ***SQAAH:*** AAB-ABB. ***BTEC ND:*** DDD.

VL51 BA Philosophy and Political Economy
Duration: 3FT Hon
Entry Requirements: ***GCE:*** AAA-AAB. ***SQAH:*** AAAAB-AAABB. ***SQAAH:*** AAB-ABB. ***BTEC ND:*** DDD.

VL5C BA Philosophy and Political Economy with Study Abroad (4 years)
Duration: 4FT Hon
Entry Requirements: ***GCE:*** AAA-AAB. ***SQAH:*** AAAAB-AAABB. ***SQAAH:*** AAB-ABB. ***BTEC ND:*** DDD.

G28 UNIVERSITY OF GLASGOW

THE UNIVERSITY OF GLASGOW
THE FRASER BUILDING
65 HILLHEAD STREET
GLASGOW G12 8QF
t: 0141 330 6062 f: 0141 330 2961
e: ugenquiries@gla.ac.uk (UK/EU undergrad enquiries only)
// www.glasgow.ac.uk

LV14 MA Archaeology/Economics
Duration: 4FT Hon
Entry Requirements: ***GCE:*** AAB. ***SQAH:*** AAAB-AABB. ***IB:*** 34.

VL41 MA Archaeology/Economics
Duration: 4FT Hon
Entry Requirements: ***GCE:*** AAB. ***SQAH:*** AAAB-AABB. ***IB:*** 34.

LV11 MA Economics/History
Duration: 4FT Hon
Entry Requirements: ***GCE:*** AAB. ***SQAH:*** AAAB-AABB. ***IB:*** 34.

LVC1 MA Economics/History
Duration: 4FT Hon
Entry Requirements: ***GCE:*** AAB. ***SQAH:*** AAAB-AABB. ***IB:*** 34.

LW13 MA Economics/Music
Duration: 4FT Hon
Entry Requirements: ***GCE:*** AAB. ***SQAH:*** AAAB-AABB. ***IB:*** 34.

LVC5 MA Economics/Philosophy
Duration: 4FT Hon
Entry Requirements: ***GCE:*** AAB. ***SQAH:*** AAAB-AABB. ***IB:*** 34.

LVD5 MA Economics/Philosophy
Duration: 4FT Hon
Entry Requirements: ***GCE:*** AAB. ***SQAH:*** AAAB-AABB. ***IB:*** 34.

CL81 MA Economics/Psychology
Duration: 4FT Hon
Entry Requirements: ***GCE:*** AAB. ***SQAH:*** AAAB-AABB. ***IB:*** 34.

LL14 MA Economics/Public Policy
Duration: 4FT Hon
Entry Requirements: ***GCE:*** AAB. ***SQAH:*** AAAB-AABB. ***IB:*** 34.

LVC2 MA Economics/Scottish History
Duration: 4FT Hon
Entry Requirements: ***GCE:*** AAB. ***SQAH:*** AAAB-AABB. ***IB:*** 34.

LVD1 MA Economics/Scottish History
Duration: 4FT Hon
Entry Requirements: ***GCE:*** AAB. ***SQAH:*** AAAB-AABB. ***IB:*** 34.

LW14 MA Economics/Theatre Studies
Duration: 4FT Hon
Entry Requirements: ***GCE:*** AAB. ***SQAH:*** AAAB-AABB. ***IB:*** 34.

LV16 MA Economics/Theology & Religious Studies
Duration: 4FT Hon
Entry Requirements: ***GCE:*** AAB. ***SQAH:*** AAAB-AABB. ***IB:*** 34.

G70 UNIVERSITY OF GREENWICH

GREENWICH CAMPUS
OLD ROYAL NAVAL COLLEGE
PARK ROW
LONDON SE10 9LS
t: 0800 005 006 f: 020 8331 8145
e: courseinfo@gre.ac.uk
// www.gre.ac.uk

XL31 BA Education and Economics
Duration: 3FT Hon
Entry Requirements: ***GCE:*** 180. ***IB:*** 24.

VL11 BA History and Economics
Duration: 3FT Hon
Entry Requirements: ***GCE:*** 180. ***IB:*** 28.

L2LC BA International Studies with Economics
Duration: 3FT Hon
Entry Requirements: ***GCE:*** 180. ***IB:*** 24.

VL51 BA Philosophy and Economics
Duration: 3FT Hon
Entry Requirements: ***GCE:*** 180. ***IB:*** 24.

B9L1 BSc Health with Economics
Duration: 3FT Hon
Entry Requirements: ***GCE:*** 160. ***IB:*** 24. ***BTEC ND:*** MMM.

H36 UNIVERSITY OF HERTFORDSHIRE
UNIVERSITY ADMISSIONS SERVICE
COLLEGE LANE
HATFIELD
HERTS AL10 9AB
t: 01707 284800 f: 01707 284870
// www.herts.ac.uk

LN16 BA Economics/Human Resources
Duration: 3FT/4SW Hon
Entry Requirements: ***GCE:*** 240.

L1N8 BA Economics/Tourism
Duration: 3FT/4SW Hon
Entry Requirements: ***GCE:*** 220.

H6L1 BSc Digital Media Technology/Economics
Duration: 3FT/4SW Hon
Entry Requirements: ***GCE:*** 220.

L1H6 BSc Economics/Digital Media Technology
Duration: 3FT/4SW Hon
Entry Requirements: ***GCE:*** 220.

L1B9 BSc Economics/Health Studies
Duration: 3FT/4SW Hon
Entry Requirements: ***GCE:*** 220-280.

L1V5 BSc Economics/Philosophy
Duration: 3FT/4SW Hon
Entry Requirements: ***GCE:*** 220.

L1C6 BSc Economics/Sports Studies
Duration: 3FT/4SW Hon
Entry Requirements: ***GCE:*** 260.

B9L1 BSc Health Studies/Economics
Duration: 3FT/4SW Hon
Entry Requirements: ***GCE:*** 220-280.

V5L1 BSc Philosophy/Economics
Duration: 3FT/4SW Hon
Entry Requirements: ***GCE:*** 220.

C6L1 BSc Sports Studies/Economics
Duration: 3FT/4SW Hon
Entry Requirements: ***GCE:*** 260.

H72 THE UNIVERSITY OF HULL
THE UNIVERSITY OF HULL
COTTINGHAM ROAD
HULL HU6 7RX
t: 01482 466100 f: 01482 442290
e: admissions@hull.ac.uk
// www.hull.ac.uk

V1L1 BA History with Economics
Duration: 3FT Hon
Entry Requirements: ***GCE:*** 300. ***IB:*** 28.

LN1F BSc Economics and Logistics
Duration: 3FT Hon
Entry Requirements: ***GCE:*** 280. ***IB:*** 28.

LN1G BSc Economics and Logistics (with Professional Experience) (4 years)
Duration: 4FT Hon
Entry Requirements: ***GCE:*** 280. ***IB:*** 28.

LNC2 BSc(Econ) Economics and Logistics (International) (4 years)
Duration: 4FT Hon
Entry Requirements: ***GCE:*** 280. ***IB:*** 28.

K12 KEELE UNIVERSITY
STAFFS ST5 5BG
t: 01782 734005 f: 01782 632343
e: undergraduate@keele.ac.uk
// www.keele.ac.uk

LP13 BA Economics and Film Studies
Duration: 3FT Hon
Entry Requirements: ***GCE:*** 300.

LV11 BA Economics and History
Duration: 3FT Hon
Entry Requirements: ***GCE:*** 300.

LLC2 BA Economics and International Relations
Duration: 3FT Hon
Entry Requirements: ***GCE:*** 320.

LW13 BA Economics and Music
Duration: 3FT Hon
Entry Requirements: ***GCE:*** 260-320.

LWC3 BA Economics and Music Technology
Duration: 3FT Hon
Entry Requirements: ***GCE:*** 280-300.

LV15 BA Economics and Philosophy
Duration: 3FT Hon
Entry Requirements: ***GCE:*** 300-320.

CL8C BSc Applied Psychology and Economics
Duration: 4FT Deg
Entry Requirements: ***GCE:*** 320.

CL81 BSc Economics and Psychology
Duration: 3FT Hon
Entry Requirements: ***GCE:*** 300-320.

K84 KINGSTON UNIVERSITY
STUDENT INFORMATION & ADVICE CENTRE
COOPER HOUSE
40-46 SURBITON ROAD
KINGSTON UPON THAMES KT1 2HX
t: 0844 8552177 f: 020 8547 7080
e: aps@kingston.ac.uk
// www.kingston.ac.uk

L1LG BA Applied Economics with International Relations
Duration: 3FT Hon
Entry Requirements: ***GCE:*** 240-320.

W8L1 BA Creative Writing with Economics (Applied)
Duration: 3FT Hon
Entry Requirements: ***GCE:*** 220-360. ***IB:*** 30.

L1W8 BA Economics (Applied) with Creative Writing
Duration: 3FT Hon
Entry Requirements: ***GCE:*** 260-360. ***IB:*** 24.

L1F9 BA Economics (Applied) with Environmental Studies
Duration: 3FT Hon
Entry Requirements: ***GCE:*** 260-360. ***IB:*** 24.

L1V1 BA Economics (Applied) with History
Duration: 3FT Hon
Entry Requirements: ***GCE:*** 260-360. ***IB:*** 24.

L1P5 BA Economics (Applied) with Journalism
Duration: 3FT Hon
Entry Requirements: ***GCE:*** BBB. ***BTEC ND:*** DDM.

L1P3 BA Economics (Applied) with Media & Cultural Studies
Duration: 3FT Hon
Entry Requirements: ***GCE:*** 240-360. ***IB:*** 24.

L1PH BA Economics (Applied) with Television & New Broadcasting Media
Duration: 3FT Hon
Entry Requirements: ***GCE:*** 260-360. ***IB:*** 24.

V1L1 BA History with Economics (Applied)
Duration: 3FT Hon
Entry Requirements: ***GCE:*** 220-360.

P5L1 BA Journalism with Economics (Applied)
Duration: 3FT Hon
Entry Requirements: ***GCE:*** 300-320. ***SQAH:*** BBCCC. ***SQAAH:*** BBC. ***IB:*** 25. ***BTEC ND:*** DDM.

P3L1 BA Media & Cultural Studies with Economics (Applied)
Duration: 3FT Hon
Entry Requirements: ***GCE:*** 240-360.

P3LC BA Television & New Broadcasting Media with Applied Economics
Duration: 3FT Hon
Entry Requirements: ***GCE:*** 220-260.

FL91 BSc Environmental Studies and Economics
Duration: 3FT Hon
Entry Requirements: ***GCE:*** 200-280. ***IB:*** 30.

FLX1 BSc Environmental Studies and Economics
Duration: 4SW Hon
Entry Requirements: ***GCE:*** 200-280.

F9L1 BSc Environmental Studies with Economics
Duration: 3FT Hon
Entry Requirements: ***GCE:*** 200-280. ***IB:*** 30.

L2LD BSc International Relations with Applied Economics
Duration: 3FT Hon
Entry Requirements: ***GCE:*** 240-360.

L14 LANCASTER UNIVERSITY
THE UNIVERSITY
LANCASTER
LANCASHIRE LA1 4YW
t: 01524 592029 f: 01524 846243
e: ugadmissions@lancaster.ac.uk
// www.lancs.ac.uk

LL12 BA Economics and International Relations
Duration: 3FT Hon
Entry Requirements: ***GCE:*** ABB. ***SQAH:*** BBBBB. ***SQAAH:*** ABB. ***IB:*** 32. ***BTEC ND:*** DDM.

L23 UNIVERSITY OF LEEDS

THE UNIVERSITY OF LEEDS
LEEDS LS2 9JT
t: 0113 343 3999
e: admissions@adm.leeds.ac.uk
// www.leeds.ac.uk

VL11 BA Economics and History

Duration: 3FT Hon
Entry Requirements: ***GCE:*** ABB. ***SQAAH:*** ABB. ***IB:*** 33.

VL51 BA Economics and Philosophy

Duration: 3FT Hon
Entry Requirements: ***GCE:*** BBB. ***SQAAH:*** BBB. ***IB:*** 32.

L1N9 BSc Economics with Transport Studies

Duration: 3FT Hon
Entry Requirements: ***GCE:*** AAB. ***SQAH:*** AAAAB. ***SQAAH:*** AAB. ***IB:*** 34.

L27 LEEDS METROPOLITAN UNIVERSITY

COURSE ENQUIRIES OFFICE
CIVIC QUARTER
LEEDS LS1 3HE
t: 0113 81 23113 f: 0113 81 23129
e: https://experience.leedsmet.ac.uk/leeds/index.do
// www.leedsmet.ac.uk

LL91 BA Global Development & Political Economy

Duration: 3FT/4SW Hon
Entry Requirements: ***GCE:*** 220. ***BTEC NC:*** DD. ***BTEC ND:*** MMM. ***OCR ND:*** D

L68 LONDON METROPOLITAN UNIVERSITY

166-220 HOLLOWAY ROAD
LONDON N7 8DB
t: 020 7133 4200
e: admissions@londonmet.ac.uk
// www.londonmet.ac.uk

LL19 BA Economics and International Development

Duration: 3FT Hon
Entry Requirements: ***GCE:*** 240. ***IB:*** 28.

LL1F BA Economics and International Relations

Duration: 3FT Hon
Entry Requirements: ***GCE:*** 240. ***IB:*** 28.

LL12 BA International Economics and International Relations

Duration: 3FT Hon
Entry Requirements: ***GCE:*** 240. ***IB:*** 28.

L72 LONDON SCHOOL OF ECONOMICS AND POLITICAL SCIENCE (UNIVERSITY OF LONDON)

HOUGHTON STREET
LONDON WC2A 2AE
t: 020 7955 7125/7769 f: 020 7955 6001
e: ug-admissions@lse.ac.uk
// www.lse.ac.uk

V3L1 BSc Economic History with Economics

Duration: 3FT Hon
Entry Requirements: ***GCE:*** AAB. ***SQAH:*** AAAAA-AAAAB. ***SQAAH:*** AAB. ***IB:*** 37.

VL31 BSc Economics and Economic History

Duration: 3FT Hon
Entry Requirements: ***GCE:*** AAB. ***SQAH:*** AAAAA-AAAAB. ***SQAAH:*** AAB. ***IB:*** 37.

L1V3 BSc Economics with Economic History

Duration: 3FT Hon
Entry Requirements: ***GCE:*** A*AA. ***SQAH:*** AAAAA. ***SQAAH:*** AAA. ***IB:*** 38.

F9L1 BSc Environmental Policy with Economics

Duration: 3FT Hon
Entry Requirements: ***GCE:*** AAB. ***SQAH:*** AAAAA-AAAAB. ***SQAAH:*** AAB. ***IB:*** 37.

LL12 BSc Government and Economics

Duration: 3FT Hon
Entry Requirements: ***GCE:*** AAB. ***SQAH:*** AAAAA-AAAAB. ***SQAAH:*** AAB. ***IB:*** 37.

LV15 BSc Philosophy and Economics

Duration: 3FT Hon
Entry Requirements: ***GCE:*** AAA. ***SQAH:*** AAAAA. ***SQAAH:*** AAA. ***IB:*** 38.

M20 THE UNIVERSITY OF MANCHESTER

OXFORD ROAD
MANCHESTER M13 9PL
t: 0161 275 2077 f: 0161 275 2106
e: ug-admissions@manchester.ac.uk
// www.manchester.ac.uk

LL91 BA Development Studies and Economics

Duration: 3FT Hon
Entry Requirements: ***GCE:*** ABB. ***SQAH:*** AABBB. ***SQAAH:*** ABB. ***IB:*** 34. ***BTEC ND:*** DDM. Interview required.

LV13 BA Economic History and Economics

Duration: 3FT Hon
Entry Requirements: ***GCE:*** ABB-BBB. ***SQAAH:*** ABB-BBB. ***IB:*** 33. ***BTEC ND:*** MMM.

M40 THE MANCHESTER METROPOLITAN UNIVERSITY
ADMISSIONS OFFICE
ALL SAINTS (GMS)
ALL SAINTS
MANCHESTER M15 6BH
t: 0161 247 2000
// www.mmu.ac.uk

PL31 BA/BSc Cultural Studies/Economics
Duration: 3FT Hon
Entry Requirements: ***GCE:*** 240. ***IB:*** 27.

LWC6 BA/BSc Economics/European Film
Duration: 3FT Hon
Entry Requirements: ***GCE:*** 240. ***IB:*** 27.

LVD1 BA/BSc Economics/History
Duration: 3FT Hon
Entry Requirements: ***GCE:*** 220. ***IB:*** 26.

LJ1X BA/BSc Economics/Logistics
Duration: 3FT Hon
Entry Requirements: ***GCE:*** 240. ***IB:*** 27.

LVD5 BA/BSc Economics/Philosophy
Duration: 3FT Hon
Entry Requirements: ***GCE:*** 220. ***IB:*** 26.

LX11 BA/BSc Economics/Teaching English as a Foreign Language
Duration: 3FT Hon
Entry Requirements: ***GCE:*** 240. ***IB:*** 27.

LNC8 BA/BSc Economics/Tourism
Duration: 3FT Hon
Entry Requirements: ***GCE:*** 240. ***IB:*** 27.

GL4C BSc Digital Media/Economics
Duration: 3FT Hon
Entry Requirements: ***GCE:*** 220. ***IB:*** 26.

LPC1 BSc Economics/Information & Communications
Duration: 3FT Hon
Entry Requirements: ***GCE:*** 220. ***IB:*** 26.

HL61 BSc Economics/Multimedia Technology
Duration: 3FT Hon
Entry Requirements: ***GCE:*** 220. ***IB:*** 26.

LC18 BSc Economics/Psychology
Duration: 3FT Hon
Entry Requirements: ***GCE:*** 280. ***IB:*** 29.

N38 UNIVERSITY OF NORTHAMPTON
PARK CAMPUS
BOUGHTON GREEN ROAD
NORTHAMPTON NN2 7AL
t: 0800 358 2232 f: 01604 722083
e: admissions@northampton.ac.uk
// www.northampton.ac.uk

W5L1 BA Dance/Economics
Duration: 3FT Hon
Entry Requirements: ***GCE:*** 220-260. ***SQAH:*** ABB-BBBC. ***IB:*** 24.
Interview required.

W4L1 BA Drama/Economics
Duration: 3FT Hon
Entry Requirements: ***GCE:*** 220-260. ***SQAH:*** ABB-BBBC. ***IB:*** 24.
Interview required.

L1W5 BA Economics/Dance
Duration: 3FT Hon
Entry Requirements: ***GCE:*** 220-260. ***SQAH:*** ABB-BBBC. ***IB:*** 24.
Interview required.

L1W4 BA Economics/Drama
Duration: 3FT Hon
Entry Requirements: ***GCE:*** 220-260. ***SQAH:*** ABB-BBBC. ***IB:*** 24.
Interview required.

L1X3 BA Economics/Education Studies
Duration: 3FT Hon
Entry Requirements: ***GCE:*** 220-260. ***SQAH:*** ABB-BBBC. ***IB:*** 24.

L1W6 BA Economics/Film & Television Studies
Duration: 3FT Hon
Entry Requirements: ***GCE:*** 220-260. ***SQAH:*** ABB-BBBC. ***IB:*** 24.

L1W1 BA Economics/Fine Art Painting & Drawing
Duration: 3FT Hon
Entry Requirements: ***GCE:*** 220-260. ***SQAH:*** ABB-BBBC. ***IB:*** 24.

L1L4 BA Economics/Health Studies
Duration: 3FT Hon
Entry Requirements: ***GCE:*** 220-260. ***SQAH:*** ABB-BBBC. ***IB:*** 24.

L1V1 BA Economics/History
Duration: 3FT Hon
Entry Requirements: ***GCE:*** 220-260. ***SQAH:*** ABB-BBBC. ***IB:*** 24.

L1B1 BA Economics/Human Bioscience
Duration: 3FT Hon
Entry Requirements: ***GCE:*** 220-260. ***SQAH:*** ABB-BBBC. ***IB:*** 24.

L1P5 BA Economics/Journalism
Duration: 3FT Hon
Entry Requirements: ***GCE:*** 220-260. ***SQAH:*** ABB-BBBC. ***IB:*** 24.

L1PH BA Economics/Media Production
Duration: 3FT Hon
Entry Requirements: ***GCE:*** 220-260. ***SQAH:*** ABB-BBBC. ***IB:*** 24.

L1P3 BA Economics/Media Studies
Duration: 3FT Hon
Entry Requirements: ***GCE:*** 220-260. ***SQAH:*** ABB-BBBC. ***IB:*** 24.

L1V5 BA Economics/Philosophy
Duration: 3FT Hon
Entry Requirements: ***GCE:*** 220-260. ***SQAH:*** ABB-BBBC. ***IB:*** 24.

L1NG BA Economics/Retailing
Duration: 3FT Hon
Entry Requirements: ***GCE:*** 220-260. ***SQAH:*** ABB-BBBC. ***IB:*** 24.

L1C6 BA Economics/Sport Studies
Duration: 3FT Hon
Entry Requirements: ***GCE:*** 220-260. ***SQAH:*** ABB-BBBC. ***IB:*** 24.

L1LX BA Economics/Third World Development
Duration: 3FT Hon
Entry Requirements: ***GCE:*** 220-260. ***SQAH:*** ABB-BBBC. ***IB:*** 24.

L1N8 BA Economics/Tourism
Duration: 3FT Hon
Entry Requirements: ***GCE:*** 220-260. ***SQAH:*** ABB-BBBC. ***IB:*** 24.

X3L1 BA Education Studies/Economics
Duration: 3FT Hon
Entry Requirements: ***GCE:*** 220-260. ***SQAH:*** ABB-BBBC. ***IB:*** 24.

W6L1 BA Film & Television Studies/Economics
Duration: 3FT Hon
Entry Requirements: ***GCE:*** 220-260. ***SQAH:*** ABB-BBBC. ***IB:*** 24.

W1L1 BA Fine Art Painting & Drawing/Economics
Duration: 3FT Hon
Entry Requirements: ***GCE:*** 220-260. ***SQAH:*** ABB-BBBC. ***IB:*** 24.

L4L1 BA Health Studies/Economics
Duration: 3FT Hon
Entry Requirements: ***GCE:*** 220-260. ***SQAH:*** ABB-BBBC. ***IB:*** 24.

V1L1 BA History/Economics
Duration: 3FT Hon
Entry Requirements: ***GCE:*** 220-260. ***SQAH:*** ABB-BBBC. ***IB:*** 24.

P5L1 BA Journalism/Economics
Duration: 3FT Hon
Entry Requirements: ***GCE:*** 220-260. ***SQAH:*** ABB-BBBC. ***IB:*** 24.

P3LC BA Media Production/Economics
Duration: 3FT Hon
Entry Requirements: ***GCE:*** 220-260. ***SQAH:*** ABB-BBBC. ***IB:*** 24.

P3L1 BA Media Studies/Economics
Duration: 3FT Hon
Entry Requirements: ***GCE:*** 220-260. ***SQAH:*** ABB-BBBC. ***IB:*** 24.

V5L1 BA Philosophy/Economics
Duration: 3FT Hon
Entry Requirements: ***GCE:*** 220-260. ***SQAH:*** ABB-BBBC. ***IB:*** 24.

N2LC BA Retailing/Economics
Duration: 3FT Hon
Entry Requirements: ***GCE:*** 220-260. ***SQAH:*** ABB-BBBC. ***IB:*** 24.

C6L1 BA Sport Studies/Economics
Duration: 3FT Hon
Entry Requirements: ***GCE:*** 220-260. ***SQAH:*** ABB-BBBC. ***IB:*** 24.

L9LC BA Third World Development/Economics
Duration: 3FT Hon
Entry Requirements: ***GCE:*** 220-260. ***SQAH:*** ABB-BBBC. ***IB:*** 24.

N8L1 BA Tourism/Economics
Duration: 3FT Hon
Entry Requirements: ***GCE:*** 220-260. ***SQAH:*** ABB-BBBC. ***IB:*** 24.

B1L1 BSc Human Bioscience/Economics
Duration: 3FT Hon
Entry Requirements: ***GCE:*** 220-260. ***SQAH:*** ABB-BBBC. ***IB:*** 24.

N84 THE UNIVERSITY OF NOTTINGHAM
THE ADMISSIONS OFFICE
THE UNIVERSITY OF NOTTINGHAM
UNIVERSITY PARK
NOTTINGHAM NG7 2RD
t: 0115 951 5151 f: 0115 951 4668
// www.nottingham.ac.uk

L160 BA Economics and International Economics
Duration: 3FT Hon
Entry Requirements: ***GCE:*** AAA-AABB. ***SQAAH:*** AAA. ***IB:*** 38.

LV15 BA Economics and Philosophy
Duration: 3FT Hon
Entry Requirements: ***GCE:*** AAA-AABB. ***SQAAH:*** AAA. ***IB:*** 38.

O33 OXFORD UNIVERSITY
UNDERGRADUATE ADMISSIONS OFFICE
UNIVERSITY OF OXFORD
WELLINGTON SQUARE
OXFORD OX1 2JD
t: 01865 288000 f: 01865 270212
e: undergraduate.admissions@admin.ox.ac.uk
// www.admissions.ox.ac.uk

LV11 BA History and Economics
Duration: 3FT Hon
Entry Requirements: ***GCE:*** AAA. ***SQAH:*** AAAAA-AAAAB. ***SQAAH:*** AAB. Interview required. Admissions Test required.

O66 OXFORD BROOKES UNIVERSITY
ADMISSIONS OFFICE
HEADINGTON CAMPUS
GIPSY LANE
OXFORD OX3 0BP
t: 01865 483040 f: 01865 483983
e: admissions@brookes.ac.uk
// www.brookes.ac.uk

LLF1 BA/BSc Economics/International Relations
Duration: 3FT Hon
Entry Requirements: ***GCE:*** BBC.

P60 UNIVERSITY OF PLYMOUTH
DRAKE CIRCUS
PLYMOUTH PL4 8AA
t: 01752 588037 f: 01752 588050
e: admissions@plymouth.ac.uk
// www.plymouth.ac.uk

L1LA BSc Economics with International Relations
Duration: 3FT/4SW Hon
Entry Requirements: ***GCE:*** 240. ***IB:*** 26. ***BTEC NC:*** DD. ***BTEC ND:*** MMM.

L2LD BSc International Relations with Economics
Duration: 3FT Hon
Entry Requirements: ***GCE:*** 240.

Q50 QUEEN MARY, UNIVERSITY OF LONDON
MILE END ROAD
LONDON E1 4NS
t: 020 7882 5555 f: 020 7882 5500
e: admissions@qmul.ac.uk
// www.qmul.ac.uk

FL71 BA Global Change: Environment, Economy & Development
Duration: 3FT Hon
Entry Requirements: ***GCE:*** 300-340. ***IB:*** 32. ***BTEC NC:*** DD. ***BTEC ND:*** DDM.

R12 THE UNIVERSITY OF READING
THE UNIVERSITY OF READING
PO BOX 217
READING RG6 6AH
t: 0118 378 8619 f: 0118 378 8924
e: student.recruitment@reading.ac.uk
// www.reading.ac.uk

LV11 BA History and Economics
Duration: 3FT Hon
Entry Requirements: ***GCE:*** 340-360. ***OCR ND:*** D

LL21 BA International Relations and Economics
Duration: 3FT Hon
Entry Requirements: ***GCE:*** 300-320.

R72 ROYAL HOLLOWAY, UNIVERSITY OF LONDON
ROYAL HOLLOWAY, UNIVERSITY OF LONDON
EGHAM
SURREY TW20 0EX
t: 01784 434455 f: 01784 473662
e: Admissions@rhul.ac.uk
// www.rhul.ac.uk

L1W3 BA Economics with Music
Duration: 3FT Hon
Entry Requirements: ***GCE:*** AAA-ABB. ***SQAH:*** AAAAA-AABBB. ***SQAAH:*** AAA-ABB. ***IB:*** 32. ***BTEC NC:*** DM. ***BTEC ND:*** DDM.

L1L2 BA Economics with Political Studies
Duration: 3FT Hon
Entry Requirements: ***GCE:*** AAA-ABB. ***SQAH:*** AAAAA-AABBB. ***SQAAH:*** AAA-ABB. ***IB:*** 32. ***BTEC NC:*** DM. ***BTEC ND:*** DDM.

S09 SCHOOL OF ORIENTAL AND AFRICAN STUDIES (UNIVERSITY OF LONDON)

THORNHAUGH STREET
RUSSELL SQUARE
LONDON WC1H 0XG
t: 020 7074 5106 f: 020 7898 4039
e: undergradadmissions@soas.ac.uk
// www.soas.ac.uk

LL91 BA Economics and Development Studies
Duration: 3FT Hon
Entry Requirements: Contact the institution for details.

LV11 BA History and Economics
Duration: 3FT Hon
Entry Requirements: Contact the institution for details.

LV16 BA Study of Religions and Economics
Duration: 3FT Hon
Entry Requirements: Contact the institution for details.

S18 THE UNIVERSITY OF SHEFFIELD

9 NORTHUMBERLAND ROAD
SHEFFIELD S10 2TT
t: 0114 222 1299 f: 0114 222 8032
e: ask@sheffield.ac.uk
// www.sheffield.ac.uk

LV15 BA Economics and Philosophy
Duration: 3FT Hon
Entry Requirements: ***GCE:*** ABB. ***SQAH:*** AAAB. ***SQAAH:*** ABB. ***IB:*** 33. ***BTEC ND:*** DDM.

S27 UNIVERSITY OF SOUTHAMPTON

HIGHFIELD
SOUTHAMPTON SO17 1BJ
t: 023 8059 4732 f: 023 8059 3037
e: admissions@soton.ac.uk
// www.southampton.ac.uk

VL51 BA Economics and Philosophy
Duration: 3FT Hon
Entry Requirements: ***GCE:*** AAB. ***IB:*** 34.

S36 UNIVERSITY OF ST ANDREWS

ST KATHARINE'S WEST
16 THE SCORES
ST ANDREWS
FIFE KY16 9AX
t: 01334 462150 f: 01334 463330
e: admissions@st-andrews.ac.uk
// www.st-and.ac.uk

LF16 BSc Economics-Environmental Geoscience
Duration: 4FT Hon
Entry Requirements: ***GCE:*** AAA. ***SQAH:*** AAAA. ***IB:*** 38.

FL61 BSc Economics-Geoscience
Duration: 4FT Hon
Entry Requirements: ***GCE:*** AAA. ***SQAH:*** AAAA. ***IB:*** 38.

LC18 BSc Economics-Psychology
Duration: 4FT Hon
Entry Requirements: ***GCE:*** AAA. ***SQAH:*** AAAA. ***IB:*** 38.

LVD1 MA Ancient History-Economics
Duration: 4FT Hon
Entry Requirements: ***GCE:*** AAA. ***SQAH:*** AAAA. ***IB:*** 38.

LV16 MA Biblical Studies-Economics
Duration: 4FT Hon
Entry Requirements: ***GCE:*** AAA. ***SQAH:*** AAAA. ***IB:*** 38.

LP13 MA Economics-Film Studies
Duration: 4FT Hon
Entry Requirements: ***GCE:*** AAA. ***SQAH:*** AAAA. ***IB:*** 38.

LL12 MA Economics-International Relations
Duration: 4FT Hon
Entry Requirements: ***GCE:*** AAA. ***SQAH:*** AAAA. ***IB:*** 38.

LVC1 MA Economics-Mediaeval History
Duration: 4FT Hon
Entry Requirements: ***GCE:*** AAA. ***SQAH:*** AAAA. ***IB:*** 38.

LV11 MA Economics-Modern History
Duration: 4FT Hon
Entry Requirements: ***GCE:*** AAA. ***SQAH:*** AAAA. ***IB:*** 38.

LV15 MA Economics-Philosophy
Duration: 4FT Hon
Entry Requirements: ***GCE:*** AAA. ***SQAH:*** AAAA. ***IB:*** 38.

CL81 MA Economics-Psychology
Duration: 4FT Hon
Entry Requirements: ***GCE:*** AAA. ***SQAH:*** AAAA. ***IB:*** 38.

LG11 MSci Applied Quantitative Finance
Duration: 4FT Hon
Entry Requirements: ***GCE:*** AAA. ***SQAH:*** AAAA. ***SQAAH:*** AA. ***IB:*** 38.

S72 STAFFORDSHIRE UNIVERSITY

COLLEGE ROAD
STOKE ON TRENT ST4 2DE
t: 01782 292753 f: 01782 292740
e: admissions@staffs.ac.uk
// www.staffs.ac.uk

LV11 BA Economics and Modern History
Duration: 3FT Hon
Entry Requirements: ***GCE:*** BCC-BB. ***IB:*** 24.

LV15 BA Economics and Philosophy
Duration: 3FT Hon
Entry Requirements: ***GCE:*** BCC-BB. ***IB:*** 24.

LL31 BA Ethics and Economics
Duration: 3FT Hon
Entry Requirements: ***GCE:*** 160-200. ***IB:*** 24.

S75 THE UNIVERSITY OF STIRLING
STIRLING FK9 4LA
t: 01786 467044 f: 01786 466800
e: admissions@stir.ac.uk
// www.stir.ac.uk

LP13 BA Economics and Film & Media
Duration: 4FT Hon
Entry Requirements: ***GCE:*** BCC. ***SQAH:*** BBBB. ***SQAAH:*** AAA-CCC. ***IB:*** 30. ***BTEC ND:*** DMM.

LV11 BA Economics and History
Duration: 4FT Hon
Entry Requirements: ***GCE:*** BCC. ***SQAH:*** BBBB. ***SQAAH:*** AAA-CCC. ***IB:*** 28. ***BTEC ND:*** MMM.

LV15 BA Economics and Philosophy
Duration: 4FT Hon
Entry Requirements: ***GCE:*** CCC. ***SQAH:*** BBBB. ***SQAAH:*** AAA-CCC. ***IB:*** 30. ***BTEC ND:*** MMM.

LC18 BA Economics and Psychology
Duration: 4FT Hon
Entry Requirements: ***GCE:*** CCC. ***SQAH:*** BBBB. ***SQAAH:*** AAA-CCC. ***IB:*** 30. ***BTEC ND:*** MMM.

LC16 BA Economics and Sports Studies
Duration: 4FT Hon
Entry Requirements: ***GCE:*** BCC. ***SQAH:*** BBBB. ***SQAAH:*** AAA-CCC. ***IB:*** 30. ***BTEC ND:*** DMM.

S78 THE UNIVERSITY OF STRATHCLYDE
GLASGOW G1 1XQ
t: 0141 552 4400 f: 0141 552 0775
// www.strath.ac.uk

LV11 BA Economics and History
Duration: 4FT Hon
Entry Requirements: ***GCE:*** ABB. ***SQAH:*** ABBB-BBBBC. ***IB:*** 34.

LN18 BA Economics and Hospitality & Tourism
Duration: 4FT Hon
Entry Requirements: ***GCE:*** ABB. ***SQAH:*** AABB-ABBBC. ***IB:*** 34.

LP15 BA Economics and Journalism & Creative Writing
Duration: 4FT Hon
Entry Requirements: ***GCE:*** AAB. ***SQAH:*** AABB-BBBBB. ***IB:*** 36. Portfolio required.

LC18 BA Economics and Psychology
Duration: 4FT Hon
Entry Requirements: ***GCE:*** ABB. ***SQAH:*** AABB-ABBBC. ***IB:*** 34.

LC1V BA Economics and Psychology
Duration: 4FT Hon
Entry Requirements: ***GCE:*** ABB. ***SQAH:*** ABBB-BBBBC. ***IB:*** 34.

S90 UNIVERSITY OF SUSSEX
UNDERGRADUATE ADMISSIONS
SUSSEX HOUSE
UNIVERSITY OF SUSSEX
BRIGHTON BN1 9RH
t: 01273 678416 f: 01273 678545
e: ug.applicants@sussex.ac.uk
// www.sussex.ac.uk

LL19 BA Economics and International Development
Duration: 3FT Hon
Entry Requirements: ***GCE:*** ABB-BBB. ***SQAH:*** AABBB-ABBBB.

LLC2 BA Economics and International Relations
Duration: 3FT Hon
Entry Requirements: ***GCE:*** ABB-BBB. ***SQAH:*** AABBB-ABBBB.

S93 SWANSEA UNIVERSITY
SINGLETON PARK
SWANSEA SA2 8PP
t: 01792 295111 f: 01792 295110
e: admissions@swansea.ac.uk
// www.swansea.ac.uk

LV13 BA Economic History and Economics
Duration: 3FT Hon
Entry Requirements: ***GCE:*** ABB. ***IB:*** 33. ***BTEC ND:*** DDM.

LV1C BA Economics and History (with a year abroad)
Duration: 4FT Hon
Entry Requirements: ***GCE:*** ABB. ***IB:*** 33. ***BTEC ND:*** DDM.

LV11 BA History and Economics
Duration: 3FT Hon
Entry Requirements: ***GCE:*** ABB. ***IB:*** 33. ***BTEC ND:*** DDM.

LC18 BSc Economics and Psychology
Duration: 3FT Hon
Entry Requirements: ***GCE:*** AAB. ***IB:*** 34.

U20 UNIVERSITY OF ULSTER

COLERAINE
CO. LONDONDERRY
NORTHERN IRELAND BT52 1SA
t: 028 7032 4221 f: 028 7032 4908
e: online@ulster.ac.uk
// www.ulster.ac.uk

W4L1 BA Drama with Economic Studies

Duration: 3FT Hon

Entry Requirements: ***GCE:*** 240. ***IB:*** 24. ***BTEC NC:*** MM. ***BTEC ND:*** MMM.

V2L1 BA Irish History with Economic Studies

Duration: 4SW Hon

Entry Requirements: ***GCE:*** 240. ***IB:*** 24. ***BTEC NC:*** MM. ***BTEC ND:*** MMM.

U80 UNIVERSITY COLLEGE LONDON (UNIVERSITY OF LONDON)

GOWER STREET
LONDON WC1E 6BT
t: 020 7679 3000 f: 020 7679 3001
// www.ucl.ac.uk

VL51 BA Philosophy and Economics

Duration: 3FT Hon

Entry Requirements: ***GCE:*** AAAe. ***SQAAH:*** AAA. ***IB:*** 38. Interview required.

W20 THE UNIVERSITY OF WARWICK

COVENTRY CV4 8UW
t: 024 7652 3723 f: 024 7652 4649
e: ugadmissions@warwick.ac.uk
// www.warwick.ac.uk

LV13 BSc Economics and Economic History

Duration: 3FT Hon

Entry Requirements: ***GCE:*** A*AAb -AAAb. ***SQAAH:*** AA. ***IB:*** 38.

W50 UNIVERSITY OF WESTMINSTER

101 NEW CAVENDISH STREET
LONDON W1W 6XH
t: 020 7915 5511 f: 020 7911 5788
e: course-enquiries@westminster.ac.uk
// www.westminster.ac.uk

LL12 BA Development Studies and International Relations

Duration: 3FT Hon

Entry Requirements: Contact the institution for details.

LV12 BA Development and History

Duration: 3FT Hon

Entry Requirements: Contact the institution for details.

Y50 THE UNIVERSITY OF YORK

ADMISSIONS AND UK/EU STUDENT RECRUITMENT
UNIVERSITY OF YORK
HESLINGTON
YORK YO10 5DD
t: 01904 433533 f: 01904 433538
e: admissions@york.ac.uk
// www.york.ac.uk

LV13 BA Economics/Economic History (Equal)

Duration: 3FT Hon

Entry Requirements: ***GCE:*** AAB. ***SQAH:*** AAAAB. ***SQAAH:*** AB. ***IB:*** 34. ***BTEC ND:*** DDD.

LV15 BA Economics/Philosophy (Equal)

Duration: 3FT Hon

Entry Requirements: ***GCE:*** AAB. ***SQAH:*** AAAAB. ***SQAAH:*** AB. ***IB:*** 34. ***BTEC ND:*** DDD.

V1L1 BA History/Economics

Duration: 3FT Hon

Entry Requirements: ***GCE:*** AAA. ***SQAH:*** AAAAA. ***SQAAH:*** AA. ***IB:*** 36. ***BTEC ND:*** DDD.

FINANCE AND OTHER COMBINATIONS

A20 THE UNIVERSITY OF ABERDEEN

UNIVERSITY OFFICE
KING'S COLLEGE
ABERDEEN AB24 3FX
t: +44 (0) 1224 273504 f: +44 (0) 1224 272034
e: sras@abdn.ac.uk
// www.abdn.ac.uk/sras

NV36 MA Divinity and Finance

Duration: 4FT Hon

Entry Requirements: ***GCE:*** BBB. ***SQAH:*** BBBB. ***IB:*** 30. ***BTEC ND:*** MMM.

NN23 MA Entrepreneurship and Finance

Duration: 4FT Hon

Entry Requirements: ***GCE:*** BBB. ***SQAH:*** BBBB. ***IB:*** 30. ***BTEC ND:*** MMM.

NV31 MA Finance and History

Duration: 4FT Hon

Entry Requirements: ***GCE:*** BBB. ***SQAH:*** BBBB. ***IB:*** 30. ***BTEC ND:*** MMM.

NVH3 MA Finance and History of Art

Duration: 4FT Hon

Entry Requirements: ***GCE:*** BBB. ***SQAH:*** BBBB. ***IB:*** 30. ***BTEC ND:*** MMM.

NLH2 MA Finance and International Relations

Duration: 4FT Hon

Entry Requirements: ***GCE:*** BBB. ***SQAH:*** BBBB. ***IB:*** 30. ***BTEC ND:*** MMM.

NV35 MA Finance and Philosophy

Duration: 4FT Hon

Entry Requirements: ***GCE:*** BBB. ***SQAH:*** BBBB. ***IB:*** 30. ***BTEC ND:*** MMM.

NK32 MA Finance and Property

Duration: 4FT Hon

Entry Requirements: ***GCE:*** BBB. ***SQAH:*** BBBB. ***IB:*** 30. ***BTEC ND:*** MMM.

B72 UNIVERSITY OF BRIGHTON

MITHRAS HOUSE
LEWES ROAD
BRIGHTON BN2 4AT
t: 01273 644644 f: 01273 642607
e: admissions@brighton.ac.uk
// www.brighton.ac.uk

N390 BSc Finance and Investment

Duration: 3FT/4SW Hon

Entry Requirements: ***GCE:*** BBC. ***IB:*** 30. ***BTEC ND:*** DMM.

C60 CITY UNIVERSITY

NORTHAMPTON SQUARE
LONDON EC1V 0HB
t: 020 7040 5060 f: 020 7040 8995
e: ugadmissions@city.ac.uk
// www.city.ac.uk

N392 BSc Investment Analysis and Insurance (3 years or 4 year SW)

Duration: 3FT/4SW Hon

Entry Requirements: ***GCE:*** AAB. ***SQAH:*** AAA-BB. ***IB:*** 35. ***BTEC ND:*** DDM.

G42 GLASGOW CALEDONIAN UNIVERSITY

CITY CAMPUS
COWCADDENS ROAD
GLASGOW G4 0BA
t: 0141 331 3000 f: 0141 331 3449
e: admissions@gcu.ac.uk
// www.gcu.ac.uk

N390 BA Finance, Investment & Risk

Duration: 4FT Hon

Entry Requirements: ***GCE:*** CCC. ***SQAH:*** BBCC. ***IB:*** 24.

H36 UNIVERSITY OF HERTFORDSHIRE

UNIVERSITY ADMISSIONS SERVICE
COLLEGE LANE
HATFIELD
HERTS AL10 9AB
t: 01707 284800 f: 01707 284870
// www.herts.ac.uk

N6N3 BA Human Resources with Finance

Duration: 3FT/4SW Hon

Entry Requirements: ***GCE:*** 260.

N8NH BA Tourism with Finance

Duration: 3FT/4SW Hon

Entry Requirements: ***GCE:*** 260.

H60 THE UNIVERSITY OF HUDDERSFIELD

QUEENSGATE
HUDDERSFIELD HD1 3DH
t: 01484 473969 f: 01484 472765
e: admissionsandrecords@hud.ac.uk
// www.hud.ac.uk

NN31 BA Financial Services

Duration: 3FT/4SW Hon

Entry Requirements: ***GCE:*** 240. ***SQAH:*** BBBB. ***IB:*** 26.

K12 KEELE UNIVERSITY

STAFFS ST5 5BG
t: 01782 734005 f: 01782 632343
e: undergraduate@keele.ac.uk
// www.keele.ac.uk

NX33 BA Educational Studies and Finance

Duration: 3FT Hon

Entry Requirements: ***GCE:*** 320.

NV31 BA Finance and History

Duration: 3FT Hon

Entry Requirements: ***GCE:*** 320.

PN33 BA Finance and Media, Communications & Culture

Duration: 3FT Hon

Entry Requirements: ***GCE:*** 280-340.

NW33 BA Finance and Music

Duration: 3FT Hon

Entry Requirements: ***GCE:*** 260-320.

NWH3 BA Finance and Music Technology

Duration: 3FT Hon

Entry Requirements: ***GCE:*** 280-300.

NV35 BA Finance and Philosophy

Duration: 3FT Hon

Entry Requirements: ***GCE:*** 300-320.

GN73 BSc Smart Systems and Finance
Duration: 3FT Hon
Entry Requirements: ***GCE:*** 300.

L27 LEEDS METROPOLITAN UNIVERSITY
COURSE ENQUIRIES OFFICE
CIVIC QUARTER
LEEDS LS1 3HE
t: 0113 81 23113 f: 0113 81 23129
e: https://experience.leedsmet.ac.uk/leeds/index.do
// www.leedsmet.ac.uk

NN8H BA Event Fundraising & Sponsorship
Duration: 3FT Ord
Entry Requirements: HND required.

L41 THE UNIVERSITY OF LIVERPOOL
THE FOUNDATION BUILDING
BROWNLOW HILL
LIVERPOOL L69 7ZX
t: 0151 794 2000 f: 0151 708 6502
e: ugrecruitment@liv.ac.uk
// www.liv.ac.uk

WN23 BA Communication, Media and Popular Music
Duration: 3FT Hon
Entry Requirements: ***GCE:*** ABB. ***SQAH:*** AABBB. ***SQAAH:*** ABB. ***IB:*** 33.

N38 UNIVERSITY OF NORTHAMPTON
PARK CAMPUS
BOUGHTON GREEN ROAD
NORTHAMPTON NN2 7AL
t: 0800 358 2232 f: 01604 722083
e: admissions@northampton.ac.uk
// www.northampton.ac.uk

JN93 BSc International Logistics & Trade Finance (top-up)
Duration: 1FT Hon
Entry Requirements: HND required.

N91 NOTTINGHAM TRENT UNIVERSITY
DRYDEN CENTRE
BURTON STREET
NOTTINGHAM NG1 4BU
t: +44 (0) 115 848 4200 f: +44 (0) 115 848 8869
e: ask.ntu@ntu.ac.uk
// www.ntu.ac.uk/

NN23 BSc Property Investment and Finance
Duration: 3FT/4SW Hon
Entry Requirements: ***GCE:*** 280. ***IB:*** 25. ***BTEC ND:*** DMM.

S30 SOUTHAMPTON SOLENT UNIVERSITY
EAST PARK TERRACE
SOUTHAMPTON
HAMPSHIRE SO14 0RT
t: +44 (0) 23 8031 9039 f: + 44 (0)23 8022 2259
e: admissions@solent.ac.uk or ask@solent.ac.uk
// www.solent.ac.uk/

N3NC BA Finance with Entrepreneurship
Duration: 3FT Hon
Entry Requirements: ***GCE:*** 200.

N3N1 BA Finance with Entrepreneurship (with foundation)
Duration: 4FT Hon
Entry Requirements: ***GCE:*** 80.

S75 THE UNIVERSITY OF STIRLING
STIRLING FK9 4LA
t: 01786 467044 f: 01786 466800
e: admissions@stir.ac.uk
// www.stir.ac.uk

NC36 BA Finance and Sports Studies
Duration: 4FT Hon
Entry Requirements: ***GCE:*** BCC. ***SQAH:*** BBBB. ***SQAAH:*** AAA-CCC. ***IB:*** 30. ***BTEC ND:*** DMM.

S78 THE UNIVERSITY OF STRATHCLYDE
GLASGOW G1 1XQ
t: 0141 552 4400 f: 0141 552 0775
// www.strath.ac.uk

NN38 BA Finance and Hospitality & Tourism
Duration: 4FT Hon
Entry Requirements: ***GCE:*** ABB. ***SQAH:*** AABB-ABBBC. ***IB:*** 34.

S93 SWANSEA UNIVERSITY
SINGLETON PARK
SWANSEA SA2 8PP
t: 01792 295111 f: 01792 295110
e: admissions@swansea.ac.uk
// www.swansea.ac.uk

G3N3 BSc Actuarial Studies
Duration: 3FT Hon
Entry Requirements: ***GCE:*** ABB. ***BTEC ND:*** DDM.

G3NH BSc Actuarial Studies (with a year abroad) (4 years)
Duration: 4FT Hon
Entry Requirements: ***GCE:*** ABB. ***BTEC ND:*** DDM.

ACCOUNTANCY AND OTHER COMBINATIONS

A20 THE UNIVERSITY OF ABERDEEN

UNIVERSITY OFFICE
KING'S COLLEGE
ABERDEEN AB24 3FX
t: +44 (0) 1224 273504 f: +44 (0) 1224 272034
e: sras@abdn.ac.uk
// www.abdn.ac.uk/sras

NV46 MA Accountancy and Divinity
Duration: 4FT Hon
Entry Requirements: ***GCE:*** BBB. ***SQAH:*** BBBB. ***IB:*** 30. ***BTEC ND:*** MMM.

NN42 MA Accountancy and Entrepreneurship
Duration: 4FT Hon
Entry Requirements: ***GCE:*** BBB. ***SQAH:*** BBBB. ***IB:*** 30. ***BTEC ND:*** MMM.

NV45 MA Accountancy and Philosophy
Duration: 4FT Hon
Entry Requirements: ***GCE:*** BBB. ***SQAH:*** BBBB. ***IB:*** 30. ***BTEC ND:*** MMM.

NK42 MA Accountancy and Property
Duration: 4FT Hon
Entry Requirements: ***GCE:*** BBB. ***SQAH:*** BBBB. ***IB:*** 30. ***BTEC ND:*** MMM.

B90 THE UNIVERSITY OF BUCKINGHAM

YEOMANRY HOUSE
HUNTER STREET
BUCKINGHAM MK18 1EG
t: 01280 820313 f: 01280 822245
e: info@buckingham.ac.uk
// www.buckingham.ac.uk

N4P9 BSc Accounting with Communication Studies (EFL)
Duration: 2FT Hon
Entry Requirements: ***GCE:*** 240. ***IB:*** 26. ***BTEC NC:*** DD. ***BTEC ND:*** MMM.

D39 UNIVERSITY OF DERBY

KEDLESTON ROAD
DERBY DE22 1GB
t: 08701 202330 f: 01332 597724
e: askadmissions@derby.ac.uk
// www.derby.ac.uk

NK41 BA Accounting and Architectural Design
Duration: 3FT Hon
Entry Requirements: ***Foundation:*** Merit. ***GCE:*** 180-240. ***IB:*** 26. ***BTEC NC:*** DM. ***BTEC ND:*** MMP.

NW42 BA Accounting and Art & Design
Duration: 3FT Hon
Entry Requirements: ***Foundation:*** Merit. ***GCE:*** 180-240. ***IB:*** 26. ***BTEC NC:*** DM. ***BTEC ND:*** MMP. Interview required. Portfolio required.

NW48 BA Accounting and Creative Writing
Duration: 3FT Hon
Entry Requirements: ***Foundation:*** Merit. ***GCE:*** 180-240. ***IB:*** 26. ***BTEC NC:*** DM. ***BTEC ND:*** MMP.

NW45 BA Accounting and Dance & Movement Studies
Duration: 3FT Hon
Entry Requirements: ***Foundation:*** Merit. ***GCE:*** 180-240. ***IB:*** 26. ***BTEC NC:*** DM. ***BTEC ND:*** MMP.

NX43 BA Accounting and Education Studies
Duration: 3FT Hon
Entry Requirements: ***Foundation:*** Merit. ***GCE:*** 180-240. ***IB:*** 26. ***BTEC NC:*** DM. ***BTEC ND:*** MMP.

NP43 BA Accounting and Film & Television Studies
Duration: 3FT Hon
Entry Requirements: ***Foundation:*** Merit. ***GCE:*** 180-240. ***IB:*** 26. ***BTEC NC:*** DM. ***BTEC ND:*** MMP.

NW4V BA Accounting and Media Writing
Duration: 3FT Hon
Entry Requirements: ***Foundation:*** Merit. ***GCE:*** 180-240. ***IB:*** 26. ***BTEC NC:*** DM. ***BTEC ND:*** MMP.

NP4H BA Accounting and Popular Culture & Media
Duration: 3FT Hon
Entry Requirements: ***Foundation:*** Merit. ***GCE:*** 180-240. ***IB:*** 26. ***BTEC NC:*** DM. ***BTEC ND:*** MMP.

NW43 BA Accounting and Popular Music Production
Duration: 3FT Hon
Entry Requirements: ***Foundation:*** Merit. ***GCE:*** 180-240. ***IB:*** 26. ***BTEC NC:*** DM. ***BTEC ND:*** MMP.

NC48 BA/BSc Accounting and Psychology
Duration: 3FT Hon
Entry Requirements: ***Foundation:*** Merit. ***GCE:*** 180-240. ***IB:*** 26. ***BTEC NC:*** DM. ***BTEC ND:*** MMP.

E28 UNIVERSITY OF EAST LONDON

DOCKLANDS CAMPUS
UNIVERSITY WAY
LONDON E16 2RD
t: 020 8223 3333 f: 020 8223 2978
e: study@uel.ac.uk
// www.uel.ac.uk

NL49 BA Accounting/Third World Development

Duration: 3FT Hon

Entry Requirements: ***GCE:*** 200. ***IB:*** 24. ***BTEC NC:*** DM. ***BTEC ND:*** MMP. ***OCR ND:*** M1 ***OCR NED:*** P1

LN94 BA Third World Development/Accounting

Duration: 3FT Hon

Entry Requirements: ***GCE:*** 200. ***IB:*** 24. ***BTEC NC:*** DM. ***BTEC ND:*** MMP. ***OCR ND:*** M1 ***OCR NED:*** P1

N4L9 BSc Accounting with Third World Development

Duration: 3FT Hon

Entry Requirements: ***GCE:*** 200. ***IB:*** 24. ***BTEC NC:*** DM. ***BTEC ND:*** MMP. ***OCR ND:*** M1 ***OCR NED:*** P1

C6N4 BSc Sports & Exercise Science with Accounting

Duration: 3FT Hon

Entry Requirements: ***GCE:*** 200. ***IB:*** 24. ***BTEC NC:*** DM. ***BTEC ND:*** MMP. ***OCR ND:*** M1 ***OCR NED:*** P1

E59 EDINBURGH NAPIER UNIVERSITY

CRAIGLOCKHART CAMPUS
EDINBURGH EH14 1DJ
t: +44 (0)8452 60 60 40 f: 0131 455 6464
e: info@napier.ac.uk
// www.napier.ac.uk

N4N2 BA Accounting with Entrepreneurship

Duration: 3FT/4FT Ord/Hon

Entry Requirements: ***GCE:*** 230.

E84 UNIVERSITY OF EXETER

LAVER BUILDING
NORTH PARK ROAD
EXETER
DEVON EX4 4QE
t: 01392 263855 f: 01392 263857/262479
e: admissions@exeter.ac.uk
// www.exeter.ac.uk/admissions

N4N2 BA Accounting with Leadership

Duration: 3FT Hon

Entry Requirements: ***GCE:*** AAA-AAB. ***SQAH:*** AAAAB-AAABB. ***SQAAH:*** AAB-ABB. ***BTEC ND:*** DDD.

N4NF BA Accounting with Leadership with European Study (4 years)

Duration: 4FT Hon

Entry Requirements: ***GCE:*** AAA-AAB. ***SQAH:*** AAAAB-AAABB. ***SQAAH:*** AAB-ABB. ***BTEC ND:*** DDD.

N4X9 BA Accounting with Leadership with Industrial Experience (4 years)

Duration: 4FT Hon

Entry Requirements: ***GCE:*** AAA-AAB. ***SQAH:*** AAAAB-AAABB. ***SQAAH:*** AAB-ABB. ***BTEC ND:*** DDD.

N4NG BA Accounting with Leadership with International Study (4 years)

Duration: 4FT Hon

Entry Requirements: ***GCE:*** AAA-AAB. ***SQAH:*** AAAAB-AAABB. ***SQAAH:*** AAB-ABB. ***BTEC ND:*** DDD.

H36 UNIVERSITY OF HERTFORDSHIRE

UNIVERSITY ADMISSIONS SERVICE
COLLEGE LANE
HATFIELD
HERTS AL10 9AB
t: 01707 284800 f: 01707 284870
// www.herts.ac.uk

NN46 BA Accounting/Human Resources

Duration: 3FT/4SW Hon

Entry Requirements: ***GCE:*** 260.

NN48 BA Accounting/Tourism

Duration: 3FT/4SW Hon

Entry Requirements: ***GCE:*** 260. ***IB:*** 24.

H72 THE UNIVERSITY OF HULL

THE UNIVERSITY OF HULL
COTTINGHAM ROAD
HULL HU6 7RX
t: 01482 466100 f: 01482 442290
e: admissions@hull.ac.uk
// www.hull.ac.uk

NJ49 BSc Accounting and Logistics

Duration: 3FT Hon

Entry Requirements: ***GCE:*** 280. ***IB:*** 28.

NJ4X BSc Accounting and Logistics (International) (4 years)

Duration: 4FT Hon

Entry Requirements: ***GCE:*** 280. ***IB:*** 28.

NJK9 BSc Accounting and Logistics (with Professional Experience) (4 years)

Duration: 4FT Hon

Entry Requirements: ***GCE:*** 280. ***IB:*** 28.

K12 KEELE UNIVERSITY
STAFFS ST5 5BG
t: 01782 734005 f: 01782 632343
e: undergraduate@keele.ac.uk
// www.keele.ac.uk

NP43 BA Accounting and Film Studies
Duration: 3FT Hon
Entry Requirements: ***GCE:*** 300-320.

NV41 BA Accounting and History
Duration: 3FT Hon
Entry Requirements: ***GCE:*** 320.

NL42 BA Accounting and International Relations
Duration: 3FT Hon
Entry Requirements: ***GCE:*** 320-340.

NW43 BA Accounting and Music
Duration: 3FT Hon
Entry Requirements: ***GCE:*** 260-320.

NJ49 BA Accounting and Music Technology
Duration: 3FT Hon
Entry Requirements: ***GCE:*** 280-320.

NV45 BA Accounting and Philosophy
Duration: 3FT Hon
Entry Requirements: ***GCE:*** 320-340.

NC48 BSc Accounting and Applied Psychology
Duration: 4FT Hon
Entry Requirements: ***GCE:*** 300-320.

NC4V BSc Accounting and Psychology
Duration: 3FT Hon
Entry Requirements: ***GCE:*** 320-340.

N38 UNIVERSITY OF NORTHAMPTON
PARK CAMPUS
BOUGHTON GREEN ROAD
NORTHAMPTON NN2 7AL
t: 0800 358 2232 f: 01604 722083
e: admissions@northampton.ac.uk
// www.northampton.ac.uk

N4D4 BA Accounting with Equine Studies
Duration: 3FT Hon
Entry Requirements: ***GCE:*** 220-260. ***SQAH:*** ABB-BBBC. ***IB:*** 24.

N4W8 BA Accounting/Creative Writing
Duration: 3FT Hon
Entry Requirements: ***GCE:*** 220-260. ***SQAH:*** ABB-BBBC. ***IB:*** 24.

N4WK BA Accounting/Drama
Duration: 3FT Hon
Entry Requirements: ***GCE:*** 220-260. ***SQAH:*** ABB-BBBC. ***IB:*** 24.
Interview required.

N4X3 BA Accounting/Education Studies
Duration: 3FT Hon
Entry Requirements: ***GCE:*** 220-260. ***SQAH:*** ABB-BBBC. ***IB:*** 24.

N4W6 BA Accounting/Film & Television Studies
Duration: 3FT Hon
Entry Requirements: ***GCE:*** 220-260. ***SQAH:*** ABB-BBBC. ***IB:*** 24.

N4L4 BA Accounting/Health Studies
Duration: 3FT Hon
Entry Requirements: ***GCE:*** 220-260. ***SQAH:*** ABB-BBBC. ***IB:*** 24.

N4P3 BA Accounting/Media Production
Duration: 3FT Hon
Entry Requirements: ***GCE:*** 220-260. ***SQAH:*** ABB-BBBC. ***IB:*** 24.

N4V5 BA Accounting/Philosophy
Duration: 3FT Hon
Entry Requirements: ***GCE:*** 220-260. ***SQAH:*** ABB-BBBC. ***IB:*** 24.

N4W3 BA Accounting/Popular Music
Duration: 3FT Hon
Entry Requirements: ***GCE:*** 220-260. ***SQAH:*** ABB-BBBC. ***IB:*** 24.

N4C8 BA Accounting/Psychology
Duration: 3FT Hon
Entry Requirements: ***GCE:*** 220-260. ***SQAH:*** ABB-BBBC. ***IB:*** 24.

N4NF BA Accounting/Retailing
Duration: 3FT Hon
Entry Requirements: ***GCE:*** 220-260. ***SQAH:*** ABB-BBBC. ***IB:*** 24.

N4C6 BA Accounting/Sport Studies
Duration: 3FT Hon
Entry Requirements: ***GCE:*** 220-260. ***SQAH:*** ABB-BBBC. ***IB:*** 24.

N4LX BA Accounting/Third World Development
Duration: 3FT Hon
Entry Requirements: ***GCE:*** 220-260. ***SQAH:*** ABB-BBBC. ***IB:*** 24.

N4N8 BA Accounting/Tourism
Duration: 3FT Hon
Entry Requirements: ***GCE:*** 220-260. ***SQAH:*** ABB-BBBC. ***IB:*** 24.

N4GK BA Accounting/Web Design
Duration: 3FT Hon
Entry Requirements: ***GCE:*** 220-260. ***SQAH:*** ABB-BBBC. ***IB:*** 24.

W8N4 BA Creative Writing/Accounting
Duration: 3FT Hon
Entry Requirements: ***GCE:*** 220-260. ***SQAH:*** ABB-BBBC. ***IB:*** 24.

W4N4 BA Drama/Accounting
Duration: 3FT Hon
Entry Requirements: ***GCE:*** 220-260. ***SQAH:*** ABB-BBBC. ***IB:*** 24.
Interview required.

X3N4 BA Education Studies/Accounting
Duration: 3FT Hon
Entry Requirements: ***GCE:*** 220-260. ***SQAH:*** ABB-BBBC. ***IB:*** 24.

W6N4 BA Film & Television Studies/Accounting
Duration: 3FT Hon
Entry Requirements: ***GCE:*** 220-260. ***SQAH:*** ABB-BBBC. ***IB:*** 24.

L4N4 BA Health Studies/Accounting
Duration: 3FT Hon
Entry Requirements: ***GCE:*** 220-260. ***SQAH:*** ABB-BBBC. ***IB:*** 24.

P3NK BA Media Production/Accounting
Duration: 3FT Hon
Entry Requirements: ***GCE:*** 220-260. ***SQAH:*** ABB-BBBC. ***IB:*** 24.

V5N4 BA Philosophy/Accounting
Duration: 3FT Hon
Entry Requirements: ***GCE:*** 220-260. ***SQAH:*** ABB-BBBC. ***IB:*** 24.

W3N4 BA Popular Music/Accounting
Duration: 3FT Hon
Entry Requirements: ***GCE:*** 220-260. ***SQAH:*** ABB-BBBC. ***IB:*** 24.

C8N4 BA Psychology/Accounting
Duration: 3FT Hon
Entry Requirements: ***GCE:*** 220-260. ***SQAH:*** ABB-BBBC. ***IB:*** 24.

N2NK BA Retailing/Accounting
Duration: 3FT Hon
Entry Requirements: ***GCE:*** 220-260. ***SQAH:*** ABB-BBBC. ***IB:*** 24.

C6N4 BA Sport Studies/Accounting
Duration: 3FT Hon
Entry Requirements: ***GCE:*** 220-260. ***SQAH:*** ABB-BBBC. ***IB:*** 24.

L9NK BA Third World Development/Accounting
Duration: 3FT Hon
Entry Requirements: ***GCE:*** 220-260. ***SQAH:*** ABB-BBBC. ***IB:*** 24.

N8N4 BA Tourism/Accounting
Duration: 3FT Hon
Entry Requirements: ***GCE:*** 220-260. ***SQAH:*** ABB-BBBC. ***IB:*** 24.

G4NK BSc Web Design/Accounting
Duration: 3FT Hon
Entry Requirements: ***GCE:*** 220-260. ***SQAH:*** ABB-BBBC. ***IB:*** 24.

S75 THE UNIVERSITY OF STIRLING
STIRLING FK9 4LA
t: 01786 467044 f: 01786 466800
e: admissions@stir.ac.uk
// www.stir.ac.uk

NC46 BAcc Accountancy and Sports Studies
Duration: 4FT Hon
Entry Requirements: ***GCE:*** BCC. ***SQAH:*** BBBB. ***SQAAH:*** AAA-CCC. ***IB:*** 30. ***BTEC ND:*** DMM.

S78 THE UNIVERSITY OF STRATHCLYDE
GLASGOW G1 1XQ
t: 0141 552 4400 f: 0141 552 0775
// www.strath.ac.uk

NN48 BA Accounting and Hospitality & Tourism
Duration: 3FT Hon
Entry Requirements: ***GCE:*** AAB. ***SQAH:*** AAAA-AAABB. ***IB:*** 36.

S93 SWANSEA UNIVERSITY
SINGLETON PARK
SWANSEA SA2 8PP
t: 01792 295111 f: 01792 295110
e: admissions@swansea.ac.uk
// www.swansea.ac.uk

G3NK BSc Actuarial Studies with Accounting
Duration: 3FT Hon
Entry Requirements: ***GCE:*** ABB. ***BTEC ND:*** DDM.

G3N4 BSc Actuarial Studies with Accounting with a year abroad
Duration: 4FT Hon
Entry Requirements: ***GCE:*** ABB. ***BTEC ND:*** DDM.

U20 UNIVERSITY OF ULSTER
COLERAINE
CO. LONDONDERRY
NORTHERN IRELAND BT52 1SA
t: 028 7032 4221 f: 028 7032 4908
e: online@ulster.ac.uk
// www.ulster.ac.uk

V2N4 BA Irish History with Accounting
Duration: 3FT Hon
Entry Requirements: ***GCE:*** 240. ***IB:*** 24. ***BTEC NC:*** MM. ***BTEC ND:*** MMM.

P5N4 BA Journalism with Accounting
Duration: 3FT Hon
Entry Requirements: ***GCE:*** 260. ***IB:*** 24. ***BTEC NC:*** MM. ***BTEC ND:*** DMM.

PS